D0206022

Reading the Text

Biblical Criticism and Literary Theory

Edited by Stephen Prickett

BLACKWELL
Oxford UK & Cambridge USA

Copyright © Basil Blackwell 1991

First published 1991

Basil Blackwell Ltd
108 Cowley Road, Oxford, OX4 1JF, UK

Basil Blackwell, Inc.
3 Cambridge Center
Cambridge, Massachusetts 02142, USA

British Library Cataloguing in Publication Data
A CIP catalogue record for this book is available from the British Library.

Library of Congress Cataloging in Publication Data

Reading the text: biblical criticism and literary theory / edited by Stephen Prickett.
    p.   cm.
    ISBN 0–631–16012–4
    1. Bible—Criticism, interpretation, etc.—History.   2. Bible and literature.
    I. Prickett, Stephen
    BS500.R3S   1991
    220.6′09—dc20   91–8919 CIP

Typeset in 10½ on 12pt Sabon
by Graphicraft Typesetters Ltd., Hong Kong
Printed in Great Britain by T. J. Press Ltd., Padstow, Cornwall

Contents

List of Contributors

Françoise Deconinck-Brossard is a Professor of English at the University of Paris X-Nanterre. She has carried out research into eighteenth-century Church history, particularly sermon literature, on which she wrote her thesis for the doctorat d'Etat at the Sorbonne (later published: 2 vols, Paris, 1984). She has also written on eighteenth-century shorthand, music and the homiletic use of the Bible. She is currently working on an edition of Locke's *Reasonableness of Christianity*. Other work in progress includes participation in a collective translation of Pepys's diary, and an anthology of English sermons.

Robert Detweiler is Professor of Comparative Literature at Emory University in Atlanta, Georgia. He has been visiting professor at the Universities of Salzburg, Hamburg and Regensburg and during 1990 held the American National Bank Chair of Humanities at the University of Tennessee. His most recent books are *Breaking the Fall: Religious Readings of Contemporary Fiction* (London and San Francisco, 1990), and *The Daemonic Imagination: Biblical Text and Secular Story* (Atlanta, 1990).

Kevin Hart is Associate Professor of Critical Theory at Monash University, Australia, where he teaches in the Department of English and the Centre for General and Comparative Literature. His most recent book is *The Trespass of the Sign: Deconstruction, Theology and Philosophy* (Cambridge, 1989). He is currently completing two monographs: *A. D. Hope* (Oxford) and *Economic Acts: Samuel Johnson and the Culture of Property* (Cambridge).

Stephen Prickett is Regius Professor of English Language and Literature at the University of Glasgow. He has previously held the Chair of English at the Australian National University in Canberra, and taught at the Universities of Minnesota and Sussex, and at Smith College, Massachusetts. His books include *Romanticism and Religion: The Tradition of Coleridge and Wordsworth in the Victorian Church* (Cambridge, 1976); *Words and the Word: Language, Poetics and Biblical Interpretation* (Cambridge, 1986); and, with Robert Barnes, *The Bible*, in the Cambridge 'Landmarks of World Literature' series.

Marjorie Reeves, formerly Official Fellow and Vice Principal, St Anne's College, is now Honorary Fellow at St Anne's College and St Hugh's College, Oxford, and a Fellow of the British Academy. She has been a visiting professor at Berkeley, California (twice) and the Chinese University of Hong Kong (twice). Her latest book is *Joachim of Fiore and the Myth of the Eternal Evangel in the Nineteenth Century* (Oxford, 1987).

Vernon K. Robbins is Professor of Religion in the Department and Graduate Division of Religion, and the Program in Classical Studies, at Emory University, Atlanta, Georgia. He was Fulbright Professor at the University of Trondheim, Norway, during 1983–4. Recently he has co-authored *Patterns of Persuasion in the Gospels* (Sonoma, CA) and *Anecdotes: From Crib to Crypt* (Sonoma, CA, 1989).

Rivkah Zim taught in the English Faculty at Cambridge University as a fellow of Fitzwilliam College and subsequently of Pembroke College. She is the author of *English Metrical Psalms: Poetry as Praise and Prayer 1535–1601* (Cambridge, 1987), as well as articles on literature of the sixteenth and nineteenth centuries. She is currently working on two new books: an edition of the poetry and letters of Thomas Sackville, Earl of Dorset, and a critical study of prisoners' writings from Boethius to Irina Ratushinskaya, and the literature of imprisonment.

Acknowledgements

Much of the credit for this book must go to Stephan Chambers, at Basil Blackwell, who originally saw the need for such a work as this, and who has given constant support to the project over its long gestation period. The present shape and balance of the book is the result of many discussions with him and with the other contributors involved. We are particularly grateful also to Professor Peter Walsh, of the Glasgow Classics Department, for reading the Preface and sharing so generously his knowledge of the literary relationship between the early Church and its cultural context.

Without the assistance of my two secretaries, Mrs Jocelyn Dawson in Australia and Miss Ingrid Swanson in Scotland, who spent long hours struggling with photocopiers and fax machines to keep in touch with constantly shifting contributors on three continents, the gestation period would have been even longer.

The publishers are grateful to Yale University Press for permission to quote from *The Complete Works of St Thomas More*, ed. and trs. C. H. Miller (New Haven and London, 1976).

Stephen Prickett
University of Glasgow 1990

Introduction

Stephen Prickett

The Bible has always been found in need of interpretation. Far from presenting a plain and transparent text, the pellucid clarity of whose original message has been accidentally muddied by time, custom and controversy, the collection of writings that has come down to most of us as the Old and New Testaments has been seen from the very beginning as presenting a peculiar order of difficulty – and therefore requiring not just interpretation, but interpretation of a very special kind. This was not primarily a matter of translation, though that has been a continual source of controversy since the Reformation; nor was it at first concerned with the facts of the contents themselves – although drawing up accurate family trees of the persons involved in the histories or 'harmonizing' the accounts of Jesus's life from the Gospels have at various times in the history of biblical criticism been held to be of great importance. It was, rather, a much more fundamental question of coming to terms with what might or might not constitute the canon of the Bible itself, and consequently, of explaining the parts in relation to the whole. Above all, it has centred on the problem of explaining the relationship between the Old and New Testaments.

Christianity was born in hermeneutics.[1] Its primal act of appropriation was the claim that the life and work of Jesus were the preordained fulfilment of earlier prophecies in the Hebrew scriptures. This was the famous 'key' without which there was no access to the Bible and, by extension at least for Protestants from the Reformation onwards, no access to salvation. As William Tyndale put it in the preface to his first English translation of the New Testament:

because the kingdom of heaven, which is the scripture and word of God, may be so locked up, that he which readeth or heareth it, cannot understand it: as Christ testifieth how that the scribes and Pharisees had so shut it up (Matt. 23) and had taken away the key of knowledge (Luke 11) that their Jews which thought themselves within, were yet so locked out, and are to this day that they can understand no sentence of the scripture unto their salvation, though they can rehearse the texts everywhere and dispute thereof as subtly as the popish doctors of dunce's dark learning, which with their sophistry, served us, as the Pharisees did the Jews.[2]

As Tyndale is quick to stress, this claim that the scriptures were a closed door that had to be unlocked was, according to the Gospels, first made by Jesus himself, but in the succeeding centuries it was systematized and formalized by a total restructuring of the existing Hebrew texts to illustrate and substantiate the Church's role as the inheritor and completion of the Jewish tradition. Similarly, for the reformers of the sixteenth century, the analogy between the first-century Jews and the Catholics of their own time was again clear. Moreover, such confidence that one was possessed of a God-given key clearly justified some attention to the lock if the fit was less than perfect. Thus even the format and arrangement of the book we have come to know as 'the Bible' is by no means hermeneutically innocent.

The Hebrew Bible is normally divided into three sections: the Torah (the five books of Moses, corresponding to what Christians call the Pentateuch); the Prophets (divided into the 'Former Prophets', that is, the 'histories' from Joshua to Kings, but not including Ruth, Esther, Chronicles, or Ezra-Nehemiah; and the 'Latter Prophets', or what Christians call the 'Prophets' simply); and a final section known as Writings, which includes the Psalms, Proverbs, Job, the Five 'Megilloth', or 'Scrolls' (Song of Songs, Ruth, Lamentations, Ecclesiastes, Esther), and Daniel, and ends with Ezra-Nehemiah and Chronicles. In the Christian Bible, however, we find that the Old Testament is commonly divided into *four* sections: the Pentateuch; the Histories (including Joshua to Kings, with Ruth following Judges, Chronicles, Ezra, Nehemiah and Esther); the Poetical Books (Job, Psalms, Proverbs, Ecclesiastes and the Song of Songs); and the Prophets (including Daniel). The difference in interpretation implied by these changes is striking. For Jews, the Torah is divine revelation, at once the foundational document both of the Bible and of their own people; the histories from Joshua to the fall of the monarchy are combined with the prophetic texts as a historical illustration of what the prophets promised and threatened; and the Writings are a somewhat open-ended group of texts, related in various ways to the practice of the Jewish religion after the exile.[3] For Christians, however, all the historical texts of what has now been retitled 'the Old Testament' go together, as it were placing the history of Israel firmly in the past; the 'poetical' books tend to be seen as a timeless inspiration for prayer and meditation; and the prophets come last, pointing to a predetermined future where the Old Testament is fulfilled by the New. In this hermeneutical appropriation the renaming is as important as the reshuffling of the contents. The mere existence of something called the 'Old' Testament transforms our expectations of the 'New'.

Nevertheless, though the New Testament is thus signalled in advance as superseding the Old, it is in many ways better seen as a continuation. In both its concepts and imagery it overtly presupposes the existence of the earlier Hebrew writings. What was necessary for the transformation of meaning then under way was to play down the literal sense of the Hebrew Scriptures in favour of figurative and literary ones. The models for this already existed in the tradition of typological and allegorical modes of interpretation within the Old Testament. Even the basic arrangement of the New Testament, when the contents were finally settled, illustrated the essentially polemical, literary and self-referential nature of the Christian Bible's construction. The four Gospels, Matthew, Mark, Luke and John, are not merely placed together, but (at least from the time of Irenaeus of Lyon in the late second century AD) always identified with the 'four living creatures' of Revelation 4, which were themselves based on the 'four living creatures' of Ezekiel 1. Just as the figurative continuities between Old and New Testaments are stressed, so too are the internal continuities of the New. The Acts of the Apostles, also supposedly written by Luke, is presented as a continuation of his Gospel. The Epistles of Paul are grouped with the 'Catholic' Epistles of James, Peter, John and Jude. Last comes the Apocalypse, or Book of Revelation, also supposedly written by the same John who wrote the Gospel and the three Epistles. Such an arrangement signals that in the Gospels we are to see the coming of the prophesied Messiah of Israel, and his founding of the 'new' Israel, the Church. In Acts we are to see the spread of this new Israel from the centre of the old, Jerusalem, to the centre of the new world, in Rome. The Epistles instruct us how the Church is to conduct itself in the world, pending the return of the Messiah. Revelation, with its series of visions of the Church's trials and tribulations in the world, is a repetition in microcosm of the whole New Testament appropriation of the Old. Its glorious and apocalyptic conclusion with the fall of Babylon (or Rome), the final defeat of Satan and the descent of the New Jerusalem from Heaven brings together, fuses and dramatically reuses some of the most powerful imagery from the prophets and the Gospels.

It is important to notice that the New Testament achieves what is, arguably, the most momentous act of appropriation in human history primarily by means of introducing a new critical theory, which, in effect, insists on a new way of reading all previous religious writings. If, as some have plausibly claimed,[4] the origins of its new hermeneutic system are rooted in the allegories of Babylon, ancient Egypt and, later, Greece, as well as the midrashic traditions of commentary on the Hebrew Scriptures, with the coming of Christianity allegorical and figural interpretation was elevated – now seemingly with divine patronage – into a total and all-embracing theory of meaning. One of the key figures in this process is Origen, who was, in turn, heavily influenced by Greek Stoic allegorizing of Homeric mythology. His work was brought to the attention of the Latin Fathers through Ambrose, who transmitted the tradition to Augustine and thus subsequently to Cassiodorus, whose sixth-century *Commentary on the Psalms* was to take allegory to unequalled extremes.

Yet the new stress on allegory was also, paradoxically, to produce a new sense of the importance of narrative. Just because the new religion began with a peculiar historical sense both of its past, and of how it differed from that past, it assigned to narrative from the earliest times a uniquely important role. The assumption that narrative has a *purpose* and an end – that it will lead the reader through however many surprises and twists to a point where eventually the meaning of all that has gone before will be made apparent – is, of course, common to both historical and allegorical literary forms. Moreover, this is so basic to our own culture (which has the novel as its characteristic art form) that it is easy to lose sight of its specifically Christian origins in that original act of appropriation. From it was to come, for instance, our modern idea of 'narrative' as distinct from the mere sequence of events we know by the term 'chronicle'. The histories of the Hebrew Bible had never been chronicles in the sense, say, of the Chinese chroniclers, for whom the succession of one Emperor after another represented simply a sequence of upwards of 5,000 years.[5] History was always related to prophecy. The historical books of the Hebrew scriptures always presupposed an explanation, a meaning, a dimly perceived divine pattern in the periodic rises and seemingly no less certain destructions of Israel. But if, for the Hebrew historians, God's purpose remained in the end arbitrary and mysterious, for the writers of the New Testament the meaning of history had been revealed. Though the Old Testament might tell its story through allegorical hints and prefigurements only to be interpreted fully in the light of the gospel, it was the task of the Gospels and of Acts to tell in narrative form the story of the coming of Jesus, his death, resurrection and of the subsequent spread of the Church throughout the Mediterranean world.

With the victory of Christianity over the pagan Roman world, however, a new problem occurred that required an equally new, and parallel, act of appropriation. That problem centred on the relationship between the biblical and classical worlds. What had to be created was not just a new sense of history,[6] but also some way of coming to terms with the pagan and secular literature of Greece and Rome. As we shall see, this relationship was a matter of continuing and deep ambivalence to many of the Church Fathers including Augustine, Jerome and Gregory the Great.[7] For Tertullian (*c*.AD 200) the matter was simple: 'What has Athens to do with Jerusalem? . . . We must seek the Lord in purity of heart . . . Since Christ Jesus, there is no room for further curiosity, since the gospel no need for further research.'[8] Similarly, for Gregory, 'the same lips cannot sound the praises of both Jupiter and Christ.' At first sight Ambrose too would seem to agree, arguing that the scriptures contained all necessary instruction,[9] yet he, on the other hand, saw nothing wrong in openly structuring his *De officiis ministrorum* for the clergy of Milan on Cicero's *De officiis*. His pupil, Augustine, likewise admits in his *Confessions* that it was Cicero's philosophy that had set him on the road to conversion by instilling in him a passion for true wisdom. Moreover, for educated members of the Roman world the Greek of the New Testament and the Septuagint could only appear crude by the literary standards of the day. Jerome, the translator of the Vulgate, himself typifies the conflict of loyalties. For him, the style of the scriptures was nothing short of 'harsh and barbarous'. Making a virtue out of necessity, he warns his readers not to expect from his translation any Ciceronian eloquence, for 'a translation made for the Church, although it may indeed have some literary merit, ought to conceal and avoid it, so as to address itself, not to the private schools of the philosophers with their handful of disciples, but rather to the whole human race.'[10] Elsewhere he wrote, 'what has Cicero to do with Paul?' Yet this vehemence only too evidently masks private fears about the cultural divide between the two worlds, which were to surface in a dream in which he appeared before the Judgement Seat of Christ at the Last Day only to be told that he was not a true Christian but in reality a mere 'Ciceronian'.[11] Even where he clearly envisages some kind of accommodation between secular learning and religious faith, his image of the former as the captive woman in Deuteronomy, who has her head shaved, eyebrows trimmed and nails pared before she is taken to wife by the true Israel (Letter 70) is, to say the least, disturbingly ambiguous.

Certainly the problem was more complex than any symbolic clipping away of pagan literary style. The classical world had contained great thinkers, writers and figures of heroic moral stature, who could not lightly be disregarded by educated Christians. Thus we find Socrates hailed by Justin Martyr (d. AD 165) as 'a Christian before Christ'. In the Middle Ages he was sometimes known as 'Saint Socrates'. Nor was this just a matter of personalities. Clement of Alexandria established a school of Christian philosophy based on Platonist theology, Aristotelian logic and Stoic ethics around AD 200. As we have seen, Origen was likewise an admirer of Stoic ethical thought. Even the content of classical literature could similarly be reread on Christian lines. Thus Virgil's fourth *Eclogue*, with its prophecy of a coming Ruler, was confidently understood as a foretelling of Christ and a parallel to Isaiah. In other cases, where the looked-for meaning was not at once obvious, it could be found through figurative readings and by allegory – and even such apparently unpromising material as Ovid's *Metamorphoses*, with the Song of Songs as the appropriate model, was given a ruthlessly Christian treatment. Thus Cassiodorus, in the sixth century, was able to accommodate classical learning to an organized programme of Christian education. The first book of his *Institutiones divinarum et saecularium litterarum* offers a syllabus of sacred reading, while the second sets out a course of study of the seven liberal arts – a knowledge of which he saw as not merely helpful but essential equipment for a proper understanding of Christian texts.[12] Boethius, his contemporary and, significantly, a layman, fighting the decay of classical culture, channelled his Christian vision of the world primarily through secular study of the seven liberal arts. Similarly, in his theological treatises his constant aim is, in his own words, 'to reconcile faith with reason' – by which he meant specifically the vision of his Greek philosophical masters. With the revival of learning associated with the ninth century, the value of classical literature, as an alternative path to truth, was almost universally accepted.[13] In its new Christian synthesis of Jewish and pagan worlds, Europe had acquired at the same time a 'key', a theory or rather set of literary critical theories by which both sacred and profane texts must now be read.

These theories were to shape the subsequent development of European literature and criticism. Until almost the end of the eighteenth century, for instance, the literal meaning of the Bible was seen as being only one among many ways of understanding it. Not merely did allegorical, figural and typological modes of reading coexist with the literal one, they were often in practice (if not in theory) accorded higher status. Since the Bible was the model for all secular literature, such ways of reading naturally also became the way in which *all* books were to be read. The allegorical levels of *The Divine Comedy* or *The Romance of the Rose* are not in any way optional additions to the basic story; they are a normal and integral part of what literature was expected to be. The idea of a primary literal meaning to a given secular text is an essentially modern one – dating, in effect, from the rise of the prose novel in the eighteenth century.

Yet, by the sixteenth century, a system of interpretation involving subtle allegorical readings dependent on a whole cultural and inter-textual network of other references was less appropriate for the new literacy of Protestantism – itself dependent on the new technology of printing – than it was for the restricted and clerical scholarly elites of the late Roman or mediaeval worlds. This is not to say that figurative readings were excluded at the Reformation – as we shall see, they were to persist as a normal mode of exegesis until well into the nineteenth century – but a system of hermeneutics that now gave primacy to the literal or 'plain' meaning of a text had insuperable difficulties with books whose traditional classification as 'apocryphal' (or 'hidden' in Greek) meant that they were to be read primarily for their secret or arcane meanings. Just as the early Church restructured the Hebrew Bible to illustrate its hermeneutic claims, so the sixteenth-century reformers excluded from their Bible many of the deuterocanonical writings that Jerome had included in the Vulgate. If this shift in modes of exegesis meant the loss of Bel and the Dragon, it also meant, for instance, that *arguments* of the Pauline Epistles, which had been submerged by a mass of associative and figural commentary, were understood afresh as what we would now call systematic theology. The effect of the new critical theory on Luther's reading of Romans was to change the course of history.

Once again, however, there are continuities. What may be a new way of reading biblical argument is closely associated with develop-ments in the theory and practice of narrative that sprang as clearly from the early Christian appropriation of the classical world as did the systems of elaborate figural readings. As part of the late Roman synthesis, the established classical literary genres of biography and history were themselves charged with a new and divinely guided sense of meaning that was soon to spill over into a new hybrid genre, hagiography. Once again Jerome was to lead the way in Latin with his *Vita S. Pauli*. Others, such as Sulpicius Severus's influential *Vita S. Martini*, for instance, quickly followed and helped to estab-lish the genre. In these lives of the saints, whose conversions, good deeds and virtuous deaths – if not martyrdoms – mirrored in miniature aspects of the life of their Saviour, the implicit expectations placed upon the narrative mode by the New Testament found their natural expression. In a closely allied vein, Augustine's *Confessions* can be read not merely for their contribution to the art of biography or for their astonishing powers of self-analysis, but for the formal assumptions about the nature of narrative they embody. Just because the supreme actant, the *real* author of the story, is the God who had already himself written the infinitely greater story of the world from the Creation to the Apocalypse, so it must be obvious to the reader (and, if necessary, *made* obvious by frequent asides by the human narrator) that the story of this individual will, as it were in microcosm, reflect the same progress and development from an upbringing in holiness and innocence, through lapse and fall, into a final state of Grace not through the merits of the person concerned but through the saving action of Christ.

In strictly formal terms there are two ways of seeing this. If, on the one hand, the secular literary forms of biography and autobiography have been taken over by a model derived from sacred literature, it is, of course, no less true, on the other, that sacred literature has been drawn towards a powerfully particularized and historic form. Though this was in one sense only an extension of the tradition already present in Hebrew writings, the Christian and classicized form in which it is handled by a writer like Augustine means that (as has often been noticed) the *Confessions* have all the internalization that we associate with the novel more than 1,000 years later. Equally important is the obvious fact that the primary meaning of the text lies in its story and associated argument, rather than in any possible figurative readings. The way is open, potentially at least, both to a secular literature and to secular theories of history. Yet, as we shall see, this peculiar tension between sacred and secular critical theory created by the Latin Christian synthesis of Jewish and classical worlds has persisted with astonishing durability to our own time. The history of the interaction of theories of biblical interpretation and literary criticism since the Reformation has been very far from simply one of progressive secularization. Rather, each has influenced the other to the point where it is as impossible to understand the history of biblical interpretation without taking into account the contemporary theories of literary criticism, as it is to understand what has been happening in literary criticism without taking account of corresponding movements in biblical criticism. We cannot hope to understand what is going on in Dante or even Chaucer without some grasp of how they themselves relate to the then current ideas of what constituted a book – derived in turn from the Bible. Spenser, Shakespeare and Milton cannot be understood in their contexts without some appreciation of the new Protestant emphasis on reading as a route to salvation. The novels of Fielding, of Jane Austen and of George Eliot are bound up with contemporary ways of reading the Bible that had their roots in the critical revolution of the eighteenth century. As we shall see, even the deconstructive modes of analysis associated with Derrida are more closely rooted in twentieth-century philosophical problems of theology and the Bible than many of his followers seem to realize. Neither metaphors of polarity nor of symbiosis, useful as they sometimes appear, seem to capture the full complexity of this long and endlessly fruitful historical interaction.

With Derrida, Hartman, Bloom, Alter and other twentieth century critics, however, we find, almost for the first time in 2,000 years, a public contribution to that interaction which is distinctively Jewish. Not merely does this constitute the resurfacing of an older and different critical tradition from a different religious perspective, with a different arrangement even of the basic texts; it also means the presence of what amounts to totally different *ways* of thinking about hermeneutics. It is, for instance, debatable how far Judaism has ever had such figures as 'theologians' in the Christian sense at all. The study of the Hebrew Scriptures has never been the prerogative of a professional group of scholars. Nor is it a solitary occupation. At one extreme are the kabbalistic teachings, which, though including such written texts as the *Zohar* (attributed to the second-century Rabbi Shimon Bar Yochai), constitute an essentially *oral* tradition in contrast with the written tradition of the Talmudic commentaries. Just as we only know of Socrates through the medium of his disciple, Plato, so we only know, for instance, of Isaac Luria (mentioned in chapter 6) through his disciples. His 'works' are, in effect, notes taken by them on the greater body of hidden knowledge that could only be imparted through the medium of direct face-to-face contact. The kabbalistic teachings later came to incorporate adaptations of Greek Platonism, Neo-Platonism and metaphysics. Such esoteric learning demanded the presence of a teacher for its spoken dialectic to be effective; a favourite image was that of Jacob wrestling with the angel. At the other extreme, the written tradition of Talmudic textual exegesis has always been applied to many different aspects of life, including other intellectual disciplines and writings presumed to communicate specific meaning, such as both law and the natural sciences. Moreover, study of the Talmud and other writings is traditionally carried out *in pairs*, so that the result automatically also tends to take on the characteristics of a dialogue or dialectic between student and student, or student and text. Such dialectic or, to use the proper Hebrew word, *pilpul*,[14] has become a noticeable feature of the intellectual heritage of Judaism since it re-emerged as a method of disputation and study in the mid-fifteenth century, and, as the critical wheel turns full circle, it has restored a typically Jewish flavour to much modern biblical and literary criticism as well as to the interaction between them – not least in certain modes of deconstruction.[15]

That continuing interaction is the subject of this book. The following pages are not intended as a collection of essays on a theme; they are, rather, conceived as a single connected history of that subtly intertwined relationship. The underlying argument is that each discipline owes more to the other than it is generally willing to acknowledge, and, perhaps more controversially, that to an astonishing degree each has been (and remains) dependent on the existence of the other for its own wellbeing. A genuinely non-literary criticism of the Bible (were that possible) would be as wrong-headed and futile as a genuinely secular and value-free theory of literary criticism. Justice to such a theme, with its necessary span of time and of disciplines, demands skills and knowledge that no single scholar could hope to possess. Our contributors include scholars trained in history, religious studies, philosophy and linguistics as well as literary criticism. Catholic, Protestant and Jewish traditions are all represented. If the process of reinterpretation that begins with the historical chapters inevitably broadens, in the two chapters concerned with the twentieth century, to more personal and subjective judgements, that is of the essence of this exercise. One's own century is always the most mysterious. It is only by putting the manifold variety of contemporary movements between biblical and literary criticism in the perspectives gained from the past that we can hope to free ourselves from the provinciality of the modern and perhaps gain some clue as to where this most extraordinary critical interaction may now be heading at the end of its first 2,000 years.

NOTES

1 On this point see also Paul Ricoeur, 'Preface to Bultmann', in *Essays on Biblical Interpretation*, trs. David Pellauer, ed. Lewis S. Mudge (Philadelphia, 1980), pp. 50–1.

2 'W. T. Unto the Reader', *Tyndale's New Testament*, ed. David Daniell (New Haven, 1989), p. 3.

3 For the different arrangements of the Hebrew and Christian Bibles see Robert Alter and Frank Kermode (eds), *The Literary Guide to the Bible* (London, 1987); Gabriel Josipovici, *The Book of God: A Response to the Bible* (New Haven, 1988); and Stephen Prickett and Robert Barnes, *The Bible*, Landmarks of World Literature Series (Cambridge, 1991).

4 See, for instance, Gareth Knight, *A History of White Magic* (London, 1978), p. 24.

5 A point made by J. H. Plumb, contrasting Greek and Chinese attitudes to the past, *The Death of the Past* (London, 1969), p. 111.

6 See again J. H. Plumb: 'History began because scholars perceived a problem which faced no other civilization – the problem of the duality of Europe's past, its conflicting ideologies, and of their different interpretations of human destiny,' ibid., p. 136.

7 See ch. 1 below, p. 13.

8 *De præscriptione hereticorum 7.*

9 See the 'Epilogue' by P. G. Walsh to G. J. Kenney (ed.), *The Cambridge History of Classical Literature*, vol. II. part 5: *The Later Principate* (Cambridge, 1982), pp. 107–8. The editor is in general greatly indebted to Professor Walsh's guidance in this area.

10 Ep. 22; 30. Cited by H. D. F. Sparks, *Cambridge History of the Bible*, vol. I, p. 524.

11 '*Ciceronianus es, non Christianus*'. Letter 22.

12 See L. W. Jones, *An Introduction to Divine and Human Readings by Cassiodorus Senator* (New York, 1966).

13 Walsh, 'Epilogue', p. 108.

14 *Pilpul* is derived from a root meaning 'to spice' or 'season' hence 'to dispute violently' or 'very ingeniously'. The *OED* gives 'pilpulist' (1859) as meaning: 'a subtle or keen disputant esp. in rabbinical argumentation'.

15 'The essential characteristic of pilpul is that it leads to a clear comprehension of the subject under discussion by penetrating into its essence and by adapting clear distinctions and a strict differentiation of the concepts. By this method a sentence or maxim is carefully studied, the various concepts which it includes are exactly determined, and all the possible consequences to be deduced from it are carefully investigated. The sentence is then examined in its relation to some other sentence harmonizing with it, the investigation being directed towards determining whether the agreement appearing on a superficial contemplation of them continues to be manifest when all the possible consequences and deductions are drawn from each one of them.' *Jewish Encyclopaedia*, new edn (New York and London, 1925), vol. X, pp. 39–43.

1

The Bible and Literary Authorship in the Middle Ages

Marjorie Reeves

For medieval writers, God was the supreme author – *auctor*, a word which, in the belief of medieval grammarians, enfolded several meanings, including the verbs *agere* (to perform) and *augere* (to make grow) and the Greek word for authority (*autentim*) – in Latin, *auctoritas*.[1] God was the creator of all material things; equally, he was the author of all history and the source of all words. Augustine embraced under the concept of 'thing' realities of every kind, including events and actions, while according to Aquinas, God was the sole *auctor* of things and could use things to signify, whereas human authors were only *auctores* of words and used words to signify.[2] In theory, all human writing flowed back to the fountain head in divine writing, that is, the Bible. Thus, in the early Middle Ages, literary theory starts from the premise that God is the one real *auctor* who writes through the human authors of the Scriptures. The Evangelists, for instance, are often portrayed with an angel or the Holy Spirit dictating to them. It was the divine *auctor* who gave his full weight to the meaning of *auctoritas* in writings and in imitation of him all literary work strove to be authoritative.

The authority of the Bible overshadowed all other works of litera-ture; its reality could be contrasted with their fiction. God's 'writing' in the Scriptures embodied the 'real' in the sense that its words recorded historical 'fact'. True, not all the words of the Bible bore this full weight of meaning – for instance, parable was not fact but didactic fiction – but the Bible was to be understood *par excellence* as the story of God's action in time, a belief sealed by the Incar-nation. God's entry into time in Jesus confirmed that there was 'meaning' in all historical happenings from the beginning of the world. Thus history was God's writing in time, supremely in sacred history, but also in secular history. 'The inspired history of Scripture is the primary source of world history,' for the sacramental nature of things is closely related to the historical. 'God has ordered the "work of Restoration" through a series of sacraments, the natural, the Mosaic, the Christian.'[3] At an early stage, therefore, students of the Scriptures perceived that to every event, person or group in history there was, so to say, a vertical point of reference as well as a horizontal. The historical fact was really there: it had its locus in time and place, but it signified more than itself. There was always a spiritual as well as a literal 'sense'.

But medieval commentators also inherited a literary theory from classical sources and believed that the aspiring exegete of biblical texts must first be trained in the seven liberal arts. According to one figure of speech, these formed a bridge by which the student gained access to the realm of theology.[4] Or again, the liberal arts constituted the substructure to divine studies.[5] Yet at first, in the early commentaries of the Fathers, there was certainly a tension between reverence for the unique status of the Bible and a sense of stylistic deficiencies when measured by the literary standards of the classics. Thus to Jerome the language of the scriptures was 'harsh and barbaric' compared with the classics.[6] The tension was resolved by elevating the Bible above the application of such human criteria. In his commentary on Job, Gregory the Great warns the reader not to look for 'literary nosegays' because, in interpreters of Holy Writ, 'the lightness of fruitless verbiage is carefully repressed, since the planting of a grove in God's temple is forbidden.' He rejects as 'unbecoming' the idea that he should 'tie down the words of the divine oracle to the rules of Donatus' (the grammarian).[7] St Augustine was ambivalent in his attitude. He found the writings of the Old Testament in his early days crude and obscure, but his literary sensitivity allowed him to delight later in the literary figures of the Bible: the Holy Spirit 'with admirable wisdom and care for our welfare, so arranged the Holy Scriptures as by the plainer passages to satisfy our hunger, and the obscure to stimulate our appetite'.[8] The root of the tension between the sacred and secular traditions lies, of course, in the question of how much the commentator should be concerned with the human authorship of the '*sacra pagina*'. Gregory allows himself to raise the problem of the human authorship and then seems to dismiss it with the words: 'It is very superfluous to inquire who wrote the work, since by faith its author is believed to have been the Holy Spirit.' Yet he returns again to the question of whether the human author was Job.[9] The human element could not be altogether denied.

'Mira profunditas!' St Augustine exclaims.[10] The overwhelming experience of biblical students in the early Middle Ages was of the vastness and inexhaustible variety of the treasure contained in the 'sacred page'. Cardinal de Lubac has assembled from the Fathers and from later exegetes a collection of the images they employed.[11] The Scriptures were a deep forest with innumerable branches, a feast prepared by divine wisdom for the nourishment of all, an infinite treasury of the Holy Spirit, a true labyrinth, a sky of profound depths, an unplumbable abyss, an immense sea for voyaging on billowing sails to infinitude, an ocean of mysteries. '*Fecunda sunt enim veritatis auctoritas*;' this remark by an unknown writer sums up the experience of many.[12] It is natural, therefore, to find the Scriptures exalted as the Queen of the Arts; '*Ista est domina artium*,' writes Haimo of Auxerre in the tenth century, and in the twelfth, Hugh of St Victor affirms: '*omnes artes subserviunt divinae sapientiae.*'[13]

Thus, to the first monks struggling to keep a torch alight in a dark age, the Bible was the great encyclopedia of knowledge, both secular and sacred. Biblical exegesis and theology were synonymous, for biblical texts formed the material of theology. This was the highest form of learning, embracing philosophy as well as theology, and using as tools all the arts of the classical heritage. Exegesis was painstaking and piecemeal, commenting sentence by sentence on grammar (which, in spite of Gregory's strictures, became almost an obsession), history, mythology, topography, and accumulating a miscellaneous collection of curious facts. Yet what seems to us a display of pedantic erudition was the foundation of the *lectio divina* which was built into the Rule of Benedictine monasticism. Two hours on weekdays were spent in Bible study – three in Lent – while on Sundays it took the place of manual work. There was as yet no conflict between exegetical learning and what might now be called spiritual meditation. Exegesis itself was an act of prayer; '*lectio* began and ended in *oratio*.'[14] The foundation of the contemplative life lay in an eager and loving concentration on every word of the biblical text itself.

There was only one truth but it was concealed in multiple forms. By the Fall, Man's understanding of what God was saying to him was deeply impaired. Thus God had to speak obliquely, adapting his Word to Man's dim understanding. The use of multiple meanings is 'God's lifting mechanism', says Gregory the Great; 'it picks Man up at the point his understanding can reach, so that as he recognizes the "outward words" he has something to hold on to while he is brought to know the meaning of their inward sense.'[15] The figural interpretation of the Old Testament forms a strong tradition. Indeed, it goes back to New Testament times, when the first Christians were struggling to find their place in a history from which they had, in a superficial sense, broken away. St Paul, in particular, desperately needed to find confirmation of Christ and the Church in the Scriptures of the Old Testament which had so influenced his youth. Thus he speaks of the hidden secrets of the Old Testament as veiled until now, even as Moses put a veil over his face so that the Israelites could not look on the revelation of God's glory: 'But their minds were blinded: for until this day remaineth the same vail untaken away in the reading of the old testament; which vail is done away in Christ' (II Cor. 3:14). Tertullian (*c*.160–*c*.225) stands in this tradition, filled with the strong sense that all the events and persons of the Old Testament are prophetic figures pointing forward. For instance, he is moved to the excitement of faith by the fact that Moses renamed Oshea, son of Nun, Joshua, which in Hebrew is the same as Jesus (Num. 13:16). For it was Joshua, not Moses, who led the Israelites into the Promised Land. This prefigured Christ's mighty act in leading the 'second people' out of the desert into the eternal life of the land flowing with milk and honey, not through the discipline of the Mosaic Law but through the grace of the Gospel.[16] Again, in the sleep of Adam, when God took Eve from his side, Tertullian sees figured the sleep of Christ in death, 'that precisely by the wound in his side should be figured the Church, the mother of all living'.[17]

This story of Adam was, of course, for Tertullian, historical fact and he emphasized constantly the historical reality of the figure as well as its fulfilment: 'Tertullian expressly denied that the literal and historical validity of the Old Testament was diminished by the figural interpretation. The Old Testament was not mere allegory: it had real literal meaning throughout, and even where there was figural prophecy, the figure had as much historical reality as what it prophesied.'[18] This conviction concerning the concrete actuality of God's prophecy through historical fact was, Eric Auerbach maintains, crucial for the future expansion of the Church. Tertullian lived in an environment where strong spiritualizing influences tended to drain away the historical realities on which Christian doctrine was based. The 'stumbling block' of the Incarnation created a strong temptation to allegorize and moralize revealed 'truth' into something which was in danger of losing touch with historical fact. The conflict turned particularly on the interpretation of the Old Testament. St Augustine warned specifically against the dangers of over-spiritualizing: 'When you hear an exposition of the mystery of the

Scriptures telling of things that took place ... Believe what is read
to have actually taken place as the reading narrates; lest, undermining the foundation of actuality, you seek as it were to build in the
air.'[19]

In the West, to a large extent, the view of Tertullian, St Augustine
and others that the Old Testament was full history and therefore full
prophecy prevailed. Its figural reality for post-Incarnational living
was vital to the faith of newly converted peoples:

Figural interpretation changed the Old Testament from a book of laws and
a history of the people of Israel into a series of figures of Christ and the
Redemption – so Celtic and Germanic peoples, for example, could accept
the Old Testament as part of the universal religion of salvation and a
necessary component of the equally magnificent and universal vision of
history conveyed to them along with this religion.... Its integral, firmly
teleological, view of history and the providential order of the world gave it
the power to capture the imagination ... of the convert nations. Figural
interpretation was a fresh beginning and rebirth of man's creative powers.[20]

Thus when the concept of multiple meanings was systematized in the
exegetical principle known as the four senses of Scripture, the historical dimension was firmly embedded in it. John Cassian (*c*.360–
435) distinguished them thus: the literal or historical sense, the
allegorical, the tropological (or moral) and the anagogical. Cassian
takes as an example the figure of Jerusalem: historically, it is the
earthly city of Jerusalem; allegorically, the Church; tropologically,
the souls of all faithful Christians; anagogically, the heavenly City of
God.[21] Tropological literally means related to the Word or doctrine
and thus carries a moral sense; anagogical concerns eternal things. A
much later popular rhyme summarized the four senses thus:

Littera gesta docet, quid credes allegoria,
Moralis quid agas, quo tendas anagogia.

The letter teaches what happened, the allegorical what to believe,
The moral what to do, the anagogical toward what to aspire.[22]

Of these senses the moral alone represents the purely spiritualizing
tendency; the other three are rooted in history. The first, the literal,
expounds concrete deeds. The fourth, the anagogical, admittedly
carries the meaning beyond time but does so by relating the actions
of persons in the here and now to that ultimate goal of history. It is
the second, the allegorical, which is of key importance. In the rhyme
quoted above it is the least well defined and, indeed, the use of the

Greek word *allegoria* could mislead, for it could easily carry the classical sense of a fictional fable or personification symbolizing an inner spiritual reality. But biblical exegetes clearly used it in the sense of figural interpretation in which the historical actuality of the figure establishes the validity of that for which it stands. Auerbach sums up the point thus:

> *Figura* is something real and historical which announces something else that is also real and historical ... Real historical figures are to be interpreted spiritually ..., but the interpretation points to a carnal, hence historical, fulfilment – for truth has become history in flesh.[23]

This is allegory in a special sense which is born directly out of the Judeo-Christian understanding of history as the work of God. It contrasts sharply with classical allegory. This second form of allegory certainly continued to be much used in the Middle Ages, as, for example, in the *Roman de la Rose* and the morality plays, but the Christian sense of history introduced this new form of allegory. Dante, as we shall see, distinguished this 'theologian's allegory' from the literary 'poet's allegory'.

The four senses of Scripture were expounded many times. Thus in the eleventh century Guibert of Nogent wrote in the preface to his commentary on Genesis:

> There are four ways of interpreting Scripture ... The first is history, which speaks of actual events, as they occurred; the second is allegory, in which one thing stands for something else; the third is tropology, or moral instruction, which treats of the ordering and arranging of one's life; and the last is ascetics, or spiritual enlightenment, through which we who are about to treat of lofty and heavenly topics, are led to a higher way of life.[24]

Then Guibert repeats Cassian's example of Jerusalem. In the twelfth century, Hugh of St Victor expounds the *Lectio divina* in the same terms. By this time, he was already stressing the importance of the literal sense, so he sees history as the basic subterranean foundation on which a second foundation of polished stones, composed of systematic doctrinal teaching (tropology) must be built to support the walls of allegory and anagogy.[25]

Thus the study of the Bible became an experience of drawing up bucketfuls of meaning from an inexhaustible well. The Scriptures were 'an encyclopedia which contained all knowledge useful to man, both sacred and profane'.[26] From this realization sprang the *Glossa Ordinaria*,[27] often called simply the Gloss. In manuscripts of the

Bible, multiple interpretations came to be written in the margins and between the lines of the sacred text. Gradually, a whole apparatus of commentary was assembled. Each book of the Scriptures was usually prefaced by a prologue or prologues of St Jerome, while successive layers of glosses to the text accumulated until, in the first part of the twelfth century, Anselm of Laon and his circle were responsible for producing what became the standard set of glosses to a large part of the Bible. But there were many anonymous glossators as well, and the whole tradition of the Gloss represents generations of biblical exegetes drawing up their buckets from the well. The Gloss became a standard textbook in the Schools, used by Peter Lombard in his famous lectures, called 'the Sentences', while by 1188 Peter Comestor was glossing the Gloss in his lectures. Once a student had worked through the seven liberal arts, the Bible, with all this apparatus, became one of the main sources of his education, supplying information on history, geography, natural history and so on, as well as the basis for theology. It carried the full weight of its divine *auctoritas*, supplemented by the authority of generations of glossators from the Fathers onwards.

Within this tradition, the allegorical sense of Scripture proved to be a peculiar and creative element in the understanding of history. Broadly speaking, until the eleventh and twelfth centuries, St Augustine's view that history had reached its climax and 'end' in the Incarnation, so that what remained was a period in which nothing significant would happen except the garnering of souls, blocked the instinct to find 'meaning' in events of post-Incarnation history. But such a pessimistic view of the time process was bound to weaken as the history of the Church and the world extended itself. God's sign-writing in the Scriptures must surely supply meaning to the experiences of the Church. So we begin to meet the figural interpretation of biblical history as the clue to the periodization and progress of Church history to the end of time.

Thus Gerhoh of Reichersberg (1093–1169), in his *De quarta vigilia noctis*, interpreted the night spent by the storm-tossed disciples on the Sea of Galilee as a *figura* of the perils through which the Church was destined to pass. In the first vigil of the night, the storm of persecution broke on the martyrs until wind and waves were temporarily calmed during the great tranquillity under Constantine. The second storm was created by Arius and other heretics against whom the confessors laboured and prevailed. In the third vigil, the ship of the Church was imperilled by inner corruption of life against which the Roman pontiffs from Gregory I to Gregory VII contended. Here, Gerhoh's stance as an ardent supporter of

Gregory VII's reforms emerges. So far the Church had outridden the storm by divine aid, but the conflict between Empire and Papacy, arising under Gregory VII, marked the onset of the greatest storm, that of the fourth vigil. Avarice was the root of evil in the Church and the strong wind of avarice now blowing was greatly to be feared. It was rising into the tempest of Antichrist, represented by the schismatics in the Church. Only Christ walking on the water could rescue his Church from being engulfed, but his aid was certain. At this point, Gerhoh's disciple points out that Christ came to his disciples in the ship and stilled the storm *before* they reached 'land' (i.e. eternal rest). This appears to mean that before Christ comes in Judgement at the end of time, he will come to rescue the still-voyaging Church. Gerhoh replies very positively that as the dawn precedes sunrise, so a clear light will prevail over the dense darkness of Antichrist before the manifest Christ appears. So Christ stills the storm and enters the boat. The distance still to be traversed before reaching the shores of eternal peace will be a time when the Church will be purged of all impurities and Christian people will be filled with great joy.[28]

Similarly Eberwin of Steinfelden, a Premonstratensian canon, uses the symbol of the six jars of wine at the marriage at Cana to work out a periodization of Church history which recognizes change within the Church's existence and views it as a 'graduated process in which the flow of the Church's history accelerates towards its end'.[29] He believed that the last age within history was now beginning in which the Church would grow in perfection through the work of a new order of the humble, surpassing all the old orders. Here 'the Incarnation is seen no longer so much as the climactic *end* of redemptive history as its *centre*.' This move away from the Augustinian view of history stimulated the urge to extend the interpretation of biblical *figurae* to Church history and to events of the present and future.

Possibly the first person to work out the full implications of the figural interpretation of history was Joachim of Fiore (*c*.1135–1202). He saw all history as the 'sign-writing' of the Triune God. The Abbot of a Benedictine (later Cistercian) monastery in Calabria, Joachim was essentially a biblical exegete who believed that by divine illumination the three-fold work of the Trinity in history could be revealed to the student who pondered on the Scriptures long and prayerfully. He called this divine illumination the *spiritualis intellectus*.[30] This gift was not the other-worldly vision of a contemplative but an understanding of the full dimensions of the

Word as it appeared clothed in historical fact. To grasp the full complexity of his scriptural interpretations, we have to realize that for Joachim this three-fold work in history did not simply take the form of three successive stages in history – as his doctrine has often been described. Through meditation on the doctrine of the Trinity in its Latin form, he came to believe that the key to the whole meaning of history lay in the mysterious inner relations of the Three Persons, each with the others. The Father 'sends' the Son; Father and Son 'send' the Spirit; or, the Son 'proceeds' from the Father; the Spirit 'proceeds' from both Father and Son. This was the doctrine of the *missio* (sending) and *processio* (proceeding).[31] Joachim's claim was that by the gift of the *spiritualis intellectus* he 'saw' the happenings of history as signs of this eternal three-fold activity. He often described this power to penetrate to the inner signification of historical facts as seeing with the eyes of the mind (*oculi mentis*),[32] while recognizing that, even with the gift of illumination, the vision was still clouded. One of his favourite texts was 'Now we see through a glass darkly (*per speculum in enigmate*), but then face to face' (1 Cor. 13:12).

God's significations were primarily revealed in sacred history. There Joachim found many 'signs'. Two of the most important were the Alpha and Omega (the first and the last) given in the Apocalypse 1:17. Joachim's strong visual imagination led him in the first place to meditate on the very shapes of these Greek letters, A, ω. He saw here a wonderful revelation: that the *missio* and *processio* of the Trinity were 'given' in these concrete forms. He then linked this New Testament sign with a famous episode in the Old Testament which was often seen as a *figura* of the Trinity, namely, the visit of the three angels to Abraham in Genesis 18, followed by the sending of two angels to rescue Lot from the doomed city of Sodom. Drawing the triangular alpha, he sets the three angels in position and then shows the *missio* figured in the two sent to Sodom. Beside this diagram he sets the fulfilment of this figure in the New Dispensation, adding to it another 'literal' fulfilment in the Hebrew Tetragrammaton or sacred name of God. This he transliterates as *IEUE*, finding to his joy that it can be divided into three parts, each containing the common E – IE, EU, UE – thus signifying at the same time the Trinity and the Unity of the Godhead. Below the alphas, he draws parallel omegas, showing the *processio* first in its Old Testament similitudes of the three patriarchs, Abraham, Isaac and Jacob, and then in its New Testament realization. Beside the Omegas he sets the round *O* to signify the Unity of the Godhead.[33]

The figures we have just studied give a close-up of Joachim's

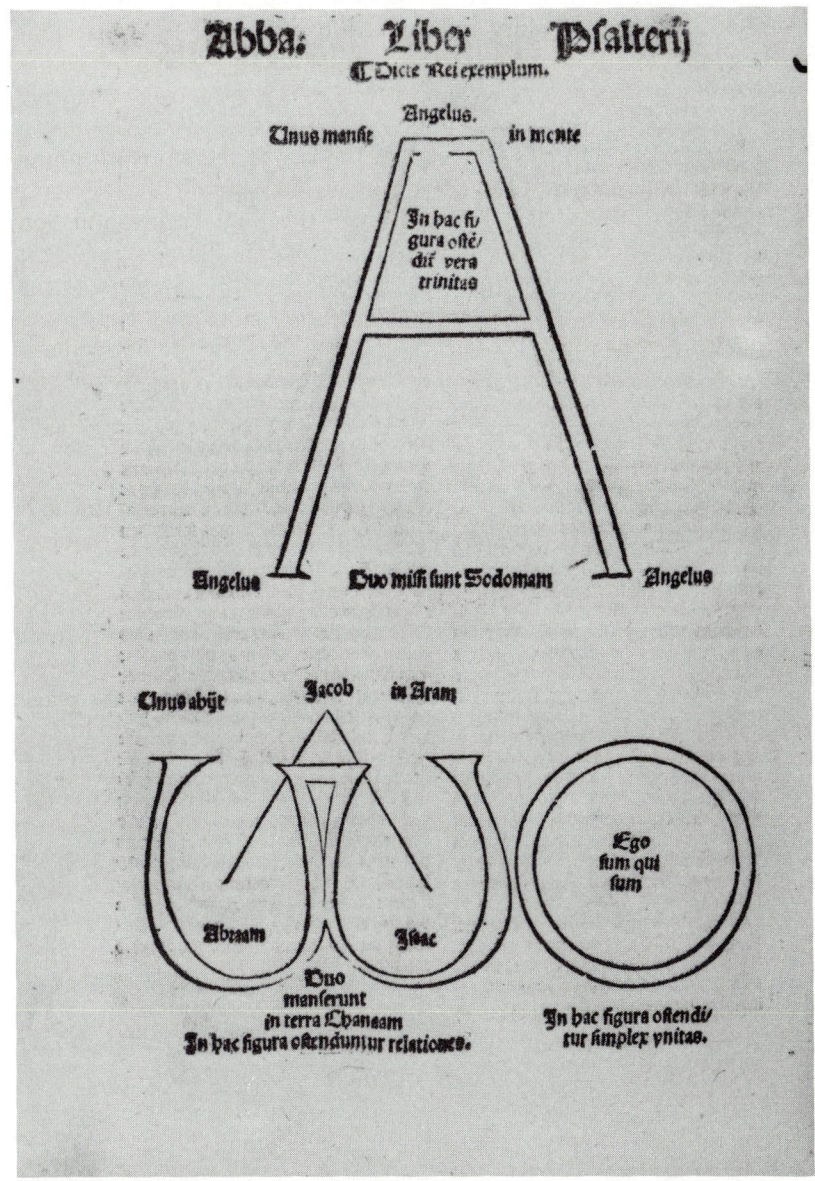

PLATE 1   Joachim of Fiore's diagram showing the angels sent to Abraham and Lot with the Alpha and Omega given in the Apocalypse, from *Psalterium decem Chordarum* (Venice, 1527), fo 256ᵛ.

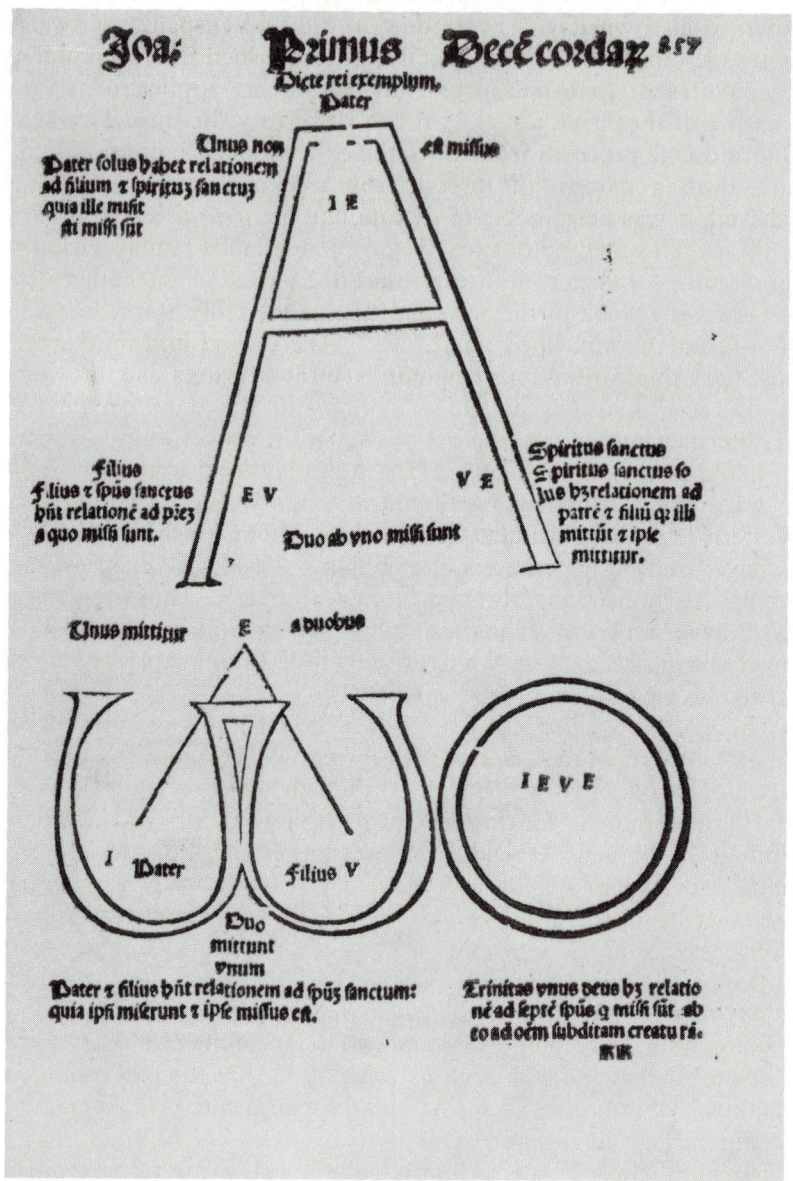

PLATE 2   The Hebrew Tetragrammaton or sacred name of God added to the
Alpha and Omega, from Joachim of Fiore, *Psalterium decem Chordarum*
(Venice, 1527), fo 257ʳ.

method, but his three main works encompass the whole of history down to his own day.[34] Everything in the Old Dispensation was a figure of things in the New – that was established interpretation as we have seen. Joachim's originality lay in his application of the doctrine of the Trinity to the process of history. Because Two send One and One proceeds from Two, the conventional 'pattern of twos' turns into a pattern of threes. From the concords of twos, he believed, it was permissible to extrapolate the *figurae* into a pattern of threes. This method of exegesis gave Joachim his famous vision of three *status* (or stages) in history: that of Law under the Father, that of Grace, the work of the Son, and that of the Holy Spirit, in a new life of illumination, liberty and love.[35] The second and third stages each have their mysterious beginnings in the previous one: the work of the Son, sent by the Father, begins in the days of the Old Testament King Uzziah; the life of the Spirit, proceeding from both Father and Son, must therefore have a double root, in the life of the Old Testament prophets, Elijah and Elisha, and in the beginnings of Western monasticism under St Benedict, whom Joachim calculated to have lived 42 generations after Elijah.[36] Besides geometrical diagrams, Joachim frequently used biological images. Thus each *status* must have a period of germination, growth and fructification, a concept which is expressed most vividly in trees of history of various forms.

The tree form[37] may have originated in Joachim's meditations on the generations of men as recorded in the Old Testament and in the genealogies of Jesus in the New Testament. In several of his trees, the Old Testament generations form the lower part of the trunk, while from the First Advent to the consummation of history they are calculated in units of 30 years to each generation. When he wishes to depict history as three connected trees in which the third should really grow out of both the first and the second, he has some difficulty. A study of the manuscripts of the *Liber de Concordia* shows various attempts to represent this figure.[38]

Numerology gave important clues to the meaning of biblical texts. Joachim found significance in his calculation that the generations of mankind fell into units of 21, 42 and 63. His vision of the whole can be summed up as in figure 1.

Joachim believed that he himself was living in the fortieth generation after the Incarnation and that the second major crisis of all history would happen within the next two generations, though he was careful to say that the length of these generations could not be calculated exactly. This crisis time would witness the greatest tribulation of the Church and the transition to the third *status* of the

1st *Etas*
2nd *Etas* — 1st *status*
3rd *Etas* — 63 generations
4th *Etas*
5th *Etas* — 2nd *status*
6th *Etas* — 63 generations
7th *Etas* — 3rd *status*

Germination — Adam to Jacob — 21 ⎱ Old Testament ⎱ Seven Seals
Fructification — Jacob to Uzziah — 21
Germination — Uzziah to Christ — 21
Fructification — Christ to Benedict — 21 ⎱ New Testament ⎱ Seven Openings
Germination — Benedict to ...
Fructification — ... to *Consummatio Seculi*

FIGURE 1   The generations of mankind

Seals: Old Dispensation	*Openings: New Dispensation*
1 Persecution of Egyptians	1 Persecution of Jews
2 Persecution of Philistines etc.	2 Persecution of Pagans,
3 Persecution of Syrians	alternatively, Arians
4 Persecution of Assyrians	3 Persecution of Goths, Vandals, etc.
5 Persecution of Chaldaeans	4 Persecution of Saracens
6 Persecution of Medes	5 Persecution of Germans
7 Persecution of Antiochus	6 Persecution of Ten Kings,
	alternatively, Saracens
	7 Persecution of Antichrist

FIGURE 2   Tribulations and persecutions

Spirit. For, in juxtaposition to the evolution of the three *status*, Joachim placed a contrasting pattern of tribulations or persecutions in a rising scale. The clue to this pattern lay in the Book sealed with Seven Seals of Apocalypse 5:1. The Seven Seals marked the seven wars or tribulations through which the People of God in the Old Dispensation had to pass; the Seven Openings marked the seven persecutions of the Church, culminating in that of the greatest Antichrist. He has variations on this pattern, but the general scheme can be summarized as in figure 2.[39]

Using another figure – that of the seven-headed dragon of the Apocalypse – Joachim plotted the persecutions of the Church according to the heads: Herod, Nero, Constantinus Arianus, Cosdroe, King of Persia (at the time of Mohammed), Mesemothus (a Muslim ruler), alternatively a German Emperor, Saladin, Antichrist.[40] The Church, like Israel, must pass through a mounting series of tribulations to the climax of persecution under the greatest Antichrist. Only beyond this would the full *status* of the Spirit be realized. The great figure for this experience was the Exodus, in which the children of Israel passed from the bondage of slaves through the wanderings and struggles of the wilderness to the final test of the crossing of Jordan and so to the blessings of the Promised Land beyond.[41]

The number 7 also gave Joachim the figure of the Seven Days of Creation, a commonly accepted symbol of the Seven Ages (*aetates*) in which the whole of history would be enacted. Five took mankind from Creation to the Incarnation; the sixth would run between the First and Second Advents, and the seventh – according to traditional interpretation – would be the Sabbath of Rest beyond time.[42] Once again, Joachim gave an original turn to this scheme by equating the

Sabbath with his third *status* and placing it within history instead of
outside. To fit this Sabbath into a pattern of seven persecutions, he
doubled the persecutions of the sixth seal and 'opening', thus height-
ening the crisis which preceded the age of tranquillity.

The figure 12 was also universally recognized as a sacred number,
with the concord of the twelve patriarchs and twelve apostles plain
for all to see. Here Joachim again added an original dimension. He
had used fives and sevens in connection with the inner relations of
the Trinity. Pondering on twelves, he seized on the detail in the Old
Testament that five tribes received their inheritance in the Promised
Land first and seven later (Joshua 18:2). This became for him a
figure of deep significance. Looking for its concords in the New
Dispensation, he matched tribes with churches, perceiving that there
were five principal churches at first, namely, Jerusalem, Antioch,
Constantinople, Alexandria and Rome, a group he associated with
St Peter, and then the seven churches of Asia, Ephesus, Smyrna,
Pergamos, Thyatira, Sardis, Philadelphia, Laodicea – to whom St
John, at the dictation of the Spirit, wrote letters in the Apocalypse.
This uneven division of the number 12 into 5 and 7 gave him, first,
an insight into the nature of the time process as containing within it
a movement from a prior to a posterior 'inheritance' and, secondly,
a sign as to the direction of that movement and the meaning of that
posterior inheritance. For the number 5 stands for the five senses,
while 7 is the number of the Gifts of the Holy Spirit. Thus there
must be a progression in history from the prior to the posterior,
from the five Tribes and Churches to the seven, from the outward
and material to the inward and spiritual, from the life of the second
status, designated in St Peter, to that of the third *status*, designated
in St John.[43]

Joachim adapted the traditional four senses of Scripture to five,
which he called historical, moral and allegorical, subdividing the
latter into tropological, contemplative and anagogical. The historical
was the *similitudo rei visibilis ad invisibilem* (the likeness of the
visible thing to the invisible).[44] The moral was close to this. The
tropological Joachim understood according to the literal meaning, as
that which pertained to the Word or doctrine. The contemplative
was related particularly to the gift of the Holy Spirit and the anagogical to the life hereafter. All these Joachim called the five general
intelligentiae through which individual human beings could ascend
from things visible and material to things invisible and spiritual.
These meanings were given for the salvation of individual souls.[45]

But Joachim needed another, a prophetic 'sense', through which
to discern the spiritual meaning of the time process itself, that is, the

working of the Trinity within the concrete events of history, always pointing towards a completion in the future. He called this special sense the *sensus typicus* and he saw it subdivided into seven *species* or *intellectus*, all of which related to the three *status* of the world's history. These seven represented seven aspects of the Trinity at work in history: Father; Son; Spirit; Father and Son; Father and Spirit; Son and Spirit; Three Persons in One.[46] Thus the *sensus typicus* required that each event or person in history should be interpreted as embodying seven types of the Trinity's activity. While in his progress through the five senses the individual human soul could pass here and now into the realm of the Spirit, the spiritual meaning of the time process as a whole could not be fully revealed until the end of time, for the prior was only completed in the posterior and history waited for the full illumination of the Spirit in the third *status* of the future.

It needed considerable ingenuity to work out these senses in relation to specific happenings in history. In book V of his *Liber de Concordia*, Joachim attempted to apply them to the Seven Days of Creation but got somewhat bogged down. One of his clearest expositions of this system of 'similitudes' deals with Hagar and Sarah, the two wives of Abraham.[47] The *intelligentia historica* teaches us that one was a bondwoman and the other was free; the moral, that one signifies carnal affection, the other, spiritual. Under the tropological sense, Hagar represents the Letter, Sarah the Spiritual Intelligence. Under the contemplative, Hagar signifies the active life, Sarah the contemplative life, while anagogically Hagar is bound to this life while Sarah points to the future life. The seven species of the *intelligentia typica* give a set of meanings on a quite different plane. Under the first, Hagar signifies the general people of Israel, Sarah the tribe of Levi set apart by God; in the second, the two represent the *ecclesia secularium* and the *ecclesia clericorum*; in the third, the *ecclesia conversorum* and the *ecclesia monachorum* of the third *status*. These three senses pertain to Father, Son and Spirit respectively. In the fourth (Father and Son), Hagar signifies the Synagogue but Sarah the Latin Church. In the fifth (Father and Spirit), Hagar is the Synagogue but Sarah the *ecclesia spiritualis*. The sixth, belonging to Son and Spirit, reveals Hagar as the Church of the sixth age, Sarah as the spiritual Church of the seventh age. In the seventh sense, pertaining to all three Persons, and therefore covering the whole of history, Hagar represents the Church of the first and second *status*, Sarah the *felicem illam ecclesiam* of the third *status*.

Finally, in a strange figure of an eagle, with captions written on its feathers, Joachim gathered up his vision of sequences in threes, fives and sevens.[48] The eagle itself was the symbol of St John, who signified for Joachim the contemplative Church of the third *status*. By the eye is the caption *Clavis David*. On the eagle's body are the great 'threes'; Abraham, Isaac, Jacob and Zacharias, John the Baptist, Christ. On the right-hand side of the head are the five senses and on the left the seven species of the *intelligentia typica*. On the tail-feathers are sequences of fives and sevens: five Patriarchs, five Apostles, seven whom God knows. Here the prophetic element becomes explicit and the detailed captions on the wing feathers carry this further in sequences of threes, fives and sevens. On the right, five feathers display the five senses in sequences of which the following are examples:

Contemplative. Abraham pater monasterii: Isaac monachus oblatialis: Jacob claustralis: quinque et septem filii: quinque generales virtutes et septem spiritales.

Anagogice. Abraham Deus Pater: Isaac Filius: Jacob Spiritus Sanctus: quinque et septem filii: duodecim milia signati.

On the left, the feathers represent the seven species of the *intelligentia typica* of which these are examples:

Third species. Abraham, abbates cassinses: Isaac, alii qui venerunt post eos in alia specie: Jacob, alii qui sunt vel futuri sunt: quinque et septem filii: quinque monasteria et septem futura.

Seventh species. Abraham, patriarche et apostoli et quidam prelati cenobiorum: Isaac, pontifices Judeorum et episcopi et quidam abbates: Jacob, prophete, doctores et quidam abbates: quinque filii: quinque tribus, quinque ecclesie, quinque monasteria: septem filii: septem tribus, septem ecclesie, septem monasteria.

There is always a progression in history: from the outward 'fives' to the spiritual 'sevens'; from patriarchs and apostles to future contemplative leaders; from tribes and churches to the monasteries of the Spirit.

The figural method was brought to its climax by Joachim in three ways: first, his belief that the inner relationships of the Trinity were mirrored in the concrete events of history; secondly, in his bold application of this method to the interpretation of contemporary events and the delineation of a pattern for the future; thirdly, in his claim that through the gift of the *spiritualis intellectus* the whole shape, future and final consummation of history could be charted.

The continuing influence and attraction of this powerful method of scriptural interpretation can be traced throughout the thirteenth century and beyond. But, alongside it, a gradual shift in attitude towards biblical texts was apparent. Institutionally, this is connected with the move of theological studies from the monastic environment to that of the 'schools', the embryonic universities. Juxtaposed to the monastic emphasis on meditation and prayer there was now set the cut and thrust of the scholastic method, characterized by the *quaestio* and *disputatio*. Overlapping from the twelfth to the thirteenth century we have three great expositors of biblical studies in the schools: Peter Comestor (d.*c*.1169), Peter the Chanter (d.1197) and Stephen Langton, who left the schools in 1206. Their commentaries were written for students. They still believed in the superiority of the spiritual senses over the literal. 'Holy Scripture is God's dining room, where the guests are made soberly drunk,' writes the Comestor; 'History is the foundation ... allegory the wall ... tropology the roof ...'[49] And the Chanter, commenting on Is. 55:2: 'Why do you spend money for that which is not bread?', says: 'You, that is, who follow the letter which killeth, not caring for the spiritual sense, and its fair morality, but for a superfluity of gloss.'[50] But the emphasis is shifting: the allegorical is sometimes replaced by the tropological sense and the Masters realize that the literal or historical sense is easier for beginners. Peter Lombard, in a sermon, characterizes the senses thus: 'The historical sense is easier, the moral (tropological), sweeter, the mystical (anagogical), sharper; the historical is for beginners, the moral for the advanced, the mystical for the perfect.'[51]

In the twelfth century, a duality of method continues to exist but by the early thirteenth century, a new literary influence was reinforcing the tendency towards a more critical and analytical approach to questions of biblical scholarship. When Aristotle's theory of the 'four causes' came into vogue this provided the form for a new type of literary prologue to a scriptural commentary.[52] Applied in this way, Aristotle's four causes gave the following guidelines for interpretation: first, the 'efficient cause', the author, involving questions of authenticity and, in the case of scriptural exegesis, the 'directions' of the divine *auctor* to the human one; secondly, the 'material cause', that is, the writer's sources; thirdly, the 'formal cause', the writer's organization of his material; fourthly, the 'final cause', the ultimate end and justification of the work, in the case of Scripture, its efficacy in leading readers to salvation.

In the long run the influence of this model on Scriptural commentary was crucial for two reasons: it focused attention on the 'letter' of the work in question and gradually shifted the emphasis from the divine author to the human. As Beryl Smalley comments:

The scheme had the advantage of focusing attention on the author of the book and on the reasons which impelled him to write. The book ceased to be a mosaic of mysteries and was seen as the product of a human, although divinely inspired, intelligence instead. The four causes ... brought the commentator considerably closer to his authors.[53]

There was little place for figural allegory here: the search for spiritual similitudes gives place to the application of literary criteria. There were, of course, anticipators of this shift in focus in the twelfth century. Perhaps the most famous was Abelard, who sought in his *Sic et Non* to reconcile the errors and contradictions of the Fathers by focusing on the historical context of their writings. Even he would not admit plain error in Scripture itself, but by seeking to explain scriptural difficulties in terms of scribes' errors and by studying the intentions of the human authors he was anticipating the new approach.[54]

The sophistication with which thirteenth- and fourteenth-century theologians used the Aristotelian categories to achieve a delicate balance between the divine and human authors is fascinating to study. Dr Minnis cites an example of a commentary on Isaiah in which two levels of authorship are distinguished (*duplex causa efficiens*):

The efficient cause is twofold, namely moving and operating. The operating cause is Isaiah, which is understood by the supposition of this word, 'he saw'. But there is also a cause which is efficient but not operating, which is noted here: 'by the spirit', namely by the Holy Spirit, which moved Isaiah that he should write.[55]

Or again, the Dominican John Russel finds a quadruple efficient cause inspiring the Apocalypse: God, Christ, the angel who visits St John, St John himself, the 'immediate' efficient cause.[56] There remained, however, a tension between the still unquestioned belief that God was the divine *auctor* of the Bible and the role of the human agent which evoked much careful discussion. In a disputation at Paris, in the late thirteenth century, Henry of Ghent analysed the relationship in terms of a craftsman who designs and directs the work and a workman who carries it out according to the rules the master has set.[57] Even if God is the first mover, or primary efficient cause, the integrity of the instrumental efficient causes must be preserved: 'Truly, mediate causes between the primary efficient cause and the ultimate effect have purposes (*intentiones*) proper to them . . .'[58] So Aquinas held that the fact that God was the unique first cause of all activity did not deny a certain degree of individuality to the human instrument.[59] Dr Minnis sums up the subtle shift of attitude under Aristotelian influence as 'a new awareness of the integrity of the individual human *auctor*'.[60]

A second influence in the later Middle Ages which worked in the same direction was the development of Hebrew studies. The Jewish tradition of scriptural exegesis emphasized the importance of the literal sense and although Christian commentators believed that rabbinical students did not fully understand the Scriptures, they were quite willing to use Jewish scholarship on the text. Thus Nicholas of Lyra, at the turn of the thirteenth/fourteenth century, supported his argument for the importance of the *sensus literalis* by reference to Jewish exegesis, complaining that earlier generations of commentators had multiplied spiritual 'senses' to the point where the literal sense was in danger of suffocation. In the prologue to his commentary on the Psalms, he focused attention on the *mens prophetae*, the inspired mind of David which God used. For 'divine inspiration works on and through the human *mens*. The man who sees visions or dreams dreams is now much more than a mere "sleeping partner" of God.'[61]

Here we must note how vital the appearance of the friars in the universities was to biblical studies. The Dominicans, in particular, centred their religious education on a modernized version of *lectio divina*.[62] But although they emphasized the moral sense of Scripture, the structure of the spiritual senses was decaying, for it had depended most on the monastic tradition. Although the friars kept alive the tradition of *lectio divina*, it took on a more intellectual character. This emerges in the great series of Dominican commentaries, culminating in those of Albertus Magnus and Thomas Aquinas. Albert the Great emphasized the importance of the Letter again and again. Miss Smalley compares his treatment of the text 'May the bones of the Twelve Prophets spring up out of their place' (Ecclus. 49:12) with that of Stephen Langton; the latter interprets the dry bones as the Letter, while the marrow and fatness are the spiritual interpretations; St Albert also compares the bones to the literal sense, not for their dryness, but because they are solid, taking their solidity from 'the truth of things'.[63] Jewish studies helped to elucidate obscure texts in Old Testament law. For example, many commentators, thinking that the literal sense was absurd, had struggled to find a spiritual sense in the precept: 'Thou shalt not boil a

kid in the milk of his dam' (Ex. 23:19). Now Aquinas, following a
suggestion of Maimonides, is able to show that the literal sense has
meaning and is not irrational. 'St Thomas had brought Christian
exegesis to a stage where the Old Testament precepts could be made
a subject of scientific study.'[64]

Yet the historical identity of the human author did not block the
spiritual meanings imparted by the Holy Spirit. The very concreteness of the historical context now receiving more emphasis was the
pledge of God's authorship, of his sign-writing in the Scriptures.
Figural interpretations were by no means dead. An example of the
blending of literal and allegorical interpretations can be seen in
Aquinas's exposition of certain psalms. Dr Minnis gives as an
instance his glossing of Psalms 10 and 20:

This psalm can be interpreted literally of David, but mystically or allegorically of Christ. But morally it can be interpreted of the just man and
heretics, as the *Glossa* expounds it.

This psalm is related of Christ who is 'the king' and David who is his
figure, and therefore it can be expounded of both: of Christ according to
truth, of David according to figure.[65]

Of the four senses of Scripture, it was the allegorical or figural
which retained most power in the later Middle Ages. The sense that
the Scriptures encompassed figurally the whole of history and the
human experience of all ages was still pervasive, for in a world
where chance and chaos often seemed to reign it was vital to be
assured of a divine pattern. Chroniclers of world history still shaped
their accounts to the Seven Days of Creation which symbolized the
Seven Ages of the World. Thus the Dominican, Vincent of Beauvais,
used this structure for his *Speculum Historiale* in the thirteenth
century.[66] The crucial point now was the interpretation of the Sixth
and Seventh Ages, especially the signs of approaching crisis at the
climax of the Sixth Age and the question of whether the Seventh Age
would fall within or outside of history. Vincent takes the accepted
Augustinian line, but his sense of imminent crisis is strong and, like
others of the period, he quotes a pseudo-Joachimist text on this
point: '*Ab anno MCC et ultra suspecta sunt mihi tempora et
momenta.*'[67] This sense of living in the End-time, overshadowed by
the imminence of Antichrist, prompted men to seek the figural
symbols of their own experience, even their own roles, in the Scriptures. A Paris academic, William of St Amour, embroiled in the
conflict of secular masters with the friars in the university, saw the

latter as the pseudo-prophets who formed one of the signs presaging the Last Things, as predicted by Christ (Matt. 24:11).[68] When the Generals of the two great mendicant orders wished to express in a joint encyclical (1255) their sense of being sent to save the world in '*novissime diebus istis in fine seculorum*', they turned to biblical symbols, finding themselves prefigured in '*duo magna luminaria, duae tubae Moyse, duo Cherubim, duo ubera sponsae, duo filii olivae splendoris, duo testes Christi . . .*'[69] When Angelo Clareno, one of the persecuted Franciscans known as Spirituals, began to write the history of their sufferings, he instinctively cast it in the form of the seven tribulations of the Church, symbolized in the seven seal-openings.[70] His sense that St Francis had inaugurated the new age led him to adapt New Testament words applied to Christ to contemporary experience in an astonishing manner: 'God has in times past spoken to us in Fathers, Apostles, Prophets, Martyrs, Doctors and Saints, but in these newest days He has spoken to us in His seraphic son Francis whom He has constituted heir of all things following . . . who, being in this world in the form of Christ crucified, humbled himself . . . wherefore God has exalted him and given him a name . . .'[71] Thus the medieval sense of history and of crucial contemporary roles within it continued to draw its inspiration from biblical allegory.

Nowhere is this more apparent than in the proliferation of pseudo-Joachimist works in the mid-thirteenth century. The most important took the form of commentaries on the prophecies of Jeremiah and Isaiah, emanating from south Italy. Here the figural method of interpreting present experience and prophesying future events was brought to a high point. The *Super Hieremiam* (*On Jeremiah*)[72] abounds in political references to the Hohenstaufen German Emperors, for *ab aquilone pandetur omne malum* (from the north appears all evil: Jer. 6:1).[73] From Isaiah are taken the prophecies: 'out of the serpent's root shall come forth a cockatrice and his fruit shall be a fiery flying serpent (Is. 14:29) and '. . . from whence come the young and old lion, the viper and the fiery flying serpent' (Is. 30:6), where the 'fiery flying serpent' is identified as Frederick II.[74] The *Super Esaiam*[75] equates the 'burdens' under which Isaiah denounced political powers of his day with contemporary counterparts. A fascinating interpretation of Jeremiah's own experience is applied to Joachim himself. After his death Joachim's exposition of the doctrine of the Trinity was condemned at the Fourth Lateran Council (1215) in favour of Peter Lombard's. Joachim's disciples clearly thought this was an unjust conspiracy against their master, seeing it prefigured in Jeremiah's persecution by the men of

Anathoth (Jer. 11:21) and in King Zedekiah's action in slashing Jeremiah's book with a knife and burning it (Jer. 36:11–23). In the New Testament, Herod and Caiaphas, the High Priest, are taken as figures of Pope Innocent III at the condemning council. The disciples of Joachim, because of this persecution, will be forced 'to flee' with the Holy Family into 'Egypt' and remain there until they can find refuge in 'Galilee', a home for the new spiritual men.[76]

The most famous of these allegorical *figurae* concerned Joachim's expectation of two new orders of spiritual men who would appear in the Last Days to lead the Church into the third *status*.[77] He had found these prefigured in many 'twos' of the Old and New Testaments and this identification was taken up with enthusiasm by the pseudo-Joachimist writers who cite as *figurae*, amongst others, the raven and dove sent out from the Ark by Noah, the two angels sent to rescue Lot from Sodom, Moses and Aaron, the two explorers sent to Canaan, Elijah and Elisha, Martha and Mary, Peter and John, the two on the road to Emmaus, Paul and Barnabas, the two witnesses in the Apocalypse.[78] For many in the thirteenth century, these *figurae* pointed obviously to the Dominicans and Franciscans. There were many other detailed applications of Holy Scripture in these so-called prophetic works of the thirteenth century. The reality of sacred history is brought under pressure to yield every possible 'sign' along the road which humanity is treading into the future. Thus, whilst on the one hand the multi-layered interpretation of Scripture was tending among professional scholars to be superceded by a more literal and critical approach to the text, on the other, the *sensus allegoricus* (in the figural sense) or *sensus typicus*, maintained a firm hold on the imagination of many, especially in the mendicant orders. It offered a method of interpreting contemporary and future history which was a defence against chaotic experience.

The greatest medieval vision of human history was cast in the form of a poem: Dante's *Divina Commedia*.[79] Anyone coming to the *Comedy* for the first time must be struck by the fact that Dante's visionary world is crowded with real people of all centuries, not personified abstractions, or abstracted categories such as 'bishop', 'king', 'lawyer'. (We must remember here that 'real' includes certain figures, such as Ulysses, whom Dante took to be historical characters but whom we regard as legendary). A crude modern reaction to Dante's use of historical persons accuses him of adapting this surprising method in order to put his enemies in hell. Nothing is further from the truth: friends and people for whom Dante felt an avowed sympathy receive due punishment in the *Inferno* along with the rest.[80] Rather, Dante is using allegory in an original way, not only to interpret God's evident signs laid up in the Scriptures, but to read the divine 'sign-writing' in human experience right down to his own contemporary situation. His purpose is to show divine judgement, mercy and providence for the future through the *figurae* of real persons and concrete happenings. But, as we have seen, the human author working on sacred history could only claim to read the spiritual 'senses' by divine inspiration. Dante's bold claim to use this method in creating a 'history' of his own could only be justified by a belief that his lone meditations on the complex mosaic of history were guided by divine illumination also. Such a claim would be akin to Joachim's belief, held in all humility, that he had been granted the gift of *spiritualis intellectus*. The view put forward here is that Dante was indeed drawing on the figural understanding of history as developed through the study of the Scriptures and most recently used by Joachim of Fiore and his followers. At the same time the new freedom given to the human author to use his own gifts in the interpretation of the divine 'senses' perhaps allowed Dante to take the bold step of viewing all history through the lens of his own 'eyes of the mind', while claiming this view as a vision from God.

It was in an earlier work, the *Convivio*, written *c.*1304, that Dante raised the question of the difference between poet's allegory and theologian's allegory, although his exposition at this point is not altogether clear. He does, however, say quite distinctly that in this work he will use poet's allegory. In each of the four existing books of the *Convivio* he takes one of his own poems and expounds its literal and allegorical meaning. The 'fictitious words' used by a poet do indeed veil an inner meaning, a truth concealed under a beautiful lie (*'una veritade ascosa sotto una bella menzogna'*).[81] The example he uses here is of Orpheus moving trees and stones with his music, which did not really happen but signifies the power of a wise man to tame and civilize. So, in the *Convivio*, the allegorical Lady of Philosophy is the presiding genius. But, remarks Dante, theologians use allegory in a different way from poets. The *'favole'* (words) of the poet belong to a different dimension from *'scritture'* – a term which Dante reserves, as a rule, for Holy Scripture.[82]

Literally the *Comedy* is also a fiction, a fictitious vision of the state of souls after death. But its fiction is that it is not a fiction. In the famous letter to Can Grande, which Dante wrote (or is supposed to have written) to his patron, the ruler of Verona, he boldly states that the *Comedy*'s spiritual meaning is *'polysemous'* (multiple in meaning) and claims for it the traditional four senses reserved for Holy Scripture. The example of this method of exposition which

Dante gives, he takes from the opening of Psalm 113: 'When Israel went out of Egypt, the house of Jacob from a people of strange language ...':

For if we consider the letter alone, the thing signified to us is the going out of the children of Israel from Egypt in the time of Moses; if the allegory, our redemption through Christ is signified; if the moral sense, the conversion of the soul from the sorrow and misery of sin to a state of grace is signified; if the anagogical, the passing of the sanctified soul from the bondage of the corruption of this world to the liberty of everlasting glory is signified. And although these mystical meanings are called by various names, they may one and all in a general sense be termed allegorical inasmuch as they are different from the literal or historical. . . . And therefore the subject of this work must be considered in the first place from the point of view of the literal meaning and next from that of the allegorical interpretation.[83]

One of the arguments used against the genuineness of this letter is that Dante could not possibly have claimed to adopt the method of the four senses because this belonged to Holy Scripture alone. Following St Thomas's distinction that only God has the power to signify by things, whereas man can only signify meaning by words, the great Dante scholar, Benedetto Nardi, concluded that no human writer could write four-fold allegory and therefore Dante could not have claimed to do so.[84] It is significant that fourteenth-century commentators turned away from the pointer in the letter and interpreted the *Comedy* in terms of straightforward personification allegory: Virgil personifies Reason, Beatrice, Theology and so on. But if Dante was a great innovator at this point, it is possible to turn the argument against the genuineness of the letter on its head: its very boldness is its claim to have been written by Dante himself. Obviously Dante was indeed writing 'words', not 'things' (or historical happenings); he could not actually do God's 'sign-writing' by making history himself nor could he arrogate to himself the role of the human *auctor* of Holy Scripture to whom the Holy Spirit dictated directly. But his own experience of history was a deeply felt one which led him to the interpretation of divine signs in contemporary events. The suggestion here is that he believed in an illumination akin to Joachim's *intellectus spiritualis* which enabled the eyes of his mind to penetrate the inner spiritual senses of God's work in history, tracing His finger in past and contemporary events and seeking to read the signs of the future.

Joachim disclaimed the title of prophet, emphasizing that the gift of spiritual understanding was grounded in the long meditations of the biblical exegete. Dante condemned the common soothsayers and diviners who fraudulently claimed to see into the future.[85] Dante's illumination – like Joachim's – was of a different order. We get a glimpse of how Dante 'read' secular history in biblical terms from an autobiographical hint in his political work *Monarchia*. He says that he once marvelled that the Roman people had been raised to world supremacy without any resistance, thinking in a superficial way that they had gained it by force, not by right. But now that, with the eyes of the mind, he had pierced to the core, all the signs convinced him that it was divine bounty which had 'provided' that supreme moment in the past when the Son of God descended into history precisely when Earth was best disposed to receive him, being at peace under the rule of the Emperor Augustus and the Roman people.[86]

It was the destiny of the Roman people which was revealed to him here. This illumination may well belong to the early days of Dante's exile from Florence when, with his own life shattered and his mind in deep confusion, he must have been searching for some political clue to the meaning of events. Out of the chaos divine guidance gave him this clue of the 'Roman people', a clue preserved from classical history but now standing for right order in society under a providentially given right monarch. In the *Monarchia*, Dante built up by the use of all possible 'signs' – philosophical, theological, classical and biblical – the case for this 'right government' decreed by providence. Through one of his biblical clues – reminiscent of Joachim's method in interpreting the generations of history – Dante established a 'concord' between the birth of David, the root from which Jesus sprang, and the birth of Rome in the coming of Aeneas to Italy, events which he makes contemporary.[87] Providence had provided two lights for the world, one spiritual, one political, and their historical origins could be seen as contemporary in time. Classical history carried its own allegorical authority, though inferior to that of Holy Scripture, as the authority of the political 'moon' was to the spiritual 'sun'.

That Dante's vision of right order in the world was no mere utopia of dreams is strikingly confirmed by his reaction to the advent of the Emperor Henry VII – Luxemburger by race but 'Roman' by title – in Italy in 1308. This event Dante saw as the work of providence: Henry was the appointed one to pacify the strife-torn cities of Italy and to erect the standard of Justice. In three letters which Dante wrote during Henry's time in Italy his daring adaptation of messianic language from the Bible would seem quite blasphemous without an understanding of his use of allegory. In the first, calling on the princes and people of Italy to receive Henry, he declared:

Behold now is the accepted time ... a new day is beginning to dawn ... for the strong lion of the tribe of Judah has ... raised up another Moses.... Rejoice, therefore, O Italy ... for soon shalt thou be the envy of the whole world, seeing that thy bridegroom ... the most clement Henry, Elect of God, Augustus and Caesar, is hastening to the wedding.[88]

In the letter addressed to Henry himself Dante is even more explicit in likening the Emperor to Christ, writing of the occasion when he was in Henry's presence: 'Then my spirit rejoiced within me when I said secretly: "Behold the Lamb of God which taketh away the sin of the world." '[89] And thirdly, castigating the Florentines for not perceiving the day of their deliverance, he writes of Henry: 'as though to him, after Christ, the prophet Isaiah had pointed the finger of prophecy when ... he declared: "Surely he hath born our griefs, and carried our sorrows." '[90] The collapse of Henry's fortunes and his death, of course, put an end to these hopes but if the *Monarchia* was written late,[91] it stands as a reaffirmation of political faith in the salvation to be brought by the 'Roman' emperor.

In the letter to Can Grande, Dante had gathered the three senses beyond the literal or historical into one category, the allegorical. Although the moral and anagogical are clearly dimensions to be read into the *Comedy*, it is the allegorical, in the figural sense developed by the biblical exegetes, that is most striking in the original use to which Dante puts it. Equally striking is the fact that there are two sources of Dante's figural inspiration – classical history as well as scriptural. They are not, of course, on a par, yet both Dante's debt to Virgil as his intellectual guide and his conviction that God's providence was working through Roman history prompted him again and again to use classical figures in conjunction with biblical. In the following brief selection of episodes from the *Comedy* the focus will be on the figural use of 'historical' characters.

But first we must note a telling little sentence at the beginning of the Can Grande letter, in which Dante places himself in a figural sequence drawn from his twin histories: 'even as the Queen of the South [i.e. the Queen of Sheba] sought Jerusalem, and as Pallas sought Helicon, so did I seek Verona.'[92] Here a concord between biblical, classical and his own contemporary role forms a 'pattern of threes' analogous to Joachim's. The opening canto of the *Inferno* gives us just such sequences. Virgil, Beatrice (representing Christ) and Dante are the chief actors. Again, when Dante questions his fitness for the tremendous role to which, according to Virgil, he is called, he sees behind him his classical and biblical counterparts: Aeneas made the journey to the underworld; St Paul, according to medieval tradition, did likewise. Is it possible, asks Dante, that he himself is summoned to emulate them?[93] 'Ma io, perche venervi? o chi 'l concede? Io non Enea, io non Paolo sono.' Thus, at the outset of the *Comedy* we are confronted with its multi-layered meaning in which one historical character or happening is resonant of others.

As Dante journeys through the circles of *Inferno* in an ever-descending spiral, two features are particularly striking: first, the concrete individualized detail of his encounters emphasizes the embodiment of universal states of sin in real, historical people. Dante, as has often been remarked, has an uncannily sharp eye for significant detail. And the philosophical thought of the thirteenth century had developed the doctrine of individual forms which gave him exactly the theological foundation he needed. St Thomas had expounded the theory that, since because of their imperfection, no one created thing or species could represent a full likeness of God, a diversity of forms had been created in order that in their totality they might approach a perfect likeness to God: '... diversity is looked upon not as an antithesis to perfection but rather as an expression of it.'[94] The potential of every person is to move towards God – or, by free will, away from him. Dante saw with peculiar intensity what he believed to be the real core of the person. He strove to delineate this both in terms of its extreme individuality and in terms of the relation of each person to the divine order of the universe. Thus the characters whom Dante recreates have carried into that eternal order where human beings finally occupy the place which they have made for themselves under God's judgement, the very 'sum' of themselves, 'that they should disclose in a single act, that character and fate that has filled out their lives.'[95] Sometimes this quintessence of a person is expressed by posture or by the fate endured, sometimes by an act of self-recollection. Dante 'was able to enter into each of his characters without ceasing to be Dante; he was able to speak their thousand languages.'[96]

But the overwhelming vision of the metaphysical order under which all diversities of forms were gathered under one unity meant that Dante's individuals frequently carried overtones of other characters drawn from experience or history or evoked as counter-types. No two persons were identical either in their choices or in God's dealings with them, yet figurally they could be related in an infinite web of connections. Thus the second striking characteristic of the *Inferno* and *Purgatorio* is that behind the selected encounters other figures often stand, giving a three-dimensional perspective to the scene. For instance, in the ante-Hell of those 'who never were alive' – the 'neither hot nor cold' of the Laodicians (Rev. 3:15) – Dante recognizes 'he who through cowardice made the great refusal'.[97] Many commentators think that this is Pope Celestine V, whose abdication let in the notorious Boniface VIII. But the figure calls up also Pontius Pilate, or the rich young ruler from Matthew 19, or Esau from the Old Testament. As Robert Hollander says: 'Each act in universal history has its past and future counterparts in other acts. It allows a polysemous interpretation that is both multitudinous and precise.'[98] The famous episode of Paolo and Francesca, which moves Dante so greatly that he loses consciousness, is redolent with allusions.[99] In the circle where carnal sinners are blown hither and thither by the winds of passion, Francesca tells how the two lovers were reading the romance of Lancelot and Guinevere together. As she recreates the scene, we see other great lovers, such as Dido and Aeneas, standing behind, while her final line contains a literary echo which, in recalling another famous book-reading episode, creates a counter-type. She ends: 'that day we read no more.' In his *Confessions*, St Augustine tells how he heard a voice beyond his garden wall saying 'Take and read.' He took up his New Testament and opened it randomly at Romans 13, where St Paul warns against the lusts of the flesh. This was the decisive moment which turned Augustine from his wanton living to become a Christian. He concludes: 'I did not wish to read any further.'[100]

As we descend through the circles the features of both sharp individualization and universal typology make their impact. Among the open sepulchres in which the heretics are entombed, one shade recognizes Dante's Tuscan accent. Farinata degli Uberti, the proud Florentine aristocrat, accosts him: 'He rose upright with breast and countenance, as if he entertained great scorn of Hell. . . . He looked at me a little and then, disdainfully, he asked me: "Who were thy ancestors?"'[101] Even in Hell, party still matters most to one of the Ghibelline Grandi. Two tyrants of north Italy, Azzolino of Romano and Obizzo of Este, are distinguished by the black hair of the one and the blond of the other.[102] The suicides – violent against themselves – are transformed into a wood of stunted and poisonous trees, perpetually torn by Harpy-birds who nest in them. Here Pier delle Vigne, the confidant of the Emperor Frederick II, embodies the psychological state of one who puts too much trust in princes: 'I am he who held both keys of Frederick's heart, and turned them, locking and unlocking so softly that from his secrets I excluded almost every other man: so great fidelity I bore to the glorious office that I lost thereby both sleep and life.' Thrown into prison by the plotting envy of other courtiers who accused him of treachery, he committed suicide: 'My soul, in its disdainful mood, thinking to escape disdain by death, made me, though just, unjust against myself.' His loyalty and his belief that it was 'just' are unimpaired even in hell, and his chief concern is that Dante should believe this: 'By the new roots of this tree, I swear to you, never did I break faith to my lord who was so worthy of honour.'[103] Dante is silenced by pity for misguided loyalty.

Among the sowers of discord, horrifically torn asunder or mutilated, Dante meets the one bitterly enshrined in Florentine memory as the instigator of the Guelf/Ghibelline feud, which tore Florence apart. He had both hands cut off and 'raising the stumps through the dim air so that their blood defiled his face, said: "Thou wilt recollect Mosca too, ah me, who said 'A thing done has an end!' which was the seed of evil to the Tuscan people."'[104] In the irony of this single sentence, recalled from Florentine legend, Dante catches all the continuing misery that human beings suffer from murderous vendettas. In the circle of evil counsellors, Ulysses tells how he led his fellow sailors to destruction. According to this story, he did not return home to Ithaca but sailed out into the ocean through the Pillars of Hercules. Urging his men on with arrogant curiosity, he voyaged south through unknown seas until, just when they thought to make landfall, the mariners and their ship were engulfed in sight of Mount Purgatory.[105] Here a counter-type is juxtaposed to the prideful journey that exceeds all bounds: 'And as he who was avenged by the bears saw Elijah's chariot at its departure, when the horses rose erect to heaven ...'[106] In this indirect allusion to Elisha, who witnessed Elijah caught up to heaven, Dante instantly captures the essence of the blessed journey to God, set against the self-destroying defiance of pride.

Finally, in the ultimate and deepest perdition of Satan's domain, treachery to lords and benefactors – a thoroughly medieval concept – is typified in the frozen horror of Satan himself, arch-traitor against God, chewing on the heads of Judas Iscariot, Brutus and Cassius.[107] The parallel here between the traitor against Christ and the conspirators against Caesar is a striking example of Dante's figural use of his twin authorities, scriptural and classical. And once again, type and anti-type are present, for Dante's detailed description of Satan's three heads 'joined at the crest' presents a parody of the Godhead in its Trinity and Unity.

The approach to the Mount of Purgatory focuses attention on another dimension of universal experience, the theme of pilgrimage or movement out of slavery towards freedom. On the sea-shore at dawn, Dante and Virgil see the Angel of God approaching across the ocean using his wings as the white sails of a ship and carrying more than 100 spirits of the lately dead. The voyagers are chanting Psalm 114: '*In exitu Israel de Egypto*' (When Israel came out of Egypt).[108] This is the latest group of souls released from the bondage of this world and about to begin their ascent of the Mountain of Purgatory towards the perfect liberty of the Sons of God. Dante here uses the very *figura* which he gave as a key to the whole poem in the letter to Can Grande: the Exodus of the Israelites from the slavery of Egypt.[109] It is the type for Dante's own pilgrimage from Florence to 'a people just and sane',[110] from Egypt to Jerusalem. It is the type for all aspiring souls who in this life 'look for a city which hath foundations, whose builder and maker is God' (Heb. 11:10).

Directing and shepherding the throng of souls on the shore is an old man who, rather surprisingly, turns out to be Cato. How, it may be asked, can Cato – a pagan, a suicide and an opponent of Caesar – be assigned this key position at the foot of Mount Purgatory? He is there, says Virgil, because he valued freedom more than life.[111] This single attribute sets him above the clash of politics as an individual who made a supreme choice. There is, here, an echo of Dante's own experience when he shed political connections and became 'a party to himself',[112] and Virgil specifically makes the connection between Cato and Dante. But there is more than this. Cato's venerable appearance is described by Dante in terms which at once recall the medieval image of Moses[113] – Moses who led that Exodus into freedom which is the type of all others. So once again we meet a three-fold pattern bringing together the classical type, the scriptural and Dante himself: all are *figurae* of aspiring souls who press towards the true Christian freedom.

In the Antepurgatory, Dante's rapid and vivid survey of contemporary or recent princes gathered in the valley of negligent rulers again illustrates both his characterization of an individual by a single detail and his reading of history as God's sign-writing.[114] 'He who sits highest and hath the semblance of having left undone what he ought to have done' is Rudolf of Hapsburg, who betrayed his God-given trust in neglecting the Imperial office. 'That snub-nosed one is beating his breast and making common cause with another who, sighing, hath made a bed for his cheek with the palm of his hand.' These are Philip III of France and Henry of Navarre, whose daughter married Philip. They are bewailing the wickedness of Philip's son, Philip the Fair, who was an arch-villain in Dante's

eyes: 'Father and father-in-law are they of the plague of France.'
The 'stout of limb' and he 'of the virile nose' are Peter III of Aragon
and Charles I of Anjou. The 'King of the simple life' is Henry
III of England, whom Dante contrasts with his energetic son,
Edward I.

The intensity with which Dante feels the significance of his own
contemporary history is revealed in two figural connections he
makes between his own times and the Passion narrative of the
Gospels. Climbing Mount Purgatory, he meets Hugh Capet, the
founder of the French dynasty, among the avaricious and prodigal.
Hugh's discourse on the deeds of his descendants leads up to de-
nunciations of contemporary Capetians.[115] First, Charles of Valois
had played a treacherous part in the coup which overturned the
'White Guelf' government in Florence, brought in the 'Blacks' and
led to the exile of Dante and other White leaders. Dante dares to
link this treachery with that of Judas: 'Forth he comes alone, without an army, and with the lance wherewith Judas jousted; and that
he couches so, that he makes the paunch of Florence to burst.' Here,
it might be felt, the personal disaster for Dante leads him to give the
episode undue importance. The second allusion is therefore all the
more striking because it goes against Dante's own experience in
casting Pope Boniface VIII in the role of Christ. In 1303, agents of
Philip the Fair of France outraged Christendom by seizing Boniface
at Anagni; the Pope died shortly afterwards. Now Boniface was one
of the simoniacal popes whom Dante denounced in the *Inferno*.[116]
He was at the root of the civil discord which was destroying
Florence; he was the evil star of Dante's personal fate. Yet here
Dante feels the sacrilege of unholy hands laid on the Vicar of Christ
so strongly that he links the episode directly with the Crucifixion,
putting into Hugh Capet's mouth the words:

> I see the fleur-de-lys enter Alagna [Anagni] and in his vicar Christ
> made captive.
> A second time I see him mocked;
> I see the vinegar and the gall renewed and him slain between living
> thieves.[117]

At the top of Mount Purgatory, in the Earthly Paradise of Man
restored to primeval innocence, Beatrice comes to Dante. But she
comes, not as the girl he once knew in Florence, but as the representative of Christ at a focal point in time for him. She comes
in the midst of a mystical procession which embraces at once the
whole of the Scriptures, the process of history and its apocalypse.[118]

First, out of the preceding brightness of light, come the Seven
Golden Candlesticks which are the Seven Gifts of the Spirit and have
seven bright banners streaming backwards over the procession. Next
come 24 elders, clothed in white and crowned with lilies. Behind
them four mystical *animalia* surround the chariot drawn by a griffon
which is the centre of the procession. To its right are three dancers
and to its left, four. Behind are two aged men, then four 'of lowly
appearance' and finally a solitary old man walking in a trance. The
procession is packed with biblical symbolism. From the Apocalypse
come the Seven Golden Candlesticks, the 24 elders and the four
'living creatures' (*animalia*) whom Dante also refers back to their
origin in Ezekiel.[119] The description of the griffon carries echos of
the Psalms and the Song of Solomon.[120] The three dancing girls,
dressed in white, green and red, are the theological virtues of Faith,
Hope and Charity from 1 Cor. 13, while the four on the other side
are the cardinal virtues, Prudence, Justice, Fortitude and Temper-
ance. The pageant as a whole sets forth the time process through the
procession of the Scriptures, with Christ (the griffon) and his Church
(the chariot) at the centrepoint of all history. The 24 elders preceding the chariot are the books of the Old Testament;[121] the four
animalia are the symbols of the four Gospels;[122] following after,
the first two are Luke, author of the Acts and likened here to
Hippocrates,[123] and Paul with a sharp sword; the four lowly ones
are the lesser epistles[124] and, last of all, the lonely visionary is St
John of the Apocalypse. Whereas the Old Testament books are
dressed in white with lily crowns for their faith in 'the evidence of
things not seen' (Heb. 11:1), the four Gospels are crowned in green
for hope and the following books of the New Testament carry red
roses and other red flowers for the fulfilment of the promises in the
new revelation of charity.

Charles Singleton stresses the point that the procession only reveals itself gradually before Dante's eyes: 'if this is the Word of God
that comes so, we see that the poet has so managed the coming of
that Word as to give us the distinct impression that it has unfolded
before our eyes, that Scripture has come into view in the due order
of its books, from the beginning to Revelation.'[125] This, says Singleton, brings into focus the whole dimension of time within which the
Word of God unfolds. Here Singleton quotes from St Bonaventura a
passage which gives the key to Dante's procession:

Holy Scripture has a length which consists of the description of the times
and ages, namely, from the beginning of the world to the day of judgement.... Thus Scripture is of great length, because in its treatment it

begins with the commencement of the world and of time, in the beginning of Genesis – and extends to the end of the world and of time, to the end of the Apocalypse.[126]

The time procession stops precisely at the point where the apparently still empty chariot is directly opposite Dante. Then the preceding figures turn to face the chariot and the griffon, so that time stands still while the eyes of all are on its centre. This is, of course, the moment of encounter for Dante. Beatrice now appears in the chariot but the acclamations which herald her coming are lauds for the Messiah, first from the Song of Solomon, *Veni sponsa de Libano*, and then *Benedictus qui venis*, the salutation to Christ as he rode into Jerusalem.[127] At this most central point an extraordinary allusion is added from Dante's other 'authority', classical history. He had already likened the chariot of the Church to the chariot of Roman emperors in triumphal procession and now he links a quotation from the *Aenead* to the Christian salutation: 'All were saying: "*Benedictus qui venis*" and strewing flowers above and around, "*manibus o date lilia plenis*"' (Oh, with full hands give lilies).[128] This heightens the solemn sense of climax, for Beatrice comes as the representative of Christ to judge Dante. Virgil, when he left Dante at the approach to the Earthly Paradise, had expressed a humanist's conviction that, after the experiences he had undergone, Dante was master of himself: 'Free, upright, and whole is thy will, and it were a fault not to act according to its prompting; wherefore I do crown and mitre thee master over thyself.'[129] But now the limits of the humanist perspective are made clear, for in an instant Dante is cast down into utter abasement by Beatrice's stern accusations: 'he turned his steps by a way not true, pursuing false visions of good ... So low sank he, that all means for his salvation were already short, save showing him the lost people.'[130] It is the moment of judgement in the midst of time which can come to Everyman and Dante actually links it with Last Judgement and End of Time.

But Dante is acutely aware that history is not yet at an end. Repentant and cleansed in the waters of Lethe, he is brought close to Beatrice who unveils his mission to him through a pageant which unites scriptural history with a vivid representation of contemporary history. The procession reforms and turns back through the forest until it halts at a tree 'despoiled of flowers and of other foliage', where everyone murmurs 'Adam'. The ravaged tree is renewed by the griffon. After an interval in which Dante sleeps, Beatrice shows him the chariot empty by the tree. An eagle swoops upon it, again rending its new leaves and flowers and smiting the chariot with full force. Then a fox leaps upon the car, but is chased away, and the eagle descends again into it, leaving it feathered with its plumage. Next a dragon attacks it, tearing away part of the bottom. In a horrible transformation, the feathered chariot sprouts seven heads and seated upon it now appears a shameless harlot to whom a giant makes love until he drags her in the monstrous car away into the forest.[131]

The symbolism of this strange pageant has been variously interpreted but the following seems to be the most plausible. The Tree of the Knowledge of Good and Evil in the Garden of Eden becomes the tree of humanity restored by Christ to new life. The eagle of the Roman Empire first ravages the tree and the chariot of the Church in presecutions and then endows the Church with the sinister feathers of worldly power in the Donation of Constantine.[132] The fox probably symbolizes heresy and the dragon schism. Finally, in a striking indictment of contemporary events, Dante represents the transformation of the Church by her worldly possessions (the feathers) into the seven-headed monster on which sits the harlot, the Papal Court. She is dragged away to captivity in Avignon by the giant, the French monarchy. Thus Dante's crisis of personal salvation leads on directly to a great statement about the course of human history and the desperate state of the contemporary Church. Beatrice commands: 'Look that thou write what thou seest when returned yonder'.[133] But his mission extends further – into prophecy. At the end of *Purgatorio*, before Beatrice leads Dante on the heavenward ascent, she utters an enigmatic prophecy to which we shall return shortly.[134]

As at the beginning of the first two cantiche, so Dante's approach to his 'crowning task' in the *Paradiso* links him again in a pattern of threes to classical and Christian *figurae*. In an invocation to Apollo, he begs that the god will draw him out of himself as he did Marsyas.[135] The story was that Apollo punished Marsyas for arrogance, after triumphing over him in a musical contest, by flaying him alive. In medieval legend, St Bartholomew is the Christian counterpart of Marsyas because he was martyred by flaying. He was often represented carrying his own skin and became a symbol of the need to slough off the old self in order to enter into new life.[136] So here Dante, overawed by his high vocation and the impossibility of his task, casts himself in the part of these two *figurae* of self-abnegation.

The successive heavens of the *Paradiso* are still peopled, to a large extent, with historical and contemporary characters carrying figural meaning for Dante. His concern is still with the salvation of societies on earth as well as with individual souls. So the heaven of Jupiter, that is, of the Just, occupies an important place.[137] The souls of the just are flying stars which gradually group themselves to form the opening words of the Book of Wisdom: '*Diligite justitiam qui judicatis terram*'; love justice you who rule the earth (Wisd. 1:1). Then further lights are pricking out in fire the head and neck of an eagle, while the last M of *terram* becomes its body and wings. The eagle's discourse on divine justice and the corrupt deeds of reigning monarchs which follows brings under paradisal scrutiny the whole sinful world of contemporary politics on the 'threshing floor which maketh us wax so fierce', as Dante describes the earth when he gazes down from the *Cielo stellato*.[138] Then, by contrast, the eagle directs Dante's attention to the lights that form his eye and eyebrows: David in the centre, Trajan, Hezekiah, Constantine, William the Good of Sicily and Ripheus, a hero of Trojan legend.[139] This is the strangest possible selection of just rulers: from classical history and legend, from the Old Testament and from post-Incarnational history. It does, indeed, appear quite arbitrary without an understanding of Dante's figural use of history. God's sign-writing was to be sought everywhere throughout the time process and could be 'read' in the obscure parts of history as well as in the more famous. Here, the independence of Dante's selection of signs is strikingly illustrated. Each fact or character could be read as an allegory of something else; each allusion is stacked with further meaning.

This method of building in further dimensions of meaning may apply to the actual form of the eagle and Dante's careful description of how it was composed.[140] It is a bizarre image: an M – probably a gothic M – which is transformed into an eagle. In one enigmatic phrase, Dante speaks of twining the M with lilies ('*pareva in prima d'ingigliarsi all' emme*'.[141] This takes us straight back to one of the most original of the Abbot Joachim's visual figures. He drew a pair of trees in which the branches, in a 5/7 pattern, represent Old Testament tribes in the first tree and New Testament churches in the second.[142] So here are the first and second *status* of scriptural history. Turned the other way up, the formalized branches actually resemble a gothic M, while they are entwined with lilies and an eagle's head now appears at the top. The whole becomes an heraldic eagle. The eagle, the lilies and the 5/7 number scheme are all clues given by Joachim pointing to the hidden third *status*. In this figure, the eye of the eagle is picked out as *Clavis David*.[143] It seems, therefore, that Joachim's figures may give us the key to a further perspective of Dante's vision: the signs of the Scriptures, when read prophetically, point forward to a coming era of the just society when the work of the Triune God will be completed in the Holy Spirit.

This prophetic theme in the *Comedy* is veiled in enigmatic symbols. Perhaps Dante grew unwilling to be more explicit after the collapse of his hopes in the Emperor Henry VII. But prophecy is still present and particularly at three key points: the opening canto of the *Inferno*, the closing canto of the *Purgatorio* and near the climax of the *Paradiso*. At the beginning of the *Inferno*, Virgil juxtaposes to the figures of the leopard, lion and wolf that bar Dante's way another animal symbol, that of a greyhound (*Veltro*) who is still to come.[144] He will not feed on land or wealth but on wisdom, love and virtue and he will chase the wolf of cupidity back to Hell. In canto 27 of the *Paradiso*, at one moment Dante is marvelling at the sweet song which seems like a smile of the universe but immediately he perceives that all Heaven is blushing, red with wrath, as St Peter begins his tremendous diatribe against the cupidity of his successors, the modern popes: 'Oh fair beginning, to what vile end must thou fall!'[145] Beatrice takes up the strain, using the metaphors of a ship and of fruits that grow cankered: 'O greed who so dost abase mortals ... the continuous drench turneth true plum fruits into cankered tubes. Faith and Innocence are found only in little children. And thou ... reflect that there is none to govern upon earth, wherefore the human household so strayeth from the path.' Then the note changes abruptly and she declares: 'that the fated season so long awaited shall turn right round the poops where the prows are, so that the fleet shall have a straight course and true fruit shall follow flower.'[146]

Leaving aside the variety of interpretations offered to explain the figure of the *Veltro*, we see that both these prophecies imply the coming of a saviour who will establish the just society, freeing it from the dominance of cupidity. The prophecy pronounced by Beatrice at the end of the *Purgatorio* is more explicit in delineating the office and task of the one who is to come but enigmatic in his designation:

Not for all time shall be without an heir the eagle that left the plumes on the car, whereby it became a monster and then a prey ... stars are already near ... that shall bring us times when a five hundred ten and five [*cinquecento dieci e cinque*], sent by God, shall slay the thief, with that giant who sins with her.[147]

So it is a true Emperor who is to come to rescue the Church from captivity. But why *cinquecento dieci e cinque*? Many have offered solutions of this riddle. The most usual puts the number into Roman numerals and then transposes the second and third to form *DV(U)X*. At this point, again, Joachim may offer a more complete explanation. This takes us back to the figural use of scriptural history common to both Joachim and Dante.

In book IV of his *Liber de Concordia*, Joachim gives one of his most striking and explicit prophecies about the leadership at the beginning of the third *status*.[148] It occurs in the context of the concords he establishes between the generations of the Old Dispensation and those of the New. In this number symbolism, the 42nd generation from Jacob and, in parallel, the 42nd generation from the Incarnation, constitute two great climaxes. In the 42nd generation after Jacob, Zorobabel, the son of Salathiel, ascended with many followers from Babylon to Jerusalem and there rebuilt the Temple which had been destroyed at the time of the Captivity. In the Church, the future 42nd generation after Christ will begin in the year that God alone knows. In this generation, when the general tribulation has been suffered and the good corn purged from all weeds, one, '*quasi novus dux*', will ascend from new Babylon and will be the universal pontiff of the new Jerusalem which is the Church ('*universalis scilicet pontifex nove Hierusalem, hoc est sancte matris ecclesie*'). Joachim also finds this *novus dux* typified in the Angel of the Apocalypse, who ascends from the rising of the sun, having the sign of the living God. Full liberty will be given to him to renovate the Christian religion. No longer will proud kings, polluted by idols and serving avarice, rule over God's people, as they have done, and do to this present day. This time will endure to the end, like a sabbath ('*velud in sabbatum*'), without war or scandal, without care or terror, because God will bless and sanctify it.

I think Joachim clearly intends the *novus dux* to be a Pope, but the title *dux* could obviously refer to a secular leader and his brief description of the sabbath age suggests the regeneration of a whole society, while he actually alludes to avarice or cupidity, Dante's *lupa*. Now the crucial fact of history here is that Zorobabel finished the rebuilding of the Temple – the symbol of the new society – in the year 515 BC. The numerical coincidence is striking. Dante had already used a concord of generations to match the birth of David with the beginnings of Rome.[149] It would be entirely in keeping with his allegorical use of Scripture to see the first Zorobabel as a *figura* of a second one to come. Joachim was certainly known to Dante: he places him in the heaven of the Sun[150] and it is almost certain that he used in the *Paradiso* not only Joachim's tree-eagles but also his figure of three circles to represent the Trinity.[151] The *Liber de*

Concordia was available in a number of manuscripts in Italy. The building of the Second Temple was an important landmark in the medieval perspective of world history, a regular milestone which appears in all world chronicles like the founding of Rome. Dante would certainly have been familiar with it. As for the system of dating by counting backwards from the Incarnation, this had been established by Eusebius whose *Cronologia*, translated into Latin by St Jerome, was a standard work for medieval chroniclers.[152] Thus the hypothesis that Dante used the first Zorobabel as the *figura* of a second Zorobabel who would rebuild earthly society seems a reasonable one. The figure would be particularly apt because the new Babylonish Captivity of the Church at Avignon was for Dante the most tragic and disastrous event of contemporary history, while the ascent from Babylon to Jerusalem once more encapsulated the theme of exodus from bondage to liberty. Finally, by a miraculous coincidence, Dante could contain the key word *DUX* in the very date he was given. The likelihood that this scriptural *figura* gives us the meaning of the *515* is strong, as is also the supposition that Dante took it from Joachim.

It was, I think, Dante's deep involvement in the tragic corruption of his own society that sent him back so constantly to his two sources of illumination, classical and scriptural history. In the long procession of historical characters he found the clues to his interpretation of present degeneracy and future *renovatio*. The theme of exodus and pilgrimage towards the true society pervades the *Comedy*. In the Empyrean, the tenth heaven, Dante's vision of this society takes the form of the celestial rose in which each redeemed soul enjoys the throne of a petal.[153] Even here history has a place, for St Bernard points to many individuals, some from the Bible and then 'rank by rank descending, even as I, naming their proper names, go down the rose petal by petal.' Augustine, Francis, Benedict and others are there, right down to the empty throne waiting for the contemporary Henry VII. Dante knows that he has come to his home. This is where he is a 'true Roman', where he passes 'from Florence to a people just and sane'.[154]

Dante represents the high point of a medieval literature which drew deeply from the well of the Scriptures. The tradition of the four-fold senses which he followed was passing out of use, as we have seen, but the work of the biblical exegetes continued in the notable commentaries of the fourteenth century. Literary theory was further developed by these in several ways. Human authorship was discussed with increasing sophistication. An outstanding example of this debt can be found in commentaries on the Book of Wisdom. Was Solomon the human author? Robert Holcot, an Oxford Dominican, assembled many opinions on this question in his popular commentary (*c*.1333–4).[155] The question of human frailty in relation to divine inspiration now exercised many minds. The key case was that of King David, psalmist and sinner. Earlier exegesis had got round the problem of David's adultery with Bathsheba by allegorizing the whole story in various ways, their sinful union being even taken as a figure of Christ's union with the Church! By the fourteenth century, such a solution offended reason and it had become possible to treat the episode literally and historically. Human authors were now seen to have differing moral roles and one of these was that of the penitent sinner, peculiarly appropriate to David in his penitential psalms.[156]

The concept of literary form – *forma tractatus* – was now increasingly developed in scriptural commentaries and the human authors' mode of proceeding – *forma tractandi* – became a focus of interest. Distinctions were made between various literary roles, such as that of author, compiler and collector.[157] Nicholas of Lyra (*c*.1270–1340) distinguished between a *compilatio*, an orderly arrangement of material by a *compilator*, and a mere *collectio*, a random gathering together.[158] The recognition that these two last categories could be applied to the Scriptures – the Book of Wisdom was a *compilatio*, while Psalms and Proverbs were *collectiones* – was paralleled in the thirteenth and fourteenth centuries by the appearance of the great compilers and collectors of literary material, such as Vincent of Beauvais, Peter Auriol and Ralph Higden. The latter felt impelled to justify his role as a *compilator* by citing precedents amongst which he includes the example of Ruth gleaning corn (Ruth 2): 'Although she followed after powerful men, the lord Boas ordered them not to despise her.' The implication is that the Lord God does not despise the humble *compilator* who follows in the footsteps of the powerful *auctores*.[159]

Finally, one of the most significant developments in the later Middle Ages was the narrowing of the gap between scriptural and pagan authorities. Of course, in so far as divine inspiration was involved, the gap was still there. But emphasis on the human author brought these writings closer together: 'when Solomon's *auctoritas* consisted in human reasoning, he was supposed to be operating on the same wavelength as Aristotle, whose *auctoritas* consisted solely in rationalisation.'[160] Miss Smalley observed that, particularly in the case of the Wisdom books of the Old Testament, commentators increasingly drew on classical literature for their philosophy, natural science, politics and ethics. Thus, in the fourteenth century, she can speak of the 'English classicising friars' – including Holcot, Lathbury and others – as those who in their scriptural exegesis drew extensively on the authors of antiquity.[161] The importance of this coming together of pagan and Christian sources for literary authors is obvious. We have already seen its operation on a different level in the individual and isolated case of Dante. But we also meet its influence in English literature:

> The 'classicising' commentaries are major repositories of scholastic literary theory. To obtain examples of this theory in practice, Chaucer and his contemporaries need have read no further than the prologues. In the prologues and in the commentaries themselves, they would have found pagan *auctoritates* being employed in the elucidation of pre-Christian ideas and mores, and the expertise of pagan sages constantly being drawn on in the interests of Christian learning.[162]

A literary author in the later Middle Ages could draw riches, pagan and Christian, from biblical scholarship and he could link himself in his authorial role with the great of both traditions, as Thomas of Usk linked himself with both Aristotle and David.[163]

One of the literary forms now identified by biblical scholars was the *forma prophetialis* which they recognized in their prologues as applying to Old Testament prophets and the Apocalypse. This could be used as a model by literary authors. Dr Minnis has demonstrated the parallels between the early thirteenth-century Apocalypse commentary attributed to Gilbert of Poitiers, which became one of the standard prologues, and John Gower's general prologue to his *Vox clamantis*.[164] Gower appeals to his namesake, the author of the Apocalypse, for guidance. He appears to follow Gilbert's distinction between three kinds of vision, using the second and third and adding to Gilbert's example of Pharaoh's dream those of Daniel and Joseph. He could not, of course, claim for himself the kind of vision or angelic visitation granted to scriptural figures, but, says Minnis, he claims this inspiration indirectly: 'the guardian angel who watches over everyone sometimes helps a man to understand the future by a special gift of insight. John Gower, it is strongly implied, is such a man.'[165] It would seem that Gower saw himself, in terms of the Aristotelian model, as 'an instrumental *causa efficiens* working under the primary *causa efficiens*, God'.[166] The parallel he is making between the vision of the seer of Patmos and his own writing is clear: the Apocalypse deals with the sufferings and corruption of the Church in the seer's time; the *Vox clamantis* deals with the suffering and corruption of the Church and society in Gower's time. Gower protests his humility with much emphasis, yet his prologue suggests that he believes he has contributed 'some personal, though God-given, insights'.[167]

Dr Minnis also points out that Gower arranged his text in seven parts, a division which at once recalls the Seven Seals of the Apocalypse and the tradition of dividing Apocalypse commentaries into seven parts. In Gower's prologue to the second book, the title there given of 'the Voice of One crying' clearly echoes the prophet John the Baptist (John 1:23). His disclaimer concerning divine *auctoritas* can be linked with the 'delicate balance' preserved in the various *artes praedicandi* between the inspiration of the preacher under the Holy Spirit and the full divine authority.

Late-medieval exegetes had come to regard many a Scriptural *auctor* in the role of preacher ... The *Vox clamantis* represents a further stage in the dissemination and development of such theory: therein a 'modern' writer adopts the stance of the preacher-prophet, likening his moral position and righteous indignation to those of the two 'ancient' preacher-prophets who are his namesakes, St John the Baptist and St John the *auctor* of the Apocalypse.[168]

By contrast, in the *Confessio amantis*, Gower was dealing with a subject on the lower plane of philosophy and ethics, although still a serious subject. In his prologue he followed the practice of recent biblical commentaries on the Wisdom books of the Old Testament in treating them as philosophical material, resting on human reason rather than written under divine inspiration. Because he was operating on this lower plane, he could bring together the Wisdom literature of the Bible and the pagan poets and philosophers: 'Solomon, Aristotle and Ovid had all used their natural reason; they were philosophers and not theologians.'[169] The *Confessio amantis* is a serious moral poem but, in tune with the theory of authorship developed by the biblical exegetes, Gower does not have to make elaborate disclaimers of *auctoritas* as in the *Vox clamantis*, where he needed to distance himself from the divinely dictated *auctoritas* of biblical preacher-prophets.

The problem of placing Langland's *Piers Plowman* within a recognized literary genre has long exercised students of the poem. Like many other great works, it contains elements of several forms. Morton Bloomfield has discussed these in his book *Piers Plowman as a Fourteenth-Century Apocalypse*.[170] He admits that the poem does not wholly fit into the category of an apocalypse but nevertheless finds its main inspiration in the apocalyptic model which

Langland drew from the Bible. He stresses the constant echoes of the Bible throughout the poem:

Piers Plowman is impregnated with the Bible and the writings of the Fathers, but more especially the Bible. It has been said of Bernard of Clairvaux that he speaks Bible as one might speak French or English. Langland speaks Bible too; phrases, echoes, and paraphrases crop up everywhere. His whole mind is steeped in the Bible; it is a real language to him.[171]

As several recent studies have shown, Langland's reading of the Bible, or perhaps more accurately, his use of biblical commentaries and concordances, underlies the whole structure and progression of the poem. The scriptural quotations and allusions are 'the matrix out of which the poem developed'.[172] The poem arises out of Langland's devotional reading, in which he expected to find 'a description of his own life and the life of his Christian society'.[173] It is clear that he read the Scriptures by the traditional method of different levels of meaning. The tropological or 'moral sense' was fundamental to his message but beyond this the allegorical and anagogical carry the imagination forward into the final 'end' towards which the human soul is groping. Here it is striking that his allegorical method is not the figural one of Dante but the literary personification inherited from classical times. Selecting, out of many, two key personifications, Holy Church and Lady Meed, we see vividly illustrated how Langland draws his images from the Bible. Holy Church descends from the Tower of Truth on the Hill to teach Will.[174] This recalls the 'tabernacle' on the 'holy hill' of Psalms such as 15 or 43 and the Mount of Transfiguration in Luke's Gospel. A homily attributed to St Augustine links Psalm 15 with the apocalyptic vision of the heavenly Jerusalem (that is, the Church) descending as the Bride of Christ (Apoc. 21:2).[175] 'The poet has the anagogical church, the Church celestial, reveal the principle of charity which is the foundation of Jerusalem. She stands as an ideal towards which the allegorical church, the Church militant, should strive.'[176] Juxtaposed to this image is that of Lady Meed whom Will first sees when told to look to the left[177] – with an implicit reference to the sheep and goats of the Last Judgement (Matt. 25:33). The whole picture of Meed, with her scarlet robes and gemmed hands, is based on that of the great Whore of Babylon in Apocalypse 17. She is the direct opposite of Holy Church. In the poem these two great figures, representing the eternal opposites of Jerusalem and Babylon, confront each other not only in the here-and-now battle for souls, but also in the eschatological warfare of End-time.

Bloomfield's characterization of *Piers Plowman* as an apocalypse has recently been reinforced by Dr Kerby-Fulton who shows the prevalence of apocalyptic texts in fourteenth-century England and links the poem with the two great apocalyptic writers, Hildegarde of Bingen and Joachim of Fiore.[178] From her detailed study, she draws out four main concerns which highlight the sense that the final crisis of history is approaching. The first of these is Langland's obsession with the conflict between true and false prophets, which is one of the signs of Last Things (Matt. 24:11, 24). Secondly, a passionate sense of the crisis in leadership and the search for a final leader of great holiness runs right through the poem. Thirdly, Langland's fascination with the life of contemplation and evangelical poverty, as enshrining the qualities of the Last Age, carries overtones of Joachim's 'new spiritual men' and the final hermit order. Fourthly, Dr Kerby-Fulton argues that, though the evidence is ambiguous, Langland expects a period of renewal in the End-time, which in the B Text is clearly placed after the battle with Antichrist, as in Joachimist prophecy. Thus a fourteenth-century poet, desperately aware of souls wandering and of a breakdown in society, draws his inspiration and vision of the true society from a multi-layered reading of the Bible and from the medieval exegetes, both traditional and radical in the Joachimist sense.

To turn briefly to Chaucer from Gower and Langland is to begin moving into a new world. True, he used the conventional distinction between an author and a compiler first developed through biblical studies. In his 'General Prologue' to the *Canterbury Tales* he declares that he is only 'rehearsing' other men's words and that his own 'wit is short'.[179] He seems to be following a writer such as Vincent of Beauvais[180] but whereas Vincent was a true compiler, Chaucer was assuming a role. No doubt there was a tinge of irony in his repetition of this common form but it was a useful literary device: as the real compilers stressed that they were only rehearsing the *ipsissima verba* of their authors, so Chaucer's narrator could pretend that these were the proper words of his fictitious characters. Yet perhaps there also remained, in the consciousness of an innovative writer who was endowing words with a new human worth, some vestige of the belief that all words take their ultimate value from God's Word. The *'retracciones'* added at the end of the *Canterbury Tales* hint at such a perception. We recall that in the Aristotelian prologue the *causa finalis* was the aim of the work. A biblical exegete saw this in terms of leading to salvation and often adopted as the highest statement of the *causa finalis* a text from Romans 15:4: 'All that is written is written for our doctrine, that by the

8   Ibid., p. 35. See also Gerald Bonner, in *Cambridge History of the Bible*, vol. I, pp. 542–3.
9   Minnis, *Medieval Theory*, p. 37.
10 de Lubac, *Exégèse Médiévale*, vol. I, p. 119, quoting St Augustine, *Confessions*, book 12, ch. 14, no 17.
11 Ibid.
12 Ibid., vol. I, p. 61.
13 Ibid., vol. I, p. 80.
14 Smalley, *Study of the Bible*, p. 27.
15 Evans, *Language and Logic*, p. 2.
16 E. Auerbach, 'Figura', trs. R. Mannheim, in Auerbach, *Scenes from the Drama of European Literature* (New York, 1959), p. 28.
17 Ibid., p. 30.
18 Ibid.
19 Ibid., p. 39.
20 Ibid., pp. 52; 56.
21 Minnis, *Medieval Theory*, p. 34.
22 Ibid. and n. 153.
23 Auerbach, 'Figura', pp. 29; 39.
24 Minnis, *Medieval Theory*, p. 34.
25 Smalley, *Study of the Bible*, p. 87.
26 Ibid., p. 26.
27 For the development of the Gloss, see ibid., pp. 46–66.
28 Gerhoh of Reichersberg, *De quarta vigilia noctis, MGH SS. Libelli de de Lite*, vol. 3, pp. 508–25.
29 For Eberwin of Steinfeld, see G. Bischoff, 'Early Premonstratensian Eschatology: The Apocalyptic Myth', in *The Spirituality of Western Christendom*, ed. E. R. Elder (Kalamazoo, 1976), pp. 53–4.
30 Joachim's use of this term was not, of course, original. It goes back at least as far as Tertullian (see Auerbach, 'Figura', p. 32), while St Augustine speaks, for example, of the Old Testament as a promise in figure and the New Testament as the *promissio spiritualiter intellecta* (*Serm.* 4:8); see ibid., pp. 32; 41. The original feature of Joachim's concept was that he believed the *spiritualis intellectus* to be the special quality of illumination in the third *status* of the Spirit, not – it must be emphasized – pertaining exclusively to it but given then in fuller measure.
31 M. Reeves, 'The Abbot Joachim's Sense of History', *1274. Année Charnière: Mutations et Continuités, Colloques Internationaux du Centre National de la Recherche Scientifique*, 558 (Paris, 1977), p. 783.
32 See M. Reeves and B. Hirsch-Reich, *The Figurae of Joachim of Fiore* (Oxford, 1972), p. 20, n. 3, for a list of references.
33 Joachim of Fiore, *Psalterium decem Chordarum* (Venice, 1527), reprinted Frankfurt a. Main, 1964, ff. 256^v–257^r; Reeves, 'The Abbot Joachim's Sense of History', pp. 783–4.
34 In addition to the *Psalterium*, these are: *Liber de Concordia* (Venice,

1519, reprinted Frankfurt a. Main, 1964; of which the first four books have been edited by E. R. Daniel, *Trans. of the American Philosophical Society*, 73, 8 (1983); references are to Daniel's edition unless otherwise specified); *Expositio in Apocalypsim* (Venice, 1527, reprinted Frankfurt a. Main, 1964).

35 The best-known statement of the three *status* under a succession of images is in *Liber de Concordia* (Venice edn), f. 112r.

36 On Joachim's calculations concerning the generations of humanity, see Reeves and Hirsch-Reich, *Figurae*, pp. 6–9; 36–8.

37 On Joachim's tree figures, see M. Reeves, 'The *Arbores* of Joachim of Fiore', in *Studies in Italian History presented to Miss E. M. Jamison*, ed. P. Grierson and J. Ward Perkins (London, 1956), pp. 124–36; Reeves and Hirsch-Reich, *Figurae*, pp. 31–8; 153–83.

38 For an analysis of these, see Reeves and Hirsch-Reich, *Figurae*, pp. 34–5.

39 For a full account of Joachim's use of the Seven Seals, see M. Reeves and B. Hirsch-Reich, 'The Seven Seals in the Writings of Joachim of Fiore', *Recherches de Théologie ancienne et médiévale*, 21 (1954), pp. 211–47.

40 See Reeves and Hirsch-Reich, *Figurae*, pp. 146–52 and pl. 2; also the figure at the beginning of Joachim, *Expositio*.

41 For a list of references to the Exodus, the Wanderings in the Wilderness and the Crossing of Jordan into the Promised Land, see Reeves and Hirsch-Reich, *Figurae*, p. 188, n. 16.

42 For the traditional view popularized by St Augustine, see M. Reeves, 'The Originality and Influence of Joachim of Fiore', *Traditio*, 36 (1980), pp. 272–3.

43 For a fuller account of this number pattern and full references, see Reeves and Hirsch-Reich, *Figurae*, pp. 13–19.

44 Joachim, *Expositio*, f. 26r.

45 See references in Reeves, 'The Abbot Joachim', p. 789.

46 Ibid.

47 Joachim, *Liber de Concordia* (Venice edn), ff. 60v–61r.

48 Joachim, *Psalterium*, f. 268r.

49 Smalley, *Study of the Bible*, p. 242.

50 Ibid., pp. 242–3.

51 Ibid., p. 245.

52 For the Aristotelian Prologue, see Minnis, *Medieval Theory*, pp. 28–9.

53 Smalley, *Study of the Bible*, p. 297.

54 On Abelard, see Minnis, *Medieval Theory*, pp. 59–62.

55 Ibid., p. 79.

56 Ibid., p. 81.

57 Ibid., p. 81.

58 Ibid., p. 83.

59 Ibid.

60 Ibid., p. 84.

61 Ibid., pp. 86; 91.
62 Smalley, *Study of the Bible*, p. 268.
63 Ibid., p. 299.
64 Ibid., p. 306.
65 Minnis, *Medieval Theory*, p. 89.
66 Vincent of Beauvais, *Speculum Historiale* (Venice, 1591).
67 Ibid., f. 488v. This popular sentence is actually a conflation of a genuine sentence from Joachim, *Liber de Concordia* (Venice edn), f. 41v and a spurious one from the pseudo-Joachimist work, *Super Hieremiam* (Venice, 1516) *Prefatio*.
68 William of St Amour actually echoes the same saying from the *Super Hieremiam*; see M. Reeves, *The Influence of Prophecy in the Later Middle Ages* (Oxford, 1969), p. 62.
69 L. Wadding, *Annales Minorum* (Rome, 1731), vol. III, p. 380. The biblical references are to Gen. 1:16; Ex. 19:16; 25:18; Song of Solomon 4:5; Zech. 4:3; Apoc. 11:3–4.
70 Angelo Clareno, OM, *Historia Septem Tribulationum*, ed. F. Tocco, *Le due prime tribolazioni dell' ordine dei minori, Rendiconti della Reale Accademia dei Lincei*, 17 (Rome, 1908), pp. 97–131; 221–36; remainder ed. F. Ehrle, *Archiv für Literatur und Kirchengeschichte des Mittelalters* (*ALKG*), 2 (1886), pp. 125–55; 256–327.
71 *ALKG*, 1 (1885), p. 558 (cf. Heb. 1:1–2; Phil. 2:6–9).
72 For reference, see n. 67.
73 *Super Hieremiam*, ff. 3v; 4r; 12r; 46r.
74 Ibid., ff. 14r; 45v.
75 *Super Esaiam* (Venice, 1517).
76 See Reeves, *Influence of Prophecy*, pp. 149–54.
77 For the main references in Joachim's works to the two new orders, see ibid., pp. 142–4.
78 Ibid., p. 158, n. 1, for the most important references.
79 The translations from the *Divina Commedia* are from the *Temple Classics* edn: Dante Alighieri, *The Divine Comedy* (London, 1901). I wish here to acknowledge my debt to Robert Hollander's book, *Allegory in Dante's Commedia* (Princeton, 1969).
80 See, for example, Dante's meeting with Cavalcante Cavalcanti, father of his friend, Guido Cavalcanti, in the circle of heretics, *Inferno*, 10:58–69, and with Brunetto Latini, one of Dante's 'masters', among the Violent against Nature, *Inferno*, 16:22–124.
81 Dante Alighieri, *Il Convivio*, ed. G. Busnelli and G. Vandelli (Florence, 1964), pt. I, p. 97.
82 Hollander, *Dante*, p. 32.
83 *Dantis Aligherii Epistolae*, ed. and trs. Paget Toynbee, 2nd edn (Oxford, 1966), p. 199.
84 B. Nardi, *Nel mondo di Dante* (Rome, 1944), p. 59.
85 *Inferno*, 20.
86 Dante Alighieri, *Monarchia*, ed. P. G. Ricci (Milan, 1965), book I, ch. 16 – book II, ch. 1.

87 Ibid., book IV, ch. 5. See J. Scott, 'La contemporaneità Enea-David', *Studi danteschi*, 49 (1972), pp. 129–34.
88 *Epistolae*, ed. Toynbee, pp. 58–9.
89 Ibid., p. 101; cf. John 1:29.
90 Ibid., p. 81; cf. Is. 53:4.
91 As argued by P. G. Ricci in his edition of *Monarchia* (n. 86), book I, pp. 158–9.
92 *Epistolae*, ed. Toynbee, p. 196.
93 *Inferno*, 2:31–2.
94 E. Auerbach, *Dante: Poet of the Secular World*, trs. R. Mannheim (Chicago, 1961), p. 84.
95 Ibid., p. 91.
96 Ibid., p. 92.
97 *Inferno*, 3:56–7.
98 Hollander, *Dante*, p. 73.
99 *Inferno*, 5:73–142.
100 See St Augustine, *Confessions*, book 8, ch. 12, and Hollander's exposition of this passage, *Dante*, pp. 112–13.
101 *Inferno*, 10:34–44.
102 Ibid., 12:109–11.
103 Ibid., 13:58–84.
104 Ibid., 28:103–8.
105 Ibid., 26:55–142. Dante was, of course, treating the legend of Ulysses as history.
106 Ibid., 26:34–6. The episode alluded to here is that of Elisha's prophecy that the children who mocked him would be eaten by bears (2 Kings 2:11; 12; 23; 24). It is typical of Dante's method that he picks such a detail – with a sidelong relevance – to identify the major episode.
107 *Inferno*, 34:28–70.
108 *Purgatorio*, 2:10–50.
109 See above, p. 36. We have already noted that the Exodus was a favorite theme of Joachim's, see above, p. 25.
110 *Paradiso*, 31:39.
111 *Purgatorio*, 1:31–93.
112 *Paradiso*, 17:69: '*parte per se stesso*'.
113 *Purgatorio*, 1:31–6.
114 Ibid., 7:9–132.
115 Ibid., 20:40–93.
116 *Inferno*, 19:54–9; also 27:66–107.
117 *Purgatorio*, 20:86–90.
118 Ibid., 29, 30.
119 Apoc. 1:12; 4:4–11; Ezek. 1:5–14.
120 Psalms 36:5, 7, 10; 57:1, 11; Song of Solomon, 5:10, 11.
121 The number 24 is arrived at by counting the Pentateuch, the historical books and the three ascribed to Solomon as one each.

122   These were, of course, accepted medieval symbols of the four Evangelists.

123   St Paul describes Luke (Col. 4:14) as 'the beloved Physician', hence Dante's likening of him to Hippocrates, the famous Greek physician. Once again, the scriptural figure is doubled with a classical one.

124   James, Peter, John, Jude.

125   Charles Singleton, *Dante Studies I* (Cambridge, MA, 1965), p. 48.

126   St Bonaventure, *Breviloquium, Opera Omnia* (Quaracchi, 1891), vol. V, p. 203, quoted Singleton, *Dante Studies I*, p. 49.

127   Song of Soloman 4:8; Matt. 21:9; Mark 11:9; Luke 19:38; John 12:13.

128   The quotation comes from *Aenead*, 6:884.

129   *Purgatorio*, 27:140–2.

130   Ibid., 30:115–38.

131   Ibid., 32.

132   The famous forged document (eighth–ninth century) in which the Emperor Constantine was supposed to have endowed the Papacy with dominion over Italy and the 'provinces, places and civitates of the Western regions'. This was treated as authoritative in the Middle Ages and formed one of the bases of Papal claims to political dominion. It was not proved to be a forgery until 100 years after Dante.

133   *Purgatorio*, 32:104–5.

134   See below, p. 48.

135   *Paradiso*, 1:13–21.

136   Dante would know the legend of Marsyas from Ovid's *Metamorphoses*, 6:385, where Marsyas cries to Apollo: 'Why do you tear me from myself?' This is turned by Dante into a prayer to Apollo: 'Enter my breast, and so infuse me with your spirit as you did Marsyas when you tore him from the cover of his limbs.' In connection with the legend of St Bartholomew, a fascinating late example is Michael Angelo's painting of him in the Last Judgement of the Sistine Chapel holding his own skin on which Michael Angelo has depicted his own face. On both these legends, see Edgar Wind, *Pagan Mysteries in the Renaissance* (London, 1958), pp. 142–5; 155–6).

137   *Paradiso*, 18; 19; 20.

138   *Paradiso*, 22:151.

139   David: see above, p. 28, for Joachim's use of David as the eagle's eye; Trajan: Roman Emperor who, in medieval legend, was saved by the prayers of Gregory the Great; Hezekiah: King of Judah, see 2 Kings 20:1–11; Constantine: see above, n. 132; William the Good: King of the Two Sicilies (1166–89); Ripheus: called by Virgil the one man amongst the Trojans most just and observant of the right (*Aenead*, 2:426).

140   *Paradiso*, 18:73–117.

141   Ibid., l. 113.

142 Reeves and Hirsch-Reich, *Figurae*, pls. 14; 15, and pp. 160–3.
143 See above, p. 28.
144 *Inferno*, 1:98–108.
145 *Paradiso*, 27:19–66.
146 Ibid., ll. 121–48.
147 *Purgatorio*, 33:37–45.
148 Joachim, *Liber de Concordia* (Venice edn), f. 56r.
149 See above, p. 37.
150 *Paradiso*, 12:140–1: '*il Calabrese abate Gioacchino, di spirito pro-fetico dotato.*'
151 See above, p. 47, for the tree-eagles, and for Dante's use of the three circles (*Paradiso*, 33:115–20), see Reeves and Hirsch-Reich, *Figurae*, pp. 323–5.
152 For a fuller statement of the argument here summarized, see M. Reeves, 'The Third Age: Dante's Debt to Gioacchino da Fiore', *Atti del II Congresso Internazionale di Studi Gioachimiti*, ed. A. Crocco (S. Giovanni in Fiore, 1986), pp. 128–39.
153 *Paradiso*, 30:124–38; 31:1–72; 32:1–39, 118–138.
154 Ibid., 31:39.
155 Minnis, *Medieval Theory*, pp. 95–6.
156 Ibid., pp. 103–10; see 2 Kings 11–12.
157 Ibid., p. 94.
158 Ibid., p. 97.
159 Ibid., p. 113.
160 Ibid., p. 115.
161 B. Smalley, *English Friars and Antiquity in the Early Fourteenth Century* (Oxford, 1960), pp. 1–2.
162 Minnis, *Medieval Theory*, p. 166.
163 Ibid., p. 163.
164 Ibid., pp. 168–71.
165 Ibid., p. 170.
166 Ibid., p. 173.
167 Ibid.
168 Ibid., p. 177.
169 Ibid., p. 182.
170 Morton Bloomfield, *Piers Plowman as a Fourteenth-Century Apoca-lypse* (New Brunswick, n.d.).
171 Ibid., p. 37.
172 J. A. Alford, 'The Role of the Quotations in *Piers Plowman*', *Speculum*, 52 (1977), p. 96.
173 J. B. Allen, 'Langland's Reading and Writing: *Detractor* and the Pardon Passus', *Speculum*, 59 (1984), p. 356.
174 D. W. Robertson and B. F. Huppé, *Piers Plowman and Scriptural Tradition* (Princeton, 1951), pp. 35–6.
175 Ibid., pp. 36–7.
176 Ibid., p. 49.
177 Ibid., pp. 50–2.

178 K. Kerby-Fulton, *Reformist Apocalypticism and 'Piers Plowman'* (Cambridge, 1990.)
179 Minnis, *Medieval Theory*, p. 193.
180 Ibid., p. 199.
181 Ibid., p. 207.

2

The Reformation: the Trial of God's Word

Rivkah Zim

A Prologue to Debate

When John Colet and Erasmus exchanged letters in October 1499 about interpretations of the metaphor in Mark 14:36, 'Father let this cup pass from me', their debate became a trial of the Word by combat in words.[1] The way in which it was conducted is as significant for the kinds of emphases and applications of biblical hermeneutics during the following century and a half as it is for the substance of their respective arguments. The writers' strategy is affective, that is, to provoke emotive and imaginative responses in order to move the will of the reader. Such an appeal to the affections, or disposition of a reader's will, often exploited striking imagery. It always tended towards the particular purpose of exciting responses which in turn could stimulate a change of mind or attitude and promote new insights or understanding.[2] Both scholars represent their debate as a clash of intellectual weapons in a battle of wits. Colet urged his opponent, as well as himself, to 'catch any sparks that may be struck out when the flints clash. For it is truth we are seeking, not the defence of a mere point of view; and perhaps, as argument meets argument, truth will shine forth, just as fire does from steel when it strikes upon steel.'[3] The truth sought was the will of God as revealed through Scripture and illuminated by their new rhetorical discourse; when hermeneutics became a process of literary warfare, biblical commentary developed into controversy and literature.

Erasmus warned Colet against taking up extreme positions 'for ... the mysteries of Scripture can yield different meanings because of their rich abundance, and we must not reject any interpretation so long as it is probable and not contrary to the faith.'[4] His com-mentary shifts from the point at issue to the nature of the debate and to the tactics his opponent has deployed in previous letters: from the local hermeneutic crux to the wider hermeneutic debate. Significantly this shift is also literary and rhetorical. The further extension of the battle metaphor (he hopes a 'bloodless fight' will not develop into 'a general massacre') deepened the seriousness of the tone, and thereby, by association, the potential significance of the battle-ground. Erasmus accused Colet of 'not acting like a theologian' but of 'making use of a sly rhetorical kind of artifice'.[5]

Colet had argued that the 'cup' to which Jesus referred was his pain at witnessing the behaviour of the Jews. This view differed from that commonly held by his contemporaries who maintained that the prayer for relief indicated that Jesus feared death. Colet rested his interpretation on the authority of Jerome as a Doctor and Father of the Church, to whom the 'truth' of Scripture had been revealed; thus he emphasized the divine nature of Jesus. Erasmus on the other hand appealed to 'circumstantial facts', to probability in a specific context, and to human experience:

The crucifixion lay threateningly close at hand ... Christ to whom there was nothing that was not known, knew what was afoot; he sought privacy, and began to be discomfited and sad, to sweat, to be deeply downcast ... If rational proofs are derived from probable inference, do not all these facts, taken together, loudly proclaim that here is a man, who stands in fear of death? The preceding passage contains a quite explicit mention of flesh and spirit, but not a word about his sorrow over the Jews.[6]

Erasmus found the traditional interpretation to be consistent with human nature and coherent with divine purpose. According to this double sense of decorum Jesus was not only behaving in character – since the prophets 'represent him as quiet, not boastful' – but more suitably for his purpose of comforting man.[7] Erasmus therefore took his stand on a principle of spiritual utility, whereby the life of Jesus provided an exemplum for man to imitate. Upon this premise, Erasmus was happy to set aside the isolated voice of Jerome's authority, 'especially since neither the substance nor the expression' in the biblical context 'affords ... the means of adducing even the slightest proof' for Colet's argument:[8] 'Surely at that moment he spoke as a man, for men, to men, and in the words of men, expressing man's fears.'[9]

My purpose in this chapter is to demonstrate from a selection of relevant examples how processes of biblical interpretation, or

hermeneutics, in the sixteenth and seventeenth centuries overlapped
with the assumptions and practices of contemporary writers. The
first part therefore considers biblical hermeneutics and the second
part examines some of the other literary repercussions of contemporary ideas about how to read the Bible. I shall argue that the
prevalence of invitations and opportunities for Protestants to search
the Scriptures in English enabled poets and preachers to exploit
readers' knowledge of the Bible, as well as their experience of the
ways in which it was read and interpreted.

I God's Word

All parties in such debates took it for granted that the 'meaning', or
message, of any biblical text was that intended by its author. Scripture had always to be interpreted 'as the intent and purpose of the
Holy Ghost was, by whom the scripture was uttered' to prophets,
scribes and apostles.[10] Several texts were commonly cited to prove
that the divine author had caused the entire Scriptures to be written
by men for man's instruction or spiritual benefit. 'All scripture is
given by inspiration of God, and is profitable for doctrine, for
reproof, for correction, for instruction in righteousness' (2 Tim.
3:16).[11] Such traditional views of the Bible and its authorship remained commonplace among Catholics and Protestants, who both
believed that 'Scripture gives us a perfect direction both for faith and
manners.'[12] However, this view was especially emphasized by many
Protestants who advised readers to 'remember that Scriptures con-
teine matter concerning' not only religion and theology but also
'commonwealthes and governments of people', families and 'the private life and doings of every man' as well as 'the common life of all
men'.[13] Humanist emphasis on the moral utility of good literature
transferred easily to Holy Scripture. In the battle against temptation,
the Bible provided 'a whole armorie of weapons, both offensive and
defensive; whereby we may save our selves and put the enemie to
flight'.[14] Emphasis on the humanity of Jesus, and on the spiritual
utility of his example for all mankind, stimulated meditative readings of the gospels for devotional purposes by a wider range of
readers than ever before.

As a result readers became more aware both of the literary qualities of Holy Scripture in which divine truth had been revealed, and
of the exploitation of rhetoric by contemporary commentators in
arguments to clarify that truth. Extended knowledge of Scripture
brought extended knowledge of the arts of language.

The Bible was seen by all parties as an external body of text, which contained within it the Word of God. This inner message, or the Word, was equated with 'the sense, interpretation, and meaning of the words' and was contained (as Jerome had argued) 'not in the leaves of [words], but in the root of reason [*non in sermonum foliis, sed in radice rationis*]'.[15] The meaning intended by the Spirit of the living God, the Word, was lodged in the organic material of the body of the text:

In every scripture there is some thing visible, and something invisible, there is a body, and a spirit or soule, the letters, sillables, and wordes be visible, as the body; but the soule, and invisible part is the sense and trueth wrapt and infoulded in the wordes, which are as the barke, ryne, or bone, the meaning within is as the roote, and juce, or as the marrow.[16]

The controversies of the period were not about the text of Scripture as such, but about its interpretation and application. In concluding his debate with Colet, Erasmus returned to the metaphor of sparks struck from flinty rocks to describe the dynamism of their intellectual encounter as a hermeneutic process: the means rather than the end of their search for 'that truth, which is buried deep within the innermost strata', and which cannot 'flash forth at once on the first feeble contact', but 'is forced out only after a long and arduous struggle'.[17] Such resonant and forceful imagery suggests that the recovery of divine truth was a kind of quarrying. Interpretation was a dangerous procedure, but such quarrying was necessary if there were to be any doctrinal building work in the future.

The Word was represented in the words of the text which could be interpreted according to different senses. For a study of the imaginative literature of the period, the implications of this concept may be simplified according to a distinction between the literal and spiritual senses, or 'understandings', of the text. The Jesuit Robert Bellarmine defined the difference between the two senses in a simile: 'As . . . the begotten Word of God hath two natures, the one human and visible, the other divine and invisible; so the written word of God hath a two-fold sense: the one outward, that is historic or literal; the other, inward, that is mystic or spiritual.'[18] He then subdivided this spiritual sense into the traditional three-fold configuration of allegorical, anagogic and tropological senses. All Christian commentators acknowledged that the doctrine of the Church had to be based on the literal sense (however interpreted) which 'alone of scripture is the whole substance of faith, and of Christian Theologie'.[19] Apart from the emphasis given to 'alone' and 'whole' neither Augustine, nor Aquinas, nor Nicholas of Lyra, would have disagreed with Luther, or with Calvin, on this point. William Whitaker, speaking for the reformed English Church in his *Disputatio de sacra scriptura* (1588), conceded Bellarmine's view, but added: 'We affirm that there is but one true, proper and genuine sense of scripture, arising from the words rightly understood, which we call the literal: and we contend that allegories, tropologies, and anagogues are not various senses, but various applications and accommodations of that one meaning.'[20]

Such theological disputes demonstrate that scholars' problems were hermeneutic rather than epistemological; Scripture defined itself, but interpreted itself only in so far as its unique authorship implied a unified purpose for its parts. This unity of purpose made it possible to gloss difficult texts with clearer ones from a different part of the whole. 'The surest mean of interpretation of scripture, is by scripture, which is the best commentarie of it selfe, when the phrase is marked, and matter, and scope, and place compared with place, hard with easie.'[21] Although interpretations based on this principle often made use of allegorical and typological readings, responsible readers of all persuasions were advised to shun 'subtile, intricate and vaine scruples, doubts, and questions'.[22]

Throughout the Middle Ages, the Councils of the Church had decreed what constituted the true sense of Scripture on the basis of a hierarchy of authority, which gave priority to certain designated Fathers of the universal Church. Their priority over all other biblical commentators was reaffirmed by the Council of Trent in its fourth session (April 1546),[23] and for Catholics, interpretation of the Bible remained the privilege of the Church. The principal grounds for doctrinal controversy arose, therefore, not only from different emphases placed by Catholics and Protestants on the authority of the Bible to determine the articles of faith but also from conflicting views about the nature of the appropriate authority for biblical interpretation.[24] A key issue, which crystallized in controversy over access to vernacular translations, was whether the divine mysteries in Holy Scripture should be mediated to man through a priesthood and the learned licensed by the Church, or whether they should be freely accessible to all the faithful.

If the message of a text could be abstracted from the mediating signs, the words arranged on the page, then no epistemological difficulty could arise when those signs were changed from one language to another. Translators were optimistic that the 'scripture and word of God is truly to every christen man of lyke worthynesse and authorite, in what language so ever the holy goost speaketh it.'[25] After all, as Miles Coverdale remarked, it is not 'as though the holy goost were not the authoure of his scriptures aswell in the Hebrue,

Greke, French, Dutche [i.e. German], and in Englysh, as in Latyn'.[26] The publication of vernacular translations effectively restricted the power of the Church to exercise its authority over interpretation since it made it more difficult to control their circulation. Thomas More was ready to concede in 1529 that a good new English Bible was feasible, but if such a translation were approved by the Church, he would have had it printed to be distributed by bishops to approved persons only; he would not 'dash rashly out holy scrypture in every lewde felowys tethe', to be interpreted without the authority of the Church.[27] While translators of the King James Bible acknowledged the difficulty inherent in interpretation 'by every translator', they argued that the ideal would allow Scripture to 'speake like it selfe, as in the language of Canaan [i.e. the biblical vernacular], that it may be understood even of the very vulgar'.[28] Most humanists distrusted the capacities of the 'vulgar', or the common people, to understand, but there was a long tradition in the Church that the Bible had special qualities which mitigated the effects of mere human inadequacy.

Augustine had observed that 'the holy scripture useth no kinde of speach which may not be found in common custom of speach amongst men.'[29] Even the stylistic register had been divinely ordained and the *sermo humilis* – 'the meannesse and homelinesse of the phrase' – was amply justified, 'sithens it is framed to our good' for its spiritual utility.[30] Since the fourth century, Christian commentators had shown themselves aware of the operation of rhetoric, and of significant literary qualities, in the discourse of the Word as transcribed by human prophets and evangelists.[31] The use of figures such as 'Anthropopathia', whereby 'an hand is applied to God to signifie his working power,' was similarly explained in terms of the Holy Spirit's horizon of expectations of 'our dulnes to conceive the thinges of God'.[32] Scripture offered readers a fine balance between carrot and stick incentives, since it had 'pleased God so wholsomly and wisely to temper the holy scriptures as by plaine places hee might satisfie hunger, and by hard places wipe away disdaine'.[33] From this traditional precept, Protestants argued that all knowledge necessary for man's salvation was 'delivered plainly in the holy Scripture', so that no soul was at risk.[34] The corollary to this was that any inscrutable passage could be dismissed in safety as an 'indifferent' matter since, although the divine message was perceived to have been mediated by human scribes in an historically transmitted text, the Holy Spirit was assumed to have exercised a supervisory role at all times. The integrity of Scripture was absolute, 'the whole ... being but as one chaine or circle'.[35]

While no one would have quibbled with the statement 'Scripture

is the rule of all trueth,' the inference drawn by some Protestant
writers that 'whatsoever truth may be proved by Scripture, it *alone*
is a sufficient witnes in stead of all other authorities and testimonies,
for it *alone* can convince the conscience,'[36] was highly contentious.
It effectively made the individual conscience – guided by the Holy
Spirit – the interpreter and judge of the meaning of the Holy Spirit.
If even 'the authority of [the] Church in expounding Scriptures' was
merely advisory, 'ministeriall, not absolute and soveraigne',[37] there
was little hope of breaking the hermeneutic circle and validating an
interpretation. The urgency of the problem increased with the
spread of Protestantism. By the 1530s it came to seem that the rule
of divine truth was 'a nose of wax', to be 'moulded and fashioned
this way and that ... howsoever ye list'.[38] Of the making of interpretations there was no end.

Whereas all agreed that the literal sense of Scripture (as opposed
to the spiritual sense) was the basis of Christian doctrine, the literal
sense itself could be interpreted either literally or figuratively. Both
the Catholic doctrine of transubstantiation, and the Zwinglian denial of the real presence, are founded on different interpretations of
the same texts: 'Take, eat; this is my body' (Matt. 26:26; cf. Mark
14:22), the words of institution for the Eucharist or Lord's Supper.
More defended the doctrine of the real presence by arguing that 'the
very lytterall truth, of the very eating and bodely receiving of Chris-
tes own veri flesh and blood' depends on the 'very true litteral sense'
of the words 'this is my body.'[39] William Tyndale defended Zwing-
li's interpretation of the words of institution as signifying a commemoration of the body of Christ by arguing that the letter of the
text signified a figurative discourse. This, he argued, was in accordance with the 'common maner of spech in many places of scripture,
and also in our mother toung';[40] the interpretation was justified by
common usage both in general and in particular. There was little
point in insisting on a literal interpretation against the evidence of
the ways in which 'words, or the things expressed in words,
denote';[41] 'it is a miserable servitude (as August[ine] saith) to take
signes for things, of which, wordes be but signes.'[42] Nevertheless,
More condemned those who thereby took away 'wyth an allegory
the very true litteral sense' of the incarnate Word.[43] Such pragma-
tism robbed religion of its fundamental mystery, and denied
miracles as well as the authority of the Church.

Erasmus and More were not alone in considering such an attack
on the authority of the Church a very dangerous precedent. The
potential dangers of singularity and individualism in new Protestant
biblical interpretations were recognized by all those with an interest

in the *status quo*: 'if every man shall have authority to give his verdict upon a controversy which shall seem and say that he hath the spirit, no certain thing shall be decreed; every man shall have his own way; no stable opinion and judgement to be rested on.'[44] By the end of the seventeenth century, the effects of this tendency had wrought revolutions in English politics, religion and literature.

To search the Scriptures

Protestants replaced the authority of the Roman Catholic Church, which claimed an absolute right to determine how Scripture should be interpreted, by that of the Holy Spirit as it operated on the conscience of an individual. English Protestants understood Luther to have said that no one could 'understand one jott or tittle of Scripture' without the Spirit, and to have advised: 'Therefore praier for inward illumination must bee joyned with outward reading and hearing.'[45] For Calvin, 'the secrete testimony of the holy ghoste' was of a higher order of proof than all human reasons, judgements, or conjectures; thus, those 'whom the holy ghost hath inwardly taught, doe wholy reste uppon the Scripture, and that . . . Scripture is to be credited for it self sake'.[46] In speaking for the reformed English Church, Whitaker asserted

we determine that the supreme right, authority, and judgment of interpreting the scriptures, is lodged with the Holy Ghost and the scripture itself. . . . We say that the Holy Spirit is the supreme interpreter of scripture, because we must be illuminated by the Holy Spirit to be certainly persuaded of the true sense of scripture.[47]

There was no question of absolute power over interpretation for any of the reformed churches, since 'The saving knowledge of heavenly truth is not in the power of any man, minister or other, no nor of Angels to give, but is the peculiar worke and gift of God.'[48] A revised, largely adminicular function was retained by the Anglican Church in matters of biblical hermeneutics – 'The word is the light, but the Church is the Lanthorne'[49] – and readers were offered appropriate guides, such as the *Theologicall Rules*, and 'Howe to take profite by reading of the holy Scriptures' published with later editions of the Geneva Bible.[50] New trials of the Word were encouraged and valued, so long as they were based on interpretations of the literal sense, but no understanding could be gained without the freely given gift of the Holy Spirit, to be invoked (but never coerced) by humble prayer.[51] Piety,

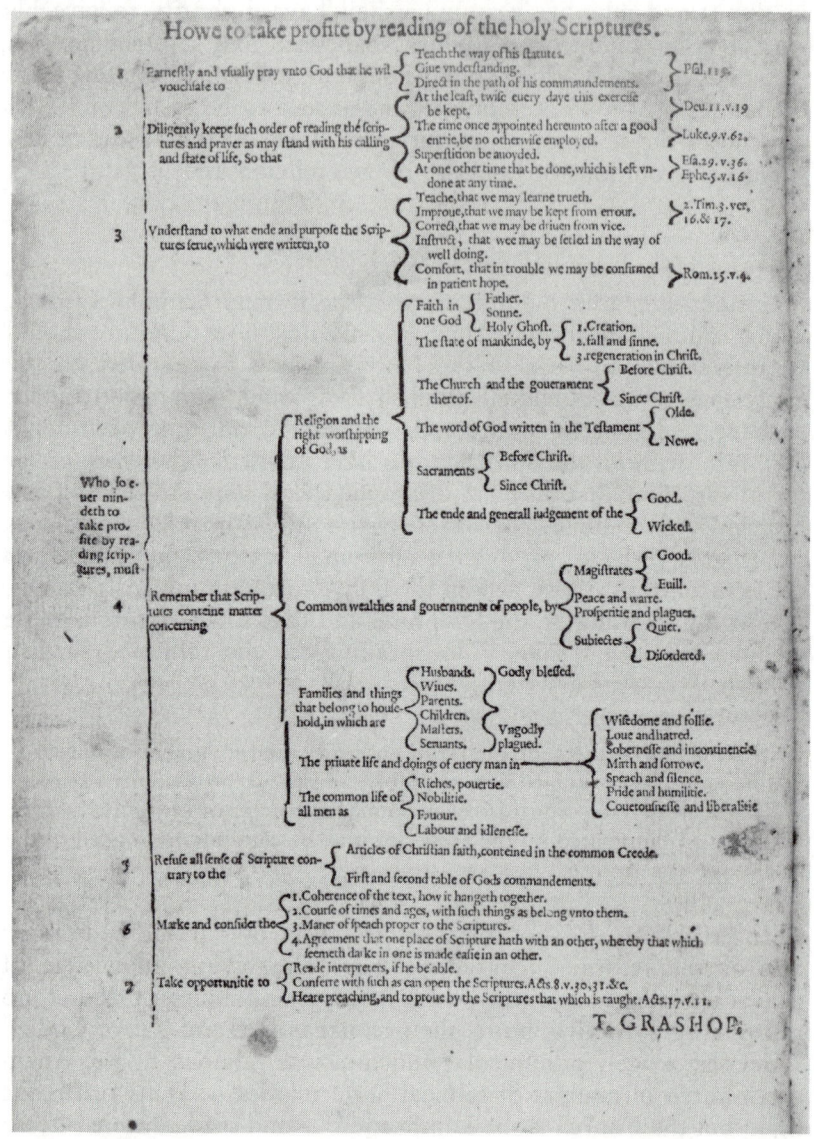

PLATE 3   The table 'Howe to take profite by reading of the holy Scriptures', from an edition of the Geneva Bible printed in London, 1599, facing fo 1ʳ. (Reproduced by kind permission of The Bodleian Library, Oxford, ref: Bibl.Eng.1599.d.1)

diligence and attentive humility were all necessary for those either hearing, or reading and studying Scripture. 'One of the greatest helpes and best meanes to understand the scripture,' wrote William Perkins, was 'to keepe a good conscience, living according to that wee know out of the word, being joyned with continuall and fervent prayer'.[52]

The first of the 1562 Homilies, appointed to be read in all English churches, was 'A Fruitful Exhortation to the Reading and Knowledge of Holy Scripture', which urged the general public not to be afraid of falling into 'error' by reading Scripture; 'Ignorance of God's word' was 'the cause of all error', and pride caused ignorance: 'the humble man may search any truth boldly in the Scripture ... And if he be ignorant, he ought the more to read and to search Holy Scripture, to bring him out of ignorance.'[53] Although it was not easy to read the Bible with proper understanding, some parts of this 'food of the soul' were more easily digested than others, since its lessons were adapted 'to the capacity both of learned and unlearned'; therefore, the Homily concluded, 'let us ruminate, and, as it were, chew the cud, that we may have the sweet juice, spiritual effect, marrow, honey, kernel, taste, comfort, and consolation of them.'[54]

There was no need for anyone to be discouraged if progress in learning was slow. 'Conference with others of heavenly things' was recognized as 'profitable', since 'with such Christ will be present to informe them'.[55] Readers of the Geneva Bible were encouraged to listen to sermons.[56] Help could also be sought from learned expositions, including paraphrases of Scripture, 'if that exposition which they give, be grounded on the scriptures'[57] – 'the well of life' – and not upon 'the stinking puddles of men's traditions, devised by men's imagination',[58] a Protestant swipe at Catholic learning. In cases of difficulty Whitaker recommended 'recourse to other persons better skilled', but warned that no learned interpretations should be accepted as authoritative by reputation alone, 'but because they are supported by the authority of scripture or by reason'.[59] In arguing against Catholic reliance on papal authority as 'sole judge of controversies', Whitaker asserted that

every one ought to rest upon his own faith and his own judgment, and not depend upon another's will and pleasure ... no one can bestow the Holy Spirit save God who infuses it in whom he will. Nor can one man render another certain in matters of religion, with whatever authority he may be invested.[60]

In cases of persistent obscurity two solutions were offered to readers. The simpler solution was to rely on the self-sufficiency of Scripture and to look for a consensus by comparing and collating different texts. The more complex solution was to appeal to the rule of faith (cf. Rom. 12:6).

While Catholic readers continued to guard against the imposition of 'private meanings' by advocating recourse to the authority of tradition manifest in the teachings of the Doctors of the Church, Protestant readers were warned to check all interpretations for themselves against 'the analogy or proportion' of faith.[61] This was subject to different definitions. The Anglican Church argued 'that no sense bee received contrary to the ten commandements, Lords prayer, and the Articles of our beliefe', which together provided the basic 'analogie of faith' in plain, straightforward statements.[62] If every place in Scripture had only one meaning, and each individual responded to the promptings of the Holy Spirit appropriately (not peculiarly), then, meaning being singular (identified with the will of God in the intention of the Holy Spirit), everyone would interpret alike, and the *orbs doctrinae christianae* would be preserved intact and unbroken.[63]

On the other hand, Whitaker had defined this analogy of faith more radically as 'nothing else but the constant sense of the general tenour of scripture ... where the meaning labours under no obscurity', and went so far as to assert that 'whatever exposition is repugnant to this analogy must be false.'[64] Radical Protestants were always prepared to assert that

Every believer has a right to interpret the scriptures for himself, inasmuch as he has the spirit for his guide, and the mind of Christ is in him; nay the expositions of the public interpreter can be of no use to him, except so far as they are confirmed by his own conscience.[65]

To be truly infused with the gift of the Spirit was to be united in spirit with the truth of the Word; but, since there was no objective test for this gift, the dangers of subjectivity in Protestant hermeneutics were not minimized. Catholics accused all Protestants of resting 'upon the singularity and wisdom'[66] of their own brains, but all Protestants were prepared to affirm that the analogy of faith, in spite of the limitations arising from its ill-defined characteristics, was a sufficient safeguard when evaluating biblical exegesis.

Among the skills required by Protestants of anyone wishing to read the text of Scripture was a sensitivity to the presence and operation of literary forms and styles. In order to understand the literal sense of the Word it was first necessary to be aware of the characteristic modes of Scripture. The *Theologicall Rules* alerted readers to literary and rhetorical procedures and to grammatical features of style in the Bible text, providing references to specific examples. The functions of different rhetorical figures were explained, as in the case of *prosopopoeia* whereby 'wee are moved more to affect the things spoken, and are more easily brought to understand them;'[67] and unfamiliar stylistic features were clarified, such as the non-copulative uses of *and*, whereby 'this particle ... beginneth the sentence absolutely without respect to any thing went before,' a feature attributed to Hebrew usage.[68] Hebraic parallelisms were recognized as having expository, and affective purposes in either representing or moving the will, especially in poetry:[69]

It is the manner of Scripture, having said a thing in one member of a sentence, to repeat the same againe in the latter member, whereof many examples in Proverbs, & Psalmes ... It is done partly by way of explication, and somtime for confirmation, somtime for expressing or exciting zeale.[70]

Other examples were drawn from a range of texts including prophetic and historical books, the first chapter of John's Gospel, and the Pauline epistles. As new translations of the Bible from the original languages appeared, so all readers were gradually made aware of the need to recognize the influence of the 'Idiomes or proprieties' of Hebrew in the Old Testament and of Greek (suffused with Hebraisms) in the New Testament, 'which being observed, bring much light, and being neglected the sense will bee troubled'.[71]

When interpreting the literal sense of the text, close attention had to be given not only to features of language and style but also (as we shall see later) to the contexts – literary and historic. Thus 'All places of Scripture have this rule common to them, that they be interpreted by the matter handled, and the phrase, and the scope or end which is aimed at, or by circumstances of time, persons, places; also by precedents and subsequents.'[72] Readers of the Geneva Bible were told to 'Marke and consider the Coherence of the text, how it hangeth together'.[73] For example, the implications of particular elements in the extended conceit of a parable should 'be expounded, and no farther strained than things agree with the principall drift' and function of the story.[74] Protestant scholars frequently cited the authority of the Fathers for such interpretative procedures.

The characteristic Reformation emphasis on personal responsibility in the matter of one's own salvation had the effect of stimulating independent thought in other areas. Similarly, emphasis on the need for literary skills in interpreting the literal sense of scripture led to literary-critical awareness in approaches to other literature.

Two case studies

The *De tristitia Christi* is Thomas More's last major work, and was written during his imprisonment in the Tower in 1535.[75] *Samson Agonistes*, probably Milton's last major poem, was published in 1671 three years before his death.[76] The *De tristitia Christi* is a Latin meditation and commentary on a harmony of the Gospels, which represents and discusses the spiritual function of human fear. *Samson Agonistes* is an English dramatic poem based on Greek form, which traces the development of Samson's understanding of the personal significance of divine prophecy. Both works are concerned with the psychology of suffering, and are infused with humanist ideas promoting Christian 'Faith and manners'; as such, parallels may be drawn between the agony experienced by the human nature represented in More's Jesus, and that portrayed in Milton's Samson. Both works represent protagonists searching to recognize the will of God from a trial of the Word, and both are literary products – albeit in very different genres – of their authors' trials of the Word. However, More explicitly denied the authority of any individual to interpret the Gospel for himself, restricting interpretation to those, such as himself, whose learning in theology and letters and whose standing with the bishops gave them licence to do so.[77] By contrast, for Milton the authority to interpret Scripture was personal, and rested on an individual's inspiration by the Holy Spirit.[78] Thus both case studies, from each end of the period under consideration, highlight (in contrasting ways) some of the key issues in contemporary biblical interpretation, and show how different approaches to reading the Bible influenced the creation of new literature.

In the *De tristitia Christi*, what begins as exposition of an historical account of Christ's agony in the garden of Gethsemane develops into a series of affective meditations in the tradition of Christ-centred piety, speeches in the first person by different *personae*, and digressions which incorporate More's personal comments on, for example, current religious controversies. These elements are somewhat loosely held together by the sequence of the Gospel narratives. By contrast with Calvin's analytical and dispassionate commentary on the harmonized Gospels, More's exegesis is highly personal and even dramatic in form and style.[79] Where Calvin describes to expound, More frequently represents Jesus in direct speech – in prayer, admonishing the inattentive apostles, or in a discourse addressed to the suffering faithful, such as More himself. More as commentator ruminates on the situation, identifying with the feelings proper to the human nature of Jesus during the night of prayer in anticipation of betrayal and death, and emphasizes the significance of his human suffering in its application to others.

More perceived the historic significance of the biblical message both for his own times, and for himself facing the prospect of death. He understood the Word by assimilating the full literary and historical context of the narrative, replete with circumstantial detail and rhetorical figures. He meditates on the words, examines other outward signs of human behaviour, and, in offering images for contemplation, employs rhetoric to stir the affections of his readers.[80]

In one of the most effective passages, the 'most lively voice' of Jesus (*'vivacissima voce'*) addresses each fearful Christian directly in the familiar second person singular. More created this speech of Jesus by selecting and reworking several biblical texts and motifs. The speech is an exhortation to faith intended to move the will by literary means through an appeal to the senses. More's Jesus addresses those readers of the Gospel, who identify with the human suffering of the biblical Jesus, through that interpretation in the *De tristitia Christi* of the message of the agony in the garden. In More's discourse, Jesus sympathizes with human frailties and finally promises an indemnity against fear.

O faint of heart, take courage and do not despair. You are afraid, you are sad, you are stricken with weariness and dread of the torment with which you have been cruelly threatened. Trust me. I conquered the world, and yet I suffered immeasurably more from fear, I was sadder, more afflicted with weariness, more horrified at the prospect of such cruel suffering drawing nearer and nearer. Let the brave man have his high-spirited [*magnanimos*] martyrs, let him rejoice in imitating a thousand of them. But you, my timorous and feeble little sheep, be content to have me alone as your shepherd, follow my leadership; if you do not trust yourself, place your trust in me. See, I am walking ahead of you along this fearful road. Take hold of the border of my garment and you will feel going out from it a power [*virtutem*] which will stay your heart's blood from issuing in vain fears, and will make your mind [*animum*] more cheerful, especially when you remember that you are following closely in my footsteps (and I am to be trusted and will not allow you to be tempted beyond what you can bear, but I will give together with the temptation a way out that you may be able to endure it) . . .[81]

When paraphrasing Isaiah 35:4 ('Be strong [take courage] and fear not'), More's representation of Jesus also fulfils this biblical injunction to speak to the fearful. The Vulgate text – '*Dicit pusillanimis: Confortamini, et nolite timere*' – is the source of More's opening: '*Confortare pusillanimis et noli desperare*'. The basis for the message of comfort is the comparison drawn between the sorrow, sadness, weariness and fear experienced by Jesus in his human nature, and that experienced by the faint-hearted: '*Times tristaris tedio et pavore concuteris*'. The parallel sequences of synonyms suggest a bond of common affliction between the individual and Jesus, which makes the argument more persuasive. The third sentence echoes the reassurance given to the Apostles in John 16:33, '*In mundum pressuram habebitis: sed confidite, ego vici mundum*' (In the world you shall have tribulation: but trust me, I conquered the world); but, whereas in the Gospel Jesus acknowledges their future suffering, More's Jesus compares his own suffering with the Christian's immediate condition: '*Confide. Ego vici mundum qui plus supra modum timui.*' This comparison enables More's Jesus to infer that the individual should follow him, because his own experience and achievement provide a powerful and relevant exemplum. More invokes the parable of the good shepherd in John's Gospel, where the sheep follow because they know the shepherd's voice, and trust that he will lay down his life to save them (John 10:4; 11). He exploits the associations of this familiar image of Jesus, enhancing its emotive qualities by using diminutives to call the sheep: '*tu timidula et imbecillis ovicula*'. The injunction to see the man who walks ahead, and to catch hold of his clothing, draws upon two incidents from the Gospels in the ministry of Jesus, which emphasize the importance of faith. In Matt. 14:26–7 the disciples see Jesus walking towards them on the waves and are afraid. Peter's attempt to follow his master's example earns him a gentle rebuke, as Jesus saves this man 'of little faith' from the fear of death (14:29–31). The chapter ends at verse 36, with Jesus healing the sick who touch the hem of his garment. These motifs of the healing touch, and the action of walking in the footsteps of the good pastor, in the context of adversity and affliction led More's imagination to focus on a parallel incident from Mark 5:27–30 and Luke 8:43–8. In this incident, a woman followed Jesus in a crowd and touched the border of his garment – '*accessit retro, et tetiget fimbriam vestimenti eius*' (Luke 8:44) – whereupon, Jesus turned to ask who had touched him, because he had felt that a power had gone out of him ('*virtutem ... exierat de illo*', Mark 5:30). The woman had been afflicted with 'an issue [*profluvio*] of blood', which stopped ('*stetit fluxus sanguinis*') as soon as she touched the garment (Mark 5:25; Luke 8:44). More took over and regenerated for his own purposes the detail of an approach from behind, the power which issued on touch (*'vestis fimbriam apprehende. Inde virtutem exire senties'*), and the effect of stopping a debilitating flow of blood (*'effluentem sanguinem sistet'*). However, the larger theme of the speech derives from the context of Matthew 14. Further scriptural borrowings are evident in the last part of this extract, which incorporates the sense and the words of Paul in 1 Cor. 10:13. More's Jesus ends his speech with a promise to 'champion your cause until you are victorious', and to reward the victor with a laurel crown after death.[82] The military metaphor, here suggested by 2 Tim. 2:1–5, evokes traditions of the faithful as the triumphant soldiers of Christ. More as commentator responds to this dramatic address by arguing that on such evidence the agony of Jesus seems intended specifically (*'non aliud quic quam euidentius'*) to lay down 'a fighting technique and a battle code for the faint-hearted soldier who needs to be swept along ... into martyrdom [*quam rapiendo in martyrium militi meticuloso*]'.[83]

The most emotionally charged of the digressions in the *De tristitia* is that relating to the controversy over the real presence in the sacrament (a controversy which, as we have seen, depended on the interpretation of the words of institution). The commentator expresses his outrage at those 'of a certain sect' who deny the real presence, and thereby 'betray' Jesus 'into the hands of sinners', much as Judas had betrayed him.[84] The commentator's incomprehension of their attitudes and his sense of the enormity of their blasphemy are expressed as he heaps up piles of clauses exciting controversy in a series of repetitions: '*contra scripturas ... contra sanctorum omnium interpretationes ... contra ... contra ...*'. This series reaches a climax in a rhetorical question which challenges the reader, as in a debate, to agree to the grounds of a similitude between those who betrayed and mocked Jesus then, and those who deny the real presence now; acceptance of the figure confirms the comparison:

When at this late date they set out to do such a thing, against the most open passages of scripture, against the clearest interpretations of all the saints, against the most constant faith of the whole church for so many centuries, against the truth most amply witnessed to by so many thousands of miracles – this group ... how little difference is there, I ask you, between them and those who took Christ captive that night?[85]

Such blasphemy is seen as a cancerous plague creeping (*serpens*) through the whole country, as the infection is spread by the spoken word:

... wherever this plague rages today most fiercely, everyone did not catch the disease in a single day. Rather the contagion spreads gradually and imperceptibly while those persons who despise it at first, afterwards can stand to hear it and respond to it with less than full scorn, then come to tolerate wicked discussions, and afterwards are carried away into error, until like a cancer ... the creeping disease finally takes over [*occupat*] the whole country.[86]

This catholic polemic is directed to rouse fear in the faithful and to urge their vigilance against an enemy occupation by microbes borne on the wind. The self-conscious commentator ends his tirade with a prayer that God 'may never allow the devil to roll the blasts [*procellas*] of this storm of his to our shores. But so much for my digression into these mysteries [*in hec mysteria*]; let us now return to the historical events [*ad hystoriam*]'.

When the commentator considers the spiritual utility for a Christian of the exemplum of Jesus's suffering, he explores More's immediate personal dilemma as a prisoner faced with a choice between denying his faith or sacrificing his life. The commentary emphasizes that 'it is not safe for just anyone to go rushing on heedlessly to the point where he cannot retrace his steps.'[87] A desire to embrace martyrdom is unnatural (as the intensity of Jesus's fear demonstrates in his request to let 'the cup' pass from him), and worse, it may be a symptom of pride. Fear safeguards against the pride of those who might seek glory contrary to the will of God, and should not be condemned: 'We should not immediately consider it cowardice for someone to feel fear and horror at the thought of torments, not even if he prudently avoids dangers (provided he does not compromise himself).'[88] More's personal involvement with the issues raised by the account of the agony in the garden focuses the underlying hermeneutic problem more sharply. How does one interpret the significance of the most relevant biblical exemplum when attempting either to determine the propriety of saving oneself (by leaning further towards a compromise), or to validate a call to witness to the truth by martyrdom? More's premise is that, although God's purpose is normally hidden from man, all is revealed '*ex archano sapientiae*',[89] when the time is right for man to know God's will. Since the will of God has already been revealed in Scripture, to search the Scriptures offers the best trial of the Word himself for a fearful man on trial. The commentator quotes Paul's assurances to the Corinthians (1 Cor. 10:13): 'For God is trustworthy. He does not allow you to be tempted beyond what you can stand, but with the temptation He also gives a way out so that you may be able to bear it.'

More tries God's Word by interrogating the text, digesting it by meditative or ruminative study, and regenerating it in terms of his own concerns and values through his own literary personality. The *De tristitia Christi* illustrates a general issue, that, however much the new writing generated in the commentary endorses old values, traditions and authorities, his reading of the text itself is provisional and personal.

In *Samson Agonistes* Milton, like More, drew from his reading of the model a concern for human nature subjected to physical temptation, and a protagonist responding to divine prophecy.[90] But by the second half of the seventeenth century, Milton could expect the readers of his poem to be familiar not only with the Hebraic ethics of his protagonist but also with a range of attitudes to the significance of the Old Testament story.[91] For several generations, Protestants had been reading the Old Testament for types of the national and personal histories of the elect, correlating their own experiences, public and private, with scriptural history. They were used to reading by themselves for themselves.

Moreover, the effects of civil war and the emergence of independent churches had stimulated a reaction to the anarchic tendencies which had come to dominate Protestant hermeneutics. Because the intellectual element in this reaction was also influenced by the impact of new developments in scientific thinking, it may be represented by Hobbes's response to 'Enthusiasme, or supernaturall Inspiration', 'occasioned by the disorders of the present time' and based upon his observations of 'Humane Nature, and the Laws Divine' in action.[92] In Hobbes's view, since the time of the Old Testament prophets,

we have no sign left, whereby to acknowledge the pretended Revelations, or Inspirations of any private man; no obligation to give ear to any Doctrine, farther than it is conformable to the Holy Scriptures, which since the time of our Saviour, supply the place, and sufficiently recompense the want of all other Prophecy; and from which, by wise and learned interpretation, and carefull ratiocination, all rules and precepts necessary to the knowledge of our duty both to God and man ... may easily be deduced.[93]

Recent experience of various groups' reliance on unorthodox interpretations, said to be inspired by the Holy Spirit, had highlighted the problems of validating such claims.[94] Hobbes's proposal, for a greater emphasis on learning and on 'carefull ratiocination', shifted the burden of validating interpretation from God to man's reason as ordained by God.

Samson Agonistes, A Dramatic Poem takes the form of a series of confrontations between the protagonist on the one hand, and either different characters or the substance of biblical prophecy on the other hand. In this way Samson interrogates his past in an attempt to explain his present condition, 'Eyeless in Gaza at the Mill with slaves' (l. 41). Samson suffers acutely as he tries to interpret and fulfil the will of God in adverse personal and national circumstances. The psychological progress of a sinner towards self-knowledge is focused through a dramatic process of soul-searching by a trial of God's Word. The dramatic form allows Milton neither authorial comment (beyond the poem's title and preface) nor an intermediary poet-narrator figure to guide a reader's interpretation, although it does offer opportunities for the characters (including the chorus) to meditate upon the action.[95] In drama there are no privileged voices.

The action begins, significantly, with a blind man seeking inspiration. Samson's thoughts are 'restless' like 'Hornets arm'd', but their attack is focused on a fundamental issue, the question:

> O wherefore was my birth from Heaven foretold
> Twice by an Angel, who at last in sight
> Of both my Parents all in flames ascended
> From off the Altar, where an Off'ring burn'd,
> As in a fiery column charioting
> His Godlike presence, and from some great act,
> Or benefit reveal'd to Abraham's race?
>
> (ll. 19–20, 23–9)

Samson's problem is a hermeneutic one: how to interpret a spectacular sign from God, which denotes other such signs needing the exposition of biblical commentators. To compare different authoritative parts of Scripture should offer a way out of the difficulty,[96] but with every reference clarification eludes him. The ascent in flames and 'charioting' (emphasized by the present participle) recalls the fiery chariot by which Elijah ascended into Heaven without suffering death. The 'column charioting' the angel's 'Godlike presence' as 'from some great act' anticipates the circumstances of Samson's catastrophe and delivery from earthly bondage. The offerring on an altar (especially in the presence of parents and an angel), and the alternative offered to 'some great act' in a 'benefit reveal'd to Abraham's race', suggest the sacrifice of at least one other precious son – Isaac (or Israel), where the 'benefit' is God's covenant. Such copious comparisons parallel the procedural difficulties in Samson's ruminations. The terms of Samson's question not only prompt expectations based on historical instances of divine intervention but also reflect upon Samson's failure to exercise free will responsibly during his lifetime.

Samson's second question is *why?*

> Why was my breeding order'd and prescrib'd
> As of a person separate to God,
> Design'd for great exploits if I must dye
> Betray'd, Captiv'd, and both my Eyes put out,
> Made of my Enemies the scorn and gaze;
> To grind in Brazen Fetters under task
> With this Heav'n-gifted strength?
>
> (ll. 30–6)

The question is appropriate to his situation, but an informed contemporary reader would respond to this dramatic situation from the perspective of the completed action – Samson's death. The reader may therefore recognize that, although Samson's premise that he must die 'the scorn' of his enemies is possible, it may not be valid.

The gap between Samson's perceptions and a reader's response to them provides the opportunity for a tragic reversal in the action. Samson pauses before his third question to emphasize the tragic ironies of his glory 'debas't', of the promised deliverer 'himself in bonds', and to command others to 'Ask for this great Deliverer now' (and thereby to interrogate God's purpose from the standpoint of Samson's uncertainty, just before he changes that standpoint: 'Yet stay, let me not rashly call in doubt Divine Prediction' (ll. 37; 42; 40; 43–4)). This shift in Samson's approach to the problem of interpreting his life alters the premise upon which he bases his next question:

> . . . what if all foretold
> Had been fulfilld but through mine own default,
> Whom have I to complain of but my self?
>
> (ll. 44–6)

Samson thereby establishes that he may accept responsibility for his 'own default' without denying the purpose of a divine prediction he cannot fathom from his own past history. The processes of Samson's mind in dramatic soliloquy (alone with himself and God's Word)[97] are self-authenticating. There is no appeal to external authorities, and any attempt to disprove his doubts about himself and 'Divine Prediction' must depend on his own efforts.

Hereafter the poem dramatizes Samson's encounters with temptations which represent different aspects of his life and personal identity: the protagonist's efforts are directed to understanding and interpreting the story of a life with no future. Such effort is not confined to Samson. Manoa questions God's purpose with regard to his own history:

> O wherefore did God grant me my request?
> Why are his gifts desirable ...?
> For this did the Angel twice descend?
> (ll. 356; 358; 361)

offering to correct the 'heavenly disposition' as he understands it,

> Alas me thinks whom God hath chosen once
> To worthiest deeds ...
> He should not so o'rewhelm, and as a thrall
> Subject him to so foul indignities,
> Be it but for honours sake of former deeds
> (ll. 368–72)

All Manoa's interpretations of the past condition his expectations for the future: they are subjective and appropriate to a hopeful father of an afflicted son. Similarly he chooses to receive 'as a Prophecy' Samson's 'words' that 'the God of Abraham' will not allow Dagon to compete 'But will arise and his great name assert' (ll. 466; 467; 472–3). The chorus acknowledges that the effects of Samson's reasoning behind his reply to the Philistine officer 'surmounts my reach' (l. 1380). The 'rouzing motions' which Samson feels, and as he reports 'dispose To something extraordinary my thoughts', will have to be taken on trust, by the reader no less than by the chorus (ll. 1382–3).[98] Samson's premise, '*If* there be aught of presage in the mind', makes his expectation doubly conditional: 'This day will be remarkable in my life By some great act, *or* of my days the last' (ll. 1387–9, my emphasis). He thereby inscribes a hermeneutic circle upon the conclusion of his argument still to be enacted. The hermeneutic dilemma within the poem reminds us of the recurrent problems of Reformation hermeneutics: what constitutes a valid interpretation of the will of God embodied in the Word? is the discourse self-sufficient? who has authority to decide?

Samson's immediate audience, the chorus, and Milton's readers are left with options (conditioned by their own beliefs) for interpreting the significance of the final catastrophe. Samson's 'or of my days the last' (l. 1389) suggests that he may try to make up for lost time – a lifetime – in a final effort to disprove his doubts, both about his interpretation of 'Divine Prediction' and about his own role as deliverer of Israel, which he believes he has disgraced so far. When Manoa receives the news of Samson's death he asks, 'How dy'd he? death to life is crown or shame' (l. 1579), as if the final act itself (rather than the report of the event interpreted by a witness) should foreclose on the contradictory options in interpretation of Samson's life story. Such foreclosure is not possible: the interrogative mode in the poem continues to both stimulate and represent a self-authenticating hermeneutic process. After the full eyewitness account the chorus and semi-chorus respond with their various interpretations of this account. The divine prediction is deemed to be fulfilled, and the moral inconvenience of 'revenge' and 'self-kill'd' is excused as 'yet glorious', and 'but tangl'd in the fold, Of dire necessity' (ll. 1660; 1664–6). The law of Nemesis which joined Samson with his enemies requires apology and thus does not preclude either option for a final judgement: death to this life may be both crown *and* shame.

When the first semi-chorus takes up the shame of the Philistines, the other semi-chorus immediately sees a contrast with the status of Samson. The first perceives the drunkenness of the Philistines to have been the visitation of a 'spirit of phrenzie' (l. 1675) sent by 'our living Dread', hence they had 'Fall'n into wrath divine, As thir own ruin on themselves to invite' (ll. 1673; 1683–4). The other semi-chorus perceives that, whereas divine wrath had stricken the enemy 'with blindness internal', Samson, though 'blind of sight', had been

> With inward eyes illuminated
> His fierie vertue rouz'd
> From under ashes into sudden flame
> (ll. 1686–7, 1689–91)

The only way to distinguish between these contrasting spirits of 'wrath divine' is by their effect. The interpreters of the catastrophe are explaining *to their own satisfaction* the significance of an historic event in terms of their own assessment of 'Divine Prediction'. The priority of the Word of God justifies their attempt, but not their interpretation.

More had demanded freedom of conscience to uphold the traditional authority of the Catholic Church. As a writer he depended on its traditions of devotional exercise and exegesis derived from the Doctors of the Church. When he dramatized the speech of Jesus in the *De tristitia Christi*, he was sustained by a faith which allowed him and a contemporary reader to assume confirmation of the guidance from God which he sought. By contrast, Milton had defined freedom of conscience in terms of liberty to read and interpret the Scriptures according to the guidance of the Holy Spirit: 'who can be at rest ... who hath not libertie to serve God and to save his own soul, according to the best light which God hath planted in him to that purpose, by the reading of his reveal'd will and the guidance of his holy spirit?'[99] When Milton wrote *Samson Agonistes* the abuse of such personal interpretation had created disillusion, and its validity had been challenged by reason as well as authority.[100] When Samson assumes confirmation of the guidance he sought, a contemporary reader would have been able to regard this as the final catastrophe of the tragedy.

New typologies

Although the premises of Catholic and Protestant approaches to the Bible differed, Protestant commentators did not discard all allegorical and typological interpretation; they continued to regard spiritual applications of the literal sense of Scripture as normal.[101] Those hermeneutic procedures which had been transferred from Scripture to the reading of secular poetry, by Dante and others,[102] also continued to flourish. Thus, typological and allegorical readings were widely assumed to be applicable to secular as well as sacred literature, and especially to those literary kinds understood to have serious moral purposes, such as epic and tragedy.[103] However, there were new typological applications whereby readings of biblical history could be seen to incorporate significance for contemporary England, and the history of the new elect nation of latterday Israelites.[104] Renewed emphasis on the historic or literal sense of the Old Testament sharpened the responses of Protestant readers to the politics of the Israelite experience, especially that narrated in the Books of Samuel and of Kings. They perceived parallels and analogues between the heroes of ancient Israel and the rulers of Protestant England. A providential order in the history of mankind from the Fall to the Reformation manifested the divine purpose.

David, as an heroic king of Israel, acquired further significance in the mythology of contemporary politics when Tudor and Stuart monarchs were eulogized as new anti-types of Old Testament leaders. In 1551 the late Henry VIII was described not only as the Moses who delivered England from 'Romishe Pharao' but also as 'an Englishe David' who 'caste the corner stone of goddes woorde'.[105] Similarly, Henry's son, Edward VI, seeking to establish the Reformation in England upon the foundations laid by his father, was

expected to become David's wise son 'Salomon ... appointed &
by special dispensacion elected to build & finishe' God's house 'by
restoring and establishing the true Christian religion'.[106]

In 1559 the English Calvinists who translated the Psalms for the
Geneva Bible dedicated their work to Elizabeth I partly in the
expectation that she would acknowledge a correspondence between
her own life before she became Queen, and the 'perils and persecutions' King David 'susteyned before he came to the royall
dignitie'.[107] Such a parallel was supposed to induce Elizabeth to
follow David's example in other respects. The praise of Elizabeth as
the redeemer of England from 'poperie' – 'the shadowe of death' –
became a feature of sermons and poems commemorating her accession day. To William Leigh, preaching towards the end of her reign,

This day is deare to England, and of all the mercies of our God, registred in
the kalender of his Love, next to that of his Sonne christ ... to bee of
blessed memorie ... The allusion is good: from our Christ, to our Queene,
for by him and her, the yoke of our burthen ... hath bene broken.[108]

The 'allusion' is sustained and not a blasphemy, because Elizabeth
is 'paraleld' with David, another anointed one, who is 'a Type of
Christ'.[109] The parallels are drawn in detail: just as 'David was the
least and last of his fathers house, so was Elizabeth' of the Tudors;
just as he was 'condemned of his brethren' so was she 'of her sister',

Saul a King persecuted David, Marie a Queene was wroth with Elizabeth.
David an exile in the holdes of Engeddi, she close prisoner in the holdes of
Wodstocke. Doeg reviled David unto Saul, so did Gardiner Elizabeth unto
Mary ... Saul in his spirit of furie purposed to have killed David play-
ing upon his harpe Winchester in his spirit of poperie purposed to have
murthered Elizabeth at her devotions by Paul Peny and James Basset.[110]

Such precise identification of an individual with a biblical type or
exemplum was also thought to assist in the process of interpreting
the Bible.

It was often argued that the personal experience of affliction –
'sanctified' by the experiences of David and of Jesus – was 'a good
helpe to the experimentall knowledge of the worde'.[111] Those 'who
come nearest in their Christian suffrings' to the afflictions of the
psalmist, which prefigure those of Jesus, 'shall best feel, & understand [the] meaning' of the Psalms.[112] Thus, George Wither dedicated his *Psalmes of David Translated Into Lyrick-Verse* (1632) to
the exiled Elizabeth Stuart, Queen of Bohemia, because 'none but

they who have bene afflicted, cann relish the sweetnes, or understand, the depth of these Raptures'.[113] Elizabeth was 'honored above
all the kings & princes of the world', in Wither's opinion, by having
had 'more occasion' in her own life 'to make personall Application'
of the Psalms to herself: 'And, because it is the greatest honour to
come so near, both to the Type & the Prototype [David and Jesus],
of our suffrings ... to beare so many marks of the Lord Jesus,' he
lists her afflictions to convince any 'skoffing Ismaelites', or others,
that 'they are the very same Afflictions, whereof (as a type of Christ)
King David complained'.[114] Thus, 'He, was exalted by God; &, yet,
cast downe. He was annointed king, & yet enjoyed not the King-
dome. He was driven from his owne possessions, & compelled to
sojourne in a forraigne Land....'[115] Like David and Jesus, so Elizabeth of Bohemia. These typological parallels do not particularize
Wither's psalm versions but such a dedication must have been intended to focus his readers' attention on the moral and devotional
applications of Psalms by individuals *in extremis*.[116] Later, Lancelot
Andrewes justified the divine right of kings by citing Old Testament
types of a Christian king. Both royalists and parliamentarians drew
on biblical accounts of the foundation and early history of the
Israelite monarchy, in debates about the validity of the monarchy in
contemporary England.[117]

The application of typology enabled a writer to exploit correspondences between his new work and a biblical sub-text in order to
invite his readers to look for hidden senses. At the same time, it
enabled the writer to evade responsibility for any particular underlying sense thus construed by the reader as interpreter of his text.
The habits of mind fostered by typology were an expedient hedge
against censorship. Shared expectations of how such readings could
operate in the contexts of kingship and the abuse of power were
used to send covert messages to kings and their councillors as early
as the mid-1520s.

The play *Godly Queen Hester* satirized Wolsey in the figure of
Haman – 'yf Aman wynkes, the lawyers shrynckes' – and may have
alluded to his plans to suppress the smaller monasteries: Haman's
threat to the pious 'Jews' who live apart from the world and own
too much land would be worth ten 'thousande pound of golde' to
the King's Treasury.[118] The King agrees to their 'suppression' but
Esther defends the piety, hospitality and care of the poor within
their communities saying that since God 'hath begunne' and 'preserved' their 'householde', 'I advise noman to be so bolde The same
to dissolve what so ever he be.'[119] The same stories were exploited
in different ways in order to derive different lessons for their

audiences.[120] Since the attack on Wolsey dominates the action of the play, the role of Mordecai is vestigial, and since Esther represents Catherine of Aragon there is (tactfully) no mention of Vashti, the King's rebellious first wife. In his poem *Hadassa or The Historie of Ester* (1633), Francis Quarles emphasized the King's dismissal of Vashti, for conjugal insubordination, in a meditation which comments in general terms on the moral and religious duty of wives to obey their husbands.[121]

In 1550, when the Protestant humanist George Buchanan was tried for heresy by the Inquisition in Lisbon, he was able to construe an interpretation of his verse drama *Baptistes*, which testified to his sympathy for the Catholic Church in England.[122] He claimed then that his tragedy on the theme of John the Baptist and Herod represented Henry VIII's tyranny and calumny against the Church, in particular (abetted by his Herodias, Anne Boleyn), the trial and execution of his Baptist, Thomas More, beheaded in 1535. Buchanan later evaded responsibility for such a reading of his play.[123] However, the political significance of the Baptist's story – whatever Buchanan's intended meaning for it – as a representation of royal tyranny was still potent in January 1643, when an English version of Buchanan's play was published by the House of Commons Committee on Printing as *Tyrannicall-Government Anatomized: Or, A discourse Concerning Evil-Councellors. Being the Life and Death of John the Baptist And Presented to the Kings most Excellent Majesty*.[124] The same play could function in different languages to different audiences in the 1540s and the 1640s as a vehicle for political dissent and attacks on current abuses of royal power. The subject would carry particular associations, as well as authority, for both audiences by virtue of being a well-known story: it was regarded as 'true' because it was biblical, and politically expedient because biblical histories were liable to such interpretations by both Protestants and Catholics.

After a century and a half of such readings and typological applications, Dryden was able to assume an experienced and widely based readership for his own contemporary political comment under cover of the story of King David's son, Absalom, and his bad councillor, Achitophel.[125] Such exploitations of types and figures from biblical history were easily adapted to other historic figures. The Earl of Essex's production of a play about Richard II on the eve of his abortive rebellion in February 1601, apparently provoked the Queen to tell William Lambarde, 'I am Richard II. Know ye not that?'[126] Contemporary readers, invited to see national and personal histories foreshadowed in biblical histories, came to expect serious literature in English to carry several layers of intended meaning. Habits of indirect reading – catching the sense at two removes (the phrase is George Herbert's) – were both reinforced by contemporary biblical hermeneutics, and condemned when abused or misapplied. Biblical truth was not simple, naked truth, except by contrast with the inflated rhetoric which, many poets claimed, abused men's wits, either by hiding the absence of any moral substance, or by veiling something noxious and likely to deprave.[127]

II Repercussions: Trials of God's Word

During this period, translations of ancient and contemporary literature, including biblical poetry, enriched the resources of English and enhanced its reputation as an expressive medium for the most subtle ideas and sensitive feelings. Translation was regarded as a national duty. In his preface to *The Courtier* (1561), Thomas Hoby appealed for every Englishman to 'store the tongue according to his knowledge and delight above other men, in some piece of learning, that wee alone of the world may not be still counted barbarous in our tongue'.[128] Tyndale had imagined opponents of vernacular Bibles denigrating the English language – 'They will say it cannot be translated into our tongue, it is so rude' – and responded by extolling the properties of English, which made it superior to Latin in interpreting the original languages of the Bible:

For the Greek tongue agreeth more with the English than with the Latin. And the properties of the Hebrew tongue agreeth a thousand times more ... The manner of speaking is both one; so that in a thousand places thou needest not but to translate it into the English, word for word; when thou must seek a compass in the Latin.[129]

By the 1580s the efforts of Tyndale and Coverdale in particular had generated several new Bibles in English.[130] The existence, but above all, the literary quality of these translations, together with the range of other interpretations available in paraphrases, expositions and commentaries, helped to enhance the status and development of the English language.

The evolution of a literary norm in the style of English prose Bibles had begun in the early 1600s, when scholars translating the Bible for King James recognized the clarity and eloquence of translations by Tyndale and Coverdale. The translators adopted these earlier versions as the stylistic models for their own new work, eschewing both the starker qualities of the Geneva Bible (1560) and the circumlocutions of the Bishops' Bible (1568). They produced thereby a text of abiding literary value, which was soundly based on the best contemporary scholarship but in what was, by 1611, already an archaic style in English prose.[131] For these reasons the prose of the King James Bible was instantly identifiable as biblical. The importance of the literary strengths of these various translations should not be overlooked in assessing the development of literary sensibilities among a wide range of people for whom the Bible in English was the primary literary experience – and for some their only literary experience.

Biblical poetry and English poetics

The emphasis Protestants gave to reading the Bible critically is reflected in numerous contemporary works on rhetoric and poetics. Those attitudes to the Bible, which included recognition of its literary qualities, and moral as well as religious teachings, were used to justify poetry and poetic composition by an appeal to biblical analogues. In particular, Philip Sidney's *Defence of Poesie* (c.1581–3) improved the status of the poet, and the value of imaginative literature in a Christian commonwealth, by reference to the poetry and prophecy of God's Holy Scriptures. He further argued for a theory of the practice of English poetry based on the precedent of biblical prophets' vernacular poetry in Hebrew verse. These arguments were an innovation in English; they could not have been advanced without the availability of the Bible in English translations sensitive to its affective qualities and rhetorical features.

Familiarity with the Bible in English often presupposed an intimate knowledge of the Psalms. As a result, their affective mode of literary procedure became well known beyond learned circles during the sixteenth century.[132] Calvin's exegesis focused on the expressive rhetoric in those psalms which provided vehicles for prayer and introspection. In 1571, his English translator, Arthur Golding, indicated the decorum for 'communication with God' as 'rather an earnest and devout lifting up of the minde, than a loud or curious utterance of the voice'. Nevertheless, he emphasized that the rhetorical discourse of the psalmist was inherently expressive: 'there be many unperfect sentences, many broken speeches, and many displaced words: according as the voice of the partie that prayed, was eyther prevented with the swiftnesse of his thoughtes, or interrupted with the vehemency of joy or greef.'[133] To present such critical observations for the benefit of readers of biblical poetry in English was a new departure in English poetics. They made the general reader conscious of the interrelationship of style, form and meaning in literary discourse: 'the maner of the handling of the matters' whereof a discourse 'treateth' was recognized as material evidence for the reconstruction of its author's intention.[134]

Calvin's critical sensitivity to biblical poetry is also evident in his *Institutio christianae religionis* (1559) where he describes the majesty and grandeur of Holy Scripture, concluding that those for whom prophetic doctrine is 'unsavorie' ought 'to be thought to have no judgement of tast'; however, 'we are even violently carried to an admiration of it rather with dignitie of matter, than with grace of woords.'[135] To prove his point, in his commentaries on the Psalms Calvin quoted several long extracts from Horace's poetry as objective testimony to the grandeur of God's creation and its humbling effect on the human heart.[136] In the *Institutio*, too, he did not hesitate to compare the affective powers of sacred and secular writings.

Reade Demosthenes or Cicero, reade Plato, Aristotle, or any other of all that sorte: I graunte they shall mervailously allure, delite, move, and ravishe thee. But if from them thou come to this holy readyng of Scriptures, wylte thou or not, it shall so lyvely move thy affections, it shall so pearce thy hearte, it shall so settle within thy bones, that in comparison of the efficacie of this feelyng all that force of Rhetoricians and Philosophers shall in maner vanysshe awaie ... the Scriptures, which doo so farre excell all gyftes and graces of mans industrie, doo breathe oute indeede a certayne divinitie.[137]

For Calvin, deeply read in the Church Fathers, especially Augustine, the affective poetry of the Holy Spirit, 'that by the ministery of men ... came to us from the very mouth of God', was nothing less than the foundation of Christian faith, since the only true faith is that which 'is sealed in our hartes by the holy gost'.[138] The written testimony of the Spirit, in which 'we undoubtedly perceive ... the strength and breathing of the divine majestie', moved the will of any reader. The Spirit therefore operated with more certainty and success than either any human will or reason: for, by its power 'we are drawn and stirred to obey, both wittingly and willingly, and yet more lively and effectually than mans wil or wit can attaine.'[139] Evidence for this inner testimony was a powerful weapon with which to rehabilitate the reputation of poets and poetry and to defend them from repetitions of Plato's objections.

Philip Sidney and other English defenders of poetry argued that since God wrote poetry mere humans could not object: 'the holy Davids Psalms are a divine Poeme ... it is fully written in meeter as all learned Hebritians agree, although the rules be not yet fully found.'[140] Above all, Sidney argued, David's 'handling his prophecie' is 'Poeticall': his mode of procedure was an art of divine poetry, 'For what else is the awaking his musical Instruments, the often and free chaunging of persons, his notable Prosopopeias, when he maketh you as it were see God comming in his majestie, his telling of the beasts joyfulnesse, and hils leaping, but a heavenly poesie ...?'[141] This art revealed David as 'a passionate lover of that unspeakable and everlasting bewtie, to be seene by the eyes of the mind, onely cleared by fayth'. The written testimony of David's vision was thus adduced to restore the reputation of poetry in England, which is 'throwne downe to so ridiculous an estimation'.[142]

Sidney further enhanced the status of the poet's imagination by analogy with the creative force of 'the heavenly maker' who 'made man to his owne likenes ... which in nothing [man] sheweth so much as in Poetry; when with the force of a divine breath, he bringeth things foorth surpassing [Nature's] doings.'[143] Among 'the chiefe both in antiquitie and excellencie' who 'did imitate the unconceiveable excellencies of God', Sidney cites 'the wryter of Jobe', David, Solomon, Moses and Deborah.[144]

Sidney's view that poetry is superior to the other human arts (also gifts of the Spirit), was similarly indebted to the currency of Calvinist ideas derived from the Fathers. The philosopher, for example, 'bestoweth but a wordish description' of how men ought to behave 'which doth neither strike, pearce, nor possesse the sight of the soule so much as [the poet] doth'.[145] By contrast, the poet 'commeth to you with words set in delightfull proportion ... with a tale, which holdeth children from play, and olde men from the Chimney corner; and pretending no more, doth intend the winning of the minde from wickednes to vertue'.[146] This inherently affective mode of procedure made poetry universally attractive and useful. An appeal to the precedent of biblical poetry in a general defence of 'poesie' – the arts of poetry – soon became commonplace in English poetics. Thomas Lodge, Puttenham and Sir John Harington all made similar references, to the Psalms especially, in their literary theory.[147]

Harington's *Briefe Apologie of Poetrie* (1591) subdivided poetry into two parts: fiction and verse.[148] Fiction was 'authorized' by examples of fables and 'a kind of Poeticall parable' which, in the cases of Demosthenes's arguments against Philip of Macedon and John Fisher's against the dissolution of the monasteries, conferred upon their authors freedom to criticize superior political powers.[149]

As Harington pointed out 'it were unreverent and almost blasphemous to say' that Nathan's literary invention reproving King David 'for his great sinne of adulterie and murther' was a 'lye', yet it was 'a peece of Poetrie'.[150] Moreover, 'did not our Saviour himself speake in parables?' The parables of Jesus were the ultimate sanction for 'a good and honest and wholesome Allegorie ... hidden in a pleasaunt and pretie fiction'.[151] Scripture was literally and figuratively 'true'. Verse was also sanctioned by biblical poetry, since (as Sidney had already reported) 'some part of the Scripture was written in verse, as the Psalmes of David, & certain other songs.' Harington concluded that 'by the authoritie of sacred Scriptures ... that great objection of lying is quite taken away & refuted.'[152]

By the seventeenth century, the theory and the practice of Protestant poetics in English had been established. Whereas Sidney and Harington had each written metrical psalms[153] as well as 'Apologies for Poetry', George Wither was one of the first English writers to provide a justification of his own poetic practice as a metrical psalmist. The preface to Wither's *The Psalmes of David Translated Into Lyrick-Verse* (1632) indicates that his intention was to observe the stylistic decorum for biblical poetry, which must 'suite the Capacitie of the Vulger' without offending 'the best Iudgments' among his readers: 'For, though the Language be plaine, it is significant ... and preserves ... the fulnes of the Sence, & the relish of the Scripture phrase.'[154] The Psalms' 'relish' was, he argued, best preserved in verse, because their 'Language of the Muses ... is not so properly exprest in the prose dialect.' He acknowledged that he had departed from the usual prose translations in some parts of his paraphrase, because

there is a poeticall emphasis, in many places, which requires such an alteration in the Grammaticall expression, as will seeme to make some difference in the judgment of the Common Reader; whereas, it giveth best life to the Author's intention; & makes that perspicuous, which was made obscure, by those meer Grammaticall Interpreters, who were not acquainted with the proprieties, & Liberties, of this kinde of writing.[155]

The properties of this kind of lyric verse justified his licence as a poetical interpreter of divine inspirations. It was his purpose in giving 'best life to the Author's intention' to 'deliver the meaning of the Originall Text, as powrefully, as plainly, & as breefly' as he could, having regard to the 'grace' and power of the 'Hebrewe ... Idioms of speach'. According to Wither, the need for a plain style was due as much to 'the grave, & simple Language' of the original

Hebrew text as to the capacities of his English 'common reader'.[156] (He makes no mention of the Augustinian tradition of a *sermo humilis* in biblical discourse.) Nevertheless, Wither neither underestimates the variety of forms and subjects in the Psalms (which are therefore 'not properly exprest in one sort of Measure'), nor does he ignore the patterns of repetition and periphrasis, the metaphorical and allegorical allusions, which, he explains, characterize this biblical poetry.[157] Wither's consciousness of the poetics of the Bible in English paraphrases led to a defiant conclusion in defence of his art: 'I regard the Censorious approbation of none, but such, as are (in their understanding, at least) both Divines and Poets.'[158] His ideal reader was a devotional poet like himself. However, by 1632 his 'common reader' would have had access to a large and varied corpus of psalm versions, and would have been able to compare different versions in order to judge 'how much the Phrases or Mysteries confine the Translator ... & what Liberties, & restraints, belong to a Lyrick-poem'.[159] For the majority of Englishmen from *c*.1560–1700, metrical psalms were the best-known English verse.

Calvin's perceptions of the eloquence of the psalmist had had repercussions for English literary theory and practice. Sidney's *Defence of Poesie* brought biblical poetics into mainstream English poetics. Alongside his psalms in poetic forms of 'that Lyricall kind' were innumerable popular versions, such as Wither's, published as 'holy songs' for the common reader and for the non-literate public too.[160] Sidney's reputation helped to establish Protestant poetics in English, thereby laying the foundations for much seventeenth-century religious poetry of different kinds. For Michael Drayton, the poetical 'truth' of Scripture was as delightful a model to imitate as 'any Poeticall fiction', and more useful since it taught divinity.[161] Wither recommended David's lamentation for Saul and Jonathan (2 Sam. 1:19–27) to readers of his *Hymns and Songs of the Church* (1623) 'as a Patterne for our Funerall Poemes'.[162] Donne praised the Sidney psalms, and Herbert's *The Temple* reflects their influence in tone and form.[163] Moreover, in so far as Sidney personalized and naturalized the learned and poetic resources of Protestant Europe, he was also following Hoby's advice to the reader of *The Courtier*, and 'storing' or stocking up the resources of English as a poetic medium.

From the mid-sixteenth century, new handbooks on rhetoric were published in English for the benefit of 'all those that be studious of Eloquence, and that reade most Eloquent Poets'.[164] These poets and orators included the human writers who had been inspired by the eloquent Spirit of God to record Holy Scripture. The general reader, as well as the learned reader of Latin, needed guidance to become eloquent and to recognize and appreciate the rhetorical detail of any written or spoken discourse. *The Garden of Eloquence Conteyning the Figures of Grammer and Rhetorick, from whence maye bee gathered all manner of Flowers, Coulors, Ornaments, Exornations, Formes and Fashions of speech* ... *Set foorth in Englishe, by Henry Pecham Minister* was dedicated to Peacham's friend and patron John Aylmer, Bishop of London, as a work which 'helpeth much for the better understanding of the holy Scriptures'. In the epistle dedicatory Peacham commended 'studyes ... to obtayne Wysedome, and Eloquence'; these he regarded as 'the onelye Ornamentes, whereby mannes lyfe is bewtifyed, and a prayse moste precyous purchased', since both were ordained by 'the Lord God ... to the mind of man' for 'the common use & utillity of mankind'.[165] Peacham's systematic definition and description of tropes and figures frequently includes examples from the Bible, which are either quoted and discussed, or listed for reference.

When individuals were encouraged to search the Scriptures in their own trials of God's Word, the humanist enterprise economy of late Elizabethan England recognized and supplied a market for methodical aids to literacy. The Cawdrays' dictionary, *A Table Alphabeticall*, which disseminated 'interpretation ... by plaine English' of loan words used in English by 1604, fulfilled an educative function for spiritual purposes.[166] It was intended both to improve the comprehension, and to stock the vocabularies, 'of Ladies, Gentlewomen, or any other unskilfull persons. Whereby they may the more easilie and better understand many hard English wordes, which they shall heare or read in Scriptures, Sermons, or elsewhere, and also be made able to use the same aptly themselves'.[167]

Robert Cawdray's *A Treasurie or Store-house of Similes: Both pleasaunt, delightfull, and profitable* (1600) was compiled 'for all estates of men in generall'.[168] His *Treasurie* is an expository handbook of Christian piety:

it containeth the explayning, and plaine opening of many grounds and principles of Christian Religion, so manifestly decyphered out, that everie one (even the very simplest and ignorantest Reader) may easily and plainely understand the true and right meaning thereof.[169]

The concept of 'right meaning' is not explored, but Cawdray assumed that, with 'better understanding therein', an 'increase of knowledge and godlinesse, even in all degrees of men', would ensue: 'For many times that thing, which cannot bee perceived or understood of Readers of Bookes, and hearers of Sermons, by a simple precept, may yet by a Similitude or plaine example, bee attained unto.'[170] The function of these similitudes is to expound a pious truism, fixing doctrine in the mind of a reader by virtue of the intrinsic qualities of metaphorical detail aptly applied. The value of 'Affliction', for example, is demonstrated by exploiting the memorable properties of biblical and native English plant life. Thus:

Like as the Palme-tree, when there is a great waight laid on it, spreadeth and florisheth the broader: or as a Camomell with treading and walking on it waxes thicker: even so a faithfull Christian, the more Affliction and persecution he suffereth for his Christ, the more is his faith increased.[171]

The biblical 'prophets' were said to have used 'similitudes' to clarify and adorn (but never to argue or prove) their sacred matter, 'giving thereby unto their matter, a certaine kind of lively gesture, and so consequently, attyring it with light, perspicuitie, easinesse, estimation, and dignitie'.[172] Like good poetry in general the similitudes of Scripture were delightful, as well as morally and spiritually profitable, because of their affective qualities, 'stirring up thereby, mens drowsie minds, and awaking slouthfull, negligent, carelesse, sluggish and retchlesse people, to the consideration and acknowledgement of the truth; and to the following and imbracing of vertue and godlinesse'.[173] In such ways, Horatian and Neo-Platonic defences of poetry, mingled with Augustinian and Calvinist concepts of biblical discourse, were mediated to people who might never have read or understood the poetics of Sidney or of Harington (Robert Cawdray's dedicatee). The priorities of the Cawdrays and Peacham were to educate English readers to read and use the most eloquent authors profitably; their books helped to cultivate the literary sensibilities of a whole nation.

Such applications of the Bible – in poetics, in rhetorical handbooks and aids to literacy and eloquence – testify to the regeneration of the religious bases of English culture through the medium of the English language and the Bible in English. Through such works, Protestant attitudes to the Bible established the credentials of vernacular poetry among English readers of the Bible, and demonstrated how to read and enjoy any literature.

These attitudes also stimulated English writers to exploit the resources of biblical poetry in major literary kinds: epic,[174] the prose sermon, the lyric, and tragic drama. The exegesis of biblical poetry in sermons and emblems created new works of art. The application of biblical hermeneutics enabled English readers of the Bible to interpret new religious allegories and tragic histories. Finally, the dramatic exploitation of biblical allusions, and discussions of hermeneutic problems in secular plays, demonstrate how far the debates, attitudes and reading practices associated with Protestant approaches to the Bible succeeded in making the English a people of the book.

Exegesis by art: lessons from the Psalms

The sermon and the emblem expound biblical texts, using different forms of art in order to persuade the wills of audiences or readers to recognize and accept doctrine derived from the text. The affective art in both the sermon and the emblem uses the cumulative effects of structural repetitions to reinforce their respective messages. Whereas the sermon is heard in public performance as an oral mode of literary discourse, reading an emblem is a private experience of words and picture seen on the page. Reading the Psalms as both an epitome of the whole Bible, and an 'Anatomy of all the partes of the Soule',[175] stimulated the creation of new literary works which expounded their authors' readings and lessons from the Psalms. The functions of such exegesis by art were to move, and thus persuade, people of the Psalms' religious teaching and spiritual value in private meditation: 'The Psalmes are the Manna of the Church. As Manna tasted to every man like that he liked best, so doe the Psalmes minister Instruction, and satisfaction, to every man, in every emergency and occasion.'[176] Golding dedicated his translation of Calvin's commentaries on the Psalms to the Earl of Oxford, but he insisted that 'the things which the holy ghost uttereth in the sacred scriptures, belong indifferently untoo all men, of what estate, degree, sex, age, or calling so ever they be without exception.'[177]

By the early seventeenth century, the English prose sermon had become an elaborate art form with several competing styles predominating in the contexts of different liturgical traditions.[178] John Donne was just one of many exponents of biblical exegesis by the rhetorical arts of preaching, whose work achieved the fame its literary quality deserved.

Donne's sermons on the Psalms show how a process of interpretation became the model for a systematic rhetorical procedure. The art of interpretation structured the sermon through a three-fold system of applications of the biblical text. He outlined the principles which shaped many of his compositions in two sermons on Psalm 38, preached at Lincoln's Inn in 1618.[179] With reference to the 'words' of Psalm 38:3 'as . . . our present object' he announces that, first, 'they are historically, and literally to be understood of David.'

Secondly, he considers their universal moral significance 'in their retrospect, as they look back upon the first Adam, and so concern Mankind collectively'. Thirdly, he tells his audience, 'we shall consider them in their prospect, in their future relation to the second Adam, in Christ Jesus,' which is their typological significance, since 'David was not onely a cleare Prophet of Christ himselfe, but a Prophet of every particular Christian.' These assumptions provided Donne with the ground plan of his sermon which then proceeds from this *divisio* in three sections. While the literal sense was never totally subordinated to any spiritual application, at the core of all Donne's thinking on the Psalms (as he explained in a sermon on Psalm 90:14) was the significance of the Passion: 'I know nothing, if I know not Christ crucified, And I know not that, if I know not how to apply him to my selfe.'[180] The historic figure of David could teach all Christians those fundamental lessons. In reading the Psalms which 'wrappeth up things in types & figures, describing them under borowed personages ... speaking of thinges too come as if they were past or present, and of things past as if they were in dooing ... every man is made a bewrayer of the secretes of his owne hart'.[181]

A variation on the pattern of exposition, which assumed that 'Historically, David; morally we; Typically, Christ is the subject of this text,'[182] is seen in the second prebend sermon preached at St Paul's in 1626. The text: 'Because thou hast been my helpe, therefore in the shadowe of thy wings will I rejoyce' (Ps. 63:7), suggested a three-fold division for 'the three parts of this Exercise', based on 'the whole compasse of Time, Past, Present, and Future'.[183] David's present condition is defined as his 'distresse ... and that lyes in the Context' of the *titulus* (or head-title) as well as the rest of the psalm. Donne asserts 'That in all those temporall calamities' which occasioned the psalm, 'David was onely sensible of his spirituall losse.' Thus the first part of the sermon compares 'temporall and spirituall afflictions' under the figure of a burden or weight, with which, unless God apply a counter weight in the promise of eternal glory,[184] 'we are waighed downe, we are swallowed up, irreparably, irrevocably, irrecoverably, irremediably' – and inevitably under this pile of ponderous syllables.[185] The second part of the sermon explains 'how David built his assurance upon that which was past; (*Because thou hast been my help*)', which establishes, in both the specific historic and general tropological applications, the need to observe 'Gods former wayes and proceedings upon us', as upon David. Trust in God's help for the future may be premised upon the 'retrospect' of past benefits. Donne enunciated as a general principle 'That it behoves us, in all our purposes, and actions, to propose to our selves a copy to write by, a patterne to worke by, a rule, or an example to proceed by', which he illustrates by applying David's words personally: 'I can propose nothing more availably, then the contemplation of the history of Gods former proceeding with me; which is Davids way here'.[186] The third division of the sermon considers how David viewed 'his prospect', and established 'his confidence for the future' in the text *'Therefore in the shadow of thy wings will I rejoyce.'* This emphasis on joy in the prospect of divine grace takes on a double significance figured in Donne's favourite image of the two hemispheres which are visible, 'If you looke upon this world in a Map'.[187] The map of Heaven, says the preacher, has two similar halves: one half is the glory of Heaven which is held over until the Resurrection, the other 'the Joy of heaven, God opens to our Discovery, and delivers for our habitation even whilst we dwell in this world', for, 'that which Christ shall say to thy soule then at the last Judgement, *Enter into thy Masters joy*, Hee sayes to thy conscience now.' The Christian understanding of the psalm text, which Donne 'opens to our Discovery' in preaching, confirms that a faithful Christian must be a joyful one with a clear conscience: 'dissected and anatomized to God, in a sincere confession, washed in the teares of true contrition, embalmed in the blood of reconciliation, the blood of Christ Jesus'. All the actions imply the preparation of a body for preservation after death, but the subject here (and throughout the sermon) is the rectified soul which, Donne argues, may have a taste of 'the very joy of Heaven' in whatever constitutes its 'true joy . . . in this world'.[188]

The parallelisms of Hebrew poetry with their inherent figures of repetition were commonly perceived to have expository and affective purposes.[189] Donne's style in exegesis is also characterized by the need to fulfil such purposes. Wherever Donne expounds his text according to a three-fold method, the style of his discourse, as well as its structure, is dominated by recurring patterns of triplets. In the following passage, each of the three main sentences is a separate unit, compounded of grammatical parallelisms and echoing sounds, which returns meaningfully to the same resting place – God.

This is the fearefull depth, this is spirituall misery, to be thus fallen from God.

But was this Davids case? was he fallen thus farre, into a diffidence in God?

No. But the danger, the precipice, the slippery sliding into that bottomlesse depth, is, to be excluded from the meanes of comming to God, or staying with God.[190]

Furthermore, each sentence is governed by the tense associated with this three-fold exposition: the present for David's historic situation; the past for the moral retrospect on his case; and implied future for the prophetic injunction, whereby David's situation is interpreted typologically as a general warning. The triple parallelism at the beginning of the last sentence represents the idea of a progressive action from 'the danger' perceived, to 'the precipice' reached, and 'the slippery sliding' enacted grammatically in the present participle. The parallelism in sense, form and rhythm in the alternative offered at the end of the last sentence aids the comprehension of a listener by suggesting an emphatic closure (or pause) in 'staying' with God, which is also imitative of the action it denotes. Even in the development of a single image, the principles, practice and purpose of Donne's exegesis by art all cohere.[191]

At the beginning of this second prebend sermon, the soothing, medicinal qualities of the Psalms are suggested by an appeal to the senses of touch and sound, as the physical properties of the metaphor – allegorically signifying Jesus – prompt parallel extensions of meaning: 'the whole booke of Psalmes is *Oleum effusum* (as the spouse speaks of the name of Christ) an Oyntment powred out upon all sorts of sores, A Searcloth that souples all bruises, A Balme that searches all wounds.'[192] Such expansiveness is part of a heuristic process which translates abstract principles into affective metaphors; it also exemplifies Donne's meditative approach to biblical poetry – here the Song of Songs (1:3) as well as the Psalms – as his literary personality ruminates on the text, digesting its 'food for the soul' several times over. The literary methods in Donne's hermeneutics ensure that the different lessons he draws from the Psalms can serve the needs and the capacities of a wide range of listeners.

The emblems of Francis Quarles also exemplify and invite a meditative approach to biblical metaphor. Quarles defined the emblem as 'a silent Parable';[193] its purpose was affective teaching and the provision of scriptural models for personal devotion. The structure of his emblems represents a new variation on the principle (if not the practice) of a four-fold method of exegesis. The emblems are composed of picture (accompanied by biblical text as motto), verse meditation, authoritative comment or prayer and concluding verse epigram. The theme developed in an emblem usually arises from meditation on a metaphor in a biblical text. The subject is commonly a reflection on the condition of the human soul, supported by divine love, but alienated from God during the course of her earthly life. The Psalms were important source texts, since they

PLATE 4   The emblem for Psalm 142:7, from Francis Quarles, *Emblemes* (London, 1635), book V, no. 10, p. 280. (Reproduced by kind permission of The Bodleian Library, Oxford, ref: Douce QQ 11)

prefigured 'all the greefes, sorowes, feares, doutes, hopes, cares, an-
guisshes, and finally all the trubblesome motions wherewith mennes
mindes are woont to be turmoyled'.[194]

The emblem for the text from Psalm 142:7 ('Bring my Soul out of
Prison, that I may praise thy Name') begins with the picture of a
birdcage, in which crouches a human form appealing to Divine Love
(a winged figure with the shining face of an angel), kneeling outside
the cage door (plate 4). An open bird trap hangs from an adjacent
tree, and a free bird soars into the sky. The speaker of the verse
meditation (in the second section of the emblem) is the psalmist,
whose words provide an analogue to the situation depicted. This
psalmist – a type for every Christian – expounds the biblical
metaphor by means of an allegorical simile:

> My Soul is like a Bird, my flesh the cage,
> Wherein she wears her weary pilgrimage
> Of hours ...
> The keyes that lock her in, and let her out,
> Are Birth and Death.[195]

The poem is more than an interpretative gloss on the picture which
is less than a representation of the message of the text.[196]

In life, within the confines of her carnal cage, the bird-like soul
'hops about',

> From pearch to pearch, from sense to reason; then
> From higher reason down to sense again:
> From sense she climbs to Faith; where for a season
> She sits and Sings; then down again to reason:
> From reason back to Faith, and straight from thence
> She rudely flutters to the perch of sense:
> From sense to hope; then hops from hope to doubt,
> From doubt to dull despair
>
> (ll. 6–14)

The imitation of the bird's restless action characterizes the condition
of the pilgrim soul, searching for freedom from the body and the
world. She begs for an early death, or release from 'the unexpired
thraldom' of her sentence to life, because she 'can find no peace'
(ll. 17–18). Only words can represent this psychological drama; the
restless quality of the repetitions, with momentary pauses, strongly
marked in this edition by colons and semi-colons, is expressive and
meaningful. Such movement can only be implied in the iconographic
contrast between the two states of the soul, as caged victim and free

bird; nevertheless, the icon of confined space illustrates the pathos of one particular moment, and reflects the soul's condition.

The speaker contrasts his present condition, wasting breath 'in sighs and sad complaint', with that of 'happier birds' who can spread their wings and sing freely, 'In choice of raptures, harmonious story Of mans Redemption, and his Makers glory' (ll. 22–3; 25–6). The souls of 'glorious Martyrs' who have departed from their 'fleshly coops' are assumed to have testified 'with Heav'n-prevailing Oratory' which the speaker would like to know how to emulate:

> . . . what rhet'rick had your tongues?
> What dextrous Art had your Elegiack songs?
> What Paul-like pow'r had your admir'd devotion
> What shackle-breaking Faith infus'd such motion
> To your strong Prayer, that could obtain the boon
> To be enlarg'd; to be uncag'd so soon?
>
> (ll. 27–8; 38; 29–34)

The lesson of the psalm is that their faith has set them free, by infusing their prayers with a power beyond rhetorical art. Finally, the speaker petitions Jesus ('Great Lord of Souls' and David's antitype) as the arbiter of every prisoner's fate.

> . . . Thou hadst thy cage, as well as I;
> And for my sake, thy pleasure was to know
> The sorrows that it brought . . .
> O set me free, and I will spend those days,
> Which now I waste in begging, in thy praise
>
> (ll. 45–50)

This last prayer returns the reader to the newly redefined and interpreted biblical text; the last two lines might serve as an additional motto for the picture.

The combination of visual and verbal images does not complete the emblem which, in its third stage of development, draws on the resources and procedures of early medieval meditation. A lengthy quotation from Anselm's *Proslogion* (or, *Faith in Search of Understanding*) develops the theme of man's estrangement from God.[197] Thus, in a series of exclamations and rhetorical questions, the extract from Anselm's colloquy expounds the matter of the speaker's complaint: 'O miserable condition of mankind, that has lost that for which he was created! Alas, what hath he lost? And what hath he found . . . Ah me, what have I enterprised? What have I done?

Whither did I go? Whither am I come?' This search for meaning focuses a reader's mind on man's relationship with his creator; its form and style stirs a reader to the compunction of sorrow, and a consideration of these questions on his own behalf. The authority of Anselm's invitation to self-scrutiny derives from his influence on the devotional tradition of the Church, but the experience of regret, which his colloquy generates, also authenticates its message in this context.

In this 1635 edition, a blank space separates the colloquy from the last component in the emblem, a four-line verse epigram. The blank on the page seems to suggest an opportunity for the meditative reader of the emblem to pause, or make notes. The epigram changes the contemplative mood, reflecting a change within the speaker of the verse meditation; true to its literary kind, the epigram is brisk in tone and witty, with a final turn,

> Paul's midnight-voice prevail'd; his musicks thunder
> Unhing'd the prison-doors, split bolts in sunder:
> And sitt'st thou here, and hang'st the feeble wing?
> And whin'st to be enlarg'd? Soul, learn to sing.

The teaching of the emblem – its lesson from the Psalms – is summarized in this final injunction. The meaning of the emblem is construed by an individual from the experience of reading it. This experience offers contrasts and confrontations, questions and answers, compounding the static icon with the dynamic word in a cumulative four-part learning process.

The combination of picture and biblical text as motto suggested a programme for meditative development in exegesis of the text. (Visual images evoke but do not develop the meaning of a text.) Similarly, Donne's initial statements of the text and division of his sermon informed his audience of his programme, without anticipating its impact in the completion of a cumulative process. In developing and reinforcing the significance of their respective lessons, both exegetes had to reconcile the utility of an instant appeal to the human will (and senses) with a need for sustained intelligibility.

The repetitions in Donne's style have already been related to his hermeneutic procedure and to his exploitation of biblical poetics: in order to present his interpretation of the psalm, Donne imitates those features inherent in the style of the Psalms themselves, which contribute to their affective mode of procedure. There are two further considerations which are extrinsic to the Psalms. In the second prebend sermon, ideas, grammatical constructions, single words or syllables are repeated. In the first place, these recurring patterns aid the memory of the preacher in his progress through the pre-planned structure.[198] In the second place, and most importantly, they help his audience to comprehend what has been said. Patterns of rhythm and sound can reinforce syntactical expectations to suggest discrete units of sense in spoken discourse. Repetition and variations on key topics help audiences to remember what they are told and allow them to anticipate significant details of the exposition from the initial outline. A reading of the Quarles emblem in its entirety, as a four-part composition, imitates that process of inter-preting the biblical text, which is reflected in the structure of the emblem itself and is substantiated by its art. First, the picture arrests attention with an image which may be looked upon as long as required; secondly, the verse meditation explicates the visual image by an allegorical simile, which initiates progress to a discovery of sense in words; thirdly, experience and understanding are confirmed by an authority; finally, the lesson is restated with epigrammatic vigour, brevity and clarity.

The processes of exegesis and reiteration by such affective tactics were creative as well as interpretative. In these sermons and em-blems, exegesis by art widened the appeal as well as the persuasive-ness and apparent authenticity of their interpreters' trials of the Word.[199]

Hermeneutics in poetry: re-creating the Passion

By the 1630s, after a century of Protestant advice and encouragement to readers of the Bible, poets could assume that their own readers would be experienced in biblical hermeneutics, and capable of applying allegorical or historical methods of interpretation to their works. 'Redemption' by George Herbert, and *Christus patiens* by Hugo Grotius (translated into English verse by George Sandys) do not expound biblical texts, but re-create their authors' reflections on the significance of the Passion, and represent their own trials of the Word.[200]

Herbert's sonnet 'Redemption' represents the significance of the Passion by using extended metaphor to affirm new-covenant theo-logy. The title of the sonnet (as published), and its position in *The Temple* (1633), among a brief sequence of Easter poems, provide the context which validates an allegorical reading. The hermeneutics of this sonnet – its process of generating meaning by pointing to its interpretation and depiction of the Christian message – is heuristic. In this case, the reading process exemplifies the uncovering of a hidden sense – the doctrinal significance of the Passion – in discovering the historic focus of the sonnet: the image of Jesus on the Cross. A reader is expected to share the speaker's satisfaction in finding and confirming the exemplary image of the Word as the poet's intended meaning. By trial and error, and step by step, the speaker's journey of discovery parallels a reader's regeneration and confirmation of the allegory by a combination of internal and external evidence. The reader's spiritual application of the speaker's literal sense is the message of the author's text; all 'Must ... be vail'd, while he that reades, divines Catching the sense at two removes' ('Jordan I', ll. 9–10).

REDEMPTION

Having been tenant long to a rich Lord,
  Not thriving, I resolved to be bold,
  And make a suit unto him, to afford
A new small-rented lease, and cancell th'old.
In heaven at his manour I him sought:
  They told me there, that he was lately gone
  About some land, which he had dearly bought
Long since on earth, to take possession.
I straight return'd, and knowing his great birth,
  Sought him accordingly in great resorts;
  In cities, theatres, gardens, parks, and courts:
At length I heard a ragged noise and mirth
  Of theeves and murderers: there I him espied,
  Who straight, Your suit is granted, said, & died.

The *prima fronte* literal sense concerns the wish of a naive tenant to persuade his rich landlord to change the terms of his lease. Circumstantial details in the first quatrain establish the speaker's situation, but lead a reader away from the doctrinal expectations suggested initially by the title 'Redemption', and the previous poem, 'Good Friday'. (The possibility of redemption through Christ is a consequence of the historic events of Good Friday.) The sonnet was originally entitled 'The Passion'.[201] Its present title focuses a reader's attention further from the protagonist of the Easter drama: the crucified Jesus. From the first line (and the printed title) a reader attends to the relationship between the speaker and his lord. The speaker's legal submission is that his old contract (issued under the old covenant) should be *bought back*, and another issued, by grace and favour (under a new dispensation). The balance between the literal and allegorical senses is restored in the second quatrain when the petitioner announces his action in seeking the lord of his manor 'in heaven'. The grammatical priority of 'heaven' is the first internal signal that the landlord–tenant conceit may be expounded allegorically: the adverbial phrase takes syntactical and psychological precedence over subject, verb and object. This invites a reader to interpret the first quatrain with the hindsight offered by the second: the first is an historic 'type' of the spiritual message developed in the second quatrain. As this quatrain develops its significance from the typological conceit, the pun on 'dearly' (l. 7) becomes prominent as an exemplar of the poem's primary message within a hidden secondary sense. ('Dearly' implies both the cost of the Passion in terms of human suffering and its theological significance as a manifestation of divine love for sinful humanity.) The sestet resolves the search within the sonnet by elaborating the paradox of the 'rich lord' of 'great birth', who pays 'dearly' to fulfil a bargain struck 'long since', at the Fall, and is finally found among thieves and murderers.

The shell of the fiction remains intact throughout; nevertheless, the context of a series of Easter poems, coupled with the tactics of the second quatrain, and the hints in the sestet which point to circumstances of the historic event, should ensure an appropriate reading for the message, or kernel, of the text. The poet assumes Christian readers practised in the arts of reading the Bible (and therefore capable of joining the speaker's search for signs of his lord), in order to interpret the doctrine of this poem themselves. 'Redemption' is what Harington had called 'a kind of Poeticall parable'.[202]

Herbert assumed a different kind of reading for 'The Sacrifice' which represents the Passion (and the events leading up to it) from the point of view of Jesus on the Cross. His affective complaint – with the refrain 'Was ever grief like mine?' – may be understood directly from the historic literal sense of its dramatic narrative addressed to all passers-by. This form of complaint was modelled on parts of the medieval liturgy for Holy Week and is also found in several Middle English lyrics.[203]

The dramatic qualities of the Easter story had stimulated liturgical re-enactments in early medieval church tropes, and civic drama, in the annual Corpus Christi cycles by fourteenth-century town guilds. In the sixteenth and seventeenth centuries, humanists grafted some of the religious applications of medieval drama on to the stock of ancient tragedy; they found a precedent among the early Church Fathers, especially Gregory Nazianzen (d.389) who was thought to have written tragic drama in Greek on Christian subjects.[204] In the preface to *Samson Agonistes*, Milton assumed that Scripture justified the moral art of tragedy, citing the 'Apostle Paul himself' who 'thought it not unworthy to insert a verse of Euripides into the text of Holy Scripture, I Cor. xv. 33'. In this defence of tragedy, Milton also cited Nazianzen's tragedy *Christ Suffering*, which he may have known through the Latin play which was based on this Greek model by Hugo Grotius.[205]

The Grotius tragedy was translated into English verse by George Sandys and published in 1640 as *Christs Passion. A Tragedy. With Annotations*; it presents a reading of the Gospel narratives informed by humanist scholarship. The play dramatizes the actions of historic personages; and the annotations (in end notes), compiled by Sandys, comment on the language, local customs and politics of first-century Jerusalem.[206] While the play omits explicit theological comment, the doctrinal significance of the Passion is nevertheless an important part of its message, and may be recognized by an experienced Christian audience responsive to the indirect statements of dramatic irony. The play emphasizes the humanity of Jesus whose agony in the garden is shown as a mental torture producing specific physiological effects (cf. Luke 22:44),[207]

> See what this Nights confederate Shadows hide:
> My Minde before my Body crucifi'd.
> Horrour shakes all my Powers: my entrailes beat,
> And all my Body flowes with purple sweat[208]

Jesus addresses Death in soliloquy, to acknowledge the greater cruelty of 'Th'anxiety and torment of the Minde'. He would like to change his lot and pray for relief, but recognizes that he is tied to a destiny which even denies him the comfort of prayer:

> [God's] purpose, fixt when yet the world was young,
> And Oracles, so oft by Prophets sung,
> Now rushing on their destinated end,
> No Orisons, nor Sacrifice can bend.[209]

As a human figure in the historical drama Jesus has significance for his contemporaries as the focus for political tensions within Judea and the city. These tensions, and sympathy for the different factions, are evoked credibly and even-handedly. On the one hand, the Chorus of Jewish Women lament their country's occupation by the Romans; at Passover (commemorating the Exodus from Egypt), these thoughts 'of servitude at home' exacerbate their misery.[210] Since the chorus interprets the tyranny of Rome over Israel as a

divine punishment, their longing for the coming of the Messiah
testifies to their misery and political oppression. On the other hand,
Pontius Pilate's soliloquy reveals his particular sense of isolation and
insecurity as the governor responsible for an unruly province:

> Farre from my friends, farre from my native Soyl
> I here in honourable Exile toyl,
> To curb a People whom the Gods disclaim[211]

Such characterization makes his willingness to be influenced by
Caiaphas all the more plausible. The potential explosiveness of the
situation in Jerusalem crowded with Passover pilgrims becomes a
factor in his decision to condemn Jesus, and so appease the Jewish
populace:

> What if the Vulgar to their weapons fall?
> Who knows the end, if once the Storme begin?
> Sure I, their Judge, egregious praise should win
> By troubling of the publique Peace . . .

His judgement is mere political opportunism: 'Is his offence not
great Whose innovation may a warre beget?'[212] The Jews exploit
this fear and appeal to his self-interest, saying 'Thy own affairs
intend' (l. 194).

After death Jesus becomes a figure of more than local political
importance. As he dies 'Night usurpes the empty Throne of Day'
(Act IV, l. 208). A new chorus of Roman soldiers considers this
disturbance in the cosmos, comparing it with the stories and personages with which they are most familiar:

> What horrid fact, before th'approach of Night,
> Deservedly deprives the World of Light!
> As when stern Atreus to his Brother gave
> His Childrens flesh, who made his owne their grave:
> Or when the Vestall Ilia's God-like Sun,
> Who our unbounded Monarchie begun,
> Was in a hundred pieces cut; by theft
> At once of Life and Funerals bereft[213]

By dramatic irony this chorus focuses the attention of a Christian
reader, or audience, on Jesus as the Light of the World, on the
eclipse of the God-like son, and the theme of a sacrificed child. In
fear, the Romans ask the 'Great Father of us all' to 'restore the Day'
and with further dramatic irony – speaking indirectly to the play's

Christian interpreters, but also in character – the soldiers continue their prayer:

> One Sacrifice seek we to expiate
> All our Offences ...
> The Bloud, which from that mangled body bled,
> Must purge our Sins, which we unjustly shed.
> O smooth thy brows! Receive the innocence
> Of one for all; and with our guilt dispence.
> For sin, what greater Ransome can we pay?
> What worthier Offering on thy Altar lay?[214]

The dramatic procedure here is to create a psychologically plausible response to the eclipse by the frightened pagan soldiers, and thereby to engage the reader's sympathy for them, stimulating reflection upon the situation from their point of view. The play's combination of narrative and oblique commentary, of soliloquy, and dialogue in the questions and answers of the women's chorus and the messengers who witness the Crucifixion, represents the attempts of its characters to understand the action in which they are involved.

The 'Annotations'[215] expound the historical circumstances of the action of the play rather than any theological significance. There is no allegorical or any other kind of spiritual interpretation in these notes attached to such *lemmata* as place names. In the note attached to 'Cedron' the assumption is that the brook and the story of the betrayal in the Garden of Gethsemane by which it flows are of the same order of reality.[216] The truth of the play's poetic fiction is confirmed by its scholarly apparatus. The notes also link the action of the play with the lives of its readers, providing a sense of the continuity of history. Events from the recent past are explained by reference to the play's representation of the biblical past. The contemporary situation of seventeenth-century Jews is specifically related to the terms of Joseph of Arimathea's curse in Act V:

Despis'd, and wretched, wander, &c.] Out of Spaine they were banished in the yeer 1500 by Ferdinand and Emanuel. Now scattred throughout the whole World, and hated by those among whom they live; yet suffered as a necessary mischiefe: subject to all wrongs and contumelies; who can patiently submit themselves to the times, and to whatsoever may advance their profit.[217]

The annotation to Joseph's remark about the tomb of Jesus completes the sense of prophetic conjecture in his words, 'Who knows but soon a holier Age may come, When all the World shall celebrate this Tombe;' and validates it by a long description which would not be out of place in a modern tourist guide to the Holy Sepulchre.[218] In these authoritative annotations the processes of historical scholarship have not merely influenced the style and attitudes manifest in the verse drama, they are also an integral part of the literary text as published: *Christs Passion. A Tragedy. With Annotations.*

The allegory of Herbert's sonnet makes it a complex artefact, but a Christian reader would have needed to bring little more than his daily experience of biblical hermeneutics to achieve a reading of the sonnet which would satisfy him. The dramatization of the narrative of the Gospels would appear to offer less of a challenge to a writer. However, the 'otherness' of history in the Grotius-Sandys tragedy offers more of a challenge to the reader, since it requires a reading which has been informed by a humanist training in classical literature, biblical scholarship and topography.

A people of the Book: Shakespeare's audience

Vernacular translations, commentaries and literary imitations of the Bible influenced the ways in which the laity approached the Bible and enriched their range of biblical reference, enabling them to recognize or identify precise phrases, images and literary contexts when they appeared in other texts. From the second half of the sixteenth century, literary allusion to the Old Testament became more frequent in English ballads and plays.[219] Shakespeare drew upon his audience's familiarity with biblical types and stories in allusions which anticipate his dramatic exposition of a plot, and can serve to remind an audience of salient details of characterization.

Knowledge of Shakespeare's contemporaries' familiarity with the Bible, and their habits of mind in reading it, can influence our reactions to a text as familiar to us as *Hamlet*. In Act I, scene ii, Claudius refers to all those who have died 'From the first corse till he that died today' (l. 105)[220] Since the first corpse was Abel's, murdered by his brother, this brings Cain, the type of fratricide, to an audience's consciousness. The allusion anticipates the ghost's evidence against Claudius presented at the end of Act I. Claudius later acknowledges his guilt as he tries to pray:

> O, my offence is rank, it smells to heaven;
> It hath the primal eldest curse upon't –
> A brother's murder
>
> (III, iii, 36–8)

As a consequence of this curse, Claudius's attempts at prayer, like Cain's labours (Gen. 4:10–12), cannot be successful. Hamlet makes the final reference to Cain, 'that did the first murder', as the grave-digger throws up a skull which 'might be the pate of a politician ... one that would circumvent God' (V, i, 75–9). In this context, the audience is reminded of Claudius, who has shown 'a will most incorrect to heaven' in circumventing God's law, and natural justice, as Cain's new anti-type.

Polonius stakes his credibility with the new King on his own diagnosis of Hamlet's 'antic disposition' as 'the very ecstacy of love' for Ophelia. Later in this same scene, Hamlet suddenly exclaims 'O Jephthah, judge of Israel, what a treasure hadst thou' (II, ii, 400). (In Judg. 11:30–40 Jephthah's irresponsible use of language – in a vow to God – inadvertently caused his daughter's life to be sacrificed.) Polonius does not see the point of this remark until Hamlet expounds 'treasure' by quoting from a popular ballad about Jephthah: 'One fair daughter and no more The which he loved passing well' (ll. 403–4).[221] Thinking that Hamlet is still in the throes of an ecstacy of love for his daughter, Polonius accepts the nomination, and acknowledges the implication: 'If you call me Jephthah, my lord, I have a daughter that I love passing well' (ll. 407–8). However, Hamlet insists that he has not understood the parallel: 'Nay, that follows not' (l. 409). The remainder of the exchange points an audience to the tragic consequences of this parallel between Polonius and Jephthah.

> *Pol:* What follows then, my lord?
> *Ham:* Why,
> > *As by lot God wot*
> and then you know,
> > *It came to pass, as most like it was.*
> The first row of the pious chanson will show you more ...
> > (ll. 410 ff.)

The first line quoted by Hamlet (rather than the first line or stanza of the ballad) is what 'will show you more': 'One fair daughter and no more'. Hamlet is merely teasing the old man, who accuses him of 'still harping on my daughter'. Shakespeare uses the quotation from the ballad to indicate to the audience that the sequence of tragic events in the ballad is 'most like' – that is, analogous with, and probable in – his play.

Shakespeare thus foreshadows the death of Ophelia, and implies that her father's rash vow to substantiate the cause of Hamlet's madness will also entail her sacrificial death. The allusion prepares an audience for Gertrude's sudden announcement of Ophelia's death; familiarity with the biblical story allowed Shakespeare's audience to comprehend and to accept it before the stage characters. In addition, the biblical parallel with Jephthah's daughter enhances Ophelia's status as a tragic victim.

There are suggestions of biblical sub-texts and allusions in most of Shakespeare's plays,[222] and since these are well documented in editors' annotations a few brief examples will suffice here. The action of *Measure for Measure* turns on a matter of legal interpretation and an issue in biblical hermeneutics. When both Angelo and Isabella take their stand on the letter rather than the spirit of the law in a Christian commonwealth, the Pauline warning in 2 Cor. 3:6, and the parable of the woman taken in adultery, become touchstones by which to judge their confrontation. The action of the play is too complex for a parable, but the religious context, and the polarization of values represented by Angelo's excessive zeal and Isabella's cloistered virtue, would have suggested biblical analogues to Shakespeare's contemporaries.[223] Similarly, the associations of Ephesus with St Paul would have been inescapable for the first audiences of *The Comedy of Errors*. Shakespeare brought the themes of the Epistle to the Ephesians into focus by choosing to set the action of the play in Ephesus (rather than Rome as in his source), and by changing the *dramatis personae* to allow comment on the duties of a Christian marriage.[224] Shakespeare's adaptations of his source would have made the parallels with Paul's comments on foreigners, the relations between parents and children, masters and servants, and husbands and wives, all the more pertinent to a Bible-reading public (cf. Eph. 2:19; 5:22–23; 6:1–9).

To Renaissance humanists and their contemporaries, the lessons of biblical history, especially its tragical histories, could be read with hindsight for their spiritual utility, and applied to individual Christian histories. Typological exploitations of biblical history in the praise and instruction of royalty – in dedications of biblical commentaries, psalm paraphrases and sermons – were familiar fare by the 1590s.[225] Shakespeare also drew upon his audiences' familiarity with the processes of biblical interpretation and their applications. In *Richard II*, the King interrogates his own past for an explanation of his present condition. He refuses to 'ravel out' the 'weav'd-up follies' which are the fabric of his personal history, and concentrates instead on the act of sacrilege committed by others in deposing him – God's anointed one (or *messiah*) and deputy on earth. In the deposition scene Richard warns Northumberland and the others

Though some of you, with Pilate, wash your hands,
Showing an outward pity – yet you Pilates
Have here deliver'd me to my sour cross,
And water cannot wash away your sin
(IV, i, 239–42)[226]

Richard then asks for a mirror in which to find the meaning of his personal history; the image which he contemplates is

> ... the very book indeed
> Where all my sins are writ, and that's myself.
> Give me that glass, and therein will I read
> (ll. 274–6)

He represents a reading of his own history in the shadow of an anointed one, and as martyr, willing his own physical destruction through his power over words as well as the simulacrum of power reflected in the glass. Richard authorizes his role by choosing the betrayed Jesus as his type. As he shatters the mirror, Richard expounds 'the moral of this sport' for Bolingbroke's benefit, in the histrionic parable which concludes with the words: 'A brittle glory shineth in this face; As brittle as the glory is the face' (ll. 287–8). The process of his interpretation of events determined the meaning he intends for his action in the context of biblical typology.

Biblical exegesis in its several literary kinds increased awareness of hermeneutic problems and practice among the laity. Just as knowledge of the religious purposes of biblical exegesis was no longer confined to a trained clerical elite, so awareness of the everyday problems in decoding different kinds of discourse, and validating their messages, was no longer restricted to those with a formal higher education. We must infer that by 1600 Shakespeare knew well what his audiences would understand and appreciate of such matters on the basis of their own experience. *Hamlet* provides two further examples indicative of his contemporaries' capacities to engage with hermeneutic issues in general. The play dramatizes reasoned attempts to resolve two extreme instances of common problems: how to validate the message of a 'portentous spirit' which is like Hamlet's father, and how to decode the discourse of a mad woman.

Since Hamlet knows that meaning is not independent of context, he repeatedly tests the moral status of speakers. In his trial of the ghost's words, Hamlet re-creates the context of his father's murder by using the play within the play. He reasons that meaning is verifiable, even when constituted by the words of a dubious spirit, since the substance, or kernel, of its message can be separated from its vehicle, or husk, and that substance can be re-created by the power of affective language and a dramatic performance. The players' oratory, which has the power to strike so to the soul, becomes instrumental to Hamlet's purpose in catching the conscience of the King, and in providing himself with 'grounds More relative' than the ghost's looks and words (II, ii, 584–601).

Shakespeare expected his audience for *Hamlet* to recognize how language may be used to communicate and to obviate ambiguity, since words signify what people agree to think they signify in the common manner of speech. The problems raised by this premise are demonstrated by the ways in which characters cope with Hamlet's deliberate displacement of normal expectations in his 'mad' discourse: a disguise or obfuscation of his intended meaning. Hamlet adopts the idiom of his 'antic disposition' in self-defence. The dramatist, his protagonist and the audience are assumed to agree that such use of language is a reasonable means to an end which is the clarification and validation of the ghost's testimony against Claudius. Hamlet's antic disposition is amusing, because the audience is in his confidence and knows better than characters like Polonius what his words signify.

The play's discussion of Ophelia's genuine mental disorder raises more fundamental questions about how the interpretative process, in general, occurs. Since normal expectations of the common grounds of significance are disturbed, Ophelia's words are not meaningful to those around her. Nevertheless, the urgency and distress with which she speaks – 'She is importunate, Indeed distract' – move others to try more strenuously than usual to reconstruct her meaning: 'Her mood will needs be pitied' (IV, v, 2–3). The audience shares their awareness of the difficulties in making sense of her efforts to communicate. It is assumed that understanding is a cumulative process of trial and error, shared between speaker and listener. The gentleman who announces Ophelia to the Queen says she

> ... speaks things in doubt
> That carry but half-sense. Her speech is nothing,
> Yet the unshaped use of it doth move
> The hearers to collection
>
> (IV, v, 6–9)

Shakespeare knew that a speaker's words 'carry but half sense' in transporting meaning. Like Montaigne – as interpreted by Florio –

his contemporaries realized that in communication 'the word is halfe his that speaketh, and halfe his that hearkeneth unto it.'[227] Ophelia's madness exacerbates the hermeneutic problems in ordinary life, just as her anxiety to speak and to be understood projects an acute form of the anxiety and difficulty common to all kinds of discourse. While 'sense' must ever be 'collected' and pieced together, it is usually possible to anticipate the action of the other party to the process. Montaigne used the simile of a tennis match between speaker and hearer, who rally the substance of a message in the air: 'As between those that play at tennis, he who keepes the hazard, doth prepare, stand, stirre and march, according as he perceives him who stands at the house, to looke, stand, remoove and strike the ball'.[228] Successful communication depends upon a similar matching of reciprocal effort within the premises or conventions of an established language game.

Ophelia cannot be clearly understood because of the random, unformulated qualities of her speech; nevertheless, her meaning can be tentatively reconstructed from the context of her doubtful words, and from the inferences her interpreters make about the drift of her 'unshaped' discourse. Such a process of interpretation is arbitrary and insecure, but it is aided by those non-verbal signs which are also ordinarily functional: 'The tune or motion of the voyce, hath some expression or signification of ... meaning,'[229] but that meaning cannot be validated. Ophelia's meaning, like everyone else's, can only be tested against the interpreters' preconceptions of her intention which is the target to be aimed at by trial and error:

> They aim at it,
> And botch the words up fit to their own thoughts,
> Which, as her winks and nods and gestures yield them,
> Indeed would make one think there might be thought,
> Though nothing sure, yet much unhappily
> (IV, v, 9–13)

Understanding Ophelia requires an act of faith on the part of her audience who presume she means something.

In life, and as reflected in the 'mirror' of Shakespearean drama, the contemporaries of More, Montaigne and Milton found that there was no complete, self-sufficient and guaranteed process by which to test conjectures about the meaning of doubtful words or discourse. Ultimately, there was no art to find the mind's construction, either in the face or in the words on a page. Meaning must always be taken on trust. When Protestant readers of the Bible placed their trust in the written record of supernatural revelations of the will of God, they prayed that their rational expectations of comprehension would be fulfilled with divine help. They allowed 'Understanding' and 'Reason' to be 'captivated', 'which in sum, is Trust, and Faith reposed in him that speaketh, though the mind be incapable of any Notion at all from the words spoken'.[230] For Hobbes, restating traditional premises in the mid-seventeenth century, this faith in the guidance of the self-authenticating Spirit of God did not entail a surrender or 'Submission of the Intellectual faculty, to the Opinion of any other man, but of the Will to Obedience, where obedience is due': to God. The Word of God was more than half his that spake it: the Word was God. There was still no rational assurance that any man's trials of the Word would always be protected from error by the guidance of the Holy Spirit, nor that such trials would be validated by the general drift of Scripture and the analogue of faith, but faith and hope were indispensable Christian virtues.

By 1600 – as *Hamlet* proves – the cultural revolution, initiated by the actions of reformers placing the Bible in the hands of ordinary people, was secure. Upon the premise that, 'as drink is pleasant to them that be dry, and meat to them that be hungry; so is the reading, hearing, searching, and studying of Holy Scripture, to them that be desirous to know God, or themselves, and to do his will,'[231] the English had become a people of the Book.

NOTES

I am especially grateful to the editor, to Dr Vincent Gillespie, Dr M. B. Parkes and Mr Stephen Wall for their advice and comments on various drafts of this chapter; I am solely responsible for the views expressed.

1 For English translations of the letters see *The Correspondence of Erasmus, Letters 1 to 141, 1484–1500*, trs. R. A. B. Mynors and D. F. S. Thomson, ed. W. K. Ferguson (Toronto, 1974), pp. 202–19; quotations are from this edition. Colet and Erasmus were both resident in Oxford at the time.

2 On the *modus affectivus* see further A. J. Minnis and A. B. Scott (eds), *Medieval Literary Theory and Criticism c.1100–c.1375 The Commentary Tradition* (Oxford, 1988), esp. pp. 200–3; also *OED*, affection *sb.* 2.

3 *Correspondence of Erasmus*, ed. Ferguson, Epistle 110, p. 212.

4 Ibid., Epistle 111, p. 213.

5 Ibid., Epistle 111, pp. 213–14.

6 Ibid., Epistle 111, pp. 214–15.

7 Ibid., Epistle 109, p. 210.

8 Ibid.
9 Ibid., Epistle 109, p. 208.
10 See Edmund Grindal, *A Fruitful Dialogue Declaring These Words of Christ: 'This is My Body'* (1576 edn) in *The Remains of Edmund Grindal*, ed. W. Nicholson, Parker Society (Cambridge, 1843), p. 40. On biblical hermeneutics and exegesis in this period see further: *The Cambridge History of the Bible: The West From the Reformation to the Present Day*, ed. S. L. Greenslade (Cambridge, 1963), pp. 21–37 and 76–93; G. Bedouelle and B. Roussel (eds), *La Bible de tous les temps: Le temps des réformes et la Bible*, (Paris, 1989), esp. pp. 763–91 for bibliography; also J. H. Bentley, *Humanists and Holy Writ: New Testament Scholarship in the Renaissance* (Princeton, 1983); G. R. Evans, *The Language and Logic of the Bible: The Road to Reformation* (Cambridge, 1985); L. G. Kelly, *The True Interpreter: A History of Translation Theory and Practice in the West* (Oxford, 1979); E. Rummel, *Erasmus's Annotations on the New Testament: From Philologist to Theologian* (Toronto, 1987), and review by J. McConica, *London Review of Books*, 2 March 1989, p. 4; W. Schwarz, *Principles and Problems of Biblical Translation: Some Reformation Controversies and their Background* (Cambridge, 1955); R. Waswo, *Language and Meaning in the Renaissance* (Princeton, 1987).
11 Cf. Rom. 15:4.
12 From Thomas Wilson's compilation *Theologicall Rules, To Guide Us in the Understanding and practise of holy Scriptures: Two Centuries: Drawne partly out of Scriptures themselves: Partly out of Ecclesiasticall writers old and new* (London, 1615), p. 3; most of the 'rules' from the writings of the Fathers were derived from the *Clavis scripturae sacrae* (1567) by the radical Lutheran theologian Matthias Flacius Illyricus. On Wilson (1563–1622) and his standing in the Church of England see further *DNB* and sources cited.
13 See 'Howe to take profite by reading of the holy Scriptures', published with editions of the Geneva Bible: plate 3; cf. below n. 50.
14 From the translators' preface to the King James Bible 1611; see A. W. Pollard (ed.), *Records of the English Bible* (Oxford, 1911), pp. 347–8. Cf. Eph. 6:14–17; also Erasmus, *Enchiridion militis Christiani* (London, 1533), ch. 2, 'The wepons of a chrysten man' (English tr. attributed to W. Tyndale), ed. A. M. O'Donnell, Early English Text Society, 282 (Oxford, 1981), pp. 44–55.
15 See William Whitaker, *Disputatio de sacra scriptura* (London, 1588), trs., W. Fitzgerald as *A Disputation on Holy Scripture Against the Papists*, Parker Society (Cambridge, 1849), 'Concerning the Interpretation of Scripture', esp., p. 402; quotations from this translation.
16 Wilson, *Theologicall Rules*, p. 46.
17 *Correspondence of Erasmus*, ed. Ferguson, Epistle 111, p. 219.
18 Quoted by Whitaker, *Disputation*, p. 404; on the immediate Augustinian sources of the simile see further B. Smalley, *The Study of the Bible in the Middle Ages*, 3rd edn (Oxford, 1984), p. 1; cf. Erasmus's

acknowledgement of Platonic and literary parallels in his *Enchiridion*, ch. 8, rule 5 (O'Donnell ed., pp. 103–35, esp. 104; 108–11).

19 From '13 Rules ... taken out of M. Luthers Works' in Wilson, *Theologicall Rules*, p. 124; for the views of Augustine, Aquinas and Nicholas of Lyra see further Smalley, *Study of the Bible*, passim.

20 Whitaker, *Disputation*, p. 404.

21 Wilson, *Theologicall Rules*, p. 16.

22 Wilson, *Theologicall Rules*, p. 14; cf. Titus 3:9.

23 For the Tridentine decree see *The Canons and Decrees of the ... Council of Trent*, trs. J. Waterworth (London and New York, 1888), pp. 17–21, esp. 19.

24 For a detailed and authoritative study of these issues see Henning Graf Reventlow, *The Authority of the Bible and the Rise of the Modern World*, trs. J. Bowden (London, 1984), part 2, 'The Crisis over the Authority of the Bible in England', esp. pp. 105–222.

25 From Miles Coverdale's epistle to the reader in *The newe testament both in Latine and Englyshe* (Southwark, 1538), sig. +2^v, +3^r.

26 Ibid. On biblical translation in England see further below and n. 131.

27 *A dyalogue of syr Thomas More ... Wherin be treatyd dyvers maters* ([London], 1529), fol. 97^r.

28 See Pollard, *Records*, p. 376.

29 Wilson, *Theologicall Rules*, p. 19.

30 Ibid.

31 For Augustine's views on the 'eloquence' of Scripture see especially *De doctrina Christiana*, IV, 6–7; see further on *sermo humilis* E. Auerbach, *Literary Language and its Public in Late Latin Antiquity and in the Middle Ages*, trs. R. Manheim (London, 1965), pp. 25–66, esp. 48–53. On medieval literary criticism of the Bible see Minnis and Scott, *Medieval Literary Theory and Criticism*, esp. pp. 197–276 and pp. 373–438, and references cited. See also above ch. 1.

32 Wilson, *Theologicall Rules*, p. 23.

33 Ibid., pp. 25–6.

34 Ibid., p. 45.

35 Ibid., p. 47.

36 Ibid., p. 5, my emphasis.

37 Ibid., p. 52. 'The authority and strong credite which scripture hath with us is from God, whose word and voice it is, so certified to our consciences by that spirit which indited it, and is not derived from the Church, whose office is faithfully to interpret and preserve this word in purity by the use of an holy ministry ...' (p. 51).

38 John Jewel, *Works*, ed. J. Ayre, Parker Society, IV (Cambridge, 1850), p. 759. On the origins and dissemination of this metaphor as applied to Scripture see H. C. Porter, 'The Nose of Wax: Scripture and the Spirit from Erasmus to Milton', *Transactions of the Royal Historical Society*, 5th ser., 14 (1964), pp. 155–74.

39 See *The answer to the first part of ... the supper* and *The answere to*

Frithes letter, in *The workes of Sir Thomas More . . . wrytten by him in the Englysh tonge* (London, 1557), pp. 1041; 835–6; cf. Porter, 'The Nose of Wax', p. 161.

40 William Tyndale, *The Supper of the Lord* (1533) in *The Whole Workes of William Tyndale, John Frith and Doctor Barnes* (London, 1573), p. 468. Cf. Waswo's discussion 'Arguments about the Word' in *Language and Meaning*, pp. 250–83.

41 Whitaker, *Disputation*, p. 405; on words and things (*res et verba*) see also p. 407.

42 Wilson, *Theologicall Rules*, p. 27.

43 More, *Workes*, p. 835.

44 James Calfhill, *An Answer to the Treatise of the Cross* (1565), ed. R. Gibbings, Parker Society (Cambridge, 1846), p. 61; on Calfhill's position in the Church see further *DNB*.

45 Wilson, *Theologicall Rules*, p. 125.

46 J. Calvin, *The Institution of Christian Religion wrytten in Latine . . . and translated into Englysh according to the authors last edition*, trs. Thomas Norton (London, 1561), I, vii, 4–5, fos 14ᵛ–15ʳ.

47 Whitaker, *Disputation*, p. 415.

48 Wilson, *Theologicall Rules*, p. 7.

49 *The Sermons of John Donne*, ed. G. R. Potter and E. M. Simpson, 10 vols (Los Angeles and London, 1953–62), vol. I, p. 205; cf. Ps. 119:105, and no. 20 of 'Thirty-Nine Articles of Religion' (1562); also above n. 37.

50 See plate 3; the table was included in editions published in 1579, 1580, 1581, 1586, 1587, 1592, 1599, 1607 and 1616, see T. H. Darlow and A. F. Moule, rev. A. S. Herbert, *Historical Catalogue of Printed Editions of the English Bible 1525–1961* (London and New York, 1968).

51 See 'Howe to take profite . . .', item 1.

52 Wilson, *Theologicall Rules*, pp. 75–6.

53 *Sermons, or Homilies, Appointed to be read in Churches* (London, 1833, rptd 1986), pp. 1–6, esp. 4–5.

54 *Homilies*, p. 6. For a discussion of the implications of this metaphor and the ruminative processes of monastic reading and meditation see J. Leclercq, *The Love of Learning and the Desire for God* (New York, 1961), pp. 18–21; 89–91. Cf. Heb. 5:12–14, and *Homilies*, p. 5.

55 Wilson, *Theologicall Rules*, p. 17.

56 See 'Howe to take profite . . .', item 7.

57 Wilson, *Theologicall Rules*, p. 16.

58 *Homilies*, p. 1.

59 Whitaker, *Disputation*, p. 473.

60 Ibid., pp. 460–1.

61 The terms *analogia*, 'rule' or 'proportion' of faith are all derived from Rom. 12:6. Cf. Tyndale's advice from the epilogue to his New Testament in English (1526): 'Marke the playne and manyfest places

of the scriptures, and in doubtfull places, se thou adde no interpreta-
cion contrary to them: but (as Paul sayth) let all be conformable and
agreynge to the fayth', Pollard, *Records*, p. 115; cf. also Porter, 'The
Nose of Wax', pp. 162–3.

62 Wilson, *Theologicall Rules*, p. 31.

63 On the danger of 'private' or idiosyncratic interpretations see also
Wilson, *Theologicall Rules*, pp. 53–4, and Whitaker, *Disputation*,
p. 410. On the phrase *orbs doctrinae* ... as a form describing the
perfection of Scripture overall see Erasmus, *Ratio seu methodus com-
pendio perveniendi ad veram theologiam* in *Opera omnia* (Basle,
1540), V, 108. Cf. also p. 69 above.

64 Whitaker, *Disputation*, p. 472 (writing in the context of a concluding
summary of his debate with the Jesuits). The examples he cites are
Catholic and Lutheran interpretations of 'This is my Body', which, he
claims, from the Church of England's point of view 'are at variance
with the analogy of faith' (p. 473).

65 See Milton, *De doctrina Christiana*, I, xxx, in *The Works of John
Milton*, Columbia edn, XVI (New York, 1934), p. 264 (Latin); p.
265 (English).

66 See the arguments used against Nicholas Ridley at his trial in Oxford
(1555) in Ridley, *Works*, ed. H. Christmas, Parker Society (Cambridge, 1841), p. 283.

67 Wilson, *Theologicall Rules*, p. 24.

68 Ibid., p. 22.

69 See further J. L. Kugel, *The Idea of Biblical Poetry: Parallelism and
its History* (New Haven and London, 1981), esp. pp. 228–31 for M.
Flacius Illyricus's perceptions in his *Clavis scripturae*; cf. also translators' notes in the margins of the Geneva Bible on Hebrew style, and
in the head notes to poetic books in I. Tremellius's new Latin translation of the Old Testament (London, 1580). On biblical Hebrew
studies (including poetry) by Christian scholars in this period see J.
Friedmann, *The Most Ancient Testimony: Sixteenth-Century Christian-
Hebraica in the Age of Renaissance Nostalgia* (Athens, Ohio, 1983);
and G. L. Jones, *The Discovery of Hebrew in Tudor England: A
Third Language* (Manchester, 1983). Both works include extensive
bibliographies.

70 Wilson, *Theologicall Rules*, p. 35.

71 Ibid., pp. 19–20.

72 Ibid., p. 32.

73 See 'Howe to take profite ...', item 6.1.

74 Wilson, *Theologicall Rules*, p. 29.

75 For a facsimile, transcription and translation of *De tristitia tedio
pavore et oratione Christi ante passionem eius* from More's holo-
graph manuscript see *The Complete Works of St Thomas More*, XIV,
2 parts, ed. and trs. C. H. Miller (New Haven and London, 1976).
Quotations are from this Yale edition. On the date and circumstances
of composition see ibid., pp. 737–45. Cf. John Gerson's version of a

harmony of the Gospels for the kind of text More used as his source: *D. Ioannis Gersonis cancellarii olim Parisiorum Monotessaron* (Cologne, 1542), esp. ch. 142 'De oratione Iesu, & sua captione, Matt. XXVI. Mar. XIIII. Lucae XXII. Ioannis XVIII' (sig. P4).

76 For a facsimile of the 1671 edition see John Milton, *Paradise Regained, Samson Agonistes* (Menston, 1968); quotations are from this edition. Cf. Milton, *Complete Shorter Poems*, ed. J. Carey (London, 1968), pp. 328–400; esp. 328–30 for a summary of arguments for dating the poem as early as ?1647–53. For a fuller review of the dating controversy, and an endorsement of the traditional date *c.*1666–70, see M. A. Radzinowicz, *Toward Samson Agonistes: The Growth of Milton's Mind* (Princeton, 1978), esp. pp. 387–407. For the biblical narrative of Samson's imprisonment and death see Judg. 16:21–36.

77 See above p. 69; on More's assimilation and exploitation of patristic commentaries see Miller's historical notes in part 2 of *Complete Works of More*, vol. XIV, ed. Miller. More was ready to put his own interpretations alongside Augustine's (see p. 297), since 'no one understands the meaning of all scriptural passages so well that there are not many mysteries hidden there which are not yet understood' (pp. 441–3). For his condemnation of 'autodidacts' see p. 445.

78 See above p. 74 and n. 65; see further J. R. Knott. *The Sword of the Spirit: Puritan Responses to the Bible* (Chicago and London, 1980), pp. 106–30 on 'Milton and the Spirit of Truth'; also Reventlow, *Authority of the Bible*, pp. 155–66. These premises of individual authority underlie Milton's arguments in *A Treatise of Civil Power in Ecclesiastical Causes* (1659) and *The Readie and Easie Way to Establish a Free Commonwealth* (1660).

79 Contrast *A Harmonie upon the three Evangelistes Matthewe, Marke, and Luke, with the Commentarie of M. John Calvine*, trs. Eusebius Paget (London, 1610), pp. 701–9: Calvin's commentary is attached to headings composed of *lemmata* extracted from the three Gospels. The Gospels are printed separately in three parallel columns, approximately six verses at a time; there is no continuous narrative of text (incorporating commentary) to compare with More's method and style.

80 See e.g. pathos in More's comments on 'Father ... let this cup pass from me', which invite the reader to meditate on the image, or mental picture, of Jesus lying prone on the bare earth (*Complete Works of More*, vol. XIV, ed. Miller, p. 115). See also meditative and affective qualities in More's digression on 'what the mind is doing while dreams take it over during sleep' (ibid., p.119), and on where the mind reaches while free-wheeling during *idle* prayer (ibid., p. 133). On the application of outward signs from behaviour and deportment 'from which our interior state of mind can be gathered (*inde mentis interne signa et argumenta colligat*)', see the description of God as the model interpreter (ibid., p. 143).

81 Ibid., pp. 101–5.

82 Ibid., p. 107.

83 Ibid., p. 109. For comparisons of More's views on the purpose of the agony with those of Erasmus and of Colet see Miller's notes and references cited ibid. (e.g., p. 1010). On the *topos* of the christian soldier see Erasmus, *Enchiridion*.

84 *Complete Works of More*, vol. XIV, ed. Miller, p. 355.

85 Ibid., p. 357.

86 Ibid., p. 359.

87 Ibid., p. 67.

88 Ibid., p. 83.

89 Ibid., p. 67.

90 For Samson's temptations see Judg. 14:15–17 and 16:4–17; for the prophecy see 13:3–5. By contrast, Francis Quarles in his verse *Historie of Samson* gives no account of Samson's sufferings as a prisoner (see London, 1638 edn, pp. 378–83).

91 On Renaissance views of Samson (including typological interpretations) see J. Wittreich, *Interpreting 'Samson Agonistes'* (Princeton, 1986), esp., pp. 174–238 and the works cited.

92 Thomas Hobbes, *Leviathan Or the Matter, Forme and Power of a Commonwealth Ecclesiasticall and Civil* (London, 1651), pp. 198, 395–6.

93 Ibid., ch. 32, 'Of the Principles of Christian Politiques', p. 198.

94 On the non-conformist groups of the Civil War period see further C. Hill, *The World Turned Upside Down* (London, 1972); W. Haller, ed. *Tracts on Liberty in the Puritan Revolution, 1638–47*, 3 vols (New York, 1934); Reventlow, *Authority of the Bible*, pp. 176–84 and works cited.

95 Contrast the form of Quarles's *Historie of Samson* (1631) in which sections of verse narrative (based on the biblical account) alternate with verse meditations where Quarles comments on the actions and attitudes of the characters.

96 See above pp. 68 and 74; cf. also George Herbert, 'The H. Scriptures II', ll. 1–6.

97 For examples of Milton's borrowings from the Psalms in his representation of Samson's self-scrutiny see Radzinowicz, *Toward 'Samson Agonistes'*, pp. 368–82.

98 Milton's 'argument', published as a head note to the poem, describes this part of the action without resolving the issue: '. . . at length perswaded inwardly that this [Philistine command 'to shew his strength at the feast'] was from God, he yields to go' (Milton, *Samson Agonistes*, p. 6).

99 *The Readie and Easie Way* (April, 1660) in *Works*, VI, p. 141.

100 See above n. 94; and Hobbes's 'Conclusion' to *Leviathan*, pp. 391–6; cf. *The Instrument of Government* (issued by the Commonwealth government 16 December 1653) articles 35–38, reprinted in S. R. Gardiner (ed.), *The Constitutional Documents of the Puritan Revol-*

ution 1625–1660, 3rd edn (Oxford, 1889, repr. 1979), pp. 405–17, esp. 416. In this context it may be noted that the verse by Euripides, which Milton claimed 'the Apostle Paul ... thought ... not unworthy to insert ... into the Text of Holy Scripture, I Cor. 15.33', begins 'Be not deceived: evil communications corrupt good manners.' St Paul continues: 'Awake to righteousness, and sin not; for some have not the knowledge of God: I speak this to your shame' (1 Cor. 15:33–4) (see 'Of that sort of Dramatic Poem which is call'd Tragedy', *Samson Agonistes*, p. 3.)

101 See above pp. 67–8; cf. 'The literal sense ... is not that which the words immediately suggest ... but rather that which arises from the words themselves, whether they be taken strictly or figuratively ... For example, the literal sense of these words "The seed of the woman shall crush the serpent's head", is this, that Christ shall beat down Satan, and break and crush all his force and power.' Whitaker, *Disputation*, p. 405.

102 See above chapter 1.

103 Much modern scholarship dealing with the influence of biblical criticism and hermeneutics on Renaissance literature has concentrated on Spenser's and Milton's applications of typology and allegory; for this reason I shall not pursue the topic further here.

On typological and numerological readings of Spenser's poetry see especially: Alastair Fowler, *Spenser and the Numbers of Time* (London, 1964); M. O'Connell, *Mirror and Veil: the Historical Dimension of Spenser's 'Faerie Queene'* (Chapel Hill, 1977); A. C. Hamilton, *The Structure of Allegory in 'The Faerie Queene'* (Oxford, 1961); A Fletcher, *The Prophetic Moment: an Essay on Spenser* (Chicago, 1971); A. B. Giametti, *Play of Double Senses: Spenser's 'Faerie Queene'* (Englewood Cliffs, NJ, 1975); I. G. MacCaffrey, *Spenser's Allegory: the Anatomy of Imagination* (Princeton, 1976).

On Milton see especially: C. A. Patrides, *Milton and the Christian Tradition* (Oxford, 1966); N. Frye, 'The Typology of Paradise Regained', *Modern Philology*, 53 (1956), pp. 227–38 repr. in A. E. Barker (ed.), *Milton: Modern Essays in Criticism* (New York, 1970), pp. 429–46; K. Cohen, *The Throne and the Chariot: Studies in Milton's Hebraism* (The Hague and Paris, 1975), esp. pp. 133–54; and see further C. A. Patrides, *An Annotated Critical Bibliography of John Milton* (Brighton, 1987).

On the apocalypse in literature and history see K. R. Firth, *The Apocalyptic Tradition in Reformation Britain 1530–1645* (Oxford, 1979); and C. A. Patrides and J. Wittreich (eds), *The Apocalypse in English Renaissance Thought and Literature: Patterns, Antecedents and Repercussions* (Manchester, 1984), esp. bibliography on pp. 369–440.

On typology see further: E. Miner (ed.), *Literary Uses of Typology from the Late Middle Ages to the Present* (Princeton, 1977); B. K. Lewalski, *Protestant Poetics and the Seventeenth-Century Religious*

Lyric (Princeton, 1979), esp. pp. 111–44; and I. Clark, *Christ Revealed: The History of the Neotypological Lyric in the English Renaissance* (Gainesville, Florida, 1982).

104   See further W. Tyndale, *The Obedience of a Christian Man* (1528) in *Doctrinal Treatises and Introductions to different portions of the Holy Scripture*, ed. H. Walter, Parker Society (Cambridge, 1848), esp. pp. 134–5; and W. Haller, *Foxe's 'Book of Martyrs' and the Elect Nation* (London, 1968).

105   From Nicholas Udall's dedication to Edward VI of *The first tome or volume of the Paraphrases of Erasmus upon the newe testament* (London, 1551), sig. *6^r and *3^v. Cf. applications of the figure of David as defender of the reformed churches in Germany, France and Geneva discussed by E. A. Gosselin, *The King's Progress to Jerusalem: Some Interpretations of David during the Reformation Period and their Patristic and Medieval Background* (Los Angeles, 1976), pp. 93–118.

106   *Paraphrases of Erasmus*, Udall's dedication, sig. *6^v.

107   *The Booke of Psalmes, wherein are contayned prayers meditations, prayses and thankesgiving* (London, 1578), sig. F3^v; the dedication, dated 10 Feb. 1559 from Geneva, was reprinted from the first edition.

108   William Leigh, *Queene Elizabeth, Paraleld in her Princely vertues, with David, Iosua, and Hezekia ... in three sermons, as they were preached three severall Queenes dayes* [i.e. 17 November, 1600, 1601, 1602] (London, 1612), p. 63. Cf. William Patten's psalm paraphrases identifying Elizabeth with David and Solomon on the occasions of the 25th and 40th anniversaries of her accession; also psalms for the accession of Mary Tudor (1553) and James Stuart (1603); see further R. Zim, *English Metrical Psalms: Poetry as Praise and Prayer* (Cambridge, 1987), pp. 133–4.

109   Leigh, *Queene Elizabeth*, p. 4.

110   Ibid., pp. 46–7.

111   Wilson, *Theologicall Rules*, p. 4.

112   George Wither, *The Psalmes of David Translated Into Lyrick-Verse according to the scope, of the Original* ([Amsterdam], 1632), sig. A3^v; cf. Calvin's claim that parallels between his own life and David's experiences had helped him to understand the Psalms: 'when I expound the inward meenings ... I intreat of things wherwith I am well acquaynted' (see Calvin's epistle to the reader, dated 23 July 1557, in *The Psalmes of David and others. With M. John Calvins Commentaries*, tr. Arthur Golding (London, 1571), sig. **2^v).

113   Wither, *Psalmes*, sig. A3^v.

114   Ibid., sig. A4^r.

115   Ibid., sig. A4.

116   For sixteenth-century examples of such applications by prisoners see Zim, *English Metrical Psalms*, pp. 80–111.

117   See, for example, Lancelot Andrewes's sermons commemorating the discovery of the Gunpowder Plot, on various texts including 'By me

kings raigne' (Prov. 18:15) from 1613, and 'My Sonne, feare thou the Lord and the King, and meddle not with them that are given to change' (Prov. 24:21–3) from 1614, both in *XCVI Sermons By the Right Honourable and Reverend Father in God, Lancelot Andrewes, Late Bishop of Winchester*, 4th edn (London, 1641), pp. 933–43, esp. 940; 945–57, esp. 949. Contrast the arguments by Milton (and the Presbyterians) that monarchy 'is against the natural law', that 'heathenish government', like that of 'the kings of the gentiles', was not appropriate for the disciples of Jesus, and that no government came 'nearer to the precept of Christ than a free Commonwealth'; see *The Readie and Easie Way*, in *Works*, VI, pp. 118–20.

118   See *A newe enterlude drawen oute of the holy scripture of godly queene Hester* (London, 1561), sig. C1ᵛ and D4ʳ; on the political context of the play, which may be dated to the 1520s, see further R. H. Blackburn, *Biblical Drama Under the Tudors* (The Hague and Paris, 1971), pp. 70–6.

119   *Godly queene Hester*, sig. E3ᵛ.

120   For different views of Esther in renaissance drama see Blackburn, *Biblical Drama*, pp. 182–8.

121   See *The Historie of Ester* in Quarles, *Divine Poems: Containing The History of Jonah. Ester. Job. Sampson. Sions Sonets. Elegies* (London, 1633), esp. pp. 108–9.

122   For the Latin text of *Baptistes, siue calumnia, tragoedia*, with a parallel English translation, see *George Buchanan Tragedies*, ed. P. Sharratt and P. G. Walsh (Edinburgh, 1983), pp. 95–164. This play (with three others on Jephthah, Medea and Alcestes) was written while Buchanan was teaching at the Collège de Guyenne in Bordeaux *c.*1539–43. Buchanan was arrested in Lisbon, tried August 1550– May 1551, and released February 1552; see J. M. Aitkin, *The Trial of George Buchanan Before the Lisbon Inquisition Including the Text of Buchanan's Defences* (Edinburgh and London, 1939), pp. 23 and 128–35; see further I. D. McFarlane, *Buchanan* (London, 1981), pp. 379–92 (on *Baptistes*) esp. 384; 131–51 (on the trial).

123   See the comments in Buchanan's autobiography (Aitkin, *Trial*, pp. xx–xxi), and the dedication to James VI of *Baptistes* (London, 1577), sig. A2, wherein he claimed the play was written to promote piety and good Latin style in his pupils. (Herod was a traditional type of tyrant, and Buchanan warns King James – also his pupil – of the misery such government causes.)

124   This edition comprises 28 pages of verse drama set as prose; there is no foundation for the attribution of this translation to Milton (see Milton, *Works*, XVIII, p. 602). Cf. publication of George Cavendish's *Negotiations of Thomas Woolsey* (first written *c.*1554–8) in 1641 and 1667 as an attack on abuses of royal power by ministers of state.

125   On Dryden's 'Absalom and Achitophel' (1681–2) see below, chapter 3.

126   For relevant portions of Lambarde's memorandum of his meeting

with the Queen (4 August 1601) and comment by Peter Ure, see the introduction to Ure's Arden edition of *King Richard II* (London, 1961, reprinted 1975), p. lix. For a wider, more detailed examination of the literary and political issues see A. Patterson, *Censorship and Interpretation: The Conditions of Writing and Reading in Early Modern England* (Madison, 1984).

127 See, for example, Philip Sidney, *The Defence of Poesie*, in *Complete Works*, ed. A. Feuillerat, vol. III (Cambridge, 1923), pp. 30–1; on the abuse of rhetoric decried by poets see Shakespeare, *Sonnets* (London, 1609), nos 82; 83; 84; 85; and George Herbert's 'Jordan' I and II, in *The Temple* (1633); cf. the 'hidden' message in Herbert's 'Coloss. 3.3' (ibid.); see also John Bunyan's offer of 'Truths' in 'mantles', or allegorical metaphors, to readers of *The Pilgrim's Progress* (1678), 'The Author's Apology'.

128 B. Castiglione, *The Book of the Courtier*, tr. T. Hoby (1561), ed. J. H. Whitfield (London, 1974), p. 5; see further on attitudes to English, R. F. Jones, *The Triumph of the English Language* (London, 1953), and C. Barber, *Early Modern English* (London, 1976), pp. 65–142.

129 Tyndale, *Obedience of a Christian Man* in *Doctrinal Treatises*, pp. 148–9; cf. the view of Joseph Addison 'that the Hebrew idioms run into the English tongue with a particular grace and beauty', *The Spectator*, 405 (14 June 1712), ed. G. G. Smith, 4 vols (London, 1945), vol. III, pp. 260–1.

130 E.g. Coverdale's Bible (incorporating Tyndale's translations), 1535; the Great Bible (revised by Coverdale), 1539; the Geneva Bible, 1560; and the Bishops' Bible, 1568. See further n. 131 below.

131 On the aims of the translators see W. Allen, *Translating for King James* (London, 1970), an edition and translation of the notes made by John Bois, a member of the final revision committee for the 1611 Bible; for the translators' preface see editions and reprints of the 1611 Bible, and Pollard, *Records*, pp. 340–77. On archaism see A. C. Partridge, *English Biblical Translation* (London, 1973), esp. pp. 115–38. On the literary and scholarly influences of earlier translators see especially C. C. Butterworth, *The Literary Lineage of the King James Bible 1340–1611* (Philadelphia, 1941, reprinted New York, 1971); D. Daiches, *The King James Version of the English Bible* (Chicago, 1941); G. Hammond, *The Making of the English Bible* (Manchester, 1982); see also C. S. Lewis, *The Literary Impact of the Authorized Version* (London, 1950).

132 See further Zim, *English Metrical Psalms*, pp. 112–51; for a guide to 90 English psalm versions and commentaries printed 1530–1601 see ibid., pp. 211–59.

133 Golding, in *Psalmes ... With ... Calvins Commentaries*, sig. *4ᵛ.

134 Ibid.; cf. 'Howe to take profite ...' item 6.3; and see above, p. 75.

135 Calvin, *Institution*, I, viii, 1, fo 16. Cf. Milton: '... Sions songs, to all true tastes excelling', *Paradise Regained* (1671), IV, 447.

136 For Calvin's quotation from Horace, *Odes* I, xxxiv, 1–8 et seq. see
    In Librum psalmorum, Iohannis Calvini commentarius (Geneva,
    1557), p. 129, and Golding's translation *Psalmes ... With ... Cal-
    vins Commentaries*, fo 106^r in the commentary on Ps. 29:3. Cf. also
    'Horacis sentence' quoted in the commentary on Ps. 46:4 (ibid., fo
    181^r).
137 Calvin, *Institution*, fo 16.
138 Ibid., fo 15^r.
139 Ibid., fo 15^v.
140 Sidney, *The Defence of Poesie*, in *Complete Works* ed. Feuillerat, vol.
    III, pp. 6–7 (quotations are from this edition). Sidney cites 'the
    testimony of great learned men, both auncient and moderne', and
    names I. Tremellius and F. Junius (see above n. 69). See further I.
    Baroway, 'Tremellius, Sidney and Biblical verse', *Modern Language
    Notes*, 49 (1934), pp. 145–9; also Kugel, *Idea of Biblical Poetry*, pp.
    152–6; 167–70; 251–8. On the implications for Sidney's metrical
    ingenuity in his psalm paraphrases see Zim, *English Metrical Psalms*,
    pp. 164–5 and works cited.
141 Sidney, *Complete Works*, ed. Feuillerat, vol. III, p. 7.
142 Ibid.
143 Ibid., pp. 8–9.
144 Ibid., p. 9.
145 Ibid., p. 14.
146 Ibid., p. 20.
147 See G. G. Smith (ed.), *Elizabethan Critical Essays*, 2 vols (Oxford,
    1904, reprinted 1971), vol. I, p. 71 for Lodge's *Defence* (1579); vol.
    II, pp. 10; 31 for Puttenham's *Arte of English Poesie* (1589); and vol.
    II, p. 207 for Harington's *Briefe Apologie* (1591). See further A. D. S.
    Fowler, 'Protestant Attitudes to Poetry, 1560–1590' (Oxford, D.Phil.
    thesis, 1957), esp. pp. 1–36 and 302–419; also Lewalski, *Protestant
    Poetics*, pp. 31–110. On the literary-critical heritage see Minnis and
    Scott, *Medieval Literary Theory* and C. C. Greenfield, *Humanist and
    Scholastic Poetics 1250–1500* (Lewisburg, 1981).
148 Harington's *Briefe Apologie* was published as a preface to his verse
    translation of Ariosto's *Orlando Furioso*; quotations taken from
    Smith, *Elizabethan Critical Essays*, vol. II, pp. 195–222.
149 Ibid., pp. 204–5; cf. above pp. 88–9 on political applications of
    new typologies.
150 Ibid., p. 205.
151 Ibid., p. 205–6.
152 Ibid., p. 207.
153 For Sidney's psalms (1–43) see his *Poems*, ed. W. A. Ringler (Ox-
    ford, 1962, reprinted 1971), pp. 270–337; for Harington's (psalms
    1–150) see Oxford, Bodleian Library, MS Douce 361.
154 Wither, *Psalmes of David*, sig. A6^r.
155 Ibid., sig. A7^r.
156 Ibid., sig. A6^v–7^r.

157 Ibid., sig. A6ᵛ; see further sig. A8ʳ for Wither's description of his method and range of sources in paraphrasing biblical poetry.
158 Ibid., sig. A8ᵛ.
159 Ibid.
160 See above n. 132.
161 See Michael Drayton, 'M.D. To the curteous Reader' in his *A Heavenly Harmonie of Spirituall Songes, and holy Himnes* (London, 1610).
162 See George Wither, *The Hymnes and Songs of the Church ... Translated and Composed by G.W.* (London, 1623), p. 23.
163 See 'Upon the Translation of the Psalmes by Sir Philip Sydney, and the Countesse of Pembroke his Sister' in John Donne, *The Divine Poems*, ed. H. Gardner, 2nd edn (Oxford, 1978), pp. 33–5; for the influence on Herbert see L. L. Martz, *The Poetry of Meditation: A Study in English Religious Literature* (New Haven and London, 1954, reprinted 1976), pp. 261–79; and C. Freer, *Music for a King: George Herbert's Style and the Metrical Psalms* (Baltimore and London, 1972).
164 Henry Peacham, *The Garden of Eloquence* (London, 1577), title page; quotations from this edition in facsimile (Menston, 1968).
165 Ibid., sig. A2ʳ.
166 Robert Cawdray, *A Table Alphabeticall, conteyning and teaching the true writing, and understanding of hard usuall English wordes, borrowed from the Hebrew, Greeke, Latine, or French &c.* (London, 1604), title page; Robert acknowledges the help of his son Thomas, a London schoolmaster.
167 Ibid., title page.
168 See Robert Cawdray, *A Treasurie or Store-house of Similes: Both pleasaunt, delightfull, and profitable* (London, 1600), title page; quotations from this edition (another edn was published 1609).
169 Ibid., sig. A2ᵛ.
170 Ibid.
171 Ibid., p. 5, no. 3. For the palm-tree simile cf. Ps. 92:12; on the properties of the camomile plant cf. Shakespeare, *1 Henry IV*, II, iv, 399; see further M. P. Tilley, *A Dictionary of the Proverbs in England in the Sixteenth and Seventeenth Centuries* (Ann Arbor, 1950), C. 34.
172 Cawdray, *Treasurie*, sig. A6ʳ and A3ᵛ; cf. above p. 75.
173 Ibid., sig. A3ᵛ–4ʳ.
174 For the major English epic poems, *The Faerie Queene* (1590, 1596) and *Paradise Lost* (1667, 1674), see the works cited in note 103 above; see also G. de Saluste du Bartas, *The Divine Weeks* translated into English verse by Joshua Sylvester (1605), ed. S. Snyder, 2 vols (Oxford, 1979). It has not been possible to discuss the epic within the scope of this single chapter. See further below for examples of the other literary kinds listed here.

175 See Calvin to the Reader in *Psalmes ... With ... Calvins Commentaries*, sig. *6ᵛ.

176 From the opening of Donne's second prebend sermon, see *Sermons*, ed. Potter and Simpson, vol. VII, p. 51.

177 *Psalmes ... With ... Calvins Commentaries*, sig. *2ʳ.

178 For contrasts between the prevailing styles among 'godly Preachers' (or Puritans) and Anglicans see Samuel Clarke, *A Collection of the Lives of Ten Eminent Divines* (London, 1662) and later enlarged editions; for a convenient selection, J. Chandos (ed.), *In God's Name: Examples of Preaching in England from the Act of Supremacy to the Act of Uniformity 1534–1662* (London, 1971); see further M. Seymour-Smith (ed.), *The English Sermon*, vol. 1: 1550–1650 (Cheadle, 1976); I. Morgan, *The Godly Preachers of the Elizabethan Church* (London, 1965); and H. Davies, *Like Angels from a Cloud: The English Metaphysical Preachers 1588–1645* (San Marino, 1986).

179 I am indebted to Evelyn Simpson's introduction to her edition of Donne's *Sermons on the Psalms and Gospels* (Berkeley, Los Angeles and London, 1963, reprinted 1974), pp. 6–8; see *Sermons*, ed. Potter and Simpson, vol. II, p. 75 for the following quotations from this sermon.

180 Ibid., vol. V, p. 276.

181 *Psalmes ... With ... Calvins Commentaries*, Golding's epistle, sig. *4ᵛ.

182 Donne, *Sermons*, ed. Potter and Simpson, vol. II, p. 97.

183 Ibid., vol. VII, pp. 51–71, esp. 52.

184 For the *pondus gloriae* metaphor, cf. 2 Cor. 4:17.

185 Donne, *Sermons*, ed. Potter and Simpson, vol. VII, pp. 52–3; 57.

186 Ibid., pp. 52; 60; 62.

187 Ibid., pp. 64; 69. For Donne's use of the map metaphor, cf. esp. 'Hymne to God my God, in my sicknesse', ll. 7–14.

188 Donne, *Sermons*, ed. Potter and Simpson, vol. VII, pp. 69; 70; 71.

189 See above p. 75 and n. 69.

190 Donne, *Sermons*, ed. Potter and Simpson, vol. VII, p. 57.

191 See further on Donne's art: E. M. Simpson, *A Study of the Prose Works of John Donne*, 2nd edn (Oxford, 1948 reprinted 1962); W. R. Mueller, *John Donne Preacher* (Princeton, 1962); D. B. Quinn, 'Donne's Christian Eloquence', *English Literary History*, 27 (1960), pp. 276–97; J. Webber, *Contrary Music: The Prose Style of John Donne* (Madison, 1963); and W. Schleiner, *The Imagery of John Donne's Sermons* (Providence, RI, 1970). For the background to Donne's preaching at St Paul's see R. C. Bald, *John Donne: A Life* (Oxford, 1970), pp. 389–469.

192 Donne, *Sermons*, ed. Potter and Simpson, vol. VII, p. 51.

193 See Quarles, *Emblemes* (London, 1635), To the Reader. See further on Quarles and the emblem tradition: R. Freeman, *English Emblem*

Books (London, 1948 reprinted 1968); K. J. Höltgen, *Francis Quarles, 1592–1644: Meditativer Dichter, Emblematiker, Royalist* (Tübingen, 1978); also Höltgen's *Aspects of the Emblem: Studies in the English Emblem Tradition and the European Context* (Kassel, 1986), esp. pp. 31–65; and E. B. Gilman, *Iconoclasm and Poetry in the English Reformation: Down Went Dagon* (Chicago and London, 1986), esp. pp. 85–116.

194 From Calvin to the Reader, *Psalmes ... With ... Calvins Commentaries*, sig. *6ᵛ.

195 Quarles, *Emblemes* (1635), book V, no. x, pp. 284–7, ll. 1–3; 5–6; quotations are from this edition.

196 Different devotional and doctrinal traditions often exploited the same or very similar images and visual compositions. Quarles, for example, used images produced by the Jesuit College in Antwerp (cf. *Typus mundi* (1627) based on H. Hugo, *Pia desideria* (Antwerp, 1624)) without compromising Protestant teachings or sensibilities in his own *Emblemes*. See further discussions in works cited n. 193 above.

197 For Anselm (d.1109) and his *Proslogion* see *The Prayers and Meditations of St Anselm*, trs. B. Ward (Harmondsworth, 1973), pp. 238–71, esp. p. 241.

198 Cf. Donne's use of the ground-plan of a building in the *divisio* of his last sermon, 'Death's Duel' (1630), on Ps. 68:20; see *Sermons*, ed. Potter and Simpson, vol. X, p. 230. See further on this *topos* F. Yates, *The Art of Memory* (London, 1966), pp. 18–20 and passim.

199 For an indication of the popularity of Quarles's *Emblems*, of which there were more than 50 editions printed before 1700, see J. Horden, *Bibliography of Francis Quarles to the Year 1800* (Oxford, 1953). For Donne's popularity as a preacher see Bald, *Donne: A Life* and other works cited n. 191 above.

200 See *The Works of George Herbert*, ed. F. E. Hutchinson (Oxford, 1941, rev. 1945), p. 40; also *Hugonis Grotii Tragoedia Christus Patiens* (Munich, 1627), and *Christs Passion. A Tragedie. With Annotations*, trs. G. Sandys (London, 1640); quotations are from these editions. See further C. Bloch, *Spelling the Word: George Herbert and the Bible* (Berkeley, Los Angeles, and London, 1985).

201 In London, Dr Williams's Library, MS Jones B62 (which contains Herbert's corrections to his English poems in his own hand), ll. 21–32 of 'Good Friday', and the sonnet 'Redemption' are separately entitled 'The Passion'; see further *Works of George Herbert*, ed. Hutchinson, pp. lii–lvi.

202 See above p. 93.

203 On 'The Sacrifice' and its background see R. Tuve, *A Reading of George Herbert* (London, 1952), pp. 19–99; see also Martz, *The Poetry of Meditation*, pp. 90–6. For the lyric complaint or *planctus* in Middle English from the fourteenth century onward, see e.g. 'Men rent me on Rode', 'Ye that pasen by the weiye', 'My folk now answere me' and 'Wofully araide' (in R. T. Davies (ed.), *Medieval*

English Lyrics: A Critical Anthology (London, 1963, reprinted 1968), nos 41; 46; 47; 106). See further V. Gillespie, 'Strange Images of Death: The Passion in Later Medieval English Devotional and Mystical Writing', in *Zeit, Tod und Ewigkeit in der Renaissance Literatur* (Salzburg, 1987), pp. 111–59.

204 Sandys's dedication of *Christs Passion* indicates that Grotius was 'not without the Example of two ancient Fathers of the Primitive Church', but in the preface to his annotations (*Christs Passion*, p. 74) he acknowledges that the attribution of the original Greek tragedy to Nazianzen is 'accounted supposititious' by some scholars; see further J. Quasten, *Patrology*, III (Utrecht, Antwerp and Westminster MD, 1960), 245–6.

205 For Milton's 'Of that sort of Dramatic Poem which is call'd Tragedy' see *Samson Agonistes*, pp. 3–5 (also reprinted in modern editions of the poem). Grotius's play *Adamus exsul* (1601) was probably known to Milton when he conceived his plans for *Paradise Lost* (see Cambridge, Trinity College MS R.3.4, facsimile edn (Menston, 1972), p. 40); in the *Second Defense* (1654) Milton mentions his pleasure at meeting Grotius in Paris in 1638. See further the discussion by G. Vossius on 'whether it bee lawfull to make a Dramatique Poem of a sacred argument' quoted in *Hugo Grotius His Sophompaneas, or Joseph. A Tragedy. With Annotations*, tr. F. Goldsmith (London, 1652), sig. A7.

206 Sandys (d.1644) travelled widely in his youth, and published an account of his journey in 1610 to Jerusalem in *A Relation of a Journey ... Foure Bookes* (London, 1615), Bk III, pp. 154–75. On Sandys's life and learning see further *DNB*; Lucius Cary, Viscount Falkland, in verses addressed 'To the Author' (*Christs Passion*, sig. A7[r]) describes Sandys as 'the English Buchanan', referring to his reputation as a metrical psalmist and to his tragic drama on biblical subjects.

207 Contrast the psychological concerns of Grotius and Sandys in their representation of the agony of Jesus with the affective imagery of Herbert:

> Therefore my soul melts, and my hearts deare treasure
> Drops bloud (the onely beads) my words to measure:
> O let this cup passe, if it be thy pleasure:
> Was ever grief like mine?
> ('The Sacrifice', ll. 21–4)

208 *Christs Passion*, I, ll. 107–10, p. 5.
209 Ibid., ll. 120–4, p. 5.
210 Ibid., l. 292, p. 12.
211 Ibid., II, ll. 153–5, p. 19.
212 Ibid., III, ll. 168–71; 173–4, pp. 33–4. Cf.

> Quid si arma vulgus sumit, & coeptas semel
> Non ponit iras? scilicet iudex pius
> Magnum merebor pace turbata decus.
> Meliusne morti dabitur? at culpa vacat.
> Quin ista magna est culpa, quod fieri potest
> Materia belli ...
> (Grotius, *Christus patiens*, p. 29)

213　*Christs Passion*, IV, ll. 375–82, p. 57. Cf.

> Quod factum scelus est? quo meruit diem
> Nondum nocte data perdere saeculum?
> Vt cum visceribus viscera condidit,
> Implevit que suis pignoribus patrem
> Ieiuni soboles effera Tantali:
> Aut cum sacrificae filius Iliae
> Terrarum domini conditor imperii
> Cum vita pariter funera perdidit
> Divisus lacero corpore centies.
> (Grotius, *Christus patiens*, pp. 45–6)

The references are to the stories of (1) Thyestes and (2) Romulus. (1) When Thyestes unwittingly feasted on the flesh of his sons, murdered by Atreus, the sun was blotted out. Cf. also the questions of the last chorus in Act 4 of Seneca's *Thyestes*. (2) When the vestal virgin's son, Romulus, disappeared suddenly from Rome there was an eclipse of the sun, which coincided with rumours that he had been taken up to heaven; he was also said to have been torn to pieces by his councillors (see Plutarch, *Life of Romulus*, iii, 2–3 and xxvii, 5–7, in Loeb edn, trs. B. Perrin (Cambridge, MA and London, 1967), vol. I, pp. 97 and 175–9.

214　*Christs Passion*, IV, ll. 416–18; 423–8, pp. 58–9.
215　Ibid., pp. 75–123.
216　See e.g. '*Cedron*] This Brook, or Torrent, runnes through the Vale of Jehosaphat between Mount Olivet and the City, close by the Garden ... where Christ was betrayed,' ibid., p. 90; cf. Sandys, *Relation of a Journey*, pp. 188–91 for a description of the Garden of Gethsemane and 'the torrent Cedron'.
217　*Christs Passion*, p. 121.
218　See ibid., p. 64, V, ll. 95–6 and pp. 122–3; cf. Sandys, *Relation of a Journey*, p. 160, for a description of the Holy Sepulchre and the activities of contemporary pilgrims at Easter.
219　For a general description see L. B. Wright, *Middle-Class Culture in Elizabethan England* (Chapel Hill, 1935, reprinted 1964), pp. 228–96; esp. 293–6 on ballads, and 325–6 on popular Old Testament histories. See further L. B. Campbell, *Divine Poetry and Drama in Sixteenth-Century England* (Cambridge, Berkeley and Los Angeles, 1959); and Blackburn, *Biblical Drama*. For an indication of the

frequency of biblical topics in plays see W. W. Greg, *A Bibliography of the English Printed Drama to the Restoration* (London, 1939–59); for ballads see H. E. Rollins, *An Analytical Index to the Ballad Entries on the Stationers' Register 1557–1709* (Cambridge, MA, 1924, reprinted 1967).

220   For this and subsequent quotations from the play see H. Jenkins's Arden edition (London, 1982).

221   For a complete text of the ballad, see ibid., pp. 475–7 and works cited.

222   See further R. Noble, *Shakespeare's Biblical Knowledge and Use of the Book of Common Prayer as Exemplified in the Plays of the First Folio* (London, 1935); N. Shaheen, *Biblical References in Shakespeare's Tragedies* (Delaware, 1987).

223   See further E. Schanzer, *The Problem Plays of Shakespeare* (London, 1963), pp. 71–106; G. Wilson Knight, '*Measure for Measure* and the Gospels', in his *The Wheel of Fire* (London, 1949, reprinted 1968), pp. 73–96; also J. W. Lever's introduction to his Arden edition of the play (1965).

224   For Shakespeare's treatment of his sources see R. A. Foakes's introduction to his Arden edition of the play (1962), esp., pp. xxiv–xxxii.

225   See above p. 86 et seq.

226   I am indebted to R. Levao's discussion in his *Renaissance Minds and Their Fictions: Cusanus, Sidney, Shakespeare* (Berkeley, Los Angeles and London, 1985), p. 321.

227   I am indebted to Waswo, *Language and Meaning*, p. 180 for this reference to Montaigne's *Essaies*. My quotations are from Florio's translation (1603) in the Everyman edition (London, 1910, reprinted 1942), vol. III, pp. 350–1.

228   Ibid., vol. III, p. 13.

229   Ibid.

230   Hobbes, *Leviathan*, ch. 32, p. 196.

231   *Homilies*, p. 1.

3

England and France in the Eighteenth Century

Françoise Deconinck-Brossard

The century that elapsed between the Glorious Revolution in Britain and the French Revolution witnessed other 'revolutions' in many fields – industry, agriculture, science. The intellectual scene, in particular, underwent a radical change in outlook. Influenced by Newton's scientific methods, eighteenth-century thinkers drifted away from deductive analysis and gradually embraced inductive reasoning, supported by empirical observation. This approach could not but undermine *a priori* assumptions and make general principles provisional by definition. Its most widespread effect was to encourage confidence in the possibilities of intellectual improvement, generate optimism and challenge authority. No proposition in any sphere, be it law, science or dogma, could be regarded as true in principle, unless it had been proved to be so. When applied to the canon of Holy Writ, in a society that could still be broadly characterized as socially and politically Christian, the new ideas were to make a profound impact on ingrained attitudes. It is worth looking at the developments of such concepts as authority and criticism in this context.

English Responses to New Criticism

In 1678, a French Oratorian, Richard Simon, who had been well acquainted with Calvinism from his early childhood in Dieppe,[1] published a book designed to contribute to the anti-Protestant controversy: *Histoire critique du Vieux Testament*.[2] In order to refute the plainness and simplicity of the Bible inferred from the heretical principle that Scripture alone was sufficient for salvation, the philologist had amassed enough critical evidence to prove the complexity of the sacred text and thus underline the need for extrascriptural tradition to expound difficult passages.

Convinced that textual criticism is a prerequisite to biblical interpretation,[3] he proceeded to describe the method of analysis he had developed and the major conclusions he had drawn. His approach was based on the distrust of received ideas, the study of grammar and the collation of different versions. Such scrupulously impartial examination of the text applied the rigorous discipline of what would now be defined as scientific objectivity to biblical interpretation.

Not unlike Descartes, he first divested himself of all previously held beliefs in the matter and insisted on the need to work with a completely unprejudiced mind.[4] Indeed, he may have realized that, without sensible criticism, it would soon be well-nigh impossible to guard scriptural texts against the scrutiny of rationalists impressed by the rise of Cartesianism in France, where the deleterious influence of free-thinkers had already been felt.

Free from the blinkers of prejudice, the critic would be able to rebuild his own basis of certitude through close analysis of the text. Richard Simon paid much attention to the many repetitions in the Pentateuch. Some he ascribed to the particular 'Genius of the Hebrew Tongue'.[5] Hence, too literal-minded an attention to synonyms, as in Ex. 32:15, 'the tables were written on both their sides; on the one side and on the other side were they written,' was unnecessary.[6] Not until Lowth's work on Hebrew prosody,[7] however, was the problem to be finally solved.

Other words could be allowed to recur simply for didactic purposes. For instance, the point of Ex. 16:36, 'now an omer is the tenth part of an ephah' might well be to clarify the meaning of the word 'omer' used three verses earlier.[8]

However, major repetitions could not be explained away as easily. The sequence of events in the Creation narrative is not arranged in an orderly fashion. It is difficult to believe that a single historian could have written the first few pages of Genesis, where the story of woman made from one of Adam's ribs seems to ignore that man and woman have already been created in the preceding chapter.[9] Through detailed examination of the text, stylistic analysis and careful consideration of the nature of narrative, the critic had come to the conclusion that the Pentateuch could not have been written by a single author.

Indeed, he only stopped short of discovering the Yahvist and Priestly traditions that were to be identified half a century later by a

semi-clandestine amateur, Jean Astruc.[10] Richard Simon's fine textual criticism had undoubtedly paved the way for the identification
of the composite materials in the first five books of the Old Testament. One cannot but admire the comments he passed on the
account of the Flood in Genesis 7. He underlined the repetition in
verse 18 of the fact that 'the waters prevailed, and were increased
greatly upon the earth' whereas verse 17 had already mentioned that
'the waters increased and bare up the ark' and verse 20 was to
repeat that 'fifteen cubits upward did the waters prevail,' only to
conclude that, had a single author written this work, he would not
have told this story in so many words.[11] The inference would not
be disowned by twentieth-century exegetes who attribute verses 17b
and 22–3 to the Yahvist tradition whereas 17a and 18–21 belong
to the Priestly document.[12]

In this embryonic documentary theory, Richard Simon questioned
the received opinion that Moses was the single author of the Pentateuch. The composite nature of the text led him to one of his
major intuitions, the hypothesis that 'public writers' or scribes had
been appointed by Moses and the prophets in order to compile their
people's archives. They could also be assumed to have edited their
predecessors' texts into the Old Testament in its present state.[13]
Though this proposition, which was much derided by many of
Simon's contemporaries, may look nowadays incomplete and
clumsy, it was in fact a brilliant insight for its time. Simon is rightly
regarded as the founding father of the historical-critical school.[14]

His basic assumption allowed for the diversity of styles in the
Pentateuch and the corrupt form of the text. The critic's prime
task would then consist in editing a collection of books not devoid of errors caused 'through length of time or negligence of
Transcribers'.[15] Such was indeed the fate of all ancient documents,
whether sacred or profane, handed down throughout the generations. Therefore, the scholar should apply the well-established rules
of textual criticism in order to find the best possible readings for
biblical and classical literature alike.[16] The method implied adequate
knowledge of the relevant languages, compilation of dictionaries,
accurate translation and collation of manuscripts.

In a later work, prudently published outside the reach of French
censorship, Simon emphasized again the need to abide by the scientific rules of what he called the 'art' of criticism, in a relatively recent
usage of the word.[17] Actually, *critique* had been in use as a noun for
almost a century. Interestingly enough, the first occurrence quoted
by dictionaries is excerpted from the works of J. Scaliger, who had
helped lay the foundations for textual criticism and exegesis in

France.[18] Much as modern historians would like to interpret it otherwise,[19] Simon seemed to be in no doubt as to which discipline would influence the other. To him, scriptural criticism had to borrow the standards of classical scholarship.

In this strictly philological approach, the sacred text lost its privileged status and became on a par with other classics. It could now undergo scientific investigation as any other ancient document. The Bible was to be considered as a collection of human, and hence fallible, interpretations of revelation, rather than an infallible narrative more or less literally transcribing the word of God. When Simon expressed the wish to transfer the secular art of textual criticism to exegesis, he was beginning to treat the Bible as literature rather than Scripture. An exegetical revolution had taken place in the post-Tridentine world.[20]

Simon's enterprise was not entirely new, however. Since the Renaissance and the Reformation, philological science had been regarded as a necessary skill by many theologians, whether Catholic or Protestant. Throughout the century, biblical studies had become more erudite and shown increasing concern for classical scholarship, culminating with the great London Polyglot Bible compiled by a Puritan divine, Brian Walton, in his enforced leisure when he was ejected from his living, and published in six volumes from 1654 to 1657. Nine languages were represented in that edition, the first ever to use the letter A for Codex Alexandrinus, thus introducing the convention of distinguishing manuscripts by Roman capitals in the *apparatus criticus*. Simon reproached Walton for systematically choosing the oldest reading, a method dating back to Tertullian's principle that oldest is truest ('*id ... verum quod sit prius traditum*').[21] Although Walton's achievement was in accordance with Catholic scholarship, Simon intended to produce a new Polyglot version, in three languages – Hebrew, Septuagint Greek and Vulgate Latin – with, he hoped, a purer Hebrew text, and marginal annotations of readings differing from these great sources.[22]

Among his predecessors, Simon very much admired the Protestant Hebraist Louis Cappel, whose major work, *Critica sacra*, compiled as early as 1632 but only published in 1650, partly with the help of an exegete from the Oratorian order, Father Morin, offered clear evidence of textual corruption in some Old Testament passages.[23] Simon held Cappel's edition of the Old Testament to be the best available, and took delight in underlining the fact that the Protestant community had not supported his project.[24]

Through the Oratorian order, Simon had also been in contact with Isaac La Peyrère (1596–1676) an eccentric millenarian with a

Calvinist upbringing, who was made to recant in order to escape the rigours of the Inquisition[25] when his theories trying to solve the inconsistencies of the Bible were circulated.[26] In his old age, he retired as a lay member at the seminary of the Oratorians at Aubervilliers, outside Paris. There he met Richard Simon, who was to write his biography soon after his death. La Peyrère believed he had found a simple solution to the mystery of the two-fold Creation narrative. The two stories described two different Creations, that of mankind as a whole and that of the Jews. He coined the word 'Preadamites' to define such men as had lived long before Adam and the Creation of the Jews.[27]

La Peyrère later wryly noted that contemporary theologians who had been used to fighting one another were so enraged by his ideas that they momentarily united in their fight against him.[28] Interestingly enough, he moved on to explain his attitude to authority, thereby clumsily giving several definitions of the word. He felt compelled to 'yield to the authority of so many authorities'.[29] The former denotes power, the latter knowledge of the doctrinal evidence to be found in patrology, council ordinances and the Catholic belief of the Christian Church. The question was not whether to submit, but which authority was to be obeyed, and eventually the writer chose that of the Roman Church.[30]

La Peyrère's preadamist theories, based on his original interpretation of Romans 5 and Genesis, implied that the biblical text, as it had been handed down through the generations, was not accurate. He underlined the discrepancies in the text, a fallible document of divine revelation transmitted through human copiers. Hence the question of the Mosaic authorship of the Pentateuch, also discussed by his contemporary Hobbes,[31] could be raised, and the tasks of future biblical criticism outlined. The original text would have to be separated from the dross of human alterations.

Although Simon was a personal friend of La Peyrère's, and was, at least indirectly, influenced by the latter's novel ideas, he strongly disagreed with preadamism, a theory based on what he regarded as poor scholarship. Another reader of La Peyrère had been Spinoza. In his *Tractatus theologico-politicus*, probably written at the time of his exclusion from the synagogue but published only eight years before Simon's critical history of the Old Testament text, the Dutch philosopher had laid down the rules for rational, scientific exegesis, based on internal evidence, and drawn the conclusion that Moses could not be the author of the Pentateuch. The same method had brought him to suspect that Esdras might have been the single narrator for the books of Joshua, Judges, Ruth, Samuel and Kings, which give an account of the history of the Jewish people from their origins to the destruction of Jerusalem. It is difficult to determine whether Simon drew his inspiration from Spinoza, or even Hobbes for that matter. The two works have often been compared, but there is no decisive evidence of the philosopher's direct inflence on the Oratorian.[32] Both found their information in the same sources, such as the twelfth-century Jewish commentator Ibn Ezra, repeatedly quoted in the *Tractatus*, and both were in contact with the same thinkers, including La Peyrère. It would be quite futile to try and trace the influence of the one on the other.[33] Each in his own way only crystallized contemporary ideas and concerns.

However, the French nineteenth-century rationalist historian Ernest Renan rightly emphasized that their works actually reveal the presence of totally different outlooks.[34] Simon's close attention to the text was mostly philological and did not question the authority or authenticity of the Bible, while Spinoza's preliminary chapters on Old Testament exegesis only shed light on the much wider political and philosophical issues of toleration and the authority of reason. It is therefore irrelevant to wonder whether the latter went further in his investigation than the former:[35] they differed widely in their points of view. The one advocated reference to internal evidence only, the other did not despise the use of external criteria.

This can partly explain why Simon often refuted Spinoza. Finding fault with the philosopher's idea of biblical inspiration[36] allowed him to raise interesting questions about the proper meaning of such words as 'authenticity' when applied to particular versions of the text, and therefore to discuss the momentous notion of the authority of Scripture.

That the sacred books were inspired did not necessarily mean God had dictated them word for word to human scribes. The critic thus warned the reader against too narrow a translation of 2 Tim. 3:16, suggesting that the beginning of the verse should mean 'all the Scripture that is given by divine inspiration is profitable' rather than 'All Scripture is given by divine inspiration and is profitable.'[37] This indication illustrates Simon's scrupulously grammatical examination of the text; one may say, however, that it is not his best example of scientific objectivity! Although modern linguists will appreciate his differentiation between defining and non-defining relative clauses, one cannot help feeling that he was bending the text to his own purpose and intimating that not every word in the Bible is inspired in the narrow sense of the word.

It is worth noting, however, that he insisted on fighting literalism. He liked to remind the reader that, short of the survival of a genuine, original copy of the Bible, the Hebrew text was the most authentic, that is to say trustworthy version of the Old Testament. Likewise, good translations from this dependable writing into Greek or Latin could be relied on.[38] Hence came the authority of the Vulgate, directly translated from Hebrew, and rightly chosen by the Council of Trent as the Bible to be used in the Roman Church for reference purposes, for the Church 'to be guided by as well in Disputes, as in Sermons and other publick Actions'.[39] In short, it could be regarded as the Catholic authorized version of Scripture. Its authority was derived not so much from the findings of biblical criticism as from the decision made by an ecclesiastical institution.[40]

Since translation is often involved in the transmission of Old and New Testament passages, Simon stressed the inherent difficulties of this activity, particularly when the source language has almost completely disappeared, as was then the case with Hebrew. True to his outlook, he emphasized the need for accurate dictionaries and grammars,[41] and insisted on the discipline of sticking to the text without trying to embellish it.[42] In order to exemplify the translator's problems, one may look at the very first words of Genesis. The received interpretation, 'in the beginning God created the heaven and the earth,' does little justice to the grammatical meaning of the Hebrew text, that should rather read 'in the beginning that God created the World, he created the Heaven and the Earth.' In other words, at the beginning of creation, God first created the heaven and the earth.[43] This analysis is in line with some modern scholarship, which questions the use of a definite article in the traditional translation and suggests that 'when God began the creation of heaven and earth' would better convey the meaning of the text.[44] Close philological examination of the following verse also brought the scholar to pass remarkably modern comments on *'terra erat inanis & vacua'*. No wonder this pioneer of biblical exegesis is the only author referred to in the preface to one of the most recent scholarly translations of the Bible into French![45]

Such findings indisputably challenged traditional criticism. No sympathy could be expected from the guardians of received interpretation. Indeed Bossuet, the powerful bishop of Meaux, suppressed Simon's *Histoire critique du Vieux Testament* as soon as he was warned of its impending publication. All the copies in the hands of the bookseller were destroyed on orders prompted by the 'eagle of Meaux' to the *Lieutenant général de police*.[46] A great peruser of the Bible, the influential prelate felt the need to defend Catholic orthodoxy against innovation and consistently censured the Oratorian's work, not through hard-heartedness, but through a sense of duty. When Simon published a new version of the New Testament 24 years later, outside the scope of his jurisdiction, the ageing bishop still found the energy to denounce him again in a vindication of the traditional views of the Roman Church on biblical criticism, with the unequivocal title of *Défense de la tradition et des Saints Pères* ('A Defence of Tradition and the Holy Fathers').[47] In the face of such censorship, Richard Simon had to leave the Oratorian order,[48] and doggedly pursued his investigation, misunderstood though he was by his contemporaries, Protestants and Catholics alike.[49]

Due to Bossuet's efficient ban, Simon's ideas were not widely circulated in France. However, two copies of the *Histoire critique* were smuggled to England by the Huguenot librarian Henri Justel, in the hope that some learned Englishman might appreciate its erudition. Simon's works were indeed almost immediately translated into English: *A Critical History of the Old Testament* as early as 1682, and the *Critical History of the Text of the New Testament* in the same year as the first edition in French, 1689.[50] The translator may have been one of Simon's friends, John Hampden, who was also an acquaintance of John Dryden.[51] Other critics have identified Henry Dickinson, a Trinity College, Cambridge, graduate, about whom very little is known, as the more likely translator.[52] Simon's major innovation in biblical criticism might have had an English audience early on.

The book did not sell well, however. Few pamphlets appeared in answer, as if scholars had been unable to deal with the challenge it presented.[53] Some divines considered Simon's assumptions as a valuable apologetical tool.[54] Others, including Stillingfleet, regarded his views as undermining scriptural authority. Among the responses prompted by the English publication of Simon's first major work is a sermon given by the Bishop at Whitehall on 23 February 1682 (Old Style).[55] Engaged throughout his career in prodigious controversial activity, Stillingfleet was to revise, in the last years of his life, an apologetic work first published in 1662, *Origines Sacrae*, asserting the historical accuracy of Scripture. So he could only feel indignation at Simon's theories. Interestingly enough, he bundled off Simon and Spinoza together in his endeavour to show that 'the Writings of Moses are genuine & sincere.' His refutation of 'a late Writer[56] in great vogue among those who are glad to find any thing that seems to reflect on the Authority of the Scriptures' is an indication of the fear that Simon's assumptions on biblical interpretation, probably 'more talked about than read',[57] might undermine the authority of the Bible. Reversing the usual typological method, the preacher argued that the authenticity of the Pentateuch could be derived from New Testament evidence of Jesus' reference to those texts: 'upon all occasions our Saviour makes use of the Authority of the Books of Moses, as well as the other parts of Scripture, not as confused heaps of Collections, but as Authentick declarations of the Will of God to mankind.' If the authenticity of the Pentateuch was warranted by the even greater authority of New Testament revelation, then there was no scope for new interpretations of the biblical texts.

Two prominent writers, however, were aware that Simon's carefully compiled textual analysis would bring a radical change to the way intelligent believers read the Bible. John Locke knew of Richard Simon, read and annotated the *Critical History of the Old Testament*, two copies of which he owned in his library.[58] The English philosopher had been in Paris when Bossuet had censured Simon's controversial work. He then remained in correspondence with Henri Justel, who promised to send him a copy of the book, as early as November 1679.[59] Although there is evidence that Locke, whose interest in biblical studies was to come to the fore, albeit anonymously, in *The Reasonableness of Christianity, As Delivered in the Scriptures* (1695),[60] and later in a paraphrase on the Pauline corpus,[61] believed in the Protestant *sola Scriptura* principle[62] that the Oratorian endeavoured to prove wrong, he admired Simon's scientific method of collecting data.

As for Dryden, he devoted the latter half of *Religio Laici* to a discussion of 'this weighty Book, in which appears / The crabbed Toil of many thoughtfull years', (ll. 234–5).[63] In an address to a young friend, the translator of Simon's momentous work, the poet voices his personal commitment to a rational faith. In order to set forth his religious ideas, he designs an appropriate poetic form, almost devoid of imagery, bared to the thread of argumentative statement, in imitation of Horace's epistles: 'And this unpolish'd, rugged Verse, I chose; / As fittest for Discourse, and nearest Prose' (ll. 453–4).

In an attempt at logical transition from the attack on deism in the first part of the poem, the author declares that his personal theology, or layman's faith, stems partly from the shock caused by the discovery of Simon's work, first in the original French, then in the English translation that triggered composition of the poem:

> Yet what they are, ev'n these crude thoughts were bred
> By reading that, which better thou hast read:
> Thy Matchless Author's work: which thou, my Friend,
> By well translating better dost commend.
>
> (ll. 226–9)

'Matchless' may be judged a carefully chosen epithet. Simon's work was indeed unique. It provided unequalled challenges that most of his contemporaries were ill equipped to answer. Although there is little evidence to suggest that the poet laureate really became acquainted with the book from an early stage, or that he had read it extensively,[64] he admired the Oratorian's craftsmanship and erudition:

> A Work so full with various Learning fraught,
> So nicely pondred, yet so strongly wrought,
> As Natures height and Arts last hand requir'd:
> As much as Man cou'd compass, uninspir'd.
>
> (ll. 244–7)

On examination of Simon's basic assumption of the corrupt state of the biblical text, however, Dryden turned to a subtle discussion of the authority of extrascriptural tradition. Where he parted with the Catholic exegete was on the interpretation of obscure passages in Holy Writ. Understandably wary of two extremes, the popish claim for infallibility and the dissenters' zeal, the poet preferred to keep to the middle course and hold on to the Anglican tenet that the simplest of believers may appreciate the plain sense of Scripture on 'essentials', that is to say, those few elements that are necessary for salvation: 'Faith is not built on disquisitions vain; / The things we *must* believe, are *few* and *plain*' (ll. 431–2).

But for the controversial couplet, 'Such an *Omniscient* Church we wish indeed; / 'Twere worth *Both Testaments*, and cast in the *Creed*' (ll. 283–4),[65] it would have been difficult for a reader of *Religio Laici* to forecast Dryden's conversion to Roman Catholicism a few years later. Although the stand taken in *The Hind and the Panther* apparently belied the layman's faith,[66] however, it should be remembered that the issues at stake had not changed. The position had shifted from the Anglican compromise to the Catholic tradition, and from plain style to vivid imagery, but the question remained the same. The crucial point was the definition of the rule of faith, now to be found in the Church guiding the believer through the maze of obscure biblical texts, rather than in the plainness of Scripture clear enough in essentials to human reason guided by the Holy Spirit:

> I think, those truths their sacred works contain,
> The church alone can certainly explain,
> That following ages, leaning on the past,
> May rest upon the Primitive at last.
> Nor wou'd I thence the word no rule infer,
> But none without the church interpreter.
>
> (II, ll. 353–8)

While conceding the centrality of the Bible to the rule of faith, the poet had now espoused the Catholic idea that tradition had an equal share with Scripture. He had been converted from the authority of inner, subjective opinion to the safeguard of objective external evidence, and from Holy Writ to Holy Church.

Religio Laici had been published barely one year after the completion of another poem equally devoid of the usual forms of poetic narration, *Absalom and Achitophel*, commonly regarded as Dryden's nondramatic masterpiece.[67] This partisan, historical, and sometimes satirical poem derived its inspiration from typological interpretation of scriptural themes. Strange as it may seem to modern readers, there was no discrepancy between Dryden's admiration for Simon's serious effort at recovering the literal sense of the Bible and his almost simultaneous use of typology. In the traditional exegetical scheme, the four senses of Scripture coexisted easily.[68] While such critics as Cappel and Simon were attached to the literal sense, which they regarded as the basis for the other three meanings, others, like Dryden, could be interested in taking scriptural texts *per figuram* as well as *per literam*. The difference should not surprise us: Simon's outlook was strictly exegetical, whereas Dryden's insight derived from his poetic creativity.

In *Absalom and Achitophel*, he applied biblical to secular history by drawing a sophisticated parallel between the contemporary constitutional crisis and the plot against King David by Absalom and Achitophel in the second book of Samuel. The idea that ancient history could shed light on modern times was based on the assumption that history could repeat itself, in so far as similar situations would bring about identical effects. Scripture narratives could therefore provide 'types' for the history of mankind, and lessons could be learnt from their analogy with contemporary events. In the words of a great Dryden scholar, 'the Word was not only Revealed but revelatory.'[69]

Besides, the poet was also drawing on a long-established tradition of political typology. Throughout the civil wars, Achitophel had been a commonplace reference to denote the evil politician and false counsellor. Comparisons between Charles II and King David had flourished. Dryden could rely on this background of typological controversy to use the scriptural frame as an effective literary device and stir the reader's imagination.

Dryden's typology, whence metaphor is derived, does not seem to imply that the contemporary relevance of 2 Samuel lies in the design of the original author. Indeed, the poet shared with such divines as South a sense of scepticism about political typology that could not be applied without 'accommodation' to a context different, and distant, from the historical background to the biblical text.[70] This is the reason why their approach may be characterized as tropological rather than merely typological. Their technique of drawing moral or figurative meanings from scriptural passages no longer suggested that such episodes were to be seen as *literally* prefiguring modern history. In that sense, one can see in their literary deployment of such tropes the beginning of the breakdown of the older typological framework.[71]

Ancients and Moderns

Although Dryden's poetry was not untainted with scepticism about the older, narrower use of typology, and he was well versed in contemporary exegetical methods, he conveyed criticism of the modern approach to textual analysis even in *Religio Laici*: 'In doubtfull questions 'tis the safest way / To learn what unsuspected Ancients say' (ll. 435–6). It is therefore worth wondering to what extent the controversy about the recent developments in biblical criticism had been influenced by the quarrel of Ancients and Moderns. Indeed, such critics as worked in the wake of Simon's intuition that Scripture should be edited with the methods of classical scholarship paradoxically applied modern techniques to ancient documents.

Among them was Richard Bentley (1662–1742),[72] 'the greatest of classical scholars',[73] best remembered nowadays for his discovery of the digamma, the Indo-european semi-vowel (sounded 'w') which alone can explain apparently irregular phonetic changes in the use of Greek throughout the ages.[74] Bentley's first published work, a dissertation appended to John Mill's edition of an eighth-century AD Byzantine chronicle, therefore entitled *Epistula ad Joannem Millium*, demonstrated the wide range of scholarly skills he had developed through the hard work of his formative years. The breadth and depth of his thought immediately gained him notoriety, both in Britain and in the international 'republic of letters'.[75] Later in his career he was to prepare editions of Horace, Terence and Homer, among others, and a new version of the New Testament. He was thus working simultaneously on classical and biblical texts. He must be assumed to have used the same skills for the latter as for the former corpus. There can be no question of trying to work out whether biblical criticism was borrowing from classical erudition. They were interacting in the same mind, in that happy age when multidisciplinary studies were still within the scope of individual humanists, who sometimes styled themselves 'polyhistorians'.[76]

In the controversy over ancient and modern learning, Bentley wrote a competent defence of the new science, the *Dissertation* demonstrating the spuriousness of a corpus of epistles attributed to the sixth century BC Sicilian tyrant, Phalaris.[77] Fraught as it is with refutation of personal charges, the work remains impressive for its erudition on many topics of classical learning and its refined critical method, appealing to the external evidence of philology, literature, history and geography. Bentley thus collected enough critical evidence to prove that the disputed text dated from perhaps the second century AD.

He was to be attacked by Swift, then secretary to Sir William Temple, champion of the Ancients, who had drawn attention to the epistles of Phalaris in an essay reviving the quarrel over 'Ancient and Modern Learning'. In *The Battle of the Books*, written at the height of the controversy in 1697 but only published in 1704 with *A Tale of a Tub*,[78] Swift satirizes the corruptions in religion and learning deriving from the excesses of modern criticism. Hermeneutical issues are raised explicitly from the beginning of the text, that is presented as edited material.[79] The *Battle* itself ends with the Ancients' victory over the Moderns, defended by Bentley and his friend Wotton.[80] However, the very last lines suggest that it may not be the end of the story.[81] Indeed, it is reasonable to find in the ending a clue to the complexity of Swift's position in the controversy. Nevertheless, it cannot be denied that, on the whole, the Ancients are shown to have the advantage. The Moderns' enterprise was launched out of 'either Folly or Ignorance'[82] – a disparaging enough statement in Swift's hand. Besides, they worship 'a malignant Deity, call'd *Criticism*', described in scathing allegory:

She dwelt on the Top of a snowy Mountain in *Nova Zembla*; there *Momus* found her extended in her Den, upon the Spoils of numberless Volumes half devoured. At her right Hand sat *Ignorance*, her Father and Husband, blind with Age; at her Left, *Pride* her Mother, dressing her up in the Scraps of Paper herself had torn. There, was *Opinion* her Sister, light of Foot, hoodwinkt and headstrong, yet giddy and perpetually turning. About her play'd her Children, *Noise* and *Impudence, Dullness* and *Vanity, Positiveness, Pedantry*, and *Ill-Manners*. The Goddess herself had Claws like a Cat: Her Head, and Ears, and Voice, resembled those of an *Ass*: Her Teeth fallen out before; Her Eyes turned inward, as if she lookt only upon herself . . . .[83]

The satire of quibbling and arrogant critics, among whom Bentley was given pride of place, was to remain a recurrent theme in Swift's less occasional writings. It is worth noting, for instance, that the scientists of Laputa in Gulliver's third voyage have one of their eyes

turned inward, like the goddess Criticism.[84] Besides, the very etymology provided by the narrator for Laputa parodies Bentley's
philological conjectures:

> The Word, which I interpret the *Flying* or *Floating Island*, is in the Original
> *Laputa*; whereof I could never learn the true Etymology. *Lap* in the old
> obsolete Language signifieth *High*, and *Untuh* a *Governor*; from which they
> say by Corruption was derived *Laputa* from Lapuntuh. But I do not
> approve of this Derivation, which seems to be a little strained. I ventured to
> offer the Learned among them a Conjecture of my own, that *Laputa* was
> *quasi Lap outed*; *Lap* signifying properly the dancing of the sun Beams in
> the Sea; and *outed* a Wing, which however I shall not obtrude, but submit
> to the judicious Reader.[85]

In fact, the name derives from the Spanish *la puta* (the whore). It
stresses Swift's political satire, referring to England's impoverish-
ment of Ireland and to some politicians' 'whorish' attitude. Since
Laputa also satirizes intellectuals, it may even be interpreted as 'the
country of thinkers' from the Latin *puto*.[86] Gulliver's lengthy discussion here serves to stress the ridicule of contemporary etymological
conjectures, such as Bentley's examination of Boyle's statement,
'That the word Tragedy may signifie Comedy' in the *Dissertation
upon the Epistles of Phalaris*.

Modern erudition is also attacked in two digressions from the
Tale published at the same time as the *Battle*:

> Every *True Critick* is a Hero born, descending in a direct Line from a
> Celestial Stem, by *Momus* and *Hybris*, who begat *Zoilus*, who begat *Tigel-
> lius*, who begat *Etcoetera* the Elder, who begat *B-tly*, and *Rym-r*, and
> *W-tton*, and *Perrault*, and *Dennis*, who begat *Etcoetera* the Younger.[87]

Swift hardly disguised his contempt for Bentley's classical scholarship!

As for the New Testament, Bentley explained the principles that
had guided his research, in the preface to his specimen critical
edition of the very last chapter in the Bible. Not unlike Simon, he
advocated a philological method based on the collation of ancient
manuscripts, in order to make up for the faults of the *editiones
principes*:

> The Author of this Edition, observing that the Printed Copies of the New
> Testament, both of the Original Greek and Antient vulgar Latin, were taken
> from Manuscripts of no great Antiquity, such as the first Editors could then
> procure; and that now by God's Providence there are MSS. in *Europe* . . .

above a Thousand Years old in both Languages; believes he may do good Service to common Christianity, if he publishes a New Edition of the *Greek* and Latin, not according to the recent and interpolated Copies, but as represented in the most antient and venerable MSS., in Greek and Roman Capital Letters.[88]

He was to revere these silent witnesses throughout his life, as the famous episode of the 1731 fire in the Cottonian Library in Ashburnham House amply shows. Bentley was seen emerging with his dressing-gown and great wig carrying the four volumes of Codex Alexandrinus in his arms, no light burden for an old man.[89] Had they been burnt, future generations of scholars would have been the poorer indeed for this irreparable loss.

True to the Protestant principle of free examination, Bentley publishes the list of readings he has chosen from, in order to allow the user to make up his own mind. But he takes care to declare that all his corrections are based on the authority of the Ancients:

The Author is very sensible, that in the Sacred Writings there's no place for Conjectures or Emendations. Diligence and Fidelity, with some Judgment and Experience, are the Characters here requisite. He declares therefore, that he does not alter one Letter in the Text without the Authorities subjoin'd in the Notes. And to leave the free Choice to every Reader, he places under each Column the smallest Variations of this Edition, either in words or Order, from the receiv'd *Greek* of *Stephanus*, and the *Latin* of the two Popes *Sixtus* V and *Clemens* VIII. So that this Edition exhibits both it Self, and the Common ones.[90]

The names of the two popes mentioned show that, in true post-Tridentine fashion, the editor was referring to the Vulgate for the Latin text. However, he seems to have agreed with Walton's idea that the older the manuscript, the nearer to the source, hence the more authoritative:

To confirm the Lections which the author places in the Text, he makes use of the old Versions, *Syriac, Coptic, Gothic* and *Aethiopic*, and all the Fathers, *Greeks* and *Latins*, within the first five centuries; ... what has crept into any copies since, is of no value or Authority.[91]

Indeed his sample edition of Revelation 22 is laid out with parallel Greek and Latin texts and full *apparatus criticus*. Unfortunately, he never completed the project, although he had spent 16 years collating almost 90 manuscripts towards this edition, partly because he was involved in controversy at Trinity, as already mentioned in the full title of the *Proposal*.[92]

The 'late' pamphleteer was Conyers Middleton, the biographer of Cicero and most brilliant scholar among his rivals. Middleton questioned some of Bentley's readings.[93] Modern critics would probably agree with the former's correction of a solecism in verse 8, but they would approve of Bentley's version of verse 5, where he had restored a correct word order. Likewise, he seems to have discovered the lection in the second verse.[94] However minor these variant readings may look, the controversy, undoubtedly inspired by personal spite in the stormy atmosphere brought about by Trinity's endemic feuds, suggests that Bentley's antagonist was implicitly accepting the scholar's critical method and only disputed his findings.

Another reason why Bentley's scheme miscarried was simply the magnitude of his design. When, in 1729, he received new collations of Codex Vaticanus, which would have meant great modifications in his work, he gave up in discouragement.[95] He too was working ahead of his time. What he really needed was a twentieth-century computer! The painstaking efforts of the greatest English scholar of the next generation, Benjamin Kennicott, who patiently listed the 683 manuscripts he had collated towards his edition of the Old Testament,[96] is the more remarkable, in comparison with Bentley's failure to complete his project.

The hair-splitting arguments resulting from close scrutiny of the text were an easy prey for satire. Bentley's scholarship was thus the butt of Pope's wit in the *Dunciad*.[97] Pope reproached Bentley's erudition for atomizing the monument of ancient literature: 'The critic Eye, that microscope of Wit, / Sees hairs and pores, examines bit by bit' (IV, ll. 233–4).

In his own notes on Homer's *Iliad*, Pope set out his preference for literary appreciation over textual criticism. His views had long been opposed to Bentley's, if the anecdote about their encounter at Dr Mead's is to be relied on. Bentley is said to have answered Pope that the latter's translation was 'a pretty poem, Mr Pope; but you must not call it Homer'.[98] Bentley sounds as if he felt his scholarship had given him superior knowledge of, hence authority on the text. If so, he introduced a new facet to the notion of authority in the field of criticism. Simon had shared with his enemies the conviction that authority lay in the text. Unlike Bentley, he never seemed to imply that expertise in textual criticism could give him any power to control the literary judgements of others.

Contrarywise, Pope stressed the need for sensitivity to the work's artistic qualities. Learning could have no bearing on the reader's search for the poetical merits of the *Iliad*. Textual criticism was irrelevant to literary judgement:

> It is something strange that of all the Commentators upon *Homer*, there is hardly one whose principal design is to illustrate the Poetical Beauties of the Author.... This has been occasion'd by the Ostentation of Men who had more Reading than Taste, and were fonder of showing their Variety of Learning in all Kinds, than their single Understanding in Poetry. Hence it comes to pass that their Remarks are rather Philosophical, Historical, Geographical, Allegorical, or in short rather any thing than Critical and Poetical.... The grand Ambition of one sort of Scholars is to encrease the Number of *Various Lections*; which they have done to such a degree of obscure Diligence, that ... we now begin to value the first Editions of Books as most correct, because they have been least corrected.... Not to add, that there is a vast deal of difference between the Learning of a Critick, and the Puzzling of a Grammarian.[99]

Indeed, Pope's translation of Homer was *not* faithful to the letter of the Greek epic, and a scholar might understandably find fault there.[100] Although the poet laureate made extensive use of earlier translators and secondary sources,[101] and his own scholarship is less open to question than has sometimes been suggested,[102] he did not share the professional man of learning's factual preoccupations or scientific scruples, believing that they might hinder the true understanding of ancient literature. He objected to literal translation in principle and disapproved of 'a servile dull Adherence to the Letter'.[103] A beautiful version 'transfusing the Spirit of the Original' would do more justice to the text for 'the Fire of the Poem is what a Translator should principally regard'.[104]

The poet did put his own principles into practice. For all its omissions, corrections and additions,[105] Pope's version brings out the spirit of the ancient tale into Augustan idiom. To take but an example, one may say that the opening lines adequately convey the style of the well-known prelude in which the Homeric writer invokes the Muse to relate the story of Achilles' anger and its ill effects:

> Achilles' Wrath, to Greece the direful Spring
> Of Woes unnumber'd, heav'nly Goddess, sing!
> That Wrath which hurl'd to *Pluto*'s gloomy Reign
> The Souls of mighty Chiefs untimely slain;
> Whose Limbs unbury'd on the naked Shore
> Devouring Dogs and hungry Vultures tore.[106]

The syntactic structure, highlighting, like the Greek original, the key-word 'wrath', from the beginning, is particularly effective and faithful to the text. Consecutive enjambments equally mirror the solemn style and length of the bard's opening sentence. Thus the translation serves well the author's purpose of bringing the reader to a closer understanding of the text, even with no access to the original. As Dr Johnson underlines, however, the artifact resulted from a gradual process of poetic improvement. Earlier versions of the first two lines, although they already resort to the same devices, lack the strength of the final rendering: 'The wrath of Peleus' son, the direful spring / Of all the Grecian woes, O Goddess sing'; or: 'The stern Pelides' rage, O Goddess, sing, / Of all the woes of Greece the fatal spring.'[107]

It would be easy to pinpoint less felicitous passages. In the episode when Athena checks Achilles in his fury, Pope's couplet, 'He said, observant of the blue-ey'd Maid; / Then in the Sheath return'd the shining Blade',[108] may not be as powerful as Dryden's 'He said; with surly faith believed her word, / And in the sheath reluctant plunged the sword.'[109] The former rendering adds the compound epithet to the goddess, though, for once, it is not rehearsed in the Homeric text, but omits the silver handle held back by the hero's heavy hand, thus skipping almost one line,[110] admittedly better translated by Dryden's very concise use of 'reluctant'. However, Pope's verse still bears comparison with the prose in his own footnotes, 'he sheaths his Sword in Obedience to her.'[111]

On the whole, Pope achieved the feat of translating the Homeric corpus into great poetry. No wonder it remained a reference version for much of the century. A French edition of *Iliad* still refers to Pope's 'excellent preface'.[112] Clearly here authority is vested in literary skill rather than dry, scientific scholarship. Hence the sly comments on Bentley's work:

> Thy mighty scholiast, whose unwearied pains
> Made Horace dull, and humbled Milton's strains.
> Turn what they will to verse, their toil is vain,
> Critics like me shall make it prose again.
> (*The Dunciad*, IV, ll. 211–4)

In this instance, textual criticism and literary judgement seem difficult to reconcile, as if the rigours of modern scholarship were incompatible with the spirit of poetry.

However indirectly the brisk exchanges in the long-standing literary debate about Ancient and Modern learning may have affected

Pope, he obviously sided against the Moderns. The French editor of Homer who, towards the end of the century, underlined the poet laureate's bias to antiquity was not mistaken.[113] The battle was not primarily concerned with scholarship, but involved momentous questions about taste. Like his fellow-Scriblerian, Swift, Pope could only respond to scientific exegesis with his own literary criticism, conveyed by satire.

Eighteenth-century Criticism in France

The literary quarrel about Ancient and Modern learning had originated in France. It focused on the classics, and particularly the Homeric corpus, regarded as authoritative texts in a country with a long tradition of interest in ancient Latin and Greek literature. One may wonder whether it reflected on other fields of criticism.

Richard Simon's theories, criticized by contemporary Protestants and Catholics incensed at the idea that Moses might not be the author of the Pentateuch, were stifled for much of the eighteenth century. Lesser-known critics, however, like Father Houbigant, another Oratorian (c.1686 or 1687 – c.1783? or 1784),[114] were trying to keep the flame of textual criticism burning, albeit in the dark. He too wanted to restore the genuine Hebrew text of the Bible, hoping that such work would provide further insights into Counter-Reformation policies, convert the Jews and win Protestants back to the Roman fold, as he explained in the first exposition of his critical principles, the *Conférences de Metz*,[115] prudently published with a Dutch imprint.

The Preface sums up the main points. First, the authority of the Vulgate is no case against biblical criticism.[116] This opinion is all the more understandable as, presumably, the author was already working on his remarkable bilingual edition of the Bible, with his own translation of the Hebrew text into Latin.[117] Besides, he underlined the insufficiency of tradition, due to its emphasis on dogmatic or unanimous interpretation.[118] This objection mirrors his textual approach, even more purely grammatical than Simon's. Houbigant did go in quest of the original text, and insisted on the need to learn the relevant languages. But he was convinced that the Massoretes' work, reproduced from one version to another since the sixteenth century, had wrongly inserted vowel marks in the Herbrew text.[119] Therefore, unlike his predecessor Simon or his own contemporary Kennicott, he did not find it necessary to collate as many manuscripts as possible. To him, they all reflected the corrupt state of an unduly vocalized document. He was thus content with the material held in the library of the Oratorian order in Paris, namely two famous copies of the Samaritan Pentateuch, nine other manuscripts with the masoretic text, and many commentaries, including a copy of Ibn Ezra.[120] This is probably one of the reasons why his edition, remarkable though it may have been for its typographical beauty,[121] was sooner forgotten than Kennicott's masterpiece. The latter, who over the years had entertained a scholarly relationship with the former and held him in high esteem, could not but locate the faults in his performance:

Quod ad Biblia attinet Clar. HOUBIGANTII, quae continent multitudinem variarum lectionum; nullo tamen plene et penitus excusso codice MSto, sed variis lectionibus hic et illic excerptis et notatis: hoc Opus, sane permagnum atque revera elegans, ad Angliam denique pervenit, exactis mensibus fere 12 post editionem dissertationis meae prius memoratae. (As far as the Rev. Houbigant's Bible is concerned, which contains a multitude of various readings, although no manuscript is thoroughly examined, but various readings have been excerpted and noted here and there, this work, really very important and elegant indeed, has at last arrived in England, almost exactly twelve months after the publication of my above-mentioned dissertation.)[122]

Houbigant's annotations, printed at the end of each chapter, do not, indeed cannot, include full details of the *apparatus criticus*. His corrections are based on linguistic criteria. The text must be made to conform to grammatical rules, since the original Hebrew Scriptures were held to be, literally, impeccable. So the philologist corrected what he considered as solecisms, barbarisms or even inconsistencies such as the sudden appearance of Elohim in Gen. 7:16, which he replaced by the tetragram, for the narrative to be coherent![123] This last emendation only shows the extent of his textual insensitivity, much greater than the intuition displayed by other critics. The chief monument of biblical criticism in eighteenth-century France thus failed to develop scientific scholarship to the full.

Meanwhile, contributors to the *Encyclopédie* only echoed well-established, conventional interpretation as illustrated by dom Calmet (1672–1757). His 22 volume exposition was the first major biblical commentary published in French within Catholic circles. A typical Benedictine's work, it aims to provide the user with an encyclopaedic survey of past and present opinion on every single chapter and verse.[124] In the general preface, the compiler explained that his team had worked in an unbiased fashion and avoided useless disputes and questions, without attacking or defending any author in particular, since they were in search for literal truth.[125] This scientific, though uncritical, outlook, aiming at objective comprehensiveness, allowed them to quote, albeit not by name, Spinoza and Simon's doubts about Mosaic authorship of the Pentateuch,[126] in contrast with their own vocal – and cautious – assertion in the preface that Moses did write the first five books in the Bible.[127]

Dom Calmet's compilation, though probably more credulous and awkward than subversive, was deemed dangerous in so far as it gave ample supply of information for radical minds. There is clear evidence that Voltaire, among others, drew on it extensively and thus acquired second-hand knowledge of biblical interpretation. A well-documented instance is the Creation narrative. Dom Calmet rightly argued that the Hebrew words for '*creavit Deus*' literally mean 'the Gods', in the plural,[128] created the earth. The compiler maintained that such a translation supported the patrological proof of the existence of Holy Trinity.[129] It is probably no coincidence that Voltaire should have used the same argument in *La Bible enfin expliquée*.[130] He could then subvert the information for his own purposes of social and political criticism. In the latter half of the century, dom Calmet's publisher therefore thought it prudent to substitute a more conventional paraphrase for the Benedictine's pluralist commentary. The result is commonly known as '*La Bible de dom Calmet*', a very pale mirror of the original work. Its clumsy attempt at opening up the text to multiple interpretation had had to be suppressed.

In point of fact, the *philosophes* often quoted biblical texts and scholarship, with which they were probably more conversant than the average late twentieth-century churchgoer! Voltaire's works are filled with biblical allusion. His discussion of the New Testament alone is scattered over about 75 writings, not to mention the correspondence.[131] Rousseau too, who had been brought up as a Protestant, had perused the Bible. Influenced by contemporary rationalism, he felt that the Scripture conception of God conformed to reason and the Enlightenment values of toleration and charity. His ethical approach led him to neglect formal criticism, however.[132] The '*vicaire savoyard*' he portrays in the *Emile* is familiar with the questions raised by the recent developments of biblical criticism; he has heard of the authorship issues but prefers to tread the path of natural religion available to all, irrespective of their level of education. Suspicious of learned exegesis and of established churches, he voices, not the scientist's faith, but the simple believer's piety. What

Rousseau anticipated here was the widening gap between the critic and the layman, which was never bridged since then.

As for Diderot, he evinced only scientific interest in biblical scholarship. Although he was familiar with the work of Simon, Spinoza and Le Clerc, he generally entrusted the composition of the religious articles in the *Encyclopédie* to more orthodox contributors who often found their information in dom Calmet's commentary.[133] The approach may have guarded the authors effectively against censorship by both church and state, but it resulted in rather bland essays.

For instance, the entry for 'Bible'[134] first lists the different versions (Hebrew, Greek, Latin, etc.) then proceeds to an enumeration of all the issues that would have to be dealt with in an introductory treatise to biblical studies.[135] On reading this passage, written in the conditional mood throughout, as if the anonymous contributor did not want to commit himself too far, one remains unsatisfied. He only records the existence of such interesting subjects as authenticity, inspiration, history, geography, biology and, last but not least, 'style', 'rhetoric' and 'idioms' – that is to say literary criticism of biblical texts – without ever elaborating upon them.

Likewise, the unsigned article on the Pentateuch does quote Simon's discussion of Mosaic authorship, only to refute it by dom Calmet's objections.[136] As every child knows, quoting other people's use of forbidden words or ideas is both safe and enjoyable. The author seems to have adopted the same tactics. Ostensibly disproving Simon's theories allowed him to inform the reader about recent developments of biblical criticism.

The *philosophes* could only object to the obscuranticism of a dominant Church that wanted to suppress criticism and impose the authority of tradition. Indeed, Renan rightly pointed out the French Catholic Church's paradoxical responsibility in fostering a trend of materialistic rationalism, very much alive to this day. Bossuet's persecution of Richard Simon, far from delivering the Church from the threat of scientific knowledge, had paved the way for sarcastic rejection of belief: 'Voltaire's success avenged Richard Simon.'[137]

There was little room in France for the English Deists' view that faith and reason could be complementary. The *philosophes'* lesser-known emulators or disciples circulating clandestine literature did look up to the English model throughout the century, and consistently quoted Toland, Collins, Mandeville and Shaftesbury,[138] but the break between reason and revelation took a much more radical form in France than across the Channel.

The themes they dealt with, and repeated so often as to make them become almost trite, may have been the same as those of their English counterparts: the need for research into semantics and history, for drawing a list of contradictory and obscure passages in the Bible, and conveying criticism – this time in the usual sense of adverse comments – of miracles, prophecies and textual authenticity. They even knew of Simon through Toland. But their approach to biblical studies was obviously tinted with anticlericalism and thus their outlook differed completely from that of even the most extreme of their English friends. Their main concern was to free their contemporaries from superstition, so they did not wish to engage in a dialogue with the Scripture text they were up against. In this respect, one may say that the interaction between biblical scholarship and literature was mostly negative in eighteenth-century France. On the other hand, it cannot be denied that criticism of the Bible, or of the Church, stirred the greatest writers' imaginations and inspired their most creative work.

Eighteenth-century Hermeneutics in England

The torch of modern exegesis was thus handed on to the Protestant countries in Northern Europe where the prevailing rationalism of the Enlightenment made it possible for biblical criticism to develop. English Latitudinarians and Low Church supporters of the Whig supremacy shared with their deist antagonists[139] the idea, based on what can be loosely characterized as Lockean epistemology, that Reason was the supreme criterion of judgement in religious matters, and did not contradict faith. Hence rational examination of the Scripture text, the main source of revelation in the Protestant tradition to which they were proud to belong, could only be profitable. The pioneers of biblical criticism are thus to be found in early and mid-eighteenth-century England.[140]

The most prominent of them was the Hebraist Robert Lowth (1710–87). A professor of poetry at Oxford (later to become Bishop of St David's, Oxford and London), he combined the scholarly and literary methods of criticism in his edition of Isaiah.[141] Through translation, he wanted to bring out the spirit of the text; as a grammarian,[142] he would not depart from the literal meaning. His outlook thus embraced both Pope's and Bentley's viewpoints, for his work required a carefully edited text:

It being then a Translator's indispensable duty faithfully and religiously to express the sense of his author, he ought to take great care, that he proceed upon just principles of Criticism, in a rational method of Interpretation;

and that the copy from which he translates be accurate and perfect in itself, or corrected as carefully as possible by the best authorities, and on the clearest result of Critical inquiry.[143]

It is worth noting that, within these few lines, new connotations of 'criticism' and 'authorities' are to be found. 'Critical inquiry' obviously refers to text editing, carried out by experts, on which literary criticism, that is to say appreciation, may be based. Lowth was privileged to live during the brief period in English literary history when it was possible to unite biblical scholarship and literary criticism. Kennicott, ever grateful for Lowth's influence on his own work, had noticed this happy conjunction, and so defined him as a citizen, not only of the republic of letters, but also of Christendom: *'Eruditissimus LOWTHUS, Praesul Londinensis admodum Reverendus; qui rempublicam et Literatam et Christianam optime demeritus est ...'* (the very erudite Lowth, the very Reverend Bishop of London, who deserves equally well of the Republic of letters and of Christendom ...).[144] However, on several occasions, one may detect passages in Lowth's works that might have forecast the specialization of the years to come, and the impending division between exegesis and hermeneutics – the latter word coming into use during the century.[145]

It was probably not a coincidence that 'philological' should have been included in the title of *Isaiah*. The author took great care to proceed with an investigation of textual problems in the available versions of the Old Testament. Like Simon, Bentley and other scholars whose work he greatly admired, Lowth suggested that the Bible should be treated no differently from other classics. The method implied patient manuscript collation and collection of data, much like Simon's techniques:

The copies of the Holy Scriptures of the Old Testament being then subject, like all other antient writings, to mistakes arising from the unskilfulness or inattention of transcribers ... it is to be considered what remedy can be applied in this case.... Hebrew Manuscripts have at length been consulted.... An infinite number of Variations have been collated, from above six hundred Manuscripts, and some antient printed Editions, collated or consulted, in most parts of Europe; and have been in part published, and the publication of the whole will, I hope, soon be completed, by the learned Dr. Kennicot, ... a Work the greatest and most important that has been undertaken and accomplished since the Revival of letters.[146]

Kennicott's achievement was remarkable indeed, as has already been mentioned. His version of the Old Testament has stood the test of time and is still occasionally referred to by late twentieth-century exegetes.[147] When Lowth recommended him to read the twenty-third chapter of 2 Samuel, according to his own account,[148] he became convinced that the Hebrew text had suffered in the hand of transcribers, then embarked on the mammoth task, financed by public subscription, of collating the maximum number of manuscripts, both in Britain and on the Continent, in order to edit the Old Testament as accurately as possible. Ten years and 9,000 pounds later, two superb folio volumes with a very clear layout were published, displaying parallel Samaritan and Hebrew texts, and detailed *apparatus criticus* in the lower half of the page. The *Index nominum* gives some idea of the critic's interchange of ideas, across national and denominational frontiers, with his British and European counterparts. Such pioneers as Cappel and Scaliger are referred to once, as a matter of course. Among contemporary exegetes, Bentley, Houbigant, two members of the German Michaelis family and – it goes without saying – Robert Lowth, are quoted several times. Michaelis and Lowth also appear in the list of subscribers. Curiously enough, however, Simon's name is not to be found in the index.

As for Robert Lowth, it is interesting to hear overtones of Simon's theses in his words. His own father, William, a well-known commentator of the Bible, had been one of Simon's few defenders, partly because they fought a common enemy, Le Clerc.[149] It is therefore reasonable to assume that Robert Lowth had been in contact with Simon's theories from an early stage.

Robert Lowth considered the Septuagint as not very reliable for Isaiah,[150] and had consulted other documents, including two annotated Bibles deposited by Archbishop Secker at the Library in Lambeth. One of these volumes was 'a Hebrew Bible of the Edition of Michaelis, Halle 1720, in 4to',[151] filled with marginal annotations in Secker's hand. It must have been the first modern *Biblia hebraica*, edited by Johann Heinrich Michaelis, Professor of Hebrew at Halle.[152] The younger biblical scholar, Johann David Michaelis, is known to have been so impressed by Lowth's second lecture, *De Sacra poesi Hebraeorum*, when he heard it at Oxford[153] that he brought out an annotated edition in 1758.[154] On his return to Germany, he also circulated Kennicott's method of comparing variants.[155] Here again, one may notice the interaction of Continental and British criticism. It was an international activity, with major ideas bouncing from the Continent to England, then back to the Continent.

What Robert Lowth is most famous for,[156] is his treatment of the Bible as literature, with his emphasis on the non-theological nature of Hebrew poetry viewed only as Oriental literature. His major discovery was that the characteristic prosody of Old Testament prophecy is based on parallelism, which he tried to bring out in his blank verse translation. When read aloud, the following sample translation of a well-known text (Is. 11:6–9) does illustrate the antiphonal structure he had analysed in his lectures on Hebrew poetry 30-odd years earlier:

> Then shall the wolf take up his abode with the Lamb;
> And the leopard shall lie down with the kid:
> And the calf, and the young lion, and the fatling shall come together;
> And a little child shall lead them.
> 7 And the heifer and the she-bear shall feed together;
> Together shall their young ones lie down;
> And the lion shall eat straw like the ox.
> 8 And the suckling shall play upon the hole of the asp;
> And upon the den of the basilisk shall the newly-weaned child lay his hand.
> 9 They shall not hurt, or destroy, in all my holy mountain;
> For the earth shall be full of the knowledge of JEHOVAH,
> As the waters that cover the depths of the sea.[157]

Although these lines do not differ widely from the Authorized Version, and in some instances reproduce it exactly, the chiastic figures in verses 7 and 8 introduce a new echoing pattern, probably related to Lowth's notion of Oriental parallelism.

Like some of his contemporaries,[158] he felt the need for a revised translation into modern English incorporating the most recent scientific discoveries about the Scripture text, as he explained in a visitation sermon:

Those heavenly stores [the Holy Scriptures] are inexhaustible: every new acquisition still leads on the further discoveries; and the most careful search will still leave enough to invite, and to reward, the repeated searches of the pious and industrious, to the latest ages.... To confirm and illustrate these holy writings, to evince their truth, to shew their consistency, to explain their meaning ... this is ... the most important end, to which our labours in the search of truth can be directed. And here I cannot but mention ... that nothing would more effectually conduce to this end, than the exhibiting of the Holy Scriptures themselves to the people in a more advantageous and just light, by an accurate revisal of our vulgar translation by public authority.[159]

The quotation had to be truncated for the critic is carried away by his sense of progress in biblical studies, typical of Enlightenment optimism, and his passion for Holy Writ. It looks as though he could not stop discussing the subject! Yet, he never seems to have used any translation but the Authorized Version in his pastoral duties, even when he preached on a text of Isaiah.

His attempt to analyse the prophetic text in formal literary terms was not only breaking new ground, but also systematically extending a long tradition of biblical criticism exemplified by his own father's well-known commentary. Indeed, the best-read expositors were not devoid of literary criticism, especially through discussions of biblical rhetoric as compared with the standard Latin and Greek classics. The popularity of such expositions of the Scriptures[160] channelled biblical criticism into a body of received interpretation that was often hinted at in contemporary secular literature.[161] Reading Scripture with the guidance of a commentary was commonplace. One will recall Dr Johnson's advice to Boswell, 'To be sure, Sir, I would have you read the Bible with a commentary.'[162] Although they would have cringed at the word and its popish overtones, his contemporaries were in fact treating such expositors as if they represented a new form of tradition. This corpus of orthodox – so to speak – exegesis incorporated several layers of interpretation, including typology and analogy, as well as general information inspired from dom Calmet's commentary translated into English.

As has been seen with Dryden, however, typology soon became obsolete, more so than analogy.[163] The latter concept emphasized the idea that Scripture cannot contradict itself. Therefore an easy passage could shed light on a more obscure verse, though not necessarily in the sense that Old Testament types had once been thought to anticipate New Testament events.

These various strata were not often regarded as conflicting methods of investigation into the meaning of the text. As in the four-fold scheme, they coexisted peacefully, particularly in sermons, on which the majority of illiterate people depended for their knowledge of the Bible. As John Sharp, Archdeacon of Northumberland, typically repeated to his congregation for almost 40 years:

Our Regard for the Scriptures provided it be *not* a superstitious one, cannot be too great; And whenever we examine them fairly & without prejudice, the Sense will generally determine, what parts of them are to be taken literally, & what passages are to be only understood in that beautiful Allegory with which Oriental Languages so much abound.[164]

The sentence encapsulates the state of contemporary criticism. It is impossible to know whether the preacher had been in contact with Lowth's theories. All we know for sure is that he was well read and

Lowth was to become his colleague at Durham, so it is not unlikely that he should have been aware of the new Orientalizing mode in biblical criticism. Anyway, there is ample evidence in the corpus of his manuscript sermons that he found it natural to apply the resources of literary or scientific analysis, however clumsily sometimes, to the interpretation of Scripture texts.[165] Likewise, one could find many examples of contemporary sermon literature echoing the disputes of biblical exegesis.[166]

Sermons, however, were not the only field of hermeneutic application. Biblical criticism also had bearing on the literary background. A celebrated example is the episode in Henry Fielding's *Joseph Andrews* in which Parson Adams enters into a discussion with a 'grave Man' he takes for a clergyman, but who is in fact a priest of the Roman Church in disguise. Moved by his interlocutor's edifying discourse, Adams cries

'Whatever you are, you have spoken my sentiments: I believe I have preached every syllable of your speech twenty times over: for it hath always appeared to me easier for a cable rope (which by the way is the true rendering of that word we have translated *camel*) to go through the eye of a needle, than, for a rich man to get into the Kingdom of Heaven.'[167]

The passage suggests that the novelist expected his readers to catch the allusion to an old debate in biblical criticism, namely the translation of a famous gospel phrase (Matt. 19:24). That the travelling parson should choose the solution usually rejected in most New Testament expositors is not of paramount importance for the general understanding of the novel. A reader who would fail to grasp the allusion would still enjoy the book, but he would surely miss an exciting detail. Minor though the trait may be, it adds a thin stroke to Adams's portrait, thus providing an interesting characterization device. The good parson, who is first introduced as 'an excellent scholar'[168] is nearly always in a minority, not only in the wider world of which he is said, from the beginning, to be ignorant,[169] but also among other learned men. Besides, the biblical text emphasizing the difficulty of a rich man entering Heaven hints at one of the main themes in the novel, so it is reasonable to maintain that allusion to the context of biblical criticism sheds light on the interpretation of the narrative.

Moreover, it is not the only instance of expanded biblical reference in the book. In a passage of purple prose, the author elaborates on the parable of the good Samaritan. When the eponymous hero is stripped and wounded by highwaymen who leave him half dead,[170]

a stage-coach comes down that way. Like the priest and the levite of the gospel story, the passengers would rather pass by on the other side. Their reluctance to share clothes or seats with the wounded man soon reveals their false charity and sexual hypocrisy. Here biblical allusion, interwoven into the narrative, obviously discloses the novelist's moral insight.

Interestingly enough, classical scholarship is also referred to extensively. Parson Adams, described from the start as 'a perfect master of the Greek and Latin languages',[171] is well read in the classics and easily confounds the hospitable Mr Wilson in his discussion of the *Iliad* over a pot of ale.[172] While his host only knows of Homer through Pope's translation, which it is apparently fashionable to quote, the curate embarks in a thorough exercise of literary criticism of *the* poet. He particularly admires the structural unity of the Homeric epic, characterized by agreement of the action to the subject, and unintentionally quotes Pope's analysis: 'for as the subject is anger, how agreeable is his action, which is war?' Clearly Fielding expected his reader to grasp allusion both to literary and biblical criticism. This should come as no surprise. Homer was regarded as the greatest of all poets, and the Bible remained *the* book of reference, so it was natural to treat these two great monuments of ancient literature in the same way. One may say that classical and biblical criticism were thus used creatively in 'literature of allusion'.[173]

To give but another well-documented instance of expanded allusion, one may recall the passage in *Humphry Clinker* in which Matthew Bramble characterizes his Yorkshire cousin, Squire Burdock, as 'a mighty fox-hunter *before the Lord*',[174] obviously a reference to Nimrod as mentioned in the table of nations (Gen. 10:8–11). The immediate context does indeed enhance the parallel with the Genesis description of the mightly hunter: 'he still keeps a pack of hounds, which are well exercised; and his huntsman every night entertains him with the adventures of the day's chace.' What Smollett really alludes to, though, is a long tradition of biblical and literary portrayal of Nimrod. Received exegesis, going back to Augustine, regards Nimrod as the presumptuous founder of Babel. From Calvin onward, his name has stood for tyranny, an interpretation that happens to be congenial with established conventions in English literature. Spenser's *Fairie Queene*, perhaps reflecting Dante, associates him with proud tyrants. To Milton, he is an encroaching despot.[175] Through his use of intertwined biblical and literary allusion, Smollett thus suggests that the Yorkshire squire is playing the domestic tyrant.

The influence of exegesis may be traced, not only through the use of implicit quotation of criticism, but also, sometimes, in the overall design of narratives. Goldsmith, no less than Fielding, echoed contemporary hermeneutic writings, not least in his problematical and puzzling novel, the 'singular tale',[176] *The Vicar of Wakefield*. There is ample evidence to suggest that the narrator's biblical diction, appropriate enough for a clergyman, often mirrors traditional exposition of the Bible. For instance, his use of commercial language to discuss morality is congenial with the commonplace trading metaphors appealing to the practice of Christian virtue, hence accumulation of spiritual capital that would bear interest in the world beyond.[177] It is only natural that the Vicar should cite other clichés such as the pride of family, philosophy of contentment, or the moral virtues of benevolence and prudence.[178] This last theme, however, relates to the general meaning of the book, undeniably based on the Job paradigm.[179] The very structure of the novel illustrates the Vicar's Job-like progress through the vicissitudes of life to the sublime of love. The author's emphasis on the sublime may be seen to parallel Lowth's stress on the sublimity of Hebrew poetry[180] and the development of contemporary aesthetic theories.[181]

Conclusion

The wheel had come full circle. Literary criticism had exerted an influence on biblical exegesis that, in turn, pervaded contemporary literature. In the process, Scripture had been secularized and modern hermeneutics had been born. The questions raised dealt with authorship of the Pentateuch, interpretations of Old Testament prophecy, the reality of New Testament miracles, the need for a revised version of the Bible, a fresh awareness of the problems arising from the use of translation, and reflection on narrative. It is probably no coincidence that the birth of modern criticism took place almost simultaneously with the rise of the novel.

The complexity of the issue should not be oversimplified. As might be expected in a century teeming with new ideas, divisions did not run along denominational, national or party-political lines. However, one should guard against an idealized vision of the 're-public of letters'. There was little neutrality or irenicism in the international community of critics. Simon and Houbigant wanted to make a case in point against Protestant theology; Ancients quarrelled with Moderns; the *philosophes* fought the Roman church and Anglican apologetes argued with Deists.

In the latter half of the century, when the Deistic debate was waning and the literary approach becoming more 'sentimental' than rational, interest in biblical studies faded away in Britain, at the very time when the resurgence of cultural nationalism and intellectual life was reviving it in Germany. The sharp renewal of interest in the early 1790s, caused by the impact in particular of the German higher criticism, was almost at once obliterated by the conservative backlash against the French Revolution. Not until the early 1820s were continental ideas again freely to be discussed in Britain, and by then it was in the context of a very different intellectual climate.

NOTES

1   The best two books about the life and works of Richard Simon have been written by modern Oratorians: Jean Steinmann (*Richard Simon: Les Origines de l'exégèse biblique*, Paris, 1960) and Paul Auvray (*Richard Simon 1638–1712: Etude bio-bibliographique avec des textes inédits*, Paris, 1974). Father Auvray's notes and documents on Richard Simon are deposited (carton VIII^3) at the Oratorian archives, 75 rue de Vaugirard, 75006 Paris. I must thank the present archivist, Father Join-Lambert, for his generous assistance.
    For a more complete bibliography of Richard Simon, see A.–M.–P. Ingold (ed.), *Essai de bibliographie oratorienne* (Paris, 1880–2), pp. 121–63.

2   Due to Bossuet's successful ban of the book (cf. infra), very few copies of the first edition are available. Unless otherwise specified, all quotations refer to the second, more imperfect, edition, *Histoire critique du Vieux Testament, par le R.P. Richard Simon, Prestre de la Congregation de l'Oratoire. Suivant la copie, imprimée à Paris*, n.p. [Elzevier, Amsterdam], 1680, in-4°, 612 pp. The original spelling has been dutifully respected.

3   '*Je suis persuadé qu'on ne peut lire la Bible avec fruit, si l'on n'est auparavant instruit de ce qui regarde la Critique du Texte*' (Simon, *Vieux Testament*, p. 2). ('It is impossible to understand thoroughly the Holy Scriptures unless we first know the different states of the Text of these Books according to the different times and places, and be instructed of all the several changes that have happened to it.') Whenever possible, a contemporary translation of Simon's *Vieux Testament* will be quoted and subsequently referred to as O.T.: *A Critical History of the Old Testament. Written Originally in French by Father Simon, Priest of the Congregation of the Oratory; And Since Translated into English, By a Person of Quality* (London, 1682, n.p.).

4   The phrase '*sans aucuns préjugés*' (without any prejudice) is repeated, see for instance Simon, *Vieux Testament*, pp. 147 and 296.

5   Ibid., p. 38 and O.T., p. 40.

6 Ibid., p. 37 and *O.T.*, p. 38: '*Ces façons de parler écrites des deux côtés, & écrites deçà et delà semblent estre les mesmes, mais énoncées differemment, & cepandant plusieurs Interpretes tant Juifs que chrestiens ont beaucoup raffiné sur ce passage ... parce qu'on n'a pas assez fait de reflexion sur le style de l'Ecriture*' ('these ways of speaking, writ on both sides, and writ on this side, and that, seem to be the same, but differently exprest; yet nevertheless many both Jewish and Christian Interpreters have been very curious upon this passage ... because they have not sufficiently considered the style of the Scripture').

7 Cf. infra pp. 158–62.

8 Simon, *Vieux Testament*, p. 37.

9 '*Peut-on s'imaginer, par exemple, qu'un Historien ait écrit l'Histoire de la Creation de l'Homme avec le peu d'ordre qui se trouve dans les premiers chapitres de la Genese, où les mesmes choses sont repetées plusieurs fois sans aucune méthode, & comme hors d'oeuvre? Et de plus aprés que l'homme & la femme ont esté créés au chap.1.verset 27. on suppose que la femme n'a pas encore esté faite, & l'on décrit au chap. suivant la maniere dont elle fut tirée de la côte d'Adam,*' ibid., p. 39. ('For example, can any one believe that an Historian shoud write the History of the Creation of Man with so little order as there is in the first Chapter of *Genesis*, where the same things are several times repeated without method, and as it were besides the purpose? and moreover after the Man and the Woman were created in the first Chapter and 27th verse, the Woman is supposed not to be made, and in the following Chapter the manner how she was taken from *Adam*'s side is described,' *O.T.*, p. 41).

10 See Georges Gusdorf, *Dieu, la nature, l'homme au siècle des Lumières* (Paris, 1972) pp. 198–200 and Adolphe Lods, 'Jean Astruc et la critique biblique au XVIIIè siècle', *Revue d'histoire et de philosophie religieuse* (Strasbourg & Paris, 1924). Eugène Ritter's 'Jean Astruc auteur des *Conjectures sur la Genèse*', *BHPF* (1916) pp. 274–87, is mostly biographical.

11 '*Il y a bien de l'apparence que si un seul auteur avoit composé cet Ouvrage, il se seroit expliqué en bien moins de paroles, principalement dans une Histoire,*' Simon, *Vieux Testament*, p. 36. ('It is probable that if onely [sic] one Authour had composed this Work he would have explained himself in fewer words, especially in a History,' *O.T.*, p. 37).

12 *Traduction oecuménique de la Bible: Ancien Testament* (Paris, 1975), hereafter referred to under the acronym widely used in the French-speaking world, *TOB*; n. *h*, p. 53. The New Testament had been published as early as 1972. A new edition of the complete Bible was published in November 1988.

13 '*J'ay aussi nommé ces Prophetes, Scribes, ainsi qu'ils sont appellés dans la Bible, ou Ecrivains publics, pour les distinguer des Ecrivains particuliers.... On remarquera ... que ces Prophetes ou Ecrivains*'

publics, n'estoient pas seulement chargés de recueillir les actes de ce qui arrivoit de leur temps, & de les mettre dans les Archives; mais ils donnoient quelquefois une nouvelle forme aux actes qui avoient esté recueillis par leur [sic] predecesseurs, en y ajoûtant ou diminuant selon qu'ils le jugeoient à propos,' Simon, *Vieux Testament*, pp. 3 and 4. ('Besides, ... these same Prophets, which may be call'd publick writers, for the distinguishing of them from other private Writers, had the liberty of collecting out of the ancient Acts which were kept in the Registers of the Republick, and of giving a new form to these same Acts by adding or diminishing what they thought fit,' *O.T.*, n.p.).

14 See for instance J(ean) C(laude) Ver(recchia), 'Exégèse', in *Dictionnaire encyclopédique de la Bible*, ed. Centre Informatique et Bible Abbaye de Maredsous (Paris, 1987), p. 453, and J(ean) M(argain), 'Simon, Richard', in ibid., p. 1209.

15 Simon, *Vieux Testament*, p. 5 and *O.T.*, n.p.

16 *'Il faut avant toutes choses établir un Texte Hebreu & en marquer les diverses leçons selon les regles de la Critique, lesquelles on a coutume d'observer dans les autres Livres,'* ibid., p. 396. ('We ought first of all to establish a Hebrew Text, and observe its various Readings according to the Rules of Criticism, as we use to do in other books', *O.T.*, book III p. 3).

17 *'Ce travail qui demande une connoissance exacte de ces Livres, & une grande recherche des Exemplaires manuscrits, s'appelle* Critique, *parce qu'on juge des meilleures leçons qu'on doit conserver dans le texte'*, preface to Richard Simon, *Histoire critique du texte du Nouveau Testament, Où l'on établit la Vérité des Actes sur lesquels la Religion Chrêtienne est fondée* (Rotterdam, 1689); ('This kind of Labour, which requires an exact knowledg [sic] of Books, joyned with a strict enquiring into the Manuscripts, is termed *Critical*; in as much as it Judges and Determines the most Authentick Readings, which ought to be inserted into the Text,' *A Critical History of the Text of the New Testament; Wherein Is Firmly Establish'd the Truth of those Acts on which the Foundation of Christian Religion is Laid* [London, 1689], n.p., subsequently referred to as *N.T.*). A few lines later he adds: *'il seroit inutile de repeter icy ce qu'on a déjà dit ailleurs touchant le mot de* Critique, *qui est un terme d'art, & qui est en quelque façon consacré aux Ouvrages où l'on examine les diverses leçons, pour rétablir les véritables.'* (It is useless to repeat here what we said in another place concerning the word *Critick* which in some sense is bestowed on all Works whose designs are to examin the various readings and establish the true.'

18 For a detailed study of Scaliger's methods, see Anthony Grafton, *Joseph Scaliger: A Study in the History of Classical Scholarship I Textual Criticism and Exegesis* (Oxford, 1983).

19 For instance A.-G.Hamman, *L'épopée du livre: Du scribe à l'imprimerie* (Paris, 1985).

20 Georges Gusdorf, in a thought-provoking book, *Les Origines de l'herméneutique* (Paris, 1988) has forceful words on the 'sterilization of hermeneutics' in Catholic thought after the Council of Trent. Even though there was a long tradition of literary analysis of the Scriptures, from the writings of such Fathers as Theodoret of Cyr, the seventeenth-century critical revolution, reviving the humanists' interest in the text as such, demystified the religious status of the Bible. The novelty consisted in focusing on the literal and historical sense that had hitherto been either despised and ignored or incorporated as one of the many hermeneutical strata. The new emphasis was on exegesis rather than hermeneutics.

21 *De praescriptione haereticorum*, XXXI, 3; what precisely Simon has to say on Walton is that 'he prefers the most ancient Copies before the modern ones because, according to him they come nigher the Original: This however is not altogether true in the Hebrew Copies of the Bible. . . . Walton herein wholly agrees, with the Opinion of the *Catholick* Church,' O.T., book III p. 163. ('*Il préfére les plus anciens Exemplaires au [sic] plus nouveaux par ce que selon lui ils approchent d'avantage des Originaux ce qui n'est pourtant pas tout-à fait vray dans les Exemplaires Hebreux de la Bible. . . . Au reste Walton s'accorde parfaitement en cela avec les sentimens de l'Eglise catholique*,' Simon, *Vieux Testament*, p. 552.)

22 Ibid., p. 585. He was to repeat the idea several years later in a tract entitled *Novum Bibliorum Polyglottorum Synopsis* (Ultrajecti, 1684).

23 It is worth noting that Milton too appreciated Cappel's earlier books and quoted them, at least once, in a discussion of the date of the first Epistle to Timothy: 'Ludovicus Capellus has successfully shown by irrefutable argument that this epistle too was composed in the reign of Claudius,' *A Defence of the People of England*, in *Complete Prose Works of John Milton*, vol. IV, 1650–1655, ed. Don M. Wolfe (New Haven and London, 1966), p. 390. I must thank the Milton scholar Roger Lejosne for drawing my attention to this fact.

24 '*Le plus sçavant ouvrage que nous ayions sur les diverses leçons & les autres changemens du Vieux Testament, est le Livre de Louïs Capelle . . . intitulé* Critica Sacra. *Il est vray que ce Livre déplût tellement à ceux de sa Religion, qu'ils en empécherent l'impression. . . . Le P. Morin de l'Oratoire . . . crût rendre un grand service à l'Eglise contre les Protestans en publiant cet ouvrage*,' Simon, *Vieux Testament*, p. 9. ('The most learned Work which we have upon the several readings and other changes of the Old Testament is the Book of *Ludovicus Capellus . . .* intituled *Critica Sacra.* 'Tis true this Book so much displeased those of his religion that they stopt the Impression of it. Father *Morin* of the Oratory thought he should doe great service for the Church against the Protestants in publishing this Work,' O.T., p. 10).

25 The *Lettre de La Peyrère à Philotime. Dans laquelle il expose les*

raisons qui l'ont obligé à abiurer la secte de Calvin qu'il professoit, &
le Liure des Preadamites qu'il auoit mis au iour. Traduit en François,
du Latin imprimé à Rome. Par l'Auteur mesme (Paris, 1658) tells a
sorry tale.

26 See Richard H. Popkin, *Isaac La Peyrère (1596–1676): His Life,*
Work and Influence (Leiden, 1987), reviewed by Anthony Grafton in
the *TLS*, 12–18 February 1988, pp. 151–2.

27 Isaac La Peyrère, *Prae Adamitae. Sive Exercitatio super Versibus*
duodecimo, decimotertio, & decimoquarto, capitis quinti Epistolae
D. Pauli ad Romanos. Quibus inducuntur Primi Homines ante Ada-
mum conditi (n.p., 1650). Although the predecessors of La Peyrère's
preadamite theories can be listed (cf. Popkin, *Isaac La Peyrère*, ch. 3),
the invention of the word may be ascribed to him.

28 '*Quoy qu'ils ayent entr'eux des sentiments contraires pour les autres*
choses, ils se sont neantmoins reünis & accordez en celle cy; d'atta-
quer mon Liure, et de le battre en ruïne,' *Lettre à Philotime*, p. 76.
(Although their opinions differ on other things, nevertheless they
have agreed and consented on this one: to attack my book and
destroy it).

29 Ibid., p. 77: '*Il a fallu absolument que i'aye cedé à l'autorité de tant*
d'autorités.' (It was absolutely necessary for me to yield to the authority of so many authorities.)

30 Ibid., p. 77: '*Et ie n'ay pas délibéré si ie cederois à l'autorité. Je n'ay*
esté en suspens, & n'ay hesité que sur ce point. A quelle autorité ie
cederois, & à laquelle ie me rendrois.' (And I did not ponder on
yielding to authority. I only wavered, and hesitated on the following
point. To which authority I would yield, and to whom I would
submit.)

31 There is evidence that La Peyrère, for over 30 years secretary then
librarian to the Prince of Condé, had met Hobbes: see Popkin, *Isaac*
La Peyrère, pp. 40–9; 72; 88–9 and *passim*.

32 Auvray, *Richard Simon*, pp. 62–4.

33 Paul Auvray convincingly argues that Richard Simon did not know of
Spinoza's *Tractatus* until after he had written his *Vieux Testament*:
'Richard Simon et Spinoza', in *Religion, Erudition et critique à la fin*
du XVIIè siècle et au début du XVIIIè, ed. Université de Strasbourg
(Paris, 1968) pp. 201–14.

On Simon's Jewish sources and Hebrew scholarship, see William
McKane, *Selected Christian Hebraists* (Cambridge, 1989), pp. 111–
50, as well as Bertram Eugene Schwarzbach, 'Les sources rabbiniques
de la critique biblique', in *Le Grand Siècle et la Bible*, ed. Jean-Robert
Armogathe (Paris, 1989, vol. 6 of the '*Bible de tous les temps*'
collection, hereafter referred to as *BTT6*), pp. 207–31. In the same
volume, John D. Woodbridge has an article on 'Richard Simon le
"père de la critique biblique"' (pp. 193–206).

34 Ernest Renan, 'L'exégèse biblique et l'esprit français', *Revue des deux*
mondes, 60 (1865), p. 240: '*je ne sais si Richard Simon avait lu*

l'ouvrage de Spinoza; en tout cas, il n'en relève pas.' (I do not know whether Richard Simon had read Spinoza's work; anyway, it is irrelevant.)

35 Madeleine Francès and Robert Misrahi discuss Renan's argument for Simon's superiority in the French edition of Spinoza's complete works, *Oeuvres complètes*, ed. Roland Caillois, Madeleine Francès and Robert Misrahi (Paris, 1954), n. 1, pp. 1463–4.

36 For instance in *Nouveau Testament*, p. 275.

37 Ibid., p. 277–8: '*On a montré ailleurs, qu'il y avoit dans l'ancienne Vulgate* inspirata & utilis, *comme il y a dans le Grec, & qu'il faut expliquer ce passage* collectivement, *et non pas* distributivement. . . . *On traduira* . . . Toute l'Ecriture qui a été inspirée est utile, *& non pas* . . . toute Ecriture inspirée de Dieu est utile.' ('But it was shown elsewhere, that in the ancient vulgar, it was *Inspirata & utilis*, i.e. *is inspired and profitable*; as it is in the Greek, and that we are to expound that Passage *collectively*, and not *distributively*. . . . The Translation will be, *All the Scripture which was given by Inspiration is profitable*, and not *All Scripture that has been given by Divine Inspiration, is profitable*,' N.T., p. 63.)

38 Simon, *Vieux Testament*, p. 296 and O.T., book II, p. 92.

39 O.T., book II, p. 93.

40 Simon, *Vieux Testament*, p. 298 and O.T., book II, p. 93: 'The Fathers of the Council examin'd not this Translation according to the rules of Criticism, thereby to judg [sic] whether it agreed with the Original, but follow'd herein the usual custom of the Church.' A few lines earlier, he had written away the contradiction with his general principles, perhaps in an attempt to appease the ecclesiastical authorities, and stated 'whether the Vulgar is the only authentick and true Scripture, seems to me to be very frivolous.'

41 Simon, *Vieux Testament*, pp. 399–403 and O.T., book III, pp. 7–14.

42 Simon, *Vieux Testament*, p. 404 and O.T., book III, p. 12.

43 Simon, *Vieux Testament*, pp. 407–8 and O.T., book III, pp. 15–16.

44 *TOB, Ancien Testament*, n. *b*, p. 43.

45 *TOB* of course. Actually, the commentators of this modern ecumenical translation wanted to praise Simon's ill-fated attempt to edit a trans-denominational version of the Bible. That this staunch anti-Protestant should have agreed to take part in the project, launched by the ministers at Charenton, only shows his overriding scientific interest in the text. Indeed the *Projet d'une nouvelle version de l'Ecriture Sainte*, written as early as 1676, conveyed the same themes as Simon's later work: the need to know the relevant languages and be familiar with the mores alluded to in order to give as faithful a translation as possible. Unfortunately, the project, started in the inauspicious decade leading up to the revocation of the Edict of Nantes, was so much ahead of its time that it was almost bound to fail.

46   Altogether 1300 copies were destroyed, the first 600 of which before
     the title page had been printed. See Bibliothèque nationale, fonds
     français n° 21743: Livres défendus, F° 166 ff., 10 April–2 August
     1678, a transcript of which is to be found in the Oratorian archives.
47   The book was only published posthumously.
48   He was expelled as early as May 1678: see Oratoratian mss. archives:
     'Extrait des ordres et délibérations du Conseil de NTRP Général',
     folio 151, 18 & 21 May 1678. Paradoxically, he remained a staunch
     defender of the Roman faith to the end, and had the word 'presbyter'
     proudly engraved on his tombstone.
49   An indefatigable polemicist, he was involved in controversies not
     only with Bossuet but also with Isaac Vossius, Canon of Windsor;
     Paul Colomiès, Librarian to the Archbishop of Canterbury; Jaques
     Basnage, a Protestant minister at Rouen then Amsterdam; and, last
     but not least, the Arminian Jean Le Clerc: see Ingold, *Bibliographie*,
     pp. 126–30.
50   Ibid., n. 12, p. 125 and n. 96, p. 136.
51   Auvray, *Richard Simon*, p. 169.
52   *The Works of John Dryden: Poems 1681–84*, ed. H. T. Swedenberg,
     Jr (Berkeley, 1972), p. 340.
53   Georges Gusdorf argues that Simon's 'religious fanaticism' may have
     hindered the diffusion of his ideas among his potential readership:
     Les Origines de l'herméneutique, pp. 114–15.
        As far as sermon literature is concerned, hardly any text seems to
     have been published in this respect, if Sampson Letsome's *Index to
     the Sermons Published since the Restoration . . .* (London, 1753) is to
     be relied on. Admittedly, as I have shown elsewhere, only a small
     proportion (1–3 per cent) of the 13,000 sermons listed dealt with
     biblical studies: see 'L'Ecriture dans la prédication anglaise', in *Le
     Siècle des Lumières et la Bible*, ed. Yvon Belaval and Dominique
     Bourel (Paris, 1986), pp. 523–43. The book, volume 7 of the '*Bible
     de tous les temps*' collection, hereafter referred to as *BTT7*, covers a
     wide range of subjects related to the use or study of the Bible in the
     eighteenth century.
54   Gerard Reedy, *The Bible and Reason: Anglicans and Scripture in
     Late Seventeenth-Century England* (Philadelphia, 1985), pp. 109–10.
55   Ms.O.81, St John's College, Cambridge; first published and tran-
     scribed by Gerard Reedy in his informative book, *The Bible and
     Reason*, Appendix I. See also Robert Todd Carroll, *The Common-
     sense Philosophy of Religion of Bishop Edward Stillingfleet 1635–
     1699* (The Hague, 1975).
56   This word replaces 'Critick' which has been crossed out; one wonders
     whether the Bishop denied Richard Simon the status of biblical
     scholar. Why he did not publish this text with his other sermons also
     remains unanswered.
57   *The Works of John Dryden*, ed. Swedenberg, vol. 2, p. 343. It is
     worth noting, by the way, that Simon's book was apparently better

known in Holland than in Britain, which explains why the French
thinker exiled in Rotterdam, Pierre Bayle, did not feel it necessary
to expound the Oratorian's theories: see Elisabeth Labrousse, *Pierre
Bayle: Tome II Hétérodoxie et rigorisme* (The Hague, 1964) p. 338,
n. 75.

58   Reedy, *The Bible and Reason*, pp. 113–14 and 175, quotes a manuscript at the Bodleian Library (f.32, fols.1–2) in which Locke
summarized Simon's argument. See also Gabriel Bonno, *Les Relations intellectuelles de Locke avec la France* (Berkeley, 1955), p. 201,
and John Harrison and Peter Laslett, *The Library of John Locke*
(Oxford, 1971), nos 2673–2682[a].

59   Henri Justel to Locke, 25 November 1679, '*Vous aurez à la fin
l'Histoire critique de la Bible avec une anticritique qui sera bonne et
qui vaudra la Critique: mais il faut attendre encore un peu et avoir
patience,*' *The Correspondence of John Locke*, ed. E. S. de Beer
(Oxford, 1976), vol. 2, p. 129. (You will eventually have the Critical
history of the Bible, with an anticritical text that will be good and as
valuable as the Critical history: but you have to wait a little and be
patient.) Justel later discussed Simon's work, reprinted in Holland, in
another letter to Locke, dated 21 May 1680: ibid., p. 163. See also
Bonno, *Les relations intellectuelles*, pp. 89, 217 and *passim*.

60   Unfortunately, there is no reliable modern edition of this significant
text so far.

61   John Locke, *A Paraphrase and Notes on the Epistles of St. Paul to
the Galatians, 1 and 2 Corinthians, Romans, Ephesians*, ed. Arthur
W. Wainwright (Oxford, 1987).

62   John Locke, *The Reasonableness of Christianity*, preface: 'the sole
Reading of the Scripture ... for the understanding the Christian
Religion'.

63   For the text of *Religio Laici*, see *The Works of John Dryden*, ed.
Swedenberg, vol. 2, pp. 98–122 and Swedenberg's notes, ibid., pp.
340–68.

64   *The Works of John Dryden*, ed. Swedenberg, vol. 2, pp. 345; 347.

65   H. T. Swedenberg believes these lines 'should be interpreted as an
ironical observation', ibid., p. 365. Even their scansion is controversial: see Pierre Legouis (ed.), *Dryden Poèmes choisis* (Paris, n.d.
[1946]), p. 57.

66   For the text of Dryden's longest poem, see *The Works of John
Dryden: vol. 3 Poems 1685–1692*, ed. Earl Miner (Berkeley, 1969),
pp. 119–200, and the editor's notes, pp. 326–459.

67   For the text, see *The Works of John Dryden*, ed. Swedenberg, vol. 2,
pp. 3–36, and the editor's notes, ibid., pp. 209–85. An illuminating
analysis of Dryden's poetry in general and *Absalom and Achitophel*
in particular is to be found in Earl Miner, *Dryden's Poetry*
(Bloomington, 1967).

68   Cf. supra ch. 1, pp. 16–19.

69   Miner, *Dryden's Poetry*, p. 114.

70 Reedy, *The Bible and Reason*, pp. 80–8.

71 The classic study is by Hans W. Frei, *The Eclipse of Biblical Narrative: A Study of Eighteenth and Nineteenth Century Hermeneutics* (New Haven and London, 1974).

72 L. D. Reynolds and N. G. Wilson maintain that it is impossible to believe Bentley did not know of Richard Simon: *D'Homère à Erasme* (Paris, 1984), p. 128.

73 G. P. Goold, 'Richard Bentley: A Tercentenary Commemoration', *Harvard Studies in Classical Philology*, 67 (1963), pp. 285–302. This article, reproducing a lecture given before the Classics Club at Harvard, is tightly packed with information. For a modern comprehensive study of Bentley's achievements, see also R. J. White, *Dr. Bentley: A Study in Academic Scarlet* (London, 1965).

74 The traditional textbook example shows that *ois* (the ewe) comes from *oFis; evidence of the former existence of the digamma in this word appears in its Latin equivalent, *ouis*. The fall of this intervocalic letter explains many a contraction and apparent irregularity in the morphology of Greek. It is a particularly important notion for one to understand the evolution from the Ionian dialect in which the Homeric poems were written to the Attic idiom used in the golden age of classic eloquence.

75 On the notion of 'republic of letters', see Annie Barnes, *Jean Le Clerc (1657–1736) et la République des lettres* (Paris, 1938), pp. 12–14 and *passim*.

76 On the concept of 'polyhistor', see ibid., p. 154.

77 For reasons of availability, I have used a nineteenth-century edition, Richard Bentley, *Dissertation upon the Epistles of Phalaris, Themistocles, Socrates, Euripides, And upon the Fables of Aesop: Also, Epistola ad Joannem Millium*, ed. Alexander Dyce (London, 1836), 2 vols.

    For a background study of the controversy, see Richard Foster Jones, 'The Background of the Battle of the Books', *Washington University Studies*, 7 (April 1920), esp. pp. 99–162.

78 Jonathan Swift, *A Tale of a Tub To Which is Added The Battle of the Books and the Mechanical Operation of the Spirit*, ed. A. C. Guthkelch and D. Nichol Smith (Oxford, 1920; 2nd edn, 1958).

79 'But, the Manuscript, by the Injury of Fortune, or Weather, being in several Places imperfect, we cannot learn to which side the Victory fell': ibid., 'The bookseller to the reader', p. 214.

80 Ibid., p. 258.

81 Ibid., p. 258: 'And now ★★★★★★★★★★★★★★★ ... *Desunt caetera.*'

82 Ibid., p. 220.

83 Ibid., p. 240.

84 Jonathan Swift, *Gulliver's Travels* ed. Paul Turner (Oxford, 1971), part III, ch. 2; p. 155.

85 Ibid., p. 158.

86 Ibid., n. 1, p. 339; n. 14, p. 341. See also Emile Pons, 'Note sur les procédés swiftiens de création linguistique dans "Les Voyages de Gulliver"' and 'Glossaire des langues gullivériennes', *Jonathan Swift: Oeuvres* (Paris, 1965), pp. 9–24. Recent Swift criticism has developed other interpretations that are not immediately relevant here (Whiggish financial chicanery, the Cartesians, or an immoral Jerusalem – see *The Scriblerian*, 20 [Spring 1988] p. 226).

87 Swift, *A Tale of a Tub*, p. 94. The book is so well known an example of the use of literary critical devices to satirize pedantry and the conceit of learning in contemporary criticism that it is unnecessary to expand on the subject.

88 *Dr. Bentley's Proposals for Printing a New Edition of the Greek Testament, And St. Hierons's Latin Version. With a Full Answer to all the Remarks of a Late Pamphleteer* (London, 1721), p. 3.

89 Adam Fox, *John Mill and Richard Bentley: A Study of Textual Criticism of the New Testament* (Oxford, 1954), p. 125.

90 *Dr. Bentley's Proposals*, p. 4.

91 Ibid., p. 4.

92 Cf. n. 88.

93 Conyers Middleton, *Some Farther Remarks, Paragraph by Paragraph, Upon Proposals Lately Publish'd for A New Edition of a Greek and Latin Testament, by Richard Bentley. Containing A Full Answer to the Editor's Late Defence of his Said Proposals, as Well as to All his Objections there Made Against my Former Remarks* (London, 1721).

94 See the discussion ibid., pp. 63–7.

95 Fox, *John Mill and Richard Bentley*, p. 125.

96 Benjamin Kennicott, *Vetus Testamentum Hebraicum, Cum Variis Lectionibus* (Oxford, 1776–80), vol. I, pp. 70–113.

97 *The Poems of Alexander Pope*, vol. 5, *The Dunciad*, ed. James Sutherland (London, 1943).

98 *The Works of Samuel Johnson* (London, 1787), vol. IV, p. 126n.

99 *The Poems of Alexander Pope*, vol. VII, *The Iliad of Homer: Books I–IX*, ed. Maynard Mack (London and New Haven, 1967), p. 82.

100 On the history of theories of translation from the sixteenth century onwards, see Roger Zuber, *Perrot d'Ablancourt et ses 'Belles Infidèles': Traduction et Critique de Balzac à Boileau* (Paris, 1968). One of the two authors mentioned in the title is Jean-Louis Guez de Balzac, not the more famous nineteenth-century novelist, of course!

101 Pope, *Iliad*, ed. Mack, pp. xxxviii–xli.

102 Ibid., pp. lxxxiii–lxxxviii.

103 Ibid., 'Preface to *The Iliad of Homer*' p. 17.

104 Ibid., p. 17.

105 For a detailed study of Pope's translation, see H. A. Mason, *To Homer through Pope: An Introduction to Homer's* Iliad *and Pope's Translation* (London, 1972) and Pope, *Iliad*, ed. Mack, pp. xciv–cv.

106 Ll. 1–6, ibid., pp. 82; 85.
107 Samuel Johnson, *The Lives of the Most Eminent English Poets; With Observations on their Works* (London, 1781), vol. IV, p. 48.
108 Pope, *Iliad*, ed. Mack bk. I, ll. 291–2, p. 100; Homer, *Iliad*, I, ll. 220–1.
109 N. A. Joukovsky, *Alexander Pope* (Harmondsworth, 1971), p. 289.
110 L. 220.
111 Pope, *Iliad*, ed. Mack, p. 99.
112 M. Bitaubé, *L'Iliade d'Homère, Avec des Remarques; Précédée de Réflexions sur Homere & sur la traduction des Poëtes* (Lyon, 1796), p. 44: '*je ne puis mieux faire ici qu'en renvoyant le lecteur à l'excellente préface de Pope sur Homere.*' (I can do no better here than refer the reader to Pope's excellent Preface on Homer.) I am grateful to M. l'abbé Perrin, *curé* at Faremoutiers, for drawing my attention to this edition. Though published one year later than Wolf's *Prolegomena ad Homerum*, it does not even mention the existence of the book that sparked off a revolution comparable in Homeric studies to what the questioning of Mosaic authorship of the Pentateuch had meant in biblical criticism.
113 Ibid., p. 25: '*Pope, si judicieux, fut ... un peu entraîné par des opinions exagérées qui portoient le sceau de l'antiquité.*' (Sensible though he was, Pope was led by excessive opinions that bore the stamp of antiquity.)
114 On Houbigant's life and works, see Ingold, *Bibliographie* pp. 62–3. The Oratorian archives in Paris hold relevant documents and manuscript material.
115 C.-F. Houbigant, *Conférences de Metz Entre un Juif, un Protestant & deux Docteurs en Sorbonne* (Leyde, 1750).
116 '*L'autenticité de la* Vulgate *ne fait pas un préjugé contre la Critique Sacrée, puisqu'elle n'en canonise point tous les sens particuliers,*' ibid., preface, n.p. (The authenticity of the Vulgate is no case against sacred criticism, since it does not canonise all its particular meanings.)
117 *Biblia Hebraica Cum notis criticis et versione latina ad notas criticas facta* (Paris, 1753).
118 '*La Tradition, qui est regardée comme l'Interprete de l'ecriture, ne suffit pas pour nous la faire entendre, puisqu'elle n'embrasse que la moindre partie des Livres Saints, & qu'elle se borne aux interprétations dogmatiques, ou à celles qui se trouvent unanimes,*' *Conférences de Metz*, preface (Tradition, which is regarded as the interpreter of Scripture, is not enough to make us understand it, since it only covers the least part of Holy Writ, & is confined to dogmatic interpretations or to those that are unanimously accepted.)
119 The 'Masorah' or 'Massora' is a collection of critical notes on the text of the Hebrew Bible, compiled mainly in Aramaic from the sixth to the tenth centuries AD by a school of biblical scholars known as the 'Masoretes' or 'Massoretes'. The 'masoretic' text is the canon of

Hebrew scriptures as set by the Massoretes. The oldest masoretic manuscript dates back to 820–50, but it only records the Pentateuch. The most ancient complete manuscript, the Aleppo codex, was copied in the first decades of the tenth century.

Several older texts, such as the Samaritan Pentateuch or the version used by the Septuagint – and the Dead Sea scrolls discovered in the mid-twentieth century – provide significant differences from the rival consonantal text on which the Massoretes based their work. Hence the temptation to 'correct' the masoretic canon.

Houbigant's position, however, was not devoid of denominational bias. On the whole, Protestant exegesis had, from the sixteenth century, supported the masoretic 'truth', while Counter-Reformation theology was based on the greater authenticity and textual superiority of the Septuagint and the Samaritan Pentateuch. One of Houbigant's – and Simon's – predecessors in the Oratorian order, Jean Morin (1591–1659), a convert from Calvinism, had, typically, taken great care to sap the authority of the Masorah.

120 Martin Lister records in his *Journey to Paris in the Year 1698* (London, 2nd edn, 1699), p. 132, that when he visited Malebranche he was shown many Greek and Hebrew manuscripts, including the famous Samaritan Pentateuch, which appeared to him as a more recent copy than that held in the Cottonian Library. Two other documents give us a good idea of the Oratorian library holdings in the period under review. An undated catalogue drawn by Richard Simon himself lists seven '*biblia manuscripta*', including '*Pentateuchus Samaritanus*', of course ('Catalogus librorum orientalium qui in bibliotheca Oratorii Parisiensis asservantur, descriptus a cel. Pat. Ric. Simon', Bibliothèque nationale mss. hebr. 1295). Another manuscript catalogue written a century later by the then archivist, Father Adry, mentions twelve '*codices orientales sacri hebraici*' ('Catalogus Manuscriptorum Codicum qui extant in Bibliothecâ Domûs Parisiensis Oratorii Domini Jesu, cum Notis Joannis Morin – Jacobi Le Long – Ricardi Simon – Car. Fr. Houbigant – Joan. Feliciss. Adry; Pars Prima, Codices Orientales [Parisiis: 1815] Oratorian archives XIX² 10A). Here the cataloguer took care to note whether the masoretic signs were thought to be written in a later hand ('*manu recentiori*' [no. 5] or '*in eo* [no. 6] *masora sed addita*') or at the same time as the text ('*in eo* [no. 7] *notae Masoreticae eodem tempore scriptae*').

121 It was set in new fount cast specially for the occasion, at the high cost of 40,000 francs, and deservedly praised for its beauty.

122 Kennicott, 'Dissertatio Generalis In Vetus Testamentum Hebraicum; Cum Variis Lectionibus, Ex Codicibus Manuscriptis et Impressis', *Vetus Testamentum Hebraicum*, p. 59.

123 Mireille Hadas-Lebel, 'Le P. Houbigant et la critique textuelle', *BTT* 7, p. 111.

124 Augustin Calmet, *Commentaire littéral sur tous les livres de l'Ancien*

et du Nouveau Testament (Paris); the first volume is dated 1707. See Patrick Marsauche, 'La Musique guérit les mélancolies: Etudes sur le commentaire de dom Calmet', *Les règles de l'interprétation*, ed. Michel Tardieu and Centre d'études des religions du Livre (Paris, 1987), pp. 195–207, and 'Historiographie et histoire des mentalités: Etude du *Commentaire Littéral* et des *Dissertations* de DOM Augustin CALMET (1672–1757)', thèse de doctorat de 3è cycle, Université de Paris X, 1982, 1 typescript vol., 259 pp., as well as 'Présentation de Dom Augustin Calmet (1672–1757): *Dissertation sur les Possesions du Démon*', BTT6, pp. 233–53.

125 Calmet, *Commentaire littéral*, vol. I, p. 2.

126 Richard Simon's name does not appear in the index to the first volume, for instance, or in the commentary upon the relevant passages in Genesis, although the preface to the Pentateuch acknowledges the fact that Moses cannot have written it completely, and that the narrative is not straightforward, which may suggest that the text was revised by several editors: ibid., vol. I, p. 13.

127 '*Le Pentateuque est l'ouvrage de Moïse. Il seroit inutile de s'étendre ici à prouver cette vérité, aprés tant d'excellens traitez que l'on a faits pour la soûtenir*', ibid., vol. I, p. 13. (The Pentateuch is Moses's work. It would be useless to enlarge here upon proof of this truth, after so many excellent treatises have been written to support it.)

128 On the plural '*elohim*' and its use in Gen. 1, see Edouard Lipinski, 'Elohim', in *Dictionnaire encyclopédique de la Bible*, pp. 404–5.

129 Ibid., p. 2, '*CREAVIT DEUS.... Dans l'Hébreu, au lieu de* Dieu créa, *on lit à la lettre*, les Dieux créa, *d'où quelques un (Origen.S. Jerom.S. Epiphan.) ont tiré une preuve de la Trinité des Personnes, dans l'unité de l'essence Divine.*' (*CREAVIT DEUS....* In the Hebrew text, instead of God created, one reads, literally, the Gods created, whence some (Origen.S.Jerom.S. Epiphan.) have drawn evidence of the Trinity of persons in the unity of one Godhead.)

130 *La Bible enfin expliquée par plusieurs aumôniers de S.M.L.R.D.P.* (London, n.p., 1776), 1: '*Du commencement les Dieux fit le Ciel & la terre.*' (From the beginning the Gods created Heaven & earth.) The note explains: '*le Texte Hébreu ... porte expressément: les Dieux fit, & non pas: Dieu créa*, Deus creavit, *comme le porte la Vulgate.*' (The Hebrew text has, literally: *the Gods made*, not: *God created*, as in the Vulgate.) Like dom Calmet, Voltaire accurately translated the verb in the singular.

131 Alfred J. Bingham, 'Voltaire and the New Testament', *SVEC*, 24 (1963), p. 184.

132 Marie-Hélène Cotoni, 'Voltaire, Rousseau, Diderot', BTT7, pp. 788–95.

133 Bertram Eugene Schwarzbach, 'L'*Encyclopédie* de Diderot et de d'Alembert', BTT 7, pp. 759–77.

134 *Encyclopédie ou Dictionnaire raisonné des sciences des arts et des*

métiers (1751–1780); facsimile ed. (Stuttgart-Bad Cannstatt, 1966), vol. II, pp. 222–7.

135 'Nous allons finir cet article par le plan d'un traité qui renfermeroit tout ce qu'on peut desirer sur les questions préliminaires de la Bible,' ibid., vol. II, p. 226, col. 2. (We shall end this entry with the plan of a treatise that would include all that one may wish to know on introductory issues about the Bible.)

136 Ibid., vol. XII, pp. 315–17.

137 Renan, 'L'exégèse biblique et l'esprit français', p. 245.

138 See Marie-Hélène Cotoni's very informative work, particularly *L'Exégèse du Nouveau Testament dans la philosophie française du dix-huitième siècle* (*SVEC* 20, Oxford, 1984).

139 It is not proper to rehearse the deist controversy here. The remarkable book on the subject is by Henning Graf Reventlow, *The Authority of the Bible and the Rise of the Modern World* (London, 1984), a translation and second edition of *Bibelautorität und Geist der Moderne, Die Bedeutung des Bibelverständnisses für die geistesgeschichtliche und politische Entwicklung in England von der Reformation bis zur Aufklärung* (Göttingen, 1980). The translator, John Bowden, needs praise, for his text reads extremely well.

140 Reventlow's book quoted above is one of the best accounts of the subject.

141 Robert Lowth, *Isaiah: A New Translation; With a Preliminary Dissertation, And Notes Critical, Philological, And Explanatory* (London, 1778) is an application of the central doctrine of Oriental parallelism that Lowth had developed in the lectures on the Sacred Poetry of the Hebrews delivered at Oxford between 1741 and 1751, published in Latin and internationally acclaimed in 1753, then translated into English in 1787. For an extended discussion of the revolutionary impact of Lowth's lectures, see Stephen Prickett, *Words and the Word: Language, Poetics and Biblical Interpretation* (Cambridge, 1986), pp. 41–3; 105–17.

142 His prescriptive *Short Introduction to English Grammar* (London, 1762) was one of the most influential handbooks of the English language.

143 Lowth, *Isaiah*, p. liii.

144 Kennicott, 'Dissertatio Generalis', *Vetus Testamentum Hebraicum*, p. 11.

145 It was first recorded in 1757. There is evidence of its use in France from 1777.

146 Lowth, *Isaiah*, pp. lxi & lxii.

147 William McKane lists a few instances of modern readings supported by Kennicott's edition, e.g. Ps. 22:17; 79:7; Prov. 19:1, and, interestingly enough, the parallelism in Prov. 10:10: 'Benjamin Kennicott: An Eighteenth-Century Researcher', *Journal of Theological Studies*, N.S., 28 (October 1977), pp. 456–7.

180 Françoise Deconinck-Brossard

148 Benjamin Kennicott, *The Ten Annual Accounts of the Collation of Hebrew MSS of the Old Testament; Begun in 1760, and Compleated in 1769* (Oxford, 1770), p. 7.

149 On Jean Le Clerc, a scholar of many interests, who never tired of vigorous polemic and enjoyed a solid fame in his time, see Barnes, *Jean Le Clerc*, and René Voeltzel, 'Jean Le Clerc (1657–1736) et la critique biblique', *Religion, érudition et critique*, pp. 33–52. See also Maria Cristina Pitassi, *Le Problème de la méthode critique chez Jean Le Clerc* (Leiden, 1987).

150 Lowth, *Isaiah*, p. lxvi.

151 Ibid., p. lxix.

152 Yvon Belaval and Dominique Bourel, 'Le Livre et sa science', *BTT7*, p. 87.

153 Anna-Ruth Löwenbrück, 'Johann David Michaelis et les débuts de la critique biblique', *BTT7*, pp. 116–17 and Gusdorf, *Les Origines de l'herméneutique*, pp. 133–4.

154 Stephen Prickett, 'Poetry and Prophecy: Bishop Lowth and the Hebrew Scriptures in Eighteenth-century England', in *Images of Belief in Literature*, ed. David Jasper (London, 1984), p. 89.

155 Löwenbrück, 'Johann David Michaelis', p. 119.

156 The only monograph so far on the Hebraist is by Brian Hepworth: *Robert Lowth* (Boston, 1978).

157 Lowth, *Isaiah*, p. 30.

158 On Challoner's revision of the Catholic 'Douai Bible', see Richard Luckett, 'Bishop Challoner: The Devotionary Writer', in *Challoner and his Church: A Catholic Bishop in Georgian England*, ed. Eamon Duffy (London, 1981), pp. 71–89. An interesting discussion of eighteenth-century biblical translation in general is to be found in Susie I. Tucker, 'Biblical Translation in the Eighteenth Century', *Essays and Studies*, 25 (1972), pp. 106–20.

159 Richard Lowth, *A Sermon Preached at the Visitation of the Honourable and Right Reverend Richard Lord Bishop of Durham, Held in the Parish-Church of St. Mary le Bow in Durham, On Thursday, July 27, 1758: Published at His Lordship's Request* (London, 1758), pp. 24–5.

160 See Marcel Brosseau, 'Essai sur les livres de spiritualité et de dévotion populaires en Angleterre de 1680 à 1760', thèse de doctorat d'Etat (U de la Sorbonne Nouvelle-Paris III, 1979), 3 typescript vols.

161 See Thomas S. Preston, 'Biblical Criticism, Literature and the Eighteenth-Century Reader', in *Books and their Readers in Eighteenth-Century England*, ed. Isabel Rivers (Leicester, 1982), pp. 97–126.

162 *Boswell's Life of Johnson*, ed. George Birkbeck Hill (Oxford, 1934) vol. III, p. 58.

163 The great book on the subject is Joseph Butler's *Analogy of Religion, Natural and Revealed, to the Constitution and Course of Nature* (1736), of which many nineteenth-century editions are still to be

found. See also Victor Harris, 'Allegory to Analogy in the Interpretation of Scriptures', *Philological Quarterly*, 45 (January 1966), pp. 1–23.

164 John Sharp, ms. sermon no. 24, n.p. The sermon was preached 70 times from 1750 to 1789. I must repeat here how grateful I am to the Durham Dean and Chapter Library for their kind help with my investigations into the Sharp corpus.

165 I have made this point elsewhere: Françoise Deconinck-Brossard, *Vie politique, sociale et religieuse en Grande-Bretagne d'après les sermons prêchés ou publiés dans le Nord de l'Angleterre 1738–1760* (Paris, 1984), vol. I, pp. 431–42.

166 Ibid., vol. I, pp. 426–9.

167 Henry Fielding, *Joseph Andrews* (Oxford, 1966), book III, ch. 8, p. 225.

168 Ibid., book I, ch. 3, p. 19.

169 Ibid., book I, ch. 3, p. 19.

170 Ibid., book I, ch. 12, pp. 46–7.

171 Ibid., book I, ch. 3, p. 19.

172 Ibid., book III, ch. 2, pp. 174–7.

173 Pope's poetry has been characterized as 'poetry of allusion'. See R. A. Brower, *Alexander Pope: The Poetry of Allusion* (Oxford, 1959).

174 Tobias Smollett, *The Expedition of Humphry Clinker*, ed. Lewis M. Knapp (London, 1966), 'To Dr. Lewis', p. 164.

175 David L. Jeffrey, 'A Dictionary of Biblical Tradition in English Literature', *Christianity & Literature*, 33 (1984), pp. 59–61.

176 Sven Bäckman, *This Singular Tale: A Study of 'The Vicar of Wakefield' and Its Literary Background* (Lund, 1971).

177 See Thomas R. Preston, 'The Uses of Adversity: Worldly Detachment and Heavenly Treasure in *The Vicar of Wakefield*', *Studies in Philology*, 81 (Spring 1984), pp. 229–51. I have shown elsewhere the frequent reference to Matt. 6:19–21 in eighteenth-century sermons: Deconinck-Brossard, *Vie politique, sociale et religieuse en Grande-Bretagne*, vol. II, pp. 587–97.

178 See for instance chapters 1, 3 and 10. The edition referred to is Oliver Goldsmith, *The Vicar of Wakefield*, ed. Arthur Friedman (Oxford, 1974).

179 On the Job-figure, see C. Battestin, 'Goldsmith: The Comedy of Job', in *The Providence of Wit: Aspects of Form in Augustan Literature and the Arts* (Oxford, 1974) pp. 193–214, and James H. Lehmann, '*The Vicar of Wakefield*: Goldsmith's Sublime, Oriental Job', *ELH* 46 (1979), pp. 97–121.

180 As Lehmann acknowledges (ibid., p. 114), however, Goldsmith's precise acquaintance with Lowth has not been identified.

181 Goldsmith is known to have reviewed Burke's popular work on the subject, *A Philosophical Inquiry into the Origin of our Ideas of the Sublime and Beautiful* in the *Monthly Review* for May 1757: see Lehmann, '*The Vicar of Wakefield*', p. 114.

4

Romantics and Victorians:
from Typology to Symbolism

Stephen Prickett

From the time of the French Revolution to the end of the nineteenth century, the history of biblical criticism in the English-speaking world is primarily one of Anglo-German relations. Which is also to say that it presents, in itself, a hermeneutic problem related to the way in which the two societies saw and understood one another, and how other societies (in particular that of Revolutionary and post-Revolutionary France) related to both.

Innovation and Conservatism

Yet the first quality that must be stressed about English writing and criticism in this period, whether biblical or secular, is its essential *conservatism*. Historians of ideas have sometimes puzzled over why (with only a few exceptions) English biblical scholars of the eighteenth century, having so fruitfully taken up the new critical methods begun and then rapidly suppressed in France, were content to leave the subsequent development of what was to be called the Higher Criticism almost entirely in German hands.[1] In what was already a highly pluralistic society, no single explanation of such a complex phenomenon can be wholly satisfactory, yet it is worth noting the irony of how often major aesthetic and intellectual innovations in England during this period were as much the product of attempts to defend an existing position as of consciously to create change. Thus, for instance, Lowth's stress on the literal meaning of biblical texts arising within a particular historical context was not, in fact, so much an endeavour to get rid of traditional polysemous typological and mystical interpretations of the Bible as to put them on a sounder

scholarly basis in response to Deist attacks on its historical authenticity.[2] Similarly, Burke's *Reflections on the Revolution in France*
was presented as no more than a commonsense restatement of
traditional beliefs.[3] Yet such features as its covertly mercantile
assumptions about the nature of freedom and its theory of the
organic nature of the state were innovative enough to set the agenda
for political debate for most of the nineteenth century. Even
Coleridge's *Church and State*, written with the avowedly reactionary
purpose of preventing Catholic Emancipation by showing how it
would violate the 'blessed accidents'[4] of the British 'Constitution',
was, through its theory of the 'Clerisy', to help set in motion
unforeseen and far-reaching changes in British social and political
life.[5]

Nowhere is this paradox of conservatism more apparent than in
the history of biblical criticism in England and its relation to the rise
of the novel. The popular reaction against the French Revolution in
England was to have the side-effect of inhibiting the introduction of
new ideas from both France and Germany for more than a generation. Though it has been argued that we must distinguish between
the French influences on English Romanticism, which were, as one
might expect, of a politically radical kind, from the German, which
were largely conservative,[6] this kind of dichotomy does not apply to
what was perhaps the most influential nexus of ideas to come out of
Germany during this period: the so-called 'Higher Criticism' of the
Bible – a term designed to distinguish its holistic approach from the
(no less important) minutiae of textual scholarship.

Perhaps the most influential French work on the history of
religion in the Revolutionary period was C. F. Volney's *Ruins of
Empire* (1791). It was a work of massive contemporary syncretistic
scholarship. All the major world religions were traced to a common
origin in the sun cults of ancient Egypt by way of Persia: 'Jews,
Christians, Mahometans, howsoever lofty be your pretensions, you
are, in your spiritual and immaterial system, only the blundering
followers of Zoroaster.'[7] Understandably, it proved an immediate
success in English radical circles. No less than three editions of
two English translations (which Volney thought unduly moderate in
tone) were brought out in 1795–6, and it was a major influence on
Tom Paine and later Shelley. Yet by the turn of the century, it was
easy enough to dismiss it – and its English derivatives – as simply
anti-clerical and infidel propaganda amounting to little more than
a species of revolutionary Jacobinism. Indeed, it was Paine's own
revolutionary attack on religion, *The Age of Reason*, that was to
cause many of the radical leaders to distance themselves from him

after 1795 and to deprive him of his early position as their natural leader.

In contrast, because the German biblical criticism was the work of Lutheran theologians and scholars who were (with the exception of Lessing) sincere Christian believers, its radical attack on traditional ways of reading the Bible was much harder to come to terms with – and was, in the long run, much more influential. So far from being divinely inspired, for them the Bible had to be read not merely as one might any other book, but specifically as the record of the myths and aspirations of an ancient and primitive Near Eastern tribe. The accounts of God's appearances and other miracles were to be seen as part of a particularly powerful (and, be it said) eclectic mythology. Many of the points made by Volney, such as that a number of the Genesis stories were discovered to have been borrowed from older Babylonian and Near Eastern mythology, and even from ancient Egypt, had in fact already appeared in the commentaries of these critics. What meaning there was to be found in such stories was moral and developmental rather than historical – illustrating what Lessing, in the title of one of his best-known books, had called *The Education of the Human Race* (1780). If such narratives were to be given a different status from those of, say, ancient Greece or Rome, it was mostly on account of their 'moral beauty' or the profoundly ethical nature of their teachings.

During the earlier part of the 1790s, the ideas of Michaelis, Reimarus, Lessing, Eichhorn, and even Herder had begun to make their way, chiefly through Unitarian channels, into progressive circles in Britain. There were even British scholars of international repute, such as the Scottish Roman Catholic priest, Alexander Geddes – the initial reception of whose work by his superiors suggests that it, too, was seen primarily as a new weapon for the conservatives in the struggle against Protestant readings of the Bible, rather than something that was eventually to destabilize the entire subject.[8] With the war against France and the accompanying anti-Jacobin backlash, Unitarianism, with its dangerous radical associations, became itself politically suspect. Joseph Priestley, the philosopher, political theorist and internationally known scientist, who was perhaps the most famous Unitarian in the country, had his house and laboratory in Birmingham burned by a mob and was forced to flee to America in 1794. Other influential academic figures suspected of Unitarian sympathies, such as William Frend (Coleridge's tutor) at Cambridge and Thomas Beddoes at Oxford, were expelled from their Fellowships. By association, the Higher Criticism was felt to be not only unchristian, but unpatriotic and politically suspect, and for almost 30 years it was virtually ignored. Not until the 1820s was the intellectual climate again sufficiently favourable for the introduction of continental ideas. It was perhaps illustrative of the priorities and standards of the time that when, in 1823, Edward Bouverie Pusey, later to be famous as a leading personality in the Tractarian Movement, wanted to find out about Lutheran theology, he could discover only two men in the whole University of Oxford who even knew any German.[9]

On the other hand, traditional biblical criticism in the same period was to exert a profound influence on the development of prose fiction. As Nicklaus Pevsner has suggested in *The Englishness of English Art*,[10] the native conservatism of the English has always been as much an aesthetic reflex as it was political or religious. It is typical that even in something as essentially innovative as the development of the eighteenth century novel there should be intermingled with startlingly new structural experiments constant reference to earlier literary models. Two examples must suffice: one from an eighteenth-century novelist who helped to shape the whole subsequent evolution of the form of the novel in England, Henry Fielding; the other, a technically less original but psychologically more penetrating early nineteenth-century novelist, Jane Austen.

Fielding, we recall, as well as being a barrister and Justice of the Peace for Westminster, had also been a successful dramatist before turning to the novel.[11] Not surprisingly, perhaps, his avowed model for *Tom Jones* is the drama – and, by implication, Shakespeare (with what combination of seriousness and irony is irrelevant!). Yet that is only one of a whole range of literary and non-literary models by which he tries to define the relation of author to reader and text in the new form he is helping to shape. After comparing himself to a pastry cook, a judge, a dramatist and a governor, Fielding at last turns explicitly to the most obvious Creator of all: the Author of the Book of Nature. Like the Almighty, he writes, the novelist *creates* his own universe with its peculiar inhabitants, laws and events. The reader is thus warned:

Not too hastily to condemn any of the Incidents in this our history, as impertinent and foreign to our main design, because thou dost not immediately conceive in what manner such incident may conduce to that design. This work may, indeed, be considered as a great creation of our own ...[12]

This is the novelist not as exegete but as a Calvinistic God. Because the reader, like fallen man, cannot appreciate the whole mysterious outworkings of the plot, he cannot judge it. At one level, of course, this is theological parody, but there is also a serious and very traditional point about textual interpretation here that a medieval writer such as Dante would have understood and appreciated. It serves too as a useful reminder of the degree to which English biblical criticism at the end of the eighteenth century was still mentally part of a continuum that stretched back through the Reformation and medieval worlds to the Church Fathers.

Similarly a standard biblical commentary of 1806, like Mrs Sarah Trimmer's *Help to the Unlearned in the Study of the Holy Scriptures*, is as firmly typological as any medieval monk's. The story of Abraham and Isaac (Gen. 22:1–14), for instance, is read primarily as a type of the Crucifixion:

Abraham spoke prophetically, ver. 8, and his words were verified; God did provide himself a lamb. Abraham's offering up his son was a type of GOD's giving his son, our LORD JESUS CHRIST, as a sacrifice for mankind. Mount Moriah, where Abraham offered up Isaac, was the place on which the house of the Lord at Jerusalem was afterwards built. We should learn from Abraham's example to be ready to submit to GOD's will in the most severe trials, and to trust always in his providence.[13]

Unless we are actually looking for it, it is easy to miss that this is actually nothing less than a standard, traditional, four-fold reading. The literal sense is too clear to need comment; the allegorical concerns Isaac as the 'lamb' of God – the 'type' of Christ, who is the antetype; the identification of Mount Moriah with the site of the later Temple at Jerusalem leads us on anagogically to the idea of the Church as founded on the blood of the lamb; while the moral instructs us accordingly how we should behave.

If one wished to find an example of a major writer insulated by education, social and political circumstances from contemporary developments in continental thought, one could hardly do better than Jane Austen. Recent critical studies and biographies have alike stressed the innate and even at times polemical conservatism of her views.[14] Two of her brothers became admirals in the Royal Navy fighting first against Revolutionary and then Napoleonic France – and she is even recorded as having confessed that her favourite reading was military history! It comes as no surprise, therefore, to find that though her stories appear at first sight to be entirely naturalistic and secular in construction, if we set them alongside Mrs Trimmer, we can see behind the secular veneer the influence of traditional modes of biblical exegesis. Critics have, for instance, long observed the so-called 'symbolism' created by the visit to Mr Rush-worth's Sotherton estate in *Mansfield Park*. It is not an accident of the novel's spiritual topography that Mary Crawford has a long discussion with Edmund, the hero, who is about to be ordained, on the role of a clergyman while the party is strolling in the part of the garden technically known as 'the wilderness'. Nor, similarly, is it accidental that when they come to the little iron gate that leads from the wilderness to the main park each member of the party acts in such a way as to foreshadow their eventual approach to marriage. (We recall, as doubtless did the author, the sexually charged couplet from Marvell's 'Coy Mistress', urging the lovers to 'tear' their 'pleasures with rough strife / Through the iron gates of life.') Thus, in chapter 10, on finding the way to further pleasure barred by the iron gate, Rushworth, who is to marry Maria Bertram, goes to get the key; Henry Crawford, who remains with her, comments on the contrast between her dissatisfaction and the beauty of the scenery: 'Your prospects, however, are too fair to justify your want of spirits. You have a very smiling scene before you.' Maria at once takes him up on the still-innocent double meaning, her language now alerting the reader to the possibility of further layers of significance in what follows:

'Do you mean literally or figuratively? Literally, I conclude. Yes, certainly, the sun shines and the park looks very cheerful. But unluckily that iron gate, that ha-ha, give me a feeling of restraint and hardship. "I cannot get out," as the starling said.' As she spoke, and it was with expression, she walked to the gate; he followed her. 'Mr Rushworth is so long fetching this key!'[15]

The reference to the caged starling in Sterne's *Sentimental Journey* strikes a whole series of further literary and figurative resonances. It was a commonplace metaphor for the soul or *anima* locked in the carnal prison of the body; in the context of the French Revolution it had acquired further connotations of restraint versus *liberté*; finally, and most pertinent here, being caged had become a familar *topos* for the condition of women trapped by love[16] – specifically, Maria's 'feeling of restraint' encapsulates succinctly her dilemma that the price of becoming mistress of the very desirable estate of Sotherton is marriage to the obnoxious and silly Rushworth. The implied appeal to Crawford to 'rescue' her takes on a further irony from the fact that the hero of the *Sentimental Journey*, though he sees himself as a modern-day knight-errant (albeit a self-deprecating and comic one), is only too willing to take advantage of his damsels in distress when occasion offers. Crawford's response is immediate and in the

light of his later seduction of her, only too clear. He persuades
Maria to squeeze round the gate, saying:

And for the world you would not get on without the key and without Mr
Rushworth's authority and protection, as I think you might with little
difficulty pass round the edge of the gate, here, with my assistance; I think
it might be done if you really wish to be more at large, and could allow
yourself to think it is not prohibited . . .[17]

Julia Bertram, who later elopes with Mr Yeats, simply scrambles
across in their wake, while Fanny, the passive if virtuous heroine,
remains on the right side, waits for Edmund – and complains of a
headache.

Much of this has been noted before – as 'symbolism'. But, of
course, it is not. It is, however ironic in its employment, old-
fashioned biblical typology of the sort that Parson Austen's daughter
was accustomed to hearing every Sunday from the pulpit, and
doubtless reading in her copy of Mrs Trimmer (or its many contemporary equivalents) on weekdays too. The four-fold senses of the
text are as much present here as they might be in any commentary
on Genesis – however much the spirit behind them may have
changed. As we have seen, the reference to the caged starling itself
carries a spiritual, a moral/political, and a personal reference ('what
shall it profit if a man, if he shall gain the whole world and lose
his own soul?' Mark 8:36). Similarly, in encountering the gate the
literal sense of the narrative is complemented by the typological:
each character acts in a way that foreshadows their later sexual
behaviour, and consequently their ordained fate within the novel.
Morally we see that waiting for legal marriage, as the 'key' to future
happiness, though it takes more time and denies immediate gratifi-
cation, is the correct course. In medieval typology, the anagogical
sense was normally taken to foreshadow a future state beyond time
– the type of a spiritual paradise. Here what is being decided is who
is to eventually inherit the 'estate' itself – and the double meaning,
now archaic, of both 'land' and 'position' is significant. By eloping
with Crawford, Maria violates both propriety and property,[18] at
once forfeiting her social status and (in jilting Rushworth) also
Sotherton; Fanny gains not just Edmund's love, but also (spiritually,
as the wife of the incumbent) Mansfield Park itself, which in the
novel has clearly idealized and even paradisal associations.

The point of these two examples is not just the truism that English
literature is permeated by biblical references, nor even that the rise
of the novel is closely associated with the private reading of the Bible

promoted by the Reformation and the improvements in printing during the sixteenth and seventeenth centuries,[19] but primarily that the enormous release of creative energy that went into the novel in the eighteenth century, though it draws heavily on biblical models, owes almost nothing at all to contemporary developments in biblical criticism. What the new aesthetic form was doing, on the contrary, was appropriating and transforming an essentially conservative and, in historical terms, old-fashioned, not to say intellectually bankrupt, mode of reading a text and creating from it a quite new kind of inner consciousness. The implications of this are even more startling if we compare what was happening in England with Germany at this same period.

Hans Frei has argued that the biblical scholarship in the two countries at the end of the eighteenth century constituted a curious polarity:

In England, where a serious body of realistic narrative literature and a certain amount of criticism of the literature was building up, there arose no corresponding cumulative tradition of criticism of the biblical writings, and that included no narrative interpretation of them. In Germany, on the other hand, where a body of critical analysis as well as general hermeneutics of the biblical writings built up rapidly in the latter half of the eighteenth century, there was no simultaneous development of realistic prose narrative and its critical appraisal.[20]

The relative weakness of the tradition of realistic prose fiction in eighteenth-century Germany is certainly very striking to an English-language reader. When Goethe, for instance, in what is often seen as the first great German novel, *Wilhelm Meister* [1796],[21] wished to give examples of leading characters from novels his entire selection was drawn not from German but from English literature: 'Grandison, Clarissa, Pamela, the Vicar of Wakefield, Tom Jones ...'[22] Moreover, in spite of a whole book of the novel being devoted to a religious consciousness with great stress, in the Moravian tradition, on reading the Bible,[23] there is little or no evidence that the metafictional structure owes anything directly either to the new critical theories or to traditional modes of polyvalent typology. On the contrary, like Fielding, Goethe's principal literary model is taken from drama – and English poetic drama to boot: *Hamlet* in fact. Thus when the critic Friedrich Schlegel wished two years later in 1798 to praise *Wilhelm Meister* as a work of art he found it natural to do so not in terms of the novel, but poetry: 'it is all poetry, high, pure poetry. Everything has been thought and uttered as though by one who is both a divine poet and a perfect artist.'[24] Similarly, Ludwig Tieck, writing in 1811, managed to compare Shakespeare with Cervantes on the premise that both are poets working in a single common medium: 'Cervantes, with great understanding and the most delicate and graceful touch, was trying to provide poetry in its orphaned state with a safe course and steady support in real life.'[25] Perhaps most disconcerting of all, Novalis praised Schlegel's *literary criticism*, as though that, too, could only be discussed as 'poetry'. Moreover, as he rapidly makes clear, this is no mere idle conceit or metaphor: 'Schlegel's writings are philosophy as lyric. His [essays on] Forster and Lessing are first-rate minor poetry, and resemble the Pindaric hymns.'[26] In such a critical climate it is small wonder that we find that the connotations of the actual words 'prose' and 'poetry' were acquiring very different flavours in the two countries, and that in Germany any discussion of the conventions of prose narrative tended to be swamped by the all-inclusive genre of 'poetics' – with correspondingly different implied conventions of reading.

To this may be added another distinctive feature of German thought as it developed during this period: a tendency to universalize and generalize at the expense of the kind of awkward particularity and detail so essential to the development of novelistic realism.[27] This symptom of the growing disjunction between the basic cast of English and German thought is exemplified, for instance, by the presence in German of two adjectives both of which must be translated into English by the single word 'poetic'. The first, *dichterisch*, is the normal word used for verse and imaginative writing in a technical sense, while the second, *poetisch*, is reserved for the kind of universalized and abstract conception of the poetic described above.[28] Because of the comparative lack of development of prose narrative and any accompanying critical theory in Germany at the end of the eighteenth century it was natural for the new wave of German critical scholars to think of the biblical narratives in 'poetic', anthropological, and mythological terms, rather than in ways drawn from the novel and prose narrative. This was as true, moreover, for those interested in the literary structure of the Bible as it was for the historical critics.

The Children of Lowth

Lowth's *Lectures on the Sacred Poetry of the Hebrews* had been republished from Göttingen in the original Latin with a preface by the biblical scholar Johann David Michaelis as early as 1758, and together with a number of other English works, such as those of Thomas Blackwell and Robert Wood on Homer, and John Brown on the origins of poetry and music[29] had helped to fuel the critical revolution in Germany. The *Lectures* were partially translated into German by C. B. Schmidt in 1793 – and published together with extracts from Herder and Sir William Jones, the philologist. As this volume showed, though such critics as Lessing and Eichhorn were chiefly interested in trying to see the biblical writings in their context, and displayed an enlightenment scepticism towards the supernatural elements of the narratives, others were still prepared to explore the Bible's literary qualities.

Johann Gottfried Herder's *The Spirit of Hebrew Poetry* (1782–3), for instance, was quick to acknowledge its debt to Lowth's pioneering work, but from the first struck a note that was sharply different from either his English antecedents or his German historicist contemporaries. The 'genius of the [Hebrew] language we can nowhere study better', he wrote in his Preface, '. . . than in its poetry, and indeed, so far as possible, in its most ancient poetry . . . Let the scholar then study the Old Testament, even if it be only as a human book full of ancient poetry, with kindred feeling and affection.'[30] But as we have already learned to expect from Germany at this period, 'poetry' for Herder was a considerably broader and more all-embracing category for him than it was for Lowth, let alone a later generation of English critics. Thus he takes it for granted that the narratives of Genesis are to be considered as 'poetry' – as is the entire book of Job – for, as he writes, 'Among the Hebrews, history itself is properly poetry'.[31] For Herder, indeed, the category of 'poetry' seems to cover all that is most ancient and profound in human nature, and he takes for granted the traditional assumption, still common in the period, that Hebrew is the most ancient of all languages. Hebrew poetry, therefore, expresses 'the earliest perceptions, the simplest forms, by which the human soul expressed its thoughts, the most uncorrupted affections that bound and guided it'.[32] Such apparent primitivism has little connection with the rather patronizing historical perspective of Eichhorn, and Herder, like Lowth, is explicitly at pains to deny any suggestion that the Bible lacked sophistication. Though the author of Job, for instance, (whom Herder, following Lowth, accepts may be Elihu the Buzite) might disregard the classical unities, 'of this,' writes Herder, 'I am inclined to believe he knew better than we do.'[33] His position is in many ways closer to that of Wordsworth – which is hardly surprising since both Herder's book and the Preface to the *Lyrical Ballads* owe their original inspiration to Lowth.

Lowth's influence on the English Romantic movement is of a significantly different kind. Though the first English translation of his *Lectures* was not published until 1787, the Preface to his translation of Isaiah, published in 1778, restates their essential arguments with much new material. Moreover *The Christian's Magazine*, a fiercely anti-Wesleyan publication, had put out an edited version in serial instalments as early as 1767. It would certainly appear that Blake had read Lowth by 1788 when he etched a short piece entitled 'All Religions are One', even if its conclusions might have startled the more conservative Oxford scholar:

PRINCIPLE 5th. The Religions of all Nations are derived from each Nation's different reception of the Poetic Genius, which is everywhere called the Spirit of Prophecy.
PRINCIPLE 6th. The Jewish & Christian Testaments are An original derivation from the Poetic Genius.[34]

Two years later, in *The Marriage of Heaven and Hell*, a prose work, produced between the writing of the *Songs of Innocence* and the *Songs of Experience*, which provides theoretical underpinning of a kind for the dialectical 'contraries' of the *Songs*, Blake elaborates a number of points that might have been taken directly from the historical criticism of Lessing or Eichhorn. In a scene where the Prophets Isaiah and Ezekiel 'dined' with him, he asks whether they did not think their visions of God 'would be misunderstood'? Isaiah replies: 'I saw no God, nor heard any, in a finite organical perception; but my senses discover'd the infinite in every thing, and as I was then perswaded, & remain confirm'd, that the voice of honest indignation is the voice of God, I cared not for consequences, but wrote.'[35] Ezekiel then explains that:

we of Israel taught that the Poetic Genius (as you now call it) was the first principle and all others merely derivative, which was the cause of our despising the Priests and Philosophers of other countries, and prophecying that all Gods would at last be proved to originate in ours & to be the tributaries of the Poetic Genius; it was this that our great poet, King David, desired so fervently & invokes so pathetic'ly, saying by this he conquers enemies and governs kingdoms; and we so loved our God, that we cursed in his name all the deities of surrounding nations, and asserted that they had rebelled: from these opinions the vulgar came to think that all nations would at last be subject to the jews.[36]

Some literary historians have found it hard to accept that Blake, the poet with the least formal education of any of the Romantics, could be the first one not merely to show evidence of having read Lowth, but also of knowledge of the German higher criticism. Yet in the early 1790s we know that he belonged to one of the few intellectual circles in the country to be in touch with Continental ideas – both French and German. He too knew William Frend, Coleridge's former Cambridge tutor who had been expelled from his Fellowship for his Unitarian views and sympathy with German biblical criticism. Blake was also a friend of Joseph Johnson, a radical London bookseller and publisher with strong Unitarian connections, and belonged to a group that met regularly at his house in St Paul's Churchyard. Among others it included Joseph Priestley, William Godwin, Mary Wollstonecraft, Tom Paine, Richard Price and Thomas Holcroft. It had been Richard Price's eulogy on the virtues of the French Revolution that had originally stimulated Burke's *Reflections*. The group was in touch with both the radical demythologizing of the German historical criticism and the current French attacks on institutionalized religion – Joseph Johnson himself was the publisher of a 1796 translation of the 3rd edition of Volney who had, we recall, offered detailed scholarly evidence to support the claim that 'all religions are one'.

But Blake's most explicit reference to Lowth's critical views is on a plate of aphorisms of 1820 known as *The Laocoön*. 'The Old and New Testaments,' he writes, 'are the Great Code of Art.'[37] In the course of a comparison of the textual problems encountered in translating Isaiah and the classics, Lowth had drawn a parallel between the moral authority of the Bible and the critical authority of Aristotle's *Poetics*, which, in spite of the possible corruption of the text was still nothing less than 'the Great Code of Criticism … the fundamental principles of which are plainly deducible from it; we still have recourse to it for the rules and laws of Epic and Dramatic Poetry, and the imperfection of the copy does not at all impeach the authority of the Legislator.'[38] For Blake, however, no such division of powers was possible. The authority of the classical world was at every level superseded by that of the Bible. The Bible is not so much the source of moral authority ('If Morality was Christianity, Socrates was the Saviour'[39]) but of *freedom* from *any* externally imposed authority, whether moral, aesthetic, or critical. Just as the new dispensation of Jesus freed the Jews from the tyranny of the Law, so Jesus also frees art from the dead hand of classical rules. 'What Jesus came to Remove was the Heathen or Platonic Philosophy, which blinds the Eye of Imagination, The Real Man.'[40] If poetry and prophecy are but one and the same thing, then it follows that 'Jesus & his Apostles & Disciples were all Artists.'[41] – a point that had implicitly been made by Lowth himself when he had described Jesus's parables as being a direct extension of the Old Testament poetic tradition.[42] Blake had, in short, produced from Lowth perhaps the nearest thing to a theory of literature ever to be devised directly from New Testament theology.

The influence of Lowth on Coleridge and Wordsworth is even better documented. We know from his own references that Coleridge used both Marsh's translation of Michaelis's *Introduction to the New Testament* and Lowth's translation of Isaiah for his 1795 *Lectures on Revealed Religion*.[43] His borrowings from the Bristol Library also include the *Lectures on the Sacred Poetry of the Hebrews*.[44] There was another intermediate source as well: Hugh Blair. Blair's *Lectures on Rhetoric and Belles Lettres* (1783) is probably the biggest single source of ideas in Wordsworth's Preface to the *Lyrical Ballads*. Blair also considered Lowth of sufficient importance to devote a whole chapter of his *Lectures* to summarizing the latter's pioneer work. Through Blair one can see how a number of the key concepts in Wordsworth's aesthetic theory had evolved from principles enunciated originally by Lowth in connection with Hebrew poetry. Thus Lowth had noted that one of the effects of his discovery of the principle of parallelism was that 'a poem translated literally from the Hebrew into the prose of any other language, whilst the same form of the sentences remain, will still retain, even as far as relates to versification, much of its native dignity, and a fair appearance of versification.' But if it is translated into Greek or Latin verse, with 'the conformation of the sentences accommodated to the idiom of a foreign language' it 'will appear confused and mutilated; [and] will scarcely retain a trace of its genuine elegance and peculiar beauty'.[45] Blair noted the obvious corollary to this: that the dignified prose of the Authorized Version actually captures the spirit of Hebrew poetry better than any verse rendering.

It is owing, in a great measure, to this form of composition, that our version, though in prose, retains so much of a poetical cast. For the version being strictly word for word after the original, the form and order of the original sentence are preserved; which by this artificial structure, this regular alternation and correspondence of parts, makes the ear sensible of a departure from the common style and tone of prose.[46]

The inference was clearly to obliterate the conventional distinction between the language of prose and that of poetry. His answer to the question 'what is poetry? and wherein does it differ from prose?' is that what separated them was not diction but emotion: 'it is the language of passion, enlivened imagination.'[47] We are here only a short step away from Wordsworth's more famous theory of poetic diction with its confident assertion that 'there neither is, nor can be, any essential different between the language of prose and metrical composition,' and its equally significant corollary, the answer to the question, 'What is a poet?', by the brilliantly complusive leap of logic that 'Poetry is the spontaneous overflow of powerful feelings.'[48]

Whatever the later differences between Wordsworth and Coleridge over the nature of poetic diction, neither was to retreat from these central Lowthian tenets of the Preface. Indeed, when Coleridge came to express his strongest disagreements with Wordsworth in the *Biographia Literaria* in 1817, he was careful also to restate the fundamental principles on which their joint venture had been founded. The account of how the *Lyrical Ballads* came to be written, in chapter 14, is followed immediately by a discussion of the nature of poetry in general. The examples of Plato, Bishop Taylor and (Thomas) Burnet furnish, for Coleridge, 'undeniable proofs that poetry of the highest kind may exist without metre, and even without the contra-distinguishing objects of a poem.' This evidence from classical Greece and seventeenth-century England is then supported by what amounts to a direct reference to Lowth, whose translation of Isaiah, we recall, he had been using more than 20 years before: 'The first chapter of Isaiah (indeed a very large portion of the whole book) is poetry in the most emphatic sense.'[49] His own formulation that follows, by echoing Blair and Wordsworth, indicates also his debts to them: 'What is poetry? is so nearly the same question with what is a poet? that the answer to the one is involved with the solution of the other.'[50] He continues his theoretical account structured in terms of what Lowth had called 'antithetical' parallelism. The poet's power:

... reveals itself in the balance or reconciliation of opposite or discordant qualities: of sameness with difference; of the general with the concrete; the idea, with the image; the individual, with the representative; the sense of novelty and freshness, with old and familiar objects; a more than usual state of emotion, with more than usual order; judgement ever awake and steady self-possession, with enthusiasm and feeling profound or vehement; and while it blends and harmonizes the natural and the artificial, still subordinates art to nature ...[51]

We can here observe the influence of Lowth at two distinct levels. On the one hand he has enabled Coleridge to cite Isaiah as an example of 'poetry in the most emphatic sense'; on the other, his formal poetic analysis of biblical prophecy in terms of parallelism has inspired a corresponding formal parallelism in Coleridge's own 'prophetic' statement of poetic theory.

More unexpected, perhaps, is Shelley's use of Lowth in his *Defence of Poetry*. Though it was not published until 1840, some 18 years after his death, and then in an edited form, Shelley's most important theoretical discussion of poetry had been written originally as a reply to a curiously ironic piece by his friend Thomas Love Peacock, entitled *The Four Ages of Poetry*.[52] In it Peacock had used the argument that because poetry was essentially a more primitive mode of expression than prose, it would eventually be totally superseded by it:

As the sciences of morals and of mind advance towards perfection, as they become more and more enlarged and comprehensive in their views, as reason gains the ascendancy in them over imagination and feeling, poetry can no longer accompany them in their progress, but drops into the background, and leaves them to advance alone.[53]

The argument is an old one, to be found in Vico, Diderot and the French *philosophes*, as well as in the late eighteenth-century Scottish tradition, and by Peacock's time it had become something of a commonplace. What Peacock does with it, however, is far from commonplace. He uses it, in effect, to invert the normal methods of historical criticism. Whereas German critics, such as Eichhorn, had stressed the 'poetic' nature of early biblical legends in order to show their primitiveness *as history*, Peacock does so to show the primitiveness of *poetry*. Since the truth or falsehood of poetry must be judged by precisely the same standards as any other kind of truth, their historical unreliability means that poetry as a medium cannot be taken seriously by modern man:

Poetry was the mental rattle that awakened the intellect in the infancy of civil society; but for the maturity of mind to make a serious business of the play-things of its childhood, is as absurd as for a full-grown man to rub his gums with coral, and to be charmed to sleep by the jingle of silver bells.[54]

Though it is not always easy to disentangle the various layers of Peacock's almost Swiftian irony, we can be fairly sure this was not his real opinion – but more likely what he most feared. What he intended was that Shelley should reply.

That reply takes the form of an extension to Lowth's analysis of

Hebrew poetry that would no doubt have stunned the conservative Bishop. Shelley begins by making clear his debt to both Lowth and Blair. 'Poets, according to the circumstances of the age and nation in which they appeared, were called, in the earlier epochs of the world, legislators or prophets: a poet essentially comprises and unites both these characters.'[55] Nor is Shelley, the atheistical disciple of Volney, here using the term 'prophet' in any merely secular sense. The whole thrust of his rhetoric is towards a barely concealed metaphorical language of divine inspiration. The phrases are unmistakable and cumulative in effect:

poetry lifts the veil from the hidden beauty of the world ... A man to be greatly good, must imagine intensely and comprehensively ... The great instrument of moral good is the imagination ... Poetry strengthens the faculty which is the organ of the moral nature of man, in the same manner as exercise strengthens a limb ... Poetry is the sword of lightning, ever unsheathed, which consumes the scabbard that would contain it ... Poetry is indeed something divine.

The sacred poetry of the Hebrews, the Book of Job, and even the 'poetry in the doctrines of Jesus Christ' are invoked as part of his argument against Peacock for the unchanging moral value of poetry. But in the process the word 'poetry' has acquired connotations more consonant with Novalis and Schlegel than with Wordsworth or Coleridge. The great minds of the past, the 'prophets' ranging from Plato to Bacon, are enlisted as 'poets' while at the same time poets such as Dante, Shakespeare and Milton become 'philosophers of the very loftiest power'. Indeed, 'all the authors of revolutions in opinion are necessarily poets as they are inventors.'[56]

The 'defence' of poetry is in effect to accept Peacock's analysis of the fate of verse, and to separate verse from poetry by finally obliterating the last vestiges of distinction between verse and prose, and claiming that prose, in so far as it is of great philosophic or moral value, is *ipso facto* 'poetry'. In this, Shelley's *Defence* must rank as one of the most radical and extraordinary critical manoeuvres ever made by a practising poet – perhaps the more so because its genesis in the article by Peacock in the obscure *Ollier's Magazine*, which had not survived beyond the opening number in 1821, was concealed both by the time-lapse before its posthumous publication and by the editorial decision of Mary Shelley to omit all references to Peacock in the published version. What was therefore intended as part of a theoretical dialogue simply could not have been seen as such by contemporary readers. Just as Blake's use of Lowth would not have been known beyond the very few who saw his laboriously hand-printed and coloured plates, so the nature of the debate that continued throughout the nineteenth century is to a large extent a private and hidden one, surfacing occasionally in works that, if they were noticed at all at the time, were perforce explained in other ways. This was certainly the case with the most interesting and serious challenge posed to Shelley by perhaps the most radical literary conservative of the entire century, Gerard Manley Hopkins.

In an essay on 'Poetic Diction', written when he was an undergraduate at Balliol College, Oxford, in 1865, for the Master, the famous classical scholar Benjamin Jowett, and not published until the twentieth century, Hopkins takes up Wordsworth's theory with implicit reference to Lowth, Coleridge, and, above all, Shelley:

The structure of poetry is that of continuous parallelism, ranging from the technical so-called Parallelism of Hebrew Poetry and the antiphons of Church music up to the intricacy of Greek or Italian or English verse. But parallelism is of two kinds necessarily – where the opposition is clearly marked, and where it is transitional rather, or chromatic. Only the first kind, that of marked parallelism is concerned with the structure of verse – in rhythm, the recurrence of a certain sequence of rhythm, in alliteration, in assonance and in rhyme. Now the force of this recurrence is to beget a recurrence or parallelism answering to it in the words or thought and, speaking roughly and rather for the tendency than the invariable result, the more marked parallelism in structure whether of elaboration or of emphasis begets more marked parallelism in the words and sense. And moreover parallelism in expression tends to beget or passes into parallelism in thought. This point reached we shall be able to see and account for the peculiarities of poetic diction. To the marked or abrupt kind of parallelism belong metaphor, simile, parable, and so on, where the effect is sought in likeness of things, and antithesis, contrast, and so on, where it is sought in unlikeness. To the chromatic parallelism belong gradation, intensity, climax, tone, expression (as the word is used in music), *chiaroscuro*, perhaps emphasis: while the faculties of Fancy and Imagination might range widely over both kinds, Fancy belonging more especially to the abrupt than to the transitional class.[57]

The passage starts with Lowth on parallelism and ends with Coleridge on Imagination. But Hopkins's argument goes beyond either in one important respect. Lowth's discovery of the principle of parallelism had been presented in the context of an argument that Hebrew poetry, with its absence of rhyme and metre, was fundamentally different in structure from its European counterparts. Hopkins now claims that both rhyme and metre are, in fact, themselves nothing less than *species* of parallelism: in short, that parallelism, so far from being a special case, peculiar to ancient Hebrew verse, is fundamental to the structure of *all* poetry. No less important for poetic theory, however, was the corollary, that if this is granted, it follows that so far from there being no essential difference between the language of poetry and that of prose, as Lowth's argument had seemed to imply, parallelism actually *accentuates* the difference, because modifications of structure produce direct corresponding modifications of meaning:

An emphasis of structure stronger than the common construction of sentences gives asks for an emphasis of expression stronger than that of common speech or writing, and that for an emphasis of thought stronger than that of common thought. And it is commonly supposed that poetry has tasked the highest powers of man's mind: this is because, as it asked for a greater emphasis of thought and on a greater scale, at each stage it threw out the minds unequal to further ascent. The diction of poetry could not then be the same with that of prose, and again of prose we can see from the other side that its diction ought not to be that of poetry.[58]

Once again we see in Hopkins that quintessentially English brand of conservatism that innovates to preserve the *status quo*. Hopkins's real target, of course, is Shelley and those like him who would defend poetry only by selling the pass altogether and obliterating the distinction between poetry and prose. If the theoretical programme implicit in that astonishing undergraduate essay is read in conjunction with the no less astonishing burst of poetry that came from Hopkins after his years of disciplinary 'elected silence' ended with the writing of 'The Wreck of the Deutschland' in 1878, one can see, in a way that was impossible for contemporaries, the degree to which his verse with all its aggressively flaunted complexity represents a massive restatement of the inseparability of poetry from verse form. That his critical theory is drawn ultimately from biblical criticism would, no doubt, only enhance his enjoyment of presenting such an argument to his tutor, Benjamin Jowett – whose essay 'On the Interpretation of Scripture' in *Essays and Reviews* (1861) had been one of the most important efforts to date to introduce historical criticism into England, and which had made him an object of considerable controversy and suspicion in Oxford. It would be interesting to speculate whether Jowett, who knew Herder's work himself, had previously introduced his brilliant student to it. Certainly the nearest published equivalent to this bold reversal of Wordsworth had been almost 80 years before in *The Spirit of*

Hebrew Poetry where Herder had also claimed that all poetry was, in one form or another, dependent on parallelism – and that, even though Hebrew verse lacked the formal structure of European, its limited number of words and consequent dependence on an exact word arrangement made it nearly incapable of translation.[59] The thrust of this argument is, however, significantly different from that of Hopkins: whereas the German sees parallelism as pointing in the end towards some kind of universal and cosmic dialectic,[60] for Hopkins it is yet another reinforcement of the individual particularity of things.

With Herder and Coleridge, however, the public aesthetic revolution inaugurated by Lowth's *Lectures* was almost complete. In the Romantic admiration for naturalness, simplicity and sublimity, and the substitution of inward feeling for rhetorical convention, we can see both the eventual triumph and the true paradox of Lowth's principles. On the one hand, his stress on the need to understand the historical context of the biblical writings had led both to a rediscovery of the Bible as history, and to the scepticism and agnosticism engendered by so much of the historical criticism; on the other, within two generations the neo-classical rules and models so much admired in the early part of the century – and not least, of course, by Lowth himself – had been largely replaced by biblical ones, so that, paradoxically, at the very moment when the historical accuracy of the Bible was being questioned as never before, its aesthetic prestige had never been higher. Yet though, as we have seen, that aesthetic prestige was being understood in increasingly different ways in Germany and England, it was still possible in a writer like Herder for a literary and theological understanding of the Bible to go hand in hand. By the time England had once again become receptive to Continental ideas, at the end of the Napoleonic Wars, such a synthesis had become far less easy.

It is hard to avoid the conclusion that the reasons for this were to an extraordinary degree contingent and accidental – depending, as they did, so much on a particular arbitrary decision by a single university administrator. In 1809, Baron Wilhelm von Humboldt, the famous philologist, was invited by Frederick William III, in the wake of his country's disastrous defeat by Napoleon, to assist in reorganizing the shattered education system by founding the new University of Berlin. One of Humboldt's greatest innovations in the new institution was to separate the humanities from the Faculty of Theology and create a Faculty of Arts (*Philosophische Facultät*).[61] Such was the prestige of the reformed German universities in the early nineteenth century, both in the humanities and theology, that this division, which was widely imitated both in Germany and in the rest of Europe, rapidly became rigidly institutionalized to the point where, in the words of one rueful commentator later in the century, it was as if a 'glacial moraine' had been constructed between the study of the Bible and of other literatures.[62] Thereafter biblical studies tended increasingly to fall into their modern mould and become a specialist matter of history, archaeology and linguistics rather than literary criticism. Though there were still brilliant generalists such as Jowett himself (who was actually Regius Professor of Greek at Oxford) they tended to become ever fewer in number. The effective result, though it was hardly apparent at the time, was to sever a 1,800 year hermeneutic tradition of polysemous textual interpretation, and to usher in a new era of biblical literalism among the very group of scholars who in the past would have been least prone to it – the biblical critics themselves – while the tradition of typological readings, together with metonymy and symbolism, separated from its roots in biblical criticism, flourished as never before in the secular climate of the nineteenth-century novel.

Coleridge

A comment of Coleridge's on Eichhorn's *Introduction to the Old Testament* (1780–3) illustrates not merely the basic difference in sensibility between the two (very different) critics, but also the ways in which German and English modes of critical thinking had themselves diverged by the beginning of the nineteenth century. When Coleridge went to Germany in 1798, it was with the intention not just of learning the language but also of studying the new historical criticism. On the advice of Thomas Beddoes, who had, we recall, been expelled from his Oxford Fellowship in 1793 for his Unitarian sympathies, Coleridge made his way to the University of Göttingen to read Eichhorn and attend his lectures. They were to make a profound impression upon him – and to change the course of his own thinking. Yet his marginal notes do not suggest altogether uncritical admiration. For example, for Eichhorn the visions of Ezekiel were to be seen as the product of conscious artistry and understood primarily in aesthetic terms: 'All these raptures and visions are in my judgement mere cover-up, mere poetical (*poetische*) fancies.'[63] In a marginal note, Coleridge challenges this whole distinction between artist and visionary:

It perplexes me to understand how a Man of Eichhorn's Sense, Learning, and Acquaintance with Psychology could form, or attach belief to, so cold-blooded an hypothesis. That in Ezeckiel's Visions Ideas or Spiritual Entities are presented in visual Symbols, I never doubted; but as little can I doubt, that such Symbols did present themselves to Ezekiel in Visions – and by a Law closely connected with, if not contained in, that by which Sensations are organized into Images and Mental Sounds in our ordinary sleep.[64]

Whether or not we accept E. S. Shaffer's claim that Eichhorn's position is intended as a corrective to an enlightenment rationalism that would dismiss Ezekiel as simply fraudulent, it is clear that the processes of aesthetic creativity are seen by him as entirely the product of conscious organization, whereas for Coleridge they operate symbolically, and involve not merely the rational powers of the mind but also the unconscious. For the Enlightenment German critic, assumptions of the uniformity of human experience have filtered out or even obliterated that sense of individual difference and uniqueness so strongly present to the English Romantic poet.

Unlike Eichhorn, Coleridge brought to his biblical criticism a sensibility formed by a prolonged exposure to *both* biblical *and* secular literature. He is, for instance, overwhelmingly conscious of writing within a culture so steeped in biblical assumptions and patterns of thought that it was no longer possible for someone within that system fully to grasp the extent of that influence or the ways in which it has come to condition his perspectives on the world.[65] Not merely ways of perceiving but also the language in which those perceptions are given shape is permeated by the Bible. It was a theme that Coleridge was to return to over and over again in his life. In the first 'Letter' of his *Confessions of an Inquiring Spirit* he defined his approach to the Bible in these words:

I take up this work with the purpose to read it for the first time as I should any other work, – as far at least as I can or dare. For I neither can, nor dare, throw off a strong and awful prepossession in its favour – certain as I am that a large part of the light and life, in and by which I see, love, and embrace the truths and the strengths co-organized into a living body of faith and knowledge ... has been directly or indirectly derived to me from this sacred volume, – and unable to determine what I do not owe to its influences.[66]

Similarly, in his *Table Talk* for 24 June 1827, for instance, among a welter of observations ranging from Shakespeare to craniology, we find this comment:

Our version of the Bible is to be loved and prized for this, as for a thousand other things, – that it has preserved a purity of meaning to many terms of natural objects. Without this holdfast, our vitiated imaginations would refine away language to mere abstractions. Hence the French have lost their poetical language; and Mr Blanco White says the same thing has happened to the Spanish.[67]

The charge that French and Spanish had entirely lost their 'poetical language' through over-refinement is at first glance a puzzling one – not least in countries where poetry continues to be written in those languages! – but Coleridge's apparent anti-Latin prejudices in fact merely echo a view that had already been expressed in France by no less an authority than Diderot, whose argument in his *Letter on the Deaf-Mutes* (1751) may well have influenced Peacock: that French, through its growing sophistication, had indeed lost its 'warmth, eloquence, and energy' and become a language of prose best fitted for science and philosophy.[68] Diderot does not, it is true, try to connect this with biblical translations! Nevertheless, Coleridge is certainly right in indirectly pointing to the very real fact that the Authorized Version of the Bible had played an incomparably bigger part in the development of English literature than any corresponding French or Spanish versions, and that it had influenced the development of the English language and its literature in certain quite fundamental ways. In particular, according to Coleridge, it had preserved a certain concreteness of expression in English that he clearly associates with the language's poetic vitality and which stands in sharp contrast with the spare and classical elegance of (say) Louis Segond's famous French version of the Bible.

As a result, Coleridge's biblical criticism, fragmentary and unsystematic as it often is, presents a unique phenomenon in the history of nineteenth-century thought. Not since Lowth had there been an approach to the Bible that so balanced an acute historical critical awareness and a poetic sensitivity to the literary nuances of the text. In the late 1820s, towards the end of his life, Coleridge began work on what he clearly hoped would be a major critical commentary which would apply the principles of the Higher Criticism in his own way to the New Testament. Though the project occupies several of his notebooks, what we have is more a series of isolated insights than a systematic work. From a historical point of view, however, the notebooks tell us much that is interesting about the intellectual climate of England, even towards the middle years of the century. In discussing Stephen's speech before his accusers (Acts 7), for instance,

Coleridge follows his own reactions with a bitter comment on the public inadmissability of what he has just written:

It reminds me of some of the rambling speeches of the first Quakers before the Magistrates – but this, I suppose, I must not acknowledge! & Why? O! because our [?] will not believe the Redeemer's words that by Babes & Sucklings (i.e. by rude and ignorant men) he would lay the foundations of his Church – and thanked his heavenly Father that he had so ordained it – no! but we must have these rude and ignorant men transmuted into consummate sages by miracle – as if this did not render our Lord's words a mere equivocation.[69]

Once again, as in the passage from Ezekiel, Coleridge has read the Bible in the light of his own psychological experience. That does not stop him being as sweeping as Eichhorn, however, in his suspicions of conscious fraud in the text:

A very useful article might be written on the History and Progress of the Vice of Lying on the Christian Church ... I would begin with Justin Martyr, Irenaeus & Tertullian, enumerating the lies that had been fabricated during the space of 90 years from the date of St. Paul's third year's residence at Rome – i.e. the concluding chapter of the Acts. The only objection to such a book is that it would comprize full half the contents of Ecclesiastic History.[70]

It is hardly surprising that Coleridge was convinced that, in the contemporary climate of opinion, his work was unpublishable. He was right. Ten years later, in 1840, some six years after his death, a collection of his essays, much more theoretical and less specific than the notebook material quoted above, was published by his nephew, Henry Nelson Coleridge, under the title *Confessions of an Inquiring Spirit*. The very personal connotations of that word 'confessions' were a deliberate attempt by H. N. Coleridge to head off trouble. His uncle's original title, 'Letters on the Inspiration of the Scriptures', had been far too descriptively accurate – not to say provocative. If this manoeuvre – together with a rather defensively pious preface – was intended to deflect criticism from the nephew, it was probably successful; it did not, however, save Coleridge's own reputation, already damaged by dark rumours about opium addiction, from taken a further dive. According to his friend and one-time disciple John Sterling, this was partly his own fault for trying to please everyone:

Great part of the obscurity of the Letters arises from his anxiety to avoid the difficulties and absurdities of the common views, and his panic terror of saying anything that the bishops and good people would disapprove. He paid a heavy price, viz. all his own candour and simplicity, in hope of gaining the favour of persons like Lady —; and you see what his reward is! A good lesson for us all.[71]

Yet Sterling, like his friend and biographer Carlyle, was here writing from a position of Lessingian agnosticism. It is also possible that, as we have seen, part of Coleridge's problem was that he was writing neither from a position of unquestioning bibliolatry nor from one of materialist scepticism, but from a real attempt to penetrate the psychology of the writers concerned.

Significantly, the predictable attack came from two quite different quarters. For the early Victorian religious public, already shaken by the suggestions of geologists and paleontologists that the dating of the Book of Genesis could not be taken at face value, Coleridge's argument from textual evidence that the Bible could not be read as a historical record of the events described could only come as further evidence that he was a crypto-infidel, seeking to destroy the Church from the inside. From a smaller but more knowledgeable group, however, there was a potentially much more damaging response. His arguments, they said, were in reality little more than a patchwork of unacknowledged plagiarisms from a previous generation of German critics such as Reimarus, and Lessing in particular. So dangerous were these suggestions considered that, when a second edition was brought out in 1849, it was prefaced by a lengthy introduction by J. H. Green defending the author from the charge of plagiarizing Lessing, and attempting to distance Coleridge from the accusations of atheism that had (correctly as it turned out) been levelled at the German.

As so often happens, the effect of such a theological furore was to divert attention from what we have seen were the much more original and important aspects of Coleridge's argument. For him the Bible was to be read as one might 'any other book', and not to be subject to what he called 'bibliolatory' – the idolizing of individual texts torn loose from their context and used as if they had a freestanding universal meaning. Similarly, its importance was not secured by divine fiat, but rather something to be discovered by practical and imaginative experience by the reader. In an earlier politico-theological work, *The Statesman's Manual*, he had described the Scriptures as: 'The living educts of the imagination ...'

giving 'birth to a system of symbols, harmonious in themselves, and consubstantial with the Truths, of which they are the conductors ... Hence ... the Sacred Book is worthily intitled the WORD OF GOD.'[72]

The inversion here is quite startling – and is deliberately intended to be. We are not, Coleridge is saying, to reverence the Bible as the Word of God because it is revealed to us by authority, but we accept its authority from our own experience because it carries for us a poetic and symbolic value – acting as a 'conductor' (in the newly coined electrical sense of that word) for divine grace and truth. In a few brief sentences, Coleridge had, in effect, stood on its head the whole hermeneutic tradition which had dominated biblical criticism since the Middle Ages. In a move that closely paralleled changes in other reading since the development of the novel, the reading of the Bible and indeed, by implication, the individual's sense of God, had been transferred from 'outer' space to 'inner'. If this process of what is commonly called 'internalization' had begun as far back as the Reformation, with its stress less on communal worship than on the individual's reading of the Bible in private, it had only come to completion with the Romantic movement. In another context, Coleridge himself had called attention to this historical process of internalization when he had observed that as late as the seventeenth century in England there was no substantive distinction in meaning between the words 'compelled' and 'obliged' – a fact which had enabled Hobbes in his *Leviathan* (1651) to deny the existence of guilt.[73] What Wesley in the middle of the eighteenth century – again partly under Moravian and pietistic influences from Germany – was to call 'the inward witness' had become for Coleridge a much more all-embracing stress on the absolute primacy of subjective experience. As we have seen, with the advantages of hindsight, there were specific and contingent historical reasons to do with the rise of the novel and accompanying critical theory why this should have happened initially in England rather than Germany – even though biblical criticism as a scholarly discipline was much more advanced in the latter country.

In particular, the work of Friedrich Schleiermacher (1768–1834) had transformed the state of hermeneutics in Germany and given to it a systematic basis that was to prove a decisive influence on the course of nineteenth-century thinking. A friend of Friedrich Schlegel, Novalis and other leading Romantics, Schleiermacher, who held the chair of Protestant theology at the University of Berlin from 1810 to 1834, was himself also a respected philologist who had translated Plato. In keeping with this background he shows a much stronger sense than Eichhorn of the creative role of the author and, correspondingly, of the work of art as an expression of the artist's creativity. Drawing on many of the same currents in German Romanticism as Coleridge, he stressed both the organic unity of a work and a concept of symbolism that allowed for an infinite range of possible interpretation. Hardly surprisingly, hermeneutics were for him not so much a matter of removing obstacles to understanding, still less of decoding a fixed meaning, but of illuminating the conditions bringing author and reader together and so making possible understanding and interpretation. There was no simple key that would unlock the Scriptures; no formula that would lay bare a final meaning: on the contrary 'understanding, is an unending task.'[74]

In relation to the Bible this raised particular historical problems. In a lecture of June 1813 he elaborated the distinction, subsequently to become a part of the German language, between the activities of the *Dolmetscher*, or interpreter, and the *Übersetzer*, or translator.[75] The former presupposes the mechanism of corresponding concepts and vocabulary that permits the practical translation essential to international trade or politics; the latter is involved with language at a level that recognizes the essential uniqueness of particular formulations and that in an absolute sense no totalizing translation is ever possible. In a later letter to the philosopher Jacobi (March 1818) he argued that the New Testament constituted the original interpretation (*Dolmetschung*) of Christian feeling but that since then such immediacy has inevitably weakened to a matter of 'translating' across the growing barriers of time and social change.[76] The recovery of that original closeness for modern Christianity is at once an impossibility and the goal for which the translator must nevertheless ceaselessly strive.

Since he was an almost exact contemporary of Coleridge's, and was influenced by many of the same ideas, it is hardly surprising that there is a strong resemblence between their approaches. They differ in that whereas Coleridge was essentially an isolated figure whose insights were scattered, unsystematic, and largely unpublished until after his death, Schleiermacher was a systematic theologian working from a respected academic power base who was expected to expound his thought directly to generations of students studying under him. It is ironic therefore that our understanding of his work has also suffered from many of the same problems that operated against Coleridge. What was published on hermeneutics during Schleiermacher's lifetime was essentially various versions of his working lecture notes, and it was not until 1958 that his manuscripts were published in their entirety. For much of the twentieth century, indeed, his work in the field has been best known through the exposition of Wilhelm Dilthey (1833–1911) who appropriated him in ways many modern scholars would now find highly questionable.[77] As a result, the immediate impact of Schleiermacher on British thought was generally slight – though, as we shall see, not altogether insignificant.

It is important to realise, however, that in England this stress on the primacy of subjective experience over external evidences or authority was not confined to Coleridge – or to that group most influenced by him, the liberal Anglicans.[78] It is no less marked, for instance, in the man widely thought of in England as the greatest religious reactionary of the nineteenth century, John Henry Newman. Though he was to return over and over again to the evils of 'liberalism', in the sense of putting the judgement of a private individual before the teachings of the Catholic Church, he was as resolute as Coleridge in his insistence that to *accept* those teachings in the first place inescapably involved a prior act of the individual conscience[79] – a point that was not so much anathema as incomprehensible to many of those on the continent, especially in Rome, who continued to feel that there was something suspiciously liberal about even Newman's critique of liberalism.

For Newman, however, the clash between his highly inward and subjective sense of self and the findings of the historical criticism was always curiously muted. Though he was one of the most formidable historians of his generation, there is little evidence that he turned his historical training on the Bible – and none at all that he accepted the naturalistic principles on which the Higher Criticism was based. When those two elements were at last brought into conjunction in Germany the result was to have profound repercussions – not least, nor, as it happened, not last, on the development of the English novel.

George Eliot and Feuerbach

Ludwig Feuerbach's *Essence of Christianity* was published in 1841 and translated into English in 1854 by a young scholar named Mary Ann Evans – better known to the world by her pen-name, George Eliot. The book had played a significant part in her own personal history. Her evangelical faith had been shattered in 1841 by reading Charles Hennell's *Enquiry Concerning the Origins of Christianity* (1838) – a work which drew heavily, via secondary sources, on German historical criticism of Eichhorn as well as the English Deist tradition.[80] It differed from most previous attacks on Christianity, however, in its tone, which was serious and even sympathetic to the ideals of the religion whose supernatural sanctions it saw as being wholly mythical. It was a tone that struck a deep chord in George Eliot's own sensibility and which was to typify the discussions of religious belief that were to play such a prominent part in her own later novels. In 1846 she was commissioned to translate Stauss's *Life of Jesus*, and eight years later, Feuerbach.

The importance of this early translation work on George Eliot's novels can scarcely be overestimated. She, more than any other single person, had been responsible for the introduction of the new and radical, post-French Revolution developments of German theological thought into English. Strauss's *Life* had created an immediate sensation at its publication. It was the first sympathetic attempt at a biography of Jesus from a *wholly* human and non-supernatural point of view. Just as the Bible was a book to be read 'like any other', so this Jesus was a man to be understood 'like any other'. *The Essence of Christianity*, however, though in some ways less immediately shocking since it did not focus narrowly on the life of its founder, was altogether broader and more searching in the scope of its enquiry.

For Feuerbach the idea of God is essentially a human projection: an abstraction of the highest and best sentiments of humanity gathered together and attributed collectively to a single mythical being who is then externalized. 'God is the highest subjectivity of man abstracted from himself ... God is the being who acts in me, with me, through me, upon me, for me, is the principle of my salvation, of my good dispositions and actions, consequently my own good principle and nature.'[81] But as human subjective consciousness, through the process of internalization already described, has progressively developed over the years, more and more of that divine abstraction has been reclaimed and reassigned to where, of course, it had in reality always belonged – the human psyche. Thus what in primitive religion was attributed to the gods, is by modern man understood as psychology. 'The course of religious development which has been generally indicated consists specifically in this, that man abstracts more and more from God, and attributes more and more to himself ... What yesterday was still religion is no longer such today; and what today is atheism, tomorrow will be religion.'[82]

As we have seen, prevailing views of the relation of supernatural religion to human consciousness are not without parallel effects on the metaphorical structure of novels of the period. George Eliot's first full-length novel, *Adam Bede*, was published five years after her translation of Feuerbach, in 1859, and, hardly surprisingly, centres on the question of the varieties of religious belief. Such relativism is in itself a comparatively new development in the history of prose fiction; what is absolutely new, however, is the effect of that relativism on what, to make the parallel with Jane Austen, we must call the 'typology' of the novel.

Chapter 15, for instance, is entitled 'Two Bed-Chambers', and contrasts the behaviour of two of the novel's principal characters, Hetty and Dinah, as they prepare for bed in the same household. Hetty seats herself in a low chair before the little chest of drawers that serves as her dressing-table and lights two candles before studying herself carefully in the mirror. As she admires her own beauty she feels the presence of 'an invisible spectator whose eyes rested on her like morning on the flowers. His soft voice was saying over and over again those pretty things she had heard in the wood; his arm was round her, and the delicate rose-scent of his hair was with her still.'[83] That Hetty, naive and self-centred, is performing her 'religious rites' at an altar of self-worship is made the more explicit in the text for us to compare her form of worship with that of Dinah, the Methodist woman preacher, who is also praying before going to bed in the next room.

Dinah delighted in her bedroom window. Being on the second storey of that tall house, it gave her a wide view over the fields. The thickness of the wall formed a broad step about a yard below the window, where she could place her chair. And now the first thing she did, on entering her room, was to seat herself in this chair, and look out on the peaceful fields beyond which the large moon was rising, just above the hedgerow elms.... Her heart was very full, for there was to be only one more night on which she would look out on those fields for a long time to come ... she thought of all the dear people whom she had learned to care for among those peaceful fields, and who would now have a place in her loving remembrance for ever. She thought of the struggles and the weariness that might lie before them in the rest of their life's journey, when she would be away from them and know nothing of what was befalling them; and the pressure of this thought soon became too strong for her to enjoy the unresponding stillness of the moonlit fields. She closed her eyes, that she might feel more intensely the presence of a Love and Sympathy deeper and more tender than was breathed from the earth and sky. That was often Dinah's mode of praying in solitude. Simple to close her eyes, and to feel herself enclosed by the Divine Presence; then gradually her fears, yearning anxieties for others, melted away like ice-crystals in a warm ocean.[84]

The contrast between each aspect of her thoughts and behaviour with those of Hetty is carefully highlighted. Whereas Hetty is looking into an old and tarnished mirror, seeing only herself, darkly, Dinah is looking through the window at the beauties of nature; whereas Hetty's vision is illuminated by two stumps of old candle, Dinah's is lit by the full moon; whereas Hetty imagines she hears the voice and feels the arms of her earthly lover, Dinah imagines herself in the arms of Christ ... etc. Recognition of the network of biblical quotations behind these images would still have been second nature to the vast majority of Eliot's readers.[85] At first glance, moreover, the formal arrangement of the comparison, together with the clue from the chapter title, would seem to suggest that, as in the passage from *Mansfield Park* we looked at earlier, the multiple senses of traditional biblical exegesis are still in evidence. And indeed this scene does prefigure the climax of the novel in very specific ways.

After her prayer, Dinah opens her well-worn Bible and reads the words from Acts, 'And they all wept sore, and fell on Paul's neck and kissed him.' Taking this as confirmation of her earlier feeling that Hetty was a 'poor thing struggling torn and bleeding' in a 'thorny thicket of sin and sorrow', 'looking with tears for rescue and finding none', she goes on impulse and knocks on Hetty's door to see if she can offer help. Though Hetty rejects her offer, the scene, and Hetty's tears, anticipate the later scene when Dinah comes to Hetty again in prison where the latter is awaiting execution for the murder of her infant.

Yet in spite of the deliberate biblical resonances of the two scenes, this is hardly a case of type and antetype. The system of correspondences that endowed the actions of the party from Mansfield Park with such resonance has in effect given way to a very different kind of symbolism. To begin with, apart from simply the different directions in which they are looking, it is not what Hetty and Dinah *do* in these scenes that matters, it is what they *think*. In other words, the typology has now become totally internalized: displayed not by an action, but by events of consciousness, states of mind. Dinah shows her moral superiority to Hetty not in what she does, but in how her mind works. Just as the external authority of the Bible or even (for Newman) of the Catholic Church had come to be dependent upon the subjectivity of individual assent, so now even the external events of the novel are seen as expressions or outworkings of the protagonists' states of consciousness. But to attach multiple meanings of the traditional kind to a thought is a very different matter from attaching them to an action. For one thing, because thoughts of this level of complexity are almost inevitably verbal, they are mediated by a novel in a much more direct way than an action can be. As we know from many forms of literature, it is not difficult for words to be ambiguous or polyvalent but it is a different kind of ambiguity from that of an action. Most commonly it arises when the person concerned is deceived in some way.

Let us look again at the meditation and prayer of each. It is difficult not to miss seeing how Hetty is deceived in her assumptions about Arthur and her consequent expectations – and several pages of some of Eliot's crudest and most heavy-handed irony are devoted to making sure we do not. But what about our heroine, Dinah? At the obvious level we are clearly meant to see how different her case is from Hetty's. Yet her religion is, of course, a textbook case of Feuerbachian projection. Her own deep love for humanity is projected into the attributes of an objective and external being who is then experienced as inspiring those feelings again in herself. In other words, despite appearances, her window is as much a 'mirror' as the unfortunate Hetty's old glass. Even the light by which she sees the tranquil landscape outside her window is 'reflected' – moonlight. If Hetty is self-deceived at one level, Dinah is also self-deceived at a much deeper one.

At first sight there seems to be no way through this morass of Feuerbachian subjectivity. Yet, besides that of Feuerbach, there were other important German influences at work in George Eliot's thought during the 1850s when *Adam Bede* was written. In November 1851, she had written to Sarah Hennell saying that she was reading ('with great amusement') Newman and reminding her to send 'Schleiermacher's little book' together with 'the M. S. translation'.[86] If this extraordinary chapter of the two bed-chambers is seen not in narrowly Feuerbachian terms but in the light of Schleiermacher's desire to focus on the conditions necessary for understanding, and his belief in the final indeterminacy of any particular interpretation, we are presented with a very different picture. The important question is then not which of the two girls is the more deceived, but one of understanding the circumstances under which each has reached her own interpretation of their situation, and, because of their utterly different perspectives, the inevitability of their mutual misunderstanding. What is important is not the truth or falsehood of each girl's vision, but the relationship between that vision and the unrepeatable context of personal circumstances from which each arises. Both must be understood by the reader with sympathy and imagination – even though in the end judgement between them must also be made. Seen thus this contrast between the two girls' acts of worship becomes, in effect, one of the most subtle and penetrating hermeneutical exercises in Victorian fiction.

Moreover, seen in this way, we have here a prime instance in which the novel has faithfully reflected the uncertainties that were increasingly to affect not merely biblical criticism but all post-Kantian epistemology. The paradigm of 'projection' that lies at the heart of Feuerbach's critique of religion (which was, of course, taken over more or less intact by both Marx and Freud) is also the paradigm for Schleiermacher's own hermeneutics. What at first sight appears to present an insoluble logical dilemma is actually the way forward' to a new level of human understanding. 'Such is the circle,' writes Paul Ricoeur, 'hermeneutics proceeds from a prior understanding of the very thing that it tries to understand by interpreting it.'[87] What is at stake from here onwards in all literature, whether biblical or secular, is nothing less than that problem of 'the hermeneutical circle': in other words, is the relation between text and reader, sense-data and perception, a closed one involving nothing more than a redescription, or is it sufficiently open for the 'new', the genuinely fresh insight or piece of information, to emerge?[88]

The contrast is neatly expressed by a comparison between Coleridge and Feuerbach who, by remarkable coincidence, both use the same image of the circulation of the blood as a description of the hermeneutical circle. For Coleridge, writing in one of his notebooks in 1829, it is an extension of the New Testament metaphor of the Church as the 'Body of Christ':

The small Artery in the Finger or the thread-like Vein in the Foot witteth not of the Blood in the Chambers of the Flesh, but a small portion thereof doth it need or can it contain – Yet by the never-resting energy of the Heart, ever expanding to acquire, and contracting to communicate, is the distant vein fed, and its needful portion renewed, and the feeding Artery receives an aiding impulse in the performance of its humble ministry.[89]

Faith renews both itself and the whole body by its constant circulation. It is not an individual possession, but (as Newman saw so clearly) belongs to a *community* which shares a common culture affecting to some degree the perception of all its members. Such a shared way of interpreting the world is not in any sense a distortion of perception, it is rather its precondition. Without such an unconscious system of predispositions, no interpretation is possible.

The Kantian basis for such an argument would be equally common to Feuerbach, but for him this points only towards a self-enclosed solipsism:

As the action of the arteries drives the blood into the extremities, and the action of the veins brings it back again, as life in general consists in a perpetual systole and diastole; so it is in religion. In the religious system man propels his own nature from himself, he throws it outward; in the religious diastole he receives the rejected nature into his heart again.[90]

The contrast provides an interesting sidelight upon the two bed-chambers scene we have been considering in *Adam Bede*. For all the apparently Feuerbachian framework of George Eliot's thinking, it is as if she is trying to articulate the former, Coleridgean, position, rather than the latter, of Feuerbach himself. Or rather, it is Hetty who is caught in the truly closed hermeneutic circle, and Dinah who, because she belongs to a community, is participating in an open circle capable of change and growth.

Matthew and Mary Augusta Arnold

It is difficult without some knowledge of the intellectual conditions in Britain summarized in the earlier part of this essay to understand the impact of an innocuously entitled volume, *Essays and Reviews* which appeared in 1861. Though the historicity of Genesis had been under challenge by both geology and paleontology since the late 1820s and Strauss and Feuerbach had been available in translation – and widely discussed – for almost a decade, it was still true that for the mass of the Victorian religious public the historical criticism of the Bible had made remarkably little impact on the way in which it was read. The preface to this new volume of essays by a number of leading academics and theologians sounded a note of caution and (for those who could hear it) of warning. While stressing the independence of its authors from one another, it added that it was 'an attempt to illustrate the advantage derivable to the cause of religious and moral truth, from a free handling, in a becoming spirit, of subjects peculiarly liable to suffer by the repetition by conventional language, and from traditional methods of treatment'. What followed was an effective and even elegant summary of the major advances in scholarship during the nineteenth century. There were articles on most of the main topics of controversy: the 'Evidences of Christianity', 'The Mosaic Cosmogony', as well as the essay already referred to by Jowett on 'The Interpretation of Scripture'. Frederick Temple, a clergyman of some distinction and Headmaster of Rugby School, attempted to give a theoretical framework to the whole by an essay with the Lessingian title of 'The Education of the World'. This latter theme, with its implications that the Bible must be understood in the light of the progressive development of the human race, not merely as between the Old and New Testaments, but as a continuing process right down to the present, was one that immediately drew secular literature once more into the debate. It was seen by its exponents as providing evidence not merely for just such a progressive development of consciousness, but also to hold the key to any contemporary and up-to-date understanding of the Bible. It was therefore appropriate that the next important popular discussion of this development should have come not from a professional theologian or even a clergyman, but from the contemporary incumbent of the Oxford Chair of Poetry once held by Robert Lowth. Though one of Matthew Arnold's favourite themes was the need to preserve what he felt to be an endangered 'high culture', the fact is that he was one of the great communicators of his day – it was he, for instance, who, as Professor of Poetry in 1857, had broken with custom and for the first time lectured in English rather than the traditional Latin. Between 1870 and 1875 he published a series of books on the difficulty of reconciling science, historical criticism and contemporary religious belief: *St Paul and Protestantism* (1870), *Literature and Dogma* (1873) and *God and the Bible* (1875). Of these, *Literature and Dogma* was to have by far the greatest impact.

As he had to be in the new internalized world reflected alike, in their own very different ways, by Coleridge, Feuerbach and Newman, Arnold begins by trying to understand the psychological basis of religious belief. For him, if Christianity was to have any chance of survival in his increasingly scientific and materialistic century, it would have to purge itself of what he called by the German name of *Aberglaube* ('extra-belief') – that incrustation of miraculous legend, superstition, and fairy-tale which constitutes such a significant part of the Bible, and which, he believed, was in danger now of strangling the basic moral truths in which, he takes it for granted, the 'real' message of Christianity lay. Yet he is conscious of the role such 'extra-belief' plays in religion.

'*Aberglaube* is the poetry of life.' That men should, by help of their imagination, take short cuts to what they ardently desire, whether the triumph of Israel or the triumph of Christianity, should tell themselves fairy-tales about it, should make these fairy-tales the basis for what is far more sure and solid than the fairy-tales the desire itself – all this has in it, we repeat, nothing that is not natural, nothing blamable ... In religion, above all, *extra-belief* is in itself no matter, assuredly, for blame. The object of religion is conduct; and if a man helps himself in his conduct by taking an object of hope and presentiment as if it were an object of certainty, he may even be said to gain thereby an advantage.[91]

What is puzzling about this, of course, is the fact that he is happy to identify this chimerical 'extra-belief' of the Bible with 'poetry' in a manner more becoming to Eichhorn or Dickens's satirical Utilitarian, Mr Gradgrind, than to Arnold, the eminent poet, critic, Professor of Poetry and man of letters. The paradox of Arnold's biblical criticism is that though, on the one hand, he seems ready to embrace the most sceptical positions of Lessing or Feuerbach, he also seems to wish, like Coleridge, to find in that very subjectivity he is most keen to see through, the seeds of some new certainty. Thus though this passage might look at first glance very much like Feuerbach, there is also a radical and deeply disconcerting difference. Biblical miracles are confidently if kindly dismissed as fairy stories, but what we are offered in their place, as something 'far more sure and solid', turns out to be nothing more than the 'desire itself'. This curious inversion of Coleridge's argument that religion begins with human 'need' in fact elevates subjectivity to new and hitherto unachieved levels of importance. Only those who could believe, with Blake's Isaiah, that 'a firm perswasion that a thing is so, makes it so' would be likely to be satisfied with such an exchange – and Arnold himself was hardly such a one, as the next paragraph makes clear.

And yet there is always a drawback to man's advantage in thus treating, when he deals with religion and conduct, what is extra-belief and not certain as if it were a matter of certainty, and in making it his ground of action. He pays for it. The time comes when he discovers that it is *not* certain; and then the whole certainty of religion seems discredited, and the basis of conduct gone.[92]

What he does *not* say, but seems nevertheless to imply, is that there *is* a certainty to religion that cannot be thus discredited if we were but to look for it in the right place. Beyond our naive desires for wish-fulfilment and our palpable projections, there seems to lurk for Arnold a continuing, if infinitely shadowy, divine presence (that 'not-ourselves which makes for righteousness') which might or might not animate the universe. However personally honest such equivocation might be, it was bound to expose him to the kind of satire brilliantly executed by, for instance, W. H. Mallock in his thinly disguised fictional character of 'Mr Luke':

'It is true that culture sets aside the larger part of the New Testament as grotesque, barbarous, and immoral; but what remains, purged of its apparent meaning, it discerns to be a treasure beyond all price. And in Christianity – such Christianity, I mean, as true taste can accept – culture sees the guide to the real significance of life, and the explanation,' Mr Luke added with a sigh, 'of that melancholy which in our day is attendant upon all clear sight.'[93]

There is, in the end, something touching, even endearing, about Arnold's studied uncertainties and evasiveness. However, his niece, Mary Augusta, better known to the literary world under her married name of Mrs Humphry Ward, though she embraced his critical principles, had no such scruples about the nature of the material in question. For her, his theological position was not merely tenable without any need for attendant melancholy, but served as the foundation for one of the best-selling novels of the century, *Robert Elsmere*. Her hero of that name is a robust young clergyman (not unlike Charles Kingsley in many respects) who, under the compelling influence of his historical studies and the Higher Criticism loses his faith in Christ as a supernatural figure. For him, the Bible comes to be not a source of facts but of 'testimony':

History depends on *testimony*. What is the nature and value of testimony at given times? In other words, did the man of the third century understand, or report, or interpret facts in the same way as the man of the sixteenth or the nineteenth? And if not, what are the differences, and what are the deductions to be made from them, if any?[94]

Behind this lies a theory of the education of mankind derived no doubt from Frederick Temple, who, as befitted a leading headmaster in the Arnoldian tradition, had elaborated and internalized Lessing's adaptation of Joachim of Fiore's three ages into a theory of divinely inspired growth. We, who live as adults in the age of the Spirit, must now be guided not by rules, nor by example, but by principles – which, among other things, now enable us to understand the significance of our own history and development.[95]

Testimony like every other human produt has *developed*. Man's power of apprehending and recording what he sees and hears has grown from less to more, from weaker to stronger, like any other of his faculties, just as the reasoning powers of the cave-dweller have developed into the reasoning powers of a Kant . . .
   To plunge into the Christian period without having first cleared the mind as to what is meant in history and literature by 'the critical method', which in history may be defined as the 'science of what is credible', and in literature as 'the science of what is rational', is to invite fiasco. The theologian in such a state sees no obstacle in accepting an arbitrary list of documents with all the strange stuff they may contain, and declaring them

to be sound historical material, while he applies to all the strange stuff of a similar kind surrounding them the most rigorous principles of modern science. Or he has to make believe that the reasoning processes exhibited in the speeches of the Acts, in certain passages of St. Paul's Epistles, or in the Old Testament quotations in the Gospels, have a validity for the mind of the nineteenth century, when in truth they are the imperfect, half-childish products of the mind of the first century, of quite insignificant or indirect value to the historian of fact, of enormous value to the historian of *testimony* and its varieties.[96]

Though in general it is always dangerous to identify an author's views too closely with those of specific characters, no one, then or now, has found any evidence to question the assumption that these were in effect Mrs Ward's own.[97] In spite of the fact that the plot of *Robert Elsmere* is not always as credible as this passage might lead one to suppose, its runaway success in the late 1880s and early 1890s reflected the power of its presentation of the issues raised by *Essays and Reviews* to a general public at last receptive to and interested in their implications. Yet its very achievement in presenting a discussion of biblical criticism in novel form, by a curious irony masks the real problem of *Robert Elsmere* – and of the Arnoldian criticism it so faithfully expresses. Far from being an avant-garde novel either in theme or structure, it was in fact yet another example of that massive English conservatism we have seen at work throughout the previous two centuries – but without that paradoxical serendipity which had in the past so often turned conservatism into implicit innovation. What is being defended by this progressive view of testimony, in effect, is less an approach to the Bible than a homogeneous theory of consciousness – with clear implications for how a book works in terms of character and narrative as a corollary. Behind the bland confidence in the critical soundness of nineteenth-century historical scholarship is a parallel but totally unconscious confidence in the conventions of nineteenth-century literary realism. For Mrs Ward, 'the science of what is credible' in the criticism of biblical history and the 'science of what is rational' in literature were part of a single continuum. That was how the world was – and must be – portrayed. That this was, in the end, itself a metaphysical position is, of course, easier to recognize with the advantages of hindsight than it was at the time. Moreover, as George Levine has convincingly argued, the apparent certainties of this aesthetic position essentially served to mask 'a fundamental uneasiness about self, society, and art.'[98]

Elsewhere, in the course of discussing Mary Shelley's secularization of the creation myth in *Frankenstein*, he highlights the corollary: 'As George Eliot turned to Feuerbach to allow her to transform Christianity into humanism with all the emotional power of religion, so the novel itself, as a genre, put its faith in a world of fact that, as Matthew Arnold pointed out, had failed us.'[99] The point is a good one, but in fact Arnold had not said quite that, but rather something even more revealing. The passage in question comes from one of his last works, *The Study of Poetry* (1880).

The future of poetry is immense, because in poetry where it is worthy of its high destinies, our race, as time goes on, will find an ever surer and surer stay. There is not a creed which is not shaken, nor an accredited dogma which is not shown to be questionable, not a received tradition which does not threaten to dissolve. Our religion has materialized itself into the fact, and in the supposed fact; it has attached its emotion to the fact, and now the fact is failing it. But for poetry the idea is everything; the rest is a world of illusion, of divine illusion. Poetry attaches its emotions to the idea; the idea *is* the fact. The strongest part of our religion today is its unconscious poetry.[100]

'The fact', we note, is not failing 'us' but 'it' – that is, religion. What we have here is, in effect, yet another chapter in that long and convoluted theoretical debate over the relationship of poetry to prose that, as we have seen, appears to have been an inescapable part of biblical hermeneutics ever since the early eighteenth century. For Lowth and his successors, such as Blair, Wordsworth and Coleridge, the Bible provided evidence that there was no essential difference in either language or content between the two; if, for Peacock and Shelley alike, this could only imply the eventual incorporation of all that was important in poetry into the factual language of prose, for Hopkins it was rather an instance of how essential form was to meaning and content; now Arnold, in an astonishing, if logical, reversal of his earlier position, proposes (with all the casualness of a *fait accompli*) that it is not the 'facts' of biblical religion but its poetry that constitutes its real essence. The reasons for this move are obvious enough. We saw earlier how, in spite of his disclaimer, he feared that the 'poetry' of *Aberglaube* might displace the moral content of the Bible. Now, implicitly, he concedes the point: what he takes to be its factual content is in the last resort indefensible, what matters, therefore, and will survive is neither the dubious 'history' nor the even more dubious miracles, but the 'poetry' – which, like Shelley, he identifies primarily with emotion. The Bible has finally been reduced (as Mallock so wittily perceived) to complete subjectivity.

It is no accident that such assumptions as to the nature of realism and subjectivity should have come to dominate literary theory at precisely the moment when the twin linguistic processes of internalization and individuation should have made the idea of a common objective reality increasingly problematic. That there might be, for instance, phenomena in nature that could not be understood without reference to the means by which they were perceived, or that matter and mind might be much more inextricably enmeshed than the neatly demarcated dualisms of nineteenth-century science could envisage, are as unthinkable as that realism in literature might not be an adequate mode of describing human experience. In short, at the very moment when historical criticism of the Bible had become the stuff of an international best-seller in the English-speaking world, the bases of that criticism were again coming under challenge, not from the theologians but from writers and critics, for whom such hidden assumptions about the nature of personality and of narrative failed to account for the actual complexities of their own perception of things.

NOTES

1 See, for instance, Henning Graf Reventlow, *The Authority of the Bible and the Rise of the Modern World*, trs. John Bowden (London, 1984).
2 See Stephen Prickett, *Words and the Word: Language, Poetics and Biblical Interpretation* (Cambridge, 1986), pp. 124–5.
3 See Stephen Prickett, *England and the French Revolution*, (London, 1989), pp. 42–61.
4 The word 'accidents' still carries for Coleridge something of its Latin force: here meaning more 'a providential ordering of events' than 'a lucky chance'.
5 See Stephen Prickett, 'Coleridge and the Idea of the Clerisy', in *Reading Coleridge: Approaches and Appreciations*, ed. Walter B. Crawford (Ithica, NY, 1979).
6 See, for instance, Marilyn Butler, *Romantics, Rebels and Reactionaries* (Oxford, 1981), Introduction.
7 C. F. Volney, *The Ruins; or A Survey of the Revolutions of Empires*, first pub. London 1795 (London, 1881), p. 83.
8 See R. C. Fuller, *Alexander Geddes* (Sheffield, 1983).
9 David Newsome, *The Parting of Friends* (London, 1966), p. 78. Cambridge was slightly better off. Herbert Marsh, the translator of Michaelis's *Introduction to the New Testament*, became Lady Margaret Professor of Divinity in 1807. Julius Hare, a fellow of Trinity in the 1820s before becoming Archdeacon of Hurstmonceaux, in Sussex, had a private library with more than 2,000 German books.
10 Niklaus Pevsner, *The Englishness of English Art* (London, 1956).

11 Pat Rogers, *Henry Fielding* (London, 1979), ch. 3.
12 Henry Fielding, *Tom Jones*, ed. R. P. C. Mutter (Harmondsworth, 1966), p. 467.
13 Sarah Trimmer, *Help to the Unlearned in the Study of the Holy Scriptures* (London, 1806), pp. 130–1.
14 See, for instance, Marilyn Butler, *Jane Austen and the War of Ideas* (Oxford, 1975), and Park Honan, *Jane Austen* (London, 1987).
15 Jane Austen, *Mansfield Park*, ed. Tony Tanner (Harmondsworth, 1966), p. 127.
16 See Lorenz Eitner, 'Cages, Prisons, and Captives in Eighteenth Century Art', in *Images of Romanticism*, ed. K. Kroeber and W. Walling (New Haven and London, 1978).
17 Austen, *Mansfield Park*, p. 127.
18 As Coleridge points out, the separation in meaning (or desynonymy) of these two words was comparatively recent: *Biographia Literaria*, ed. J. Shawcross (Oxford, 1907), vol. 1, p. 61.
19 See, for instance, Gabriel Josipovici, *The Book of God: A Response to the Bible* (New Haven, 1988), ch. 2.
20 Hans W. Frei. *The Eclipse of Biblical Narrative: A Study in Eighteenth and Nineteenth Century Hermeneutics* (New Haven and London, 1974), p. 142.
21 It was in fact begun as early as 1777, and the passage quoted was written some time between then and 1785.
22 Johann Wolfgang von Goethe, *Wilhelm Meister's Apprenticeship and Travels*, trs. Thomas Carlyle, 2 vols, (Centenary Edn. Carlyle: *Works*, London, 1896–1903, vols XXIII & XXIV). vol. 1, p. 345.
23 Ibid., book VI, 'Confessions of a Fair Saint'.
24 Friedrich Schlegel, 'On Goethe's *Meister*' (1798), in *Dialogue on Poetry and Literary Aphorisms*, ed. and trs. Ernst Behler and R. Struc (Pennsylvania and London, 1968). Cited in Kathleen Wheeler (ed.), *German Aesthetic and Literary Criticism* (Cambridge, 1984), p. 64.
25 Ludwig Tieck, 'The Old English Theatre', in Wheeler, *German Criticism*, p. 120.
26 Novalis, 'Miscellaneous Writings' (1797), ibid., p. 92.
27 See, for instance, Hans Frei: 'On the one hand, historicism was the apprehension of the specificity and irreducibly historical particularity of cultural change. But on the other hand as a movement in German thought it led to the very opposite of this apprehension, to a vast universalization in defining the content of historical change. One reason why historicism failed to move towards realistic depiction was the enormous universalizing tendency we have observed in Herder and which reached its philosophical epitome in Hegel's descriptive explanation of spirit or reason as the unitary moving force of history. In a more moderate form this spiritualizing, universalizing tendency, for which life, spirit, self-consciousness, or some other mode of man's self-grasp as generically unique is the subject of culture and history, has remained the same ever since.' Frei, *Eclipse of Biblical Narrative*, pp. 213–14.

28 For a detailed discussion of these and related meanings of 'poetic', especially in Anglo-German cross-fertilizations, see Prickett, *Words and the Word*, ch. 2.

29 Thomas Blackwell, *Enquiry into the Life and Writings of Homer* (London, 1735), translated into German by J. H. Voss, 1766; Robert Wood, *On the Original Genius and Writings of Homer* (privately printed 1769, republished and enlarged, 1775); John Brown, *Dissertation on the Rise Union and Power, the Progressions, Separations and Corruptions of Poetry and Music* (London, 1763), translated into German, 1769.

30 J. G. Herder, *The Spirit of Hebrew Poetry*, trs. James Marsh (Burlington, Vermont, 1833), pp. 22–3. [First published Dessau, 1782–3; Marsh's translation based on 3rd edn 1822, Marburg]

31 Ibid., p. 37.

32 Ibid., pp. 45–6.

33 Ibid., p. 104.

34 *Complete Writings of William Blake*, ed. Geoffrey Keynes (Oxford, 1966), p. 98.

35 Ibid., p. 153.

36 Ibid., pp. 153–4.

37 Ibid., p. 777.

38 Robert Lowth, *Isaiah: A New Translation* [first pub. 1778], fifth edn (Edinburgh, 1807), vol. 1, p. lxxviii.

39 *Laocoön*, in *Complete Writings of William Blake*, ed. Keynes, p. 775.

40 *Annotations to Berkeley's 'Siris'* (1820), in ibid., p. 775.

41 *Laocoön*, in ibid., p. 777.

42 Robert Lowth, *Lectures on the Sacred Poetry of the Hebrews*, tr. G. Gregory (London, 1787), vol. 1, p. 224.

43 S. T. Coleridge, *Lectures on Politics and Religion* (1795), ed. Lewis Patton and Peter Mann, (London and New Jersey, 1971), p. 153.

44 See George Whalley, 'The Bristol Library Borrowings of Southey and Coleridge 1793–8', *The Library*, 5th Series, 4 (1950), p. 123.

45 Lowth, *Lectures*, vol. 1, pp. 71–2.

46 Hugh Blair, *Lectures on Rhetoric and Belles Lettres* [first pub. 1783], 2 vols (Edinburgh, 1820), vol. 2, pp. 270–1.

47 Ibid., vol. 2, pp. 212–13.

48 William Wordsworth, 'Preface to the *Lyrical Ballads*', [1798–1800], ed. R. L. Brett and A. R. Jones, revised impression (London, 1965), pp. 253; 266.

49 Coleridge, *Biographia Literaria*, vol. 2, p. 11.

50 Ibid., vol. 2, p. 12.

51 Ibid., vol. 2, p. 12.

52 For a discussion of some of the ironies of this article see Stephen Prickett, 'Peacock's *Four Ages* Recycled', *British Journal of Aesthetics*, Spring, 1982.

53 Thomas Love Peacock and P. B. Shelley, *The Four Ages of Poetry and A defence of Poetry*, ed. H. F. B. Brett-Smith (Oxford, 1953), p. 9.

54   Ibid., p. 18.
55   Ibid., p. 88.
56   Ibid., pp. 29–30.
57   *A Hopkins Reader*, ed. John Pick (Oxford, 1953), p. 80.
58   Ibid., pp. 80–1.
59   Herder, *Spirit of Hebrew Poetry*, vol. 1, pp. 40–2.
60   Ibid., p. 208.
61   See Prickett, *Words and the Word*, p. 1.
62   Hermann Usener (1888), see ibid., p. 1.
63   '*Alle Entzückungen und Visionen sind, meinem Urtheil nach, blosse Einkleidung, blosse poetische Dichtungen.*' Johann Gottfried Eichhorn *Einleitung in das Alte Testament*, 3 vols (Leipzig 1780–3), vol. III, p. 188. Annotated by S. T. Coleridge (copy in British Library). Cited by E. S. Shaffer, *'Kubla Khan' and The Fall of Jerusalem: The Mythological School in Biblical Criticism and Secular Literature 1770–1880* (Cambridge, 1975), p. 88.
64   Ibid., pp. 88–9.
65   See Prickett, *Words and the Word*, ch. 1.
66   S. T. Coleridge, *Confessions of an Enquiring Spirit*, 2nd edn (London, 1849), p. 9.
67   S. T. Coleridge, *Table Talk*, ed. H. N. Coleridge (London, 1852), p. 43.
68   See Hans Aarsleff, 'Introduction to Wilhelm von Humboldt', in *On Language*, trs. Peter Heath (Cambridge, 1988). p. lvii.
69   Notebook No. 37 (British Museum Add. Ms. 47,532), p. 26. For a detailed discussion of Coleridge's late biblical studies, see Stephen Prickett, *Romanticism and Religion: The Tradition of Coleridge and Wordsworth in the Victorian Church* (Cambridge, 1976), ch. 2.
70   Notebook no. 39 (B.M. Ms. 47,534), p. 52.
71   Thomas Carlyle, *Life of John Sterling* (London, 1893), p. 364.
72   S. T. Coleridge, 'The Statesman's Manual', *Lay Sermons*, ed. R. J. White [Bollingen Series LXXV] (London and New Jersey, 1972), pp. 28–9.
73   S. T. Coleridge, *Philosophical Lectures*, ed. Kathleen Coburn (London, 1949), Lecture V, p. 174. For an extended discussion of this process and, in particular, the ideas of Owen Barfield, see Prickett, *Words and the Word*, pp. 86–94.
74   *Hermeneutics, the Handwritten Manuscripts*, ed. H. Kimmerle, trs. J. Duke and J. Forstmann (Missoula, MT, 1977), p. 41 (Sect. A, Bibl.). For a general account of Schleiermacher's hermeneutics see Kurt Mueller-Vollmer (ed.) *The Hermeneutics Reader* (Oxford, 1986), ch. 2.
75   'Über die verschiednen Methoden des Übersetzens', *Das Problem des Übersetzens*, ed. H. J. Storig (Darmstadt, 1973). Cited by T. H. Curran in 'Schleiermacher: True Interpreter', *The Interpretation of Belief: Coleridge, Schleiermacher and Romanticism*, ed. David Jasper (London 1986), pp. 97–8.

76 Ibid., p. 99.
77 See, for instance, Werner G. Jeanrond, 'The Impact of Schleier-
    macher's Hermeneutics on Contemporary Interpretation Theory',
    Jasper, *The Interpretation of Belief*, p. 83.
78 For a definition of this term and an account of them see Duncan
    Forbes, *The Liberal Anglican Idea of History* (Cambridge, 1952).
79 J. H. Newman, *A Grammar of Assent*, 1870. For a longer discussion
    of this point, see Prickett, *Romanticism and Religion*, ch. 6.
80 See Shaffer, '*Kubla Khan*' *and The Fall of Jerusalem*, pp. 230–2.
81 Ludwig Feuerbach, *The Essence of Christianity*, trs. George Eliot,
    (New York, 1957), p. 31.
82 Ibid., pp. 31–2.
83 George Eliot, *Adam Bede*, ed. Stephen Gill (Harmondsworth, 1980),
    p. 195.
84 Ibid., p. 202.
85 E.g. I Cor. 13:13.
86 *Selections from George Eliot's Letters*, ed. Gordon S. Haight (New
    Haven, 1985), p. 86.
87 Paul Ricoeur, *The Symbolism of Evil*, trs. Emerson Buchanan (New
    York, 1967), p. 232.
88 The literature on this problem is too extensive to list here, but see, for
    instance, Paul Ricoeur, *The Rule of Metaphor*, trs. Robert Czerny,
    with Kathleen McLaughlin and John Costello S.J. (Toronto, 1977),
    and Prickett, *Words and the Word*, esp. ch. 5.
89 S. T. Coleridge, Notebook No 37, 1829 (B.M. ms. 47,532), p. 60.
90 Feuerbach, *Essence of Christianity*, p. 31.
91 Matthew Arnold, *Literature and Dogma*, (1873) popular edn (Lon-
    don, 1895), pp. 80–1.
92 Ibid.
93 W. H. Mallock, *The New Republic* (Chatto, London, n.d.), p. 31.
94 Mrs Humphry Ward, *Robert Elsmere* (1888), ed. Clyde de L. Ryals
    (Lincoln, Neb., 1967), p. 199.
95 'The Education of the World', *Essays and Reviews*, 9th edn (London,
    1861).
96 Ward, *Robert Elsmere*, p. 317.
97 See Stephen Prickett, 'Biblical Prophecy and Nineteenth Century His-
    toricism: the Joachimite Third Age in Matthew and Mary Augusta
    Arnold', *Literature and Theology*, 2, 2 (September), 1988, pp. 219–
    36.
98 G. Levine, *The Realistic Imagination: English Fiction from 'Franken-
    stein' to 'Lady Chatterley'* (Chicago, 1981), p. 12.
99 George Levine, 'The Ambiguous Heritage of Frankenstein', in *The
    Endurance of Frankenstein: Essays on Mary Shelley's Novel*, ed.
    George Levine and U. C. Knoepflmacher (Berkeley, 1979), p. 7.
100 *Complete Prose Works of Matthew Arnold*, ed. R. H. Super (Michi-
    gan, 1960–77), vol. IX, p. 161. The essay was originally published as
    the General Introduction to *The English Poets*, ed. T. H. Ward.

5

From New Criticism to Poststructuralism: Twentieth-Century Hermeneutics

Robert Detweiler and Vernon K. Robbins

The modern relationship between biblical and literary scholarship is highly complex and readily leads to confusion, not least because the same terminology may refer to different interpretive procedures and goals. Such divergence is not surprising, given the growing fragmentation of scholarship described at the end of the previous chapter; as the disciplines became more specialized and isolated from each other, it was inevitable that they would develop different and even contradictory meanings for shared terms. A prime example of this confusion resides in the very term 'literary criticism'. In literary scholarship the term generally means the whole, usually academic, enterprise of praxis, of interpreting 'serious' works of literature, including the Bible, by employing, more or less self-consciously, some kind of formalist, historical, psychological or structuralist method. In line with this approach, the interpreter distinguishes between literary criticism and literary theory or poetics, which refers to the more abstract investigations of hermeneutical principles and assumptions underlying actual interpretation.

Within biblical scholarship, however, literary criticism has meant research concerned with authorship of texts. First, it has meant the identification of literary sources used by an author who composed a biblical text. This literary interest differs from text criticism, which is designed to establish the early wording of a text by comparing its variant manuscripts to remove scribal errors, additions and revisions. It also differs from form criticism, which is designed to detect the influence of oral as well as written traditions in a biblical text. In this mode, then, literary criticism is concerned with previously written texts that have influenced the sequential order, general organization or wording of a biblical text. Second, literary criticism has meant identification of the stylistic and thematic unity of a biblical text. This approach, on the one hand, may be closely aligned with source criticism, since it may distinguish material containing the author's style and themes from material containing styles and themes perceived to be from previously written material the author incorporated into the text. On the other hand, this approach may presuppose the authorial unity of the existing text and display the particular theological emphases residing in its style and themes. This approach, focusing on unity of style and theme, enables the interpreter to distinguish between the theological views of different authors and provides the framework for writing a history of theological developments within Israel, Judaism and early Christianity. Thus, biblical and literary critics today must be scrupulous in their definitions of hermeneutical terms, procedures and goals.

Another example of the complexity of our subject resides in the juxtaposition of the term 'literary' with 'biblical' in the opening sentence. A particular literary critic from an English department who engages in Bible interpretation may be as actively engaged in the activities of a synagogue or church as a particular biblical critic who teaches in a school of theology or department of religion, yet the differences in their scholarship will be more directly related to their participation in their respective fields of research than to their participation in a particular religious community. A literary critic functions within a field of interpretation of 'serious' literature in the world. This literature often has, but need not have, religious themes, content, or dimensions, but whether it does or not, all of the texts, including biblical texts, are approached in a manner consonant with the current interests in the discipline of modern literary criticism.

A modern biblical critic, in contrast, interprets the Bible and other literature within a framework of theology and historical study of religion. This has two consequences. First, even where literature does not have explicit religious themes, content or dimensions, the biblical critic regularly uses it as a medium for exhibiting religious and theological issues. Second, biblical literature is considered to be primarily characterized by religious and theological issues. Therefore, the biblical critic considers an interpretive strategy arising from any one discipline outside the field of religion and theology to be 'reductionist', i.e., it reduces its interest to literary, anthropological, sociological, or psychological aspects of the text rather than focusing on the primary religious and theological aspects that give the text its special status as religious text. It is one of the less remarked ironies of the twentieth century that although both biblical and literary critics would now take it for granted that they approach the Bible as they would 'any other text', their strategies for doing so are arguably more different than at any period during the past.

The situation is complicated further by differences in commitment to history of religion *or* history of theology in biblical studies. Biblical interpreters regularly consider the major achievement of nineteenth-century interpretation to have been the liberation of biblical interpretation from the shackles of 'dogmatic theology'. Biblical study achieved its academic status through widespread commitment to the historical-critical method which provided the framework for intensive research, nuanced debate and widespread consensus.[1] Profound tensions persisted, however, between very different combinations of history of theology and history of religion within the historical-critical approach. German Bible interpreters like Gerhard Ebeling, Ernst Käsemann, Wolfhart Pannenberg, Jürgen Moltmann and Peter Stuhlmacher limit the conversation to the relation of historical method and theology as established by the Protestant Reformation and Ernst Troeltsch, and they have dominated the discussion.[2] The work of interpreters like Carsten Colpe, Gerd Theissen, Klaus Berger, Norman Gottwald, René Girard and Burton Mack suggests that the profoundest issues arise out of a history of religions approach informed by social and anthropological analyses, but these voices have been kept on the margins by a coalition of Protestant and Catholic interpreters who are convinced that the major issues lie in the arena of historical method and theological belief.

Most, but not all, biblical scholars who have an interest in modern literary criticism have a greater investment in theology than in the history of religions. For such interpreters literary criticism is a secular discipline, and herein lies the major issue. Edgar McKnight, a New Testament scholar with theological rather than history of religions interests, formulates it in the following manner:

> The Bible assumes the sacred and makes no attempt to accommodate readers who do not share this assumption. The critical approach, on the other hand, *methodologically* ignores the sacred; and critical assumptions and approaches make it difficult to image the sacred.... Indeed, the indirect image of the sacred gained from a literary approach may challenge the explicit teaching concerning the sacred gained from particular passages.[3]

For a person with a commitment to history of religions issues, in contrast, the most significant problems do not emerge from secular methods that do not accommodate the sacred, since no method is free from historical context and since historical-critical scholarship has specialized for over a century in approaching the sacred with a general hermeneutic that uses methods perceived to be applicable to all literature.[4] The issue, rather, is a use of methods that open issues for discussion in the broader field of academic discourse, rather than limiting the field to theological debates that exclude the wider intellectual community. Burton Mack, a representative of this latter position, formulates the issue in this manner:

Religious symbols ... articulate a displaced system (imaginary, ideal, 'sacred,' marked off) as a counterpoint to the way things usually go. The inevitable incongruence between the symbol system and the daily round provides a space for discourse.... [T]he trick must be to find a way to locate particular texts at specific junctures of social formation in order to be able to assess their mutual interrelations.[5]

Here we see a biblical critic who considers it possible to formulate the issues in a manner that goes right to the heart of debates in the field of poststructural literary criticism. He considers the issues in biblical interpretation to be related in a primary way to the complex issues in the field of literary criticism itself. Thus, significant tensions have arisen within biblical criticism as a result of dramatic challenges to the historical-critical method, much as tensions have appeared in the disciplines of philosophy, history and literary criticism where established approaches have become the target of structuralist and poststructuralist critiques. In an environment where a significant conversation has begun among literary critics and biblical critics, the discussions reveal a wide variety of approaches to the Bible.

There is yet one more issue that presents confusion, namely, the term *Bible*. As we have seen, historical criticism as performed by biblical critics was based on interpretation of the Christian Bible, the Old and New Testaments. The discipline was created by Protestant scholars and fully adopted by Catholic scholars during the 1940s.[6] Literary criticism shared this same view of the Bible, as evidenced by the approach of Northrop Frye's *The Great Code*.[7] But this situation has changed. Three recent literary studies, Robert Alter's *The Art of Biblical Narrative*,[8] Meir Sternberg's *The Poetics of Biblical Narrative*,[9] and Harold Bloom's *Ruin the Sacred Truths*[10] consider the Bible to be the Jewish Bible, the corpus which was traditionally called the Old Testament.

This emergence of Jewish interpreters has radically changed the field of literary criticism of the Bible. Although, for generations, people assumed 'the Judeo-Christian tradition' to be the natural context of both biblical and literary hermeneutics, that context until the past two decades was far more Christian than Judaic. The instruction in the Torah (the word means 'instruction' in Hebrew) precedes Christian teaching by centuries, and midrash[11] is at least as old as the fourth century CE, but these activities had no strong role in modern times in Christian-oriented seminaries, schools of theology and divinity schools, or in college and university religion departments, and they were still less influential in the literature-and-religion interdiscipline. Now, as Hebrew and Jewish Studies programs proliferate in higher education and bring such studies closer to the cultural mainstream, one finds the attention paid to the Jewish sacred texts starting to balance the old stress on the Christian canon (less so, of course, in Christian seminaries), and simultaneously a new awareness of Jewish Scripture in the study of literature-and-religion as well as literature-and-the-Bible.

Evidence of the change is extensive. In 1986, two Jewish scholars, Geoffrey Hartman and Sanford Budick, edited a collection of essays entitled *Midrash and Literature*.[12] In 1987 the Jewish scholar Robert Alter and Frank Kermode edited *The Literary Guide to the Bible* and in the process faced at least obliquely the problems of canon/sacred texts for Jews, Protestants, Catholics and 'secularists' (the editors' term) – since, for the first three of these, the Bible does not consist entirely of the same texts. Two Jewish scholars are editors of influential publications in the United States, William Scott Green, of the *Journal of the American Academy of Religion*, and Ed Greenstein, of *Semeia Studies*.

Our sketch of such change brings into view the new interdisciplinary scene of our discourse. Until recently, among literary critics there was little sense of any difference, such as we described above, between religion and theology. The name 'literature-and-theology' was interchangeable with 'literature-and-religion', and from the perspective of biblical studies both were thought of as subfields of something called either theology or religious studies.

These things are changing rapidly, and we can see how by attending to the newer relationship between biblical and literary hermeneutics. We used to say that the interaction between the two kinds of scholarship consisted mainly in three efforts:

1 Biblical scholars interpreting biblical texts with the aid of approaches borrowed from literary critics – e.g., structuralist or narratological or reader-response strategies – yet generally still based on historical criticism.

2 Literary scholars interpreting the Bible via their various methods and relating their readings to those of other 'serious' literary texts.
3 Literary scholars interpreting literature other than the Bible in terms of the influence of the Bible on the composition and understanding of those texts.

Things have become much more complicated. Nowadays literary critics such as Robert Alter and Meir Sternberg, with competence in the languages of the biblical texts, address those texts in ways that employ literary critical approaches to challenge and qualify the readings of biblical scholars – mainly those who still rely on historical methods. Biblical critics such as the New Testament scholar John Dominic Crossan and the Old Testament scholar Hugh White[13] are offering similar challenges from within the biblical/religious studies establishment. A few biblical scholars such as Crossan and Robert Funk have even ventured interpretations of secular literature, focusing on texts by authors such as Franz Kafka and Jorge Luis Borges.

But the changes are even more radical than this. The study of sacred Scripture by Western scholars at home in the Jewish and Christian traditions now includes increasing attention to texts of the other 'world' religions, native religions and new religions. The implications of this greatly broadened base of investigation are stunning. Whereas such scholarship has been undertaken in the past mainly via the approaches of comparative religion and anthropology of religion, we can anticipate that traditional and innovative methods of biblical and literary hermeneutics will be applied more and more to texts of Islam, Hinduism and Buddhism, for example (often to those texts in translation by scholars not familiar with the original languages); and that 'indigenous' methods of interpreting those texts will likewise be tried out on the Hebrew and Christian Bibles. We can expect further, thanks to increasingly sophisticated research in the oral literary traditions as conducted, for instance, by Walter Ong,[14] that the study of native religions such as those of Amerindians will become more important to Bible/religion and literary scholars. An example of such a book already in print and worthy of attention by religious studies and literary scholars is William K. Powers's 1986 *Sacred Language*, a translation and explication of the North American Lakota Indians' sacred song texts.[15] Finally, as the media both create and discover novel religious movements – some of them quasi and meta-religious and involving everything from New Age to Elvis-worship – we can await information on how new belief systems are formed. All of these expansions and extensions of sacred text study (and study of sacred texts in the making) should be welcomed and taken seriously by those involved in biblical and literary hermeneutics.

Our task here, however, is not to project what the study of biblical and literary interpretation might become but to describe what it is and has been in the twentieth century. Stephen Prickett has referred earlier to George Levine's pregnant suggestion that 'the bland confidence ... of nineteenth century critical scholarship' concealed 'a fundamental uneasiness' about self, society, and art.[16] The emergence of this uneasiness into a full blown crisis is the story of modern hermeneutics, both biblical and literary, and their interrelationship not only in Britain but in France, Germany, and America as well – the four cultures to which we must, for reasons of space, limit our study. Because of our nationality and training, our discussion will necessarily favour an American perspective on literary and biblical hermeneutics.

In varying ways, the breakdown of German historicism, French rationalism and Anglo-American empiricism and positivism has marked hermeneutics, while the decline of realism has characterized (less spectacularly) creative literature, and both of these have occupied the theorists. But things are, as usual, more complicated than this. Twentieth-century biblical interpretation has been mainly a matter of dynamics within the dominant nineteenth-century historical-critical approach, which was only seriously challenged from the outside during the late sixties. Similarly literary interpretation by the 1920s had turned its attention to what we might call the humane literariness of the text or to the literary text itself as incarnation of cultural sensitivity apart from the sway of historical considerations, and it was not until the sixties that this focus was distracted by other objects for examination.

Having generalized thus, we can venture more detail. Within the field of biblical hermeneutics, the reign of historical criticism was marked by two sometimes interrelated and sometimes conflicting impulses – one the enterprise of scientific history close to or even a part of empirical methodology. the other an extension of Hegelian universalizing history as philosophy. Whereas the first impulse brought forth a continual refinement of text, source, form, *Gattung* and redaction criticism, the second impulse moved through the influence of the Tübingen school to a crisis in the 1920s that produced a half-century of various stages leading to a new crisis that presently informs biblical studies. The initial crisis emerged from the 'radical empiricism' of Husserl's phenomenology, a reaction to the Cartesian rationalism that generated both empirical science and speculative idealism – followed hard upon by Heidegger's philosophy of Being. The stages this crisis precipitated were existentialist interpretation, the New Hermeneutic, structuralism (in a paradoxical way), narratology/reader-response criticism and, most recently, the strategies of poststructuralism.

Within the discipline of literary criticism, the dominance of various 'close readings' (Eastern European formalism, Leavisite organicism, French *explication de text*, above all the New Criticism) was challenged over the four decades between the twenties and the sixties by the 'extrinsic' approaches based on Marxism, psychoanalysis, myth studies, comparatism, as well as an eclecticism produced by great mavericks such as Kenneth Burke. This hegemony, however, was not broken until the advent of structuralism and was not displaced until the growth of poststructuralist thought in the late seventies – an ascension that has brought on a crisis in literary interpretation at least as severe as that in biblical studies. As we shall see, it was also the phenomenological incursion during the first third of the century that led eventually to the deconstructive modes of the last third.

It is obvious from this sketch that while the reactions to historical criticism in biblical studies and to the various strategies of close reading in literary criticism do not result in parallel stages, there are nonetheless important connections between the two, and many of these connections can be elucidated in terms of Bible/religion and literature interaction. We can start with T. S. Eliot as a dominant figure who, from the end of World War I through mid-century, represented the sort of text-oriented criticism that sought to establish a balanced literature-and-religion relationship: one that would not merely duplicate the old Arnoldian substitution of poetry for religion and that would maintain a high regard for the Christian Bible on its own terms without treating it as 'literature', which is to say as any other classical work of literature. It was also, above all, Eliot the artist who composed poetry and drama replete with religious and biblical resonances that encouraged religious explication and that inspired the early stage of religious-literary hermeneutics characterized by the search for the sacramental, redemptive and other numinous meanings of the text's figurative, dramatic or narrative-rhetorical language.

Eliot's germinal 1935 essay, 'Religion and Literature'[17] – a text that, it could be said, launched the modern literature-and-religion enterprise – argues a crucial interdependence of the disciplines of theology and literary criticism. In the secular era, Eliot says, 'Christian' critics need to rely finally on the authority of theology, for it is the values propounded by theology that underlie great literature, even though the critic must employ literary norms to discern what literature is. Or as David Jasper neatly summarizes the argument, 'literature requires the assessment of ethical theological standards which operate only in conditions already defined by literary standards.'[18] Jasper calls this a paradox, but it is also a circular argument typical of Eliot's criticism, and one that has dogged the literature-and-religion effort for decades.

It was not until the assertion in modern hermeneutics of the linguistic paradigm over the historical one, beginning in the sixties, that Eliot's shadow faded: as it became clearer that religious-theological language is as metaphorical as that of literature and hence provides no firm foundation on which to ground literary interpretation – and hence, also, that a more promising approach would lie in comparing the metaphoricity of both discourses in the context of an awareness of ideologies and interpretive communities at work.

Eliot also insisted that reading the Bible mainly as literature is to mistake the source of its historical-cultural influence, for its authority has depended not on its literary stature but on its status as divine revelation. Thus, 'that men of letters now discuss it as "literature" probably indicates the *end* of its literary influence.'[19]

A counterpart to T. S. Eliot, representing the kind of imperfect parallel one finds between biblical and literary criticism, is Rudolf Bultmann (1884–1976), whose career and influence spanned the same period of time as Eliot's. Bultmann, like Eliot, presupposed that the Bible should not be read as literature but as divine revelation. He also presupposed that the source of its historical-cultural influence was its religious content, which he pursued with the method of *Sachkritik*. In this he was following William Wrede, who had 'demanded that the New Testament be understood in its own terms,' and that '[t]he New Testament writings did not constitute a history of teachings, or doctrines, or of theology which took place at a literary level.'[20] This means that Bultmann, like Eliot, shifted 'the locus of meaning in a text, the object of interpretation, from the author to the "subject matter".'[21] One must immediately add that Bultmann and Eliot went in separate ways from this point on as they addressed what they considered to be the pertinent issues in their respective fields of study. But their beginning point shares amazing similarities, not least of which is a shift from the author to the text – a conviction that what is in the text must take precedence over historical information one may have about an author. Indeed, they would have argeed that historical information about an author might actually interfere with one's interpretation of that which is present in the text.

Eliot, and by implication Bultmann, could not have been more wrong about the importance of the literary nature of the Bible for its influence in the latter part of the twentieth century. Recently, both literary and biblical critics have recognized the importance of the Bible's literary nature upon all who read it and upon 'men of letters' who have carried its presuppositions, images and visions forward in their own creative work. Both Eliot and Bultmann failed to see that the Bible's stature as a culture's sacred text, if it could be saved at all in the secular age, would be saved by a thoroughgoing literary investigation that would disclose the Bible's awesome resourcefulness as model and structure of Western thought.

No significant study of literature from the side of Bible and religion scholars took place among Eliot's Anglo-American contemporaries, nor did literary study of the Bible receive attention among Bultmann's followers. There was, however, one major difference. Eliot and his fellow 'men of letters' were largely ignorant of, or at least unconcerned with, the most significant development of modern philosophy taking place on the Continent during their lifetimes, one that would have a profound effect on future religious and literary hermeneutics. First Husserlian, then Heideggerian phenomenology, with its emphasis on the intentional structures of subjectivity and consciousness, led away from the supposed objectivity of empirical science and of scientific history as part of that empiricism and toward the existentialist thought that would, in various guises, radically change the next stages of religious and literary hermeneutics. Bultmann, of course, was in the midst of this discussion and contributed to it from the side of biblical criticism.

The philosopher Martin Heidegger was, in significant ways, an interpreter of literature, and so also was Bultmann. Both as young men conducted studies of classical texts, employing the methods of the venerable Germanic philology, itself a historicizing strategy that attempted to trace the true meaning of terms to their origins in the original languages. Heidegger transformed and dehistoricized this approach into a formidable hermeneutical tactic by creating German-language terms, often neologisms, out of those etymologies that he intended as the basis of a new kind of philosophical reflection. In the later years of his career he merged this method with close, densely metaphorical readings of modern poets such as Stefan George and Georg Trakl to carry out a program of 'poetic thinking' as a still more radical alternative to traditional philosophy.

Bultmann, guided not only by Heidegger but by his own pupil

Hans Jonas, tested the limitations of classical philology and discovered that it could not disclose the truly primal language of poetry but only project the circumstances, through more and less accurate reconstructions, in which such language took shape. Hence he appropriated Heidegger's existential categories to draw forth this primal language out of its 'mythic' (which for Bultmann means the world view of its speakers) context and restore its vitality for modern readers.

Whereas for Schleiermacher the task had been for the interpreter to project himself into the role of the biblical text's author and thereby bridge the gap between the past and present, for Bultmann it was for the reader to encounter the text itself existentially, which meant to respond in faith to the 'kerygma', the proclamation of the first-century church expressed in its mythological language, in ways dependent neither upon historical reconstruction of the life of Jesus nor upon theological demonstration of the 'truth' of Christianity.

Bultmann's approach was, in fact, a phenomenology of faith, a 'reduction' of the nature of faith to its existential dimensions. But in this process of reduction the mythological language in which the kerygma of the New Testament Gospels is entangled is not excised. This is not possible, nor is it what Bultmann meant by his term 'demythologizing'. But if Bultmann refuses to let 'the mythological kerygma ... disintegrate into a symbolic representation of religious piety',[22] or be explained historically, what is left? The reader or hearer of the Gospels must *interpret* the mythic language of proclamation, obviously without believing in the first-century world picture it embraces, but also without subjecting it to the literal-mindedness of modern scientific thinking. The demythologizing effort as Bultmann intends it, in other words, is more of a critique of the scientific world view – if this is assumed to be existentially meaningful – than it is of New Testament myth. Rather than subjecting the kerygma to analysis, one should respond to it as transcendental Word trying to break through the resilience of modern self-understanding. We shall see later how Paul Ricoeur deals with this same issue of myth, kerygma and modern self-understanding in terms of 'false-consciousness'.

That Bultmann's demythologizing has been so consistently misinterpreted results, for the most part, from its author's inadequate understanding of the nature of language. Bultmann did not follow Heidegger into 'poetic thinking' (and one should perhaps be grateful that he did not), and he did not appreciate the intensely symbolic nature of religious language that could, given a chance, body forth his existential categories for modern persons in ways that would enhance rather than impoverish the power of proclamation. Only one New Testament scholar contemporary with Bultmann recognized the potential of the 'mythopoeic' language of kerygma – the American Amos Wilder. Wilder was a harbinger of the present rapprochement of biblical and literary interpretation – minus the apparatus of structural linguistics – and we will treat him later in that context. But for now we will turn to Paul Tillich as a prominent theologian whose aesthetic sense made him more attractive, if ultimately perhaps less significant, to literature-and-religion scholars than Bultmann.

Paul Tillich, who was, like Heidegger and Bultmann, a child of German Romanticism and nineteenth-century liberalism (as he himself confesses),[23] sought for self-identity and fulfilment via the transformations effected by transcendent language but was far more receptive than the other two to the possibilities of that language inhabiting ordinary, 'broken' experience. He first encountered Heidegger's thought in 1925 in Marburg, when Heidegger was a philosophy professor there and Tillich, a member of the theology faculty, was beginning work on his *Systematic Theology*. Here, he reveals, is where 'existentialism in its twentieth century form crossed my path. It took years before I became aware of the impact of this encounter on my own thinking. I resisted, I tried to learn, I accepted the new way of thinking more than the answers it gave.'[24] Because Tillich, fleeing the Third Reich, took up teaching in the United States in 1935, he became a strong influence on religious and theological hermeneutics in America and in the postwar years functioned effectively as a bridge between American and German religious thought. Actually, Tillich propounded a version of religious existentialism that owed a great deal to Heidegger. His theology explored the meaning of concepts such as finitude, freedom and despair as elements of the human dilemma: that we are destined to die, and thus discover that our potential for self-realization is severely limited, leads to a sense of meaningless existence. His projection of Christ as the 'New Being', perfect humanity who did not give in to despair in spite of his finitude nor abuse his freedom to attempt autonomous living but rather lived in continuity with God, 'the ground of Being', is obviously non-Heideggerian. It illustrates how, like Bultmann, Tillich wished to provide a Christian solution to the existential crisis – how he, in fact, like Bultmann stressed the crisis in order to render the solution more urgent.

Terms such as the 'New Being' suggest Tillich's sensitivity to symbolic language, and Tillich's aesthetics, focusing on the nature of the symbol, made his thought particularly attractive to a generation of literature-and-religion scholars, such as the prolific Nathan A. Scott, Jr., beginning work for the most part in the fifties. Tillich's essay 'Protestantism and Artistic Style', published in 1955 and discussing the predominant 'expressive style' of the first half-century, indicates how his writing could inspire religious-aesthetic interpretation:

The attempts to re-create religious art have led mostly to a rediscovery of the symbols in which the negativity of man's predicament is expressed. The symbol of the Cross has become the subject matter of many works of art. . . . Symbols, such as resurrection, have not yet found any adequate artistic representation, and so it is with the other traditional 'symbols of glory'.

Although he goes on to warn that 'no premature solutions should be tried,' it is clear that he would welcome 'redemptive' art works.[25] Tillich's theory of symbols seems naive in the era that has absorbed structural linguistics, and it displays no awareness of Saussure's work on signs that had been accomplished, after all, two decades before Tillich left for America, but at the time it seemed revelatory. His distinction between signs as not sharing 'in any way in the reality and power of that to which they point' and symbols as participating in the 'meaning and power'[26] of that to which they point prepared for his definition of religious symbols as opening up a 'dimension of ultimate reality [which] is the dimension of the Holy'.[27] Facile as this definition may seem today, it challenged religiously oriented artists and critics to create and interpret such symbols in modern art (the sort that Tillich preferred over that of earlier periods) as modes of participation in transformational reality.

Tillich's resort to unwieldy existentialist terminology reveals his conviction that, like Bultmann's myth-encumbered kerygma, religious symbols are untranslatable,[28] and (unlike Bultmann but with a similar Christian hermeneutical concern) he tried to fashion the biblical Jesus-the-Christ as the ultimate religious symbol who points beyond himself to an ultimate reality, in whose New Being humans can share, and who is untranslatable into any philosophical or theological formula. Tillich's aesthetics, in other words, are determined by his theological agenda; he is little concerned with the formal features of an art work itself. Yet because he claims to take aesthetics with 'ultimate' seriousness, he should be willing to subject his theology to the disinterestedness of the art object, and that he does not do.

Tillich's aesthetics, we should point out, concentrated on the visual arts rather than on literature. Kelsey remarks that 'Tillich does not show how such an aesthetic [as he employs it to interpret paintings] can be applied to works of literature.'[29] Hence the appropriation of Tillich's thought by literary critics is generally bothered not only by the theological distortions of his aesthetics but also by the lack of a literary hermeneutical model from Tillich himself. Finally, although we have treated Tillich in a general context of hermeneutics cognizant of the problematics of myth, Tillich actually added little to a modern critical understanding of myth. For him, symbol and myth were virtually synonymous: 'Myths are symbols of faith combined in stories about divine-human encounters.'[30] It would remain for scholars such as Paul Ricoeur and Northrop Frye to disclose religious meaning in the myths themselves rather than through them.

Though one could argue that the New Hermeneutic was a relatively short-lived movement of the fifties and sixties in theological and biblical studies, it is our contention that it set the stage for the current interaction of biblical and literary interpretation. It intensified the attempt of Bultmann and his followers somehow to reconcile the claims of existential and historical criticism; it recognized more acutely than earlier approaches the centrality of language in the interpretation debate and helped usher in the so-called shift of paradigms of twentieth-century thought from the historical to the linguistic; it turned critical interest significantly from text to interpreter; it drew the British and the French more directly into what had been a German-American exchange; and it accelerated the awareness that theology and biblical studies need not necessarily be carried out in a confessional framework.

We will begin by considering the first and the last of these observations together. One reason why the discussion moved beyond the concerns of 'believing' theologians was that the attention paid to hermeneutical theory itself, beginning – not surprisingly – with Heidegger, recalled the crucial interaction of philosophy and theology in the genesis of modern hermeneutics in the nineteenth century. Wilhelm Dilthey, Heidegger, Heidegger's student Hans-Georg Gadamer, and the French phenomenologist Paul Ricoeur represent a century-long tradition of philosophical hermeneutics that surrounds and sometimes merges with theology and biblical studies. It was first Dilthey who, beginning with Schleiermacher's insights, sought to develop a hermeneutical method that would distinguish humanities interpretation from that of the natural sciences and who stressed personal experience as germane to interpretation. Hermeneutics for Dilthey also came to include, beyond considerations of text interpretation, the interrogation of how understanding itself takes place, an emphasis which points to the phenomenological appropriation of hermeneutics by Heidegger and Ricoeur posed in questions such as, how does one's being-in-the-world influence understanding, and what are the intentional marks of understanding?[31] As Heidegger reports:

[T]he title 'hermeneutics' was familiar to me from my study of theology. At that time I was especially tormented by the question as to the relation between the word of Holy Scripture and theological speculative thought. It was, if you will, the same relation, namely that between language and being, only concealed and unavailable to me, so that I sought in vain on many detours and blind alleys for a guiding thread. . . . Later I found this title *Hermeneutik* again in Wilhelm Dilthey in his theory of those humane sciences which are historiological in character. Dilthey was familiar with hermeneutics from the *same* source, his study of theology, especially his study of Schleiermacher.[32]

Bultmann's version of this struggle appears in, for example, the early pages of *Jesus Christ and Mythology*. There, after inquiring into the 'modern study of history, which does not take into account any intervention of God or of the devil or of demons in the course of history,'[33] he describes the preaching of Jesus as 'concealed under the cover of mythology' that does not open up to a historical approach but that will reveal its 'deeper meaning via *demythologizing* – an unsatisfactory word, to be sure. Its aim is not to eliminate the mythological statements but to interpret them. It is a method of hermeneutics.'[34]

Gadamer, still the leading hermeneutical philosopher in Germany in the late eighties, in a 1962 response to Ernst Fuchs's development of Bultmann's hermeneutics shows how a sympathetic non-theologian could contribute to the dialogue by recasting the discourse in non-theological language. Commenting on Fuchs's argument that a translation of a biblical text 'should create the same room that the text sought to create as the Spirit spoke to it,' Gadamer declares this as evidence that 'the word has primacy over the text, for the word is language event.' 'Language event' in the New Hermeneutic replaces the Bultmannian 'kerygma' and is intended at least as dramatically as Bultmann's term. As Gadamer says, 'the relation between word and thought is not that of belatedly catching up with thought by means of the word expressing it. Rather the word is like a flash of lightning that strikes.'[35]

Gadamer, who has influenced reader-oriented literary criticism via the work of Wolfgang Iser of the 'Constance School', among others, embodies the tension between the subjective and objective aspects of hermeneutics. In his *Truth and Method*[36] he opposes the interpreter's participation in the language event (his familiar 'fusion of horizons' of reader and text) with the distanciation of the old hermeneutical objectivity. Yet he does not come down on either side but attempts a mediation. Above all, he does not make an easy identification of the historical with objectivity and the existential with subjectivity. An admission of the reader's prejudices that constitute a pre-understanding of the text signals to the reader the impossibility of scientific-objective interpretation that historians have striven for; yet Gadamer's concentration on what the text has meant to generations of readers places the interpretive process in the context of history, in effect by stressing the history of 'prejudicial' readings of the text.

Similarly, Gadamer's concern with dialogical interpretation is existential, for such dialogue means a sharing of decisive moments – but this is not merely subjectivity in action. Gadamer encourages not a focus of the dialogue partners on each other but rather their common attention to the text. This very gesture of relinquishing individual control over the text (as if one could ever truly control it), in favour of offering one's reading to another's critique, moves to overcome subjective manipulation and toward what would eventually be defined more clearly by Stanley Fish as the interpretive community.[37]

Gadamer's hermeneutics also stresses the centrality of language as the arena where history and existence join. An interpretation is a historically important moment, a linguistic encounter that transcends our ordinary linguistic categories, and a totalizing experience. The hermeneutical experience is absorbed into the ontological one; through the language of the text we learn who we are at a particular juncture in time. As David Linge states it, for Gadamer 'language is the medium in which past and present actually interpenetrate. Understanding as a fusion of horizons is an essentially linguistic process; indeed, these two – language and the understanding of transmitted meaning – are not two processes, but are affirmed by Gadamer as one and the same.'[38] And: 'Since our horizons are given to us prereflectively, we always possess our world linguistically ... there is no "world in itself" beyond its presence as the subject matter of a particular language community.'[39]

Gadamer's work significantly marked the New Hermeneutic in Germany and the United States especially, and we will describe in some detail how the proponents of it elaborated the newer awareness of language into their interpretation theory and praxis. It would be proper also to turn now to the work of Paul Ricoeur, who at about this time was launching a philosophical hermeneutic in France shaped in good measure by Heidegger's thought. Yet because Ricoeur's writing has been, and remains, so massively influential, we shall suspend discussion of it until we come to our survey of structuralist and poststructuralist hermeneutics and describe from that vantage point, retrospectively, how he has accompanied, guided and challenged the hermeneutical shifts of some three decades.

The two names synonymous with the New Hermeneutic are those of the Germans Ernst Fuchs and Gerhard Ebeling, and we will discuss their influence in detail. Both stress the emergence of language itself as the focus and foundation of the interpretive act – and almost simultaneously they recognize that language as such a foundation is inadequate. These insights derive from Heidegger, as did Bultmann's, yet whereas Bultmann turned away from the 'problematics' of language toward a search for the existential meaning 'behind' it, Fuchs and Ebeling absorbed the Heidegger of *On the Way to Language* and sought to translate his investigations of language as the articulation of Being into projects of biblical exegesis, christology and preaching. Even though Fuchs, at least, sees this effort as an extension of Bultmann's program, it is also post-Bultmannian in its addressing of language itself as a transforming force, since Bultmann persisted in employing language mainly as a vehicle for such transformation.

In ways that anticipate the structuralist revolution beginning in France a few years later, language, for Fuchs, takes on ontological as well as kerygmatic qualities. Jesus is understood literally as the *Word* of God, so that word is, after a fashion, apotheosized; but Jesus is also incarnated precisely in and as language, so that when Fuchs refers to the 'linguisticality of existence'[40] he is challenging history as the paradigmatic modality and replacing it with a Christ-born and borne language as ontology.

Because language itself is thus christological, Funk can refer to 'language events' (*Sprachereignisse*), denoting a shift in the status of language as object, as tool, to that of other, that which we encounter and over which we exert little control. Language is, indeed, revelatory. It speaks *us* even as we employ it as a means of communication. This relationship to language generates self-disclosure and self-understanding but also inspires community. As Robinson puts it:

The language event can also be described as carrying out the assembling function of being to which Heidegger had called attention. Theologically speaking, proclamation is such a language event in which the body of Christ is constituted, assembled. The church as assembly takes place in the language event of proclamation. Here the distinctively Protestant definition of the church in terms of the preaching of the word has been restated in terms of the new hermeneutic's understanding of language.[41]

This kind of preaching, furthermore, reverses the strategy of Schleiermacher's hermeneutics. In that tradition, the 'carrying-over' (*übersetzen*) attempted was into the world and mind-set of the text proclaimed. In the New Hermeneutic the effort is just the opposite: to bring the text to life by translating it into contemporary expression as one shares with the community one's encounter with the text.[42]

As Fuchs himself says, struggling with the problem of Christians troubled by the fact of death:

Is there something that is able to bring our life into the light of a truth that also really fits us? This something is to be found only within the sphere of language. . . . [L]anguage presses in upon us before or behind objects, in everything that affirms or rejects us. Hence *it is precisely language that belongs to our human nature*. And since only man has the capacity to be himself by giving himself to another, the language of man belongs in the sphere of love.[43]

Love responds to death, in other words, and does so via the language of the community of faith which is the fundamental medium of all human understanding.

As editor of the *Zeitschrift für Theologie und Kirche*, revived in 1950, Ebeling was in a position to influence the mid-century theology scene significantly. He did so by programmatically recasting theology and biblical criticism in terms of a hermeneutics that judged traditional (historical) criticism as moribund and in need of a mode of address to the world not unlike Bonhoeffer's 'religionless Christianity'. Yet as a Luther scholar, Ebeling also returned hermeneutics to the Reformation stress on the word of God which is more than Scripture, and described a tension in early mid-twentieth-century theology between the emphasis on the word of God at the expense of hermeneutics (the Barthian position) and the emphasis on hermeneutics at the expense of the word of God (the Bultmannian position). Ebeling aimed to reconcile these and to make the reconciliation relevant to modern interpreters.

For Ebeling, hermeneutics 'embraces both linguistic tradition and encounter with reality'.[44] It deals with a demythologized word of

God that is not 'any special supernatural word (and incidentally, God does not mean any separate, special Reality), but true, proper, finally valid word.'[45] This word informs a theological hermeneutics that has much in common with the nontheological kind, yet it also challenges nontheological hermeneutics, maintaining that 'God's word is the ultimate ground of understanding because it is here in the last analysis that word is encountered as word and understanding as understanding.'[46] Here the structure of the word is defined not as mere statement but 'in the pregnant sense of participation and communication'[47] – as word event. In good Lutheran fashion, Ebeling wants the event to take place in preaching, but not in the sermon as the interpretation of Scripture that concentrates on 'the historical task of understanding', for to do so would not confirm the text 'in its historical givenness as proclamation that has taken place'.[48] Like Fuchs, Ebeling intends to make Scripture active in the present, so that the sermon as 'execution of the text' urges understanding of 'the present reality *coram Deo*',[49] which is the same as 'in its radical futurity' – Ebeling's expression of Fuch's concern for making existence bounded by death fiducially meaningful.

Ebeling agrees that such a hermeneutics is existentialist (and thus in the tradition of Heidegger and Bultmann), so long as the event character of word of God is emphasized, but he was involved in other efforts to relate the New Hermeneutic to the broader community of interpretation. One of Ebeling's colleagues at the University of Zurich was the highly regarded Germanist/literary critic Emil Staiger, probably best known for his *Die Kunst der Interpretation*,[50] in which his aggressive correspondence with Heidegger demonstrates the limitations of Heidegger's literary readings. 'The presence of Professor Staiger at the University of Zürich,' argues Robinson, 'immediately gives to Ebeling's hermeneutic a universe of discourse shared with the humanities. The practical relevance of this rapport is enhanced when one recalls that many theological students, planning to teach in the public schools, divide their studies between theology and literature.'[51]

Though they were very alert to the 'reality' of the world mediated by the word event over against the illusory reality of historical thinking, neither Fuchs nor Ebeling engaged the language of poetry in any notable ways to bridge the gap between the existential and historical modes, preferring the language of homiletics instead. But a friendly American critic of, and participant in, the New Hermeneutical dialogue who did comprehend the place and power of poetry in the modern arena of interpretation was the New Testament scholar and literary critic, Amos Wilder.

Amos Wilder preceded by a quarter of a century the current generation of scholars pursuing professional competence in both biblical and literary interpretation – and he established his credentials in theology as well. Educated in biblical studies at both Oxford and Yale and familiar with German theological scholarship, Wilder like few others also demonstrated the sensibilities and convictions of a literary critic. Indeed, Wilder's oft-repeated complaint that 'both scholars and general readers have failed to do justice to ... the operations of the imagination in the Scriptures – to the poetry, the imagery, and the symbolism,'[52] is all the more telling because it is uttered by someone inside the 'guild' of biblical interpretation.

Wilder's hermeneutical position often appears to echo that of Fuchs and Ebeling. For example, when he argues in 'The Uses of a Theological Criticism' that 'a Christian criticism' can 'coincide at many points with any grounded hermeneutical criticism ... but can also alert such criticism to the resonances of a profounder anthropology,'[53] he could well be reinforcing the language-event theology, in its engagement with existential proclamation, of the New Hermeneutic.

But Wilder also pursues a vigorous literary interpretive agenda, both in terms of applying literary critical categories to biblical exegesis and of urging biblical scholars to read and learn from the fictions of literary artists, above all the modern ones. His literary criticism of the Bible is a brilliant sublation – a simultaneous rejection and fulfilment – of Eliot's (and others') decree that Scripture should not be read as literature because (*qua* Eliot) such interpretation fails to recognize the unique nature of Scripture (e.g., its call to judgement and to ethical behaviour) that transcends the standards and concerns of literature. Wilder, too, stresses the difference of the biblical texts, their uniqueness. He grants, in studies such as *The Language of the Gospel: Early Christian Rhetoric*,[54] that the Gospels cannot be categorized according to classical genres and even that they are 'subliterary', yet he sees their singularity far more positively than Eliot in literary-critical terms. The Gospel of Mark, for example, introduces a new genre shaped by the early Church via its liturgy, its celebration of 'cult-legends'[55] telling the 'faith-story of Christ as a pattern of meaning, of life-orientation'.[56] Similarly, Wilder argues, the biblical categories of acts, apocalypse, epistle, prophecy, etc. cannot be subsumed under standard generic classifications but must be appreciated and interpreted for and as what they uniquely are.

Wilder also produced innovative readings of the New Testament parables. His discussion of their realistic settings, rhetorical deftness and eschatological urgency is done in a context that honours the influence of the rabbinic tradition, compares them to Greek genres and draws on modern literature and depth psychology as well. It is exemplary of imaginative, deeply informed biblical-literary criticism that accomplishes the New Hermeneutical programme, at least in one way, better than the New Hermeneuts themselves; his writing is challenging to scholars but also addressed to general readers and thus 'proclaims' the biblical texts existentially to the modern world.

Wilder, finally, pioneered the analysis of the parables as extended metaphors and as narrative entities inviting scrutiny both in terms of their 'symbolic realism' and their mythic/storytelling (oral and written) dimensions. Just how generative Wilder's approach was will become apparent as we sketch in later pages the current narratological and poststructuralist strategies applied to biblical texts and discover the old master's anticipation.

Wilder was, of course, also formed by the New Criticism, and it was that virtually hegemonistic mode that drove him to insist on addressing the text itself in terms of its literary components and in the faith that such a focus would, finally, allow the world's complexity and its redemptive energies to shine through. Yet his immersion in existential philosophy and theology tempered the relatively naive faith of the New Critics in the reliability of language, artistic and otherwise, and prepared him – and us – for the travails of interpretation in an age that knows itself condemned to use a language that it cannot trust – forever writing 'under erasure'.

Robert W. Funk in *Language, Hermeneutic, and Word of God*, carries Wilder's programme forward in an environment of the New Hermeneutic. After an analysis of 'language as event' in Bultmann, Heidegger, Fuchs and Ebeling and of 'the language of theology' in Van Buren, Ogden and Ott, he analyzes language as it occurs in parable and in letter. Language in parable, he argues, is metaphor. This means that a parable is open-ended temporally: '[i]t opens onto a vibrant nexus, whose movement it seeks to reflect in its "tensive" language.'[57] The 'existential tenor' of the parable, then, belongs to the imagination, which is the mode of cognition that stands closest to event. This means that:

> The metaphor, like the parable, is incomplete until the hearer is drawn into it as participant; this is the reason the parables are said to be argumentative, calling for a transference of judgment. Metaphor and parable sustain their existential tenor because they participate in immediacy, an immediacy pertaining to the future as well as to the present and past.[58]

The letter, in contrast, 'is a more complex language-gesture than the parable.'[59] If the language of the parable is 're-flective', Funk suggests, 'the Pauline letter can be characterized as language in the mode of primary reflectivity.'[60] Paul, according to Funk, is reflecting on the fate of the proclamation of the kerygma among his readers. This has two poles: (a) what the proclamation intends, and (b) the way in which the proclamation is being heard. Paul tries to juxtapose what is to be heard with what is being heard within a language that brings each to bear on the other. This means, for Funk, that Paul's language is a 'theological language'. It presupposes a 'foundational language tradition' like the parable which 'founds a world', and 'intends a "world" in which faith is ingredient.'[61] With this a primary difference appears in the language of the parable and the letter.

Jesus and faith refer themselves to something which does not 'appear' at all in the 'world' intended by the parable. Since that something does not 'appear,' it can only be referred to the source of the speaking and the source of the seeing. Jesus calls for faith while God remains hidden.[62]

In Paul's reflective language, that which is hidden in the 'field of the parable' is brought into view in the everyday world. When this happens, the totality of significations in parabolic language is 'fragmented with the result that God and Christ are on their way to becoming entities, and the various objects in the mundane field are also subject to consideration in isolation (Who is my neighbor?).'[63] Funk carries this work on the parables and letter further in *Parables and Presence*[64] and develops a manner of analysing the healing miracle stories that he considers to be appropriate for the narrative movement that occurs in them.[65] Then, following this line of understanding further, he develops a 'sentence grammar' to analyse longer segments of texts in Mark, Luke and John, in *The Poetics of Biblical Narrative*.[66]

Dan O. Via, Jr, drawing heavily on the work of Wilder, Funk, Fuchs and Ebeling, turned the discussion decisively away from the New Hermeneutic by studying the parables as aesthetic objects.[67] In conversation with critics such as Murray Krieger, Northrop Frye and Philip Wheelwright, he 'viewed the parables as having an internal pattern that was the clue to their meaning in any situation.'[68] Using Aristotle's distinction between tragic and comic plots, he interprets parables with a falling plot line as tragic and with a rising plot line as comic.

William A. Beardslee has extended the work of Wilder in a slightly different way, using the tradition of Aristotle's *Rhetoric* and *Poetics* to merge literary study with rhetorical study. Starting with the Gospel form, Beardslee, using Wilder's observations, discusses the nature of story as re-enactment and as hope. One of the most important occurrences in 'the Gospel process', he suggests, is 'the concretization of myth, a concretization impelled by the transposition of the future into the present'.[69] The language in proverb, in contrast, 'expresses a flash of insight which sees the "order" in a certain kind of happening'.[70] In the New Testament, the beatitude or macarism, as a special kind of proverb, is transported into various contexts where it 'has power not only to bring a fortunate situation to expression, but even to work on the situation'.[71] Beyond the Gospel form is the Book of Acts, and to understand this kind of literature, Beardslee suggests, one must understand Greek and Hellenistic history-writing as well as Hebraic history-writing. The result is an awareness that Luke was moving his language toward the style of self-conscious literary authorship that contains a highly developed 'organizing pattern' and uses 'the narrow escape' to highlight the quest theme and emphasize its unfinished character.[72] Finally, 'apocalyptic' is a form that 'embodies a profound thirst for total presence', a thirst 'for total victory, the all-inclusive transformation of reality'.[73] The Book of Revelation, as the central, literary expression of Christian apocalyptic, brings the reader into a world in which:

All is different.... Here there is no effort to hold the imagination to the world of concrete human existence. Except in the letters to the seven churches, the images are, with remarkable consistency, distortions and intensifications of everyday reality, 'unreal,' in a word, mythical. The book's concentration on the end serves to release the imagination from concrete reality; because they are pictures of the 'not yet,' the images are free to go their own way, rather than being conformed to concrete human existence.[74]

With the work of Wilder, Funk, Via and Beardslee at the end of the 1960s, biblical study began to take a decisive turn as insights from modern literary criticism appeared in the midst of various kinds of interpretations. The scene became very complex, however, as structural analysis stormed the field of biblical studies during the 1970s, and during the 1980s the complexity has grown as discussions have interwoven formalist, structuralist and poststructuralist approaches with various forms of traditional criticism.

Before turning to the fortunes of biblical and literary interpretation in our own age, we will, briefly, treat the New Critical interpretations of literature and religion that paralleled those of existentialist and New Hermeneutical exegesis and occasionally interacted with them. Even though these readings were addressed far more to secular texts – poetry, fiction and drama – than to biblical ones, biblical influence is usually present, and it is appropriate to include discussion of representative critics writing in this mode. Not least, we wish to show how the formalist concern with the text itself, far from being abandoned by post-formalist modes, survived even as it was absorbed into broader and more sophisticated hermeneutical operations.

The New Criticism (John Crowe Ransom's 1941 book of that name gave the term its currency)[75] flourished in the United States roughly from the mid-thirties to the late sixties and had its counterparts early on in Eastern European formalism and, later, in the practice of 'close reading' in Great Britain and on the Continent. It provided the foundation and context for the establishing of literature-and-religion as an interdiscipline, more or less recognized and accepted (sometimes barely tolerated), by literary critics who wished to focus on the text itself rather than on distractions to text interpretation generated by history, biography, philosophy, psychology, etc., but who also wanted the text-attentive approach to retain an ethical flavour. Indeed, the morality of good literature was axiomatic for many of the New Critics, who accepted Henry James's dictum that great art is *always* moral. If religion rather than moral philosophy was the exceptional discipline for such critics, the one permitted to influence the otherwise 'objective' attitude toward the text, it was because they felt a personal Christian persuasion that transcended interpretive disinterestedness.

This is a markedly different stance from the Arnoldian one that sought to replace an enervated Victorian religion with poetry as the new substance for reflexes of faith, and from the 'Cambridge English' positions of I. A. Richards (often considered the progenitor of the New Criticism) or F. R. Leavis, who believed that the best literature incorporated the deepest values of an era and hence should be taught as a means of inspiring persons to surpass the quotidian norm. Poetry, Richards concludes, can do for us what religion and philosophy no longer can, that is tell us 'what to feel' and 'what to do'; it alone is 'capable of saving us'.[76]

The 'believing' New Critics who are our concern here considered Christianity a living religion embodied in the great texts, so that a scrupulous reading of them would disclose either their numinosity or the representation of lives in need of redemption or both. One sees, with the benefit of hindsight, the flaws in this approach. For example, to insist that great literature must by definition be morally concerned and thus congenial to Christian interpretation is to make a facile identification of art and morality and to fashion an instrument of exclusion: any literature/art one does not wish to deal with can be labelled ethically wanting and hence unworthy. Nevertheless, the effort of the Christian-oriented New Critic to have it both ways, to find Christian belief exemplified in the very structure of poetic (i.e., literary) language, produced impressive criticism, and we will sketch the contributions of four scholars more and less closely connected to this 'school'.

In the work of the American Cleanth Brooks one finds an insistence that literary language, while representing an objective reality that concretely exists, has a special metaphoric nature that defies paraphrase and demands instead the critic's attention to literary-rhetorical concepts such as ambiguity, analogy, irony and paradox. To read a poem in ways that elucidate the structuring and meaning-creating action of these concepts is not to summarize it but to demonstrate the impossibility of paraphrase by describing how clashing, even irreconcilable components of the poem are made to balance in tension with each other. Such display of the reconciliation of opposites (a theory borrowed from Coleridge) confirms the objective nature of the poem itself. The use of irony, paradox and so on to interpret a poem does not mean that they are an integral part of the poem's nature.

This elevation of the literary work via its extraordinary language brings it close to the special nature of the Christian Word, and Brooks is led to make specific connections. For example, in *The Hidden God* he writes that 'we read literary works not so much for instruction in ideas as to learn – through a kind of dramatic presentation – what it feels like to hold certain beliefs, including the pressure exerted against belief.'[77] One observes here a close relationship between the tension of a poem in its organization of opposites, the critic's imaginative exposition of that tension as inherent in the poem's metaphoric structure, and the Christian's sense of the balanced tension of his/her faith exercised in and by the poem.

In his essay published in 1962, at about the same time as *The Hidden God,* and entitled 'Christianity, Myth, and the Symbolism of Poetry',[78] Brooks takes the side of Eliot and contra Arnold (and Richards) that poetry does not provide redemption yet does offer us the means for comprehending other belief systems – a position consistent with his view of the literary text as autonomous yet reflecting a Christian ontology that is, at last, our true reality.

R. W. B. Lewis, like Brooks a professor at Yale in his time, has been equally forceful in his disclosures of the religious impulse animating much poetry and fiction, although Lewis vigorously denies any intention of practising Christian apologetics. He is, in fact, highly critical of approaches that assign theological relevance to literary works without preparing for and grounding such meaning in thorough textual analysis. In his frequently anthologized essay, 'Hold on Hard to the Huckleberry Bushes', Lewis fulminates against facile Christian interpretation and offers as a more authentic model his own quest for the religious dimensions of literature – a search characterized by uncertainty and ambiguity. In Lewis's own terms, 'What is open to doubt is not the value of a theological approach to literature, but the value of approaching this particular body of [American] literature with any set of terms and doctrines that has been fully and finally elaborated, historically, once and for all.'[79] The exhortation to work through the text's structure and patterns, the alertness to ambiguity, reveal Lewis's formalist reflexes. In his books *The American Adam* and *The Picaresque Saint*,[80] the careful tracing of motifs and imagery, the alertness to myth and history in the plots and lives of fictional personae and real people, and the tenacious sleuthing of the religious energies and complexes determining individual and communal behaviour show an exemplary New Critic cum historian of ideas in action.

Lewis's better-known British namesake, C. S. Lewis, while not a New Critic in any programmatic sense, certainly shared many of their assumptions. An outspoken apologist for (and popularizer of) an intelligent layperson's Christianity, at the same time both an erudite humanities scholar and a popular novelist, Lewis was perhaps too versatile to be appreciated as he should have been by the academy. Like R. W. B. Lewis, C. S. Lewis eschewed precipitous theological readings of literature, but unlike the American Lewis, he did preach vigorously a Christian criticism that would work its way exhaustively through the text at hand in order to earn the right to theological and confessional pronouncements. His depiction of the need for the critic to enter the world of the text, to submit himself to the text, is not unlike the New Hermeneutical attitude (although there are no direct connections), yet Lewis immerses himself in the mythic and metaphoric atmosphere of literary texts rather than of Scripture (which Lewis, like Eliot, will not read literarily – 'the New Testament has nothing at all to tell us of literature')[81] and engages a certain Christian playfulness in his treatment of these texts that the 'unbeliever', he says, cannot.

The Christian will take literature a little less seriously than the cultured Pagan; he will feel less uneasy with the purely hedonistic standard for at least many kinds of work. The unbeliever is always apt to make a kind of religion of his aesthetic experiences; . . . he has to obey a mystical amoral law called his artistic conscience; and he commonly wishes to maintain his superiority to the great mass of mankind who turn to books for mere recreation. But the Christian knows from the outset that the salvation of a single soul is more important than the production or preservation of all the epics and tragedies in the world.[82]

Lewis's interpretive theory, developed in works such as *An Experiment in Criticism*, is foreshadowed and exemplified brilliantly in his earlier books, *The Allegory of Love* and *A Preface to Paradise Lost*.[83] In the first of these especially he demonstrates the utility of learning otherness in its poetic-religious depth by explicating the complexities of courtly love in its late-medieval idiom and setting; in the second he shows how theology can be legitimately practised by the literary critic with a comprehensive (if nonprofessional) knowledge of the Bible who is willing to enter the daunting arena of Milton scholarship.

The work of Nathan Scott is grounded in the New Criticism but complicated considerably by his familiarity with Continental-American phenomenology, the New Hermeneutic, existentialism and (more recently) the structuralist-poststructuralist discussion. It is, in fact, hard to say whether Scott is a theologian of culture (as Vernon Ruland calls him)[84] practising literary criticism or a literary critic drawing on theology. At any rate, he appears equally comfortable with both approaches, although his influence has been far greater as a religion and theology-oriented literary critic.

Scott's theology is more sophisticated than that of Brooks and R. W. B. Lewis, more 'catholic' than that of C. S. Lewis, and highly informed by Bonhoeffer's religionless Christianity, Tillich's theology of culture and the later Heidegger's poetic ontology. In spite of a liking for the ponderous Germanic style, Scott is invariably readable, and his distillations of Continental theology and philosophy, applied to myriad texts of mostly modern poetry, drama and fiction, have no doubt done more to spread awareness of the always embattled literature and religion field than the work of any other such critic. His 1976 *The Poetry of Civic Virtue* is a representative study. Here, addressing the writing of T. S. Eliot, André Malraux and W. H. Auden, he argues that these artists have nurtured the *polis* in ways that counter the misconception of all Modernist writers as sequestered away from communal interaction and creating their art out of a self-indulgent alienation. Implicit in Scott's exposition is a vision of *homo politicus* taking responsibility for building 'civic virtue' through individual acts of sacrifice and friendship, and the model is, at core, Christian.[85]

Robert C. Tannehill has carried forward a New Critical programme more completely than any other biblical scholar during the 1970s and 1980s. Informed by the New Hermeneutic, and engaged in discussion with structuralists, he nevertheless has maintained a course of interpretation that focuses on the internal conversations within the texts that provide its overall coherence and unity. His earliest work appropriating modern literary criticism as a guide was 'The Magnificat as Poem',[86] in which he carefully follows patterns of repetition, antithesis and progression that produce tensive relations and poetic disclosure. Then, in *The Sword of His Mouth*, he analyzes 'forceful and imaginative language' in synoptic sayings that reveal organic unity within pattern and tension. Calling for new terminology as he analyzes the unit on Turning the Other Cheek as a 'focal instance'[87] and interprets various sayings as 'antithetical aphorisms',[88] he works from individual sayings to clusters and finally toward sayings where a narrative setting contributes to their imaginative force. From this work, he turns to the 'pronouncement story' or apophthegm in the Gospels and divides them into six types of stories based on correction, commendation, objection, quest, inquiry and description.[89] Then he turns to narrative analysis of christology in the Gospel of Mark[90] before producing complete volumes on the narrative unity of the Gospel of Luke and the Acts of the Apostles.[91]

In Hebrew Bible interpretation, David M. Gunn has pursued a similar program of analysis, beginning with the fate of King Saul and working subsequently with the story of King David, Joshua and Judges, and Ruth.[92] It has been unusual for an interpreter of the Hebrew Bible to be guided by New Criticism, however, since the recent developments began with structural and linguistic studies by Edmund Leach and Roman Jakobson,[93] and to this field of interpretation we now turn.

Structuralism broke the dominance of formalisms such as the New Criticism in literary studies and posed the most serious challenge, at that point in the century, to historicism in biblical studies. It was also the movement that brought biblical and literary scholars closer together than the New Hermeneutic or the New Criticism had done. From the perspective of the 1990s, structuralism looks like a remarkably restrictive and prescriptive approach, with its own formalist biases, but at its zenith it seemed a refreshing advance beyond the repetitiousness of New Critical and historicist exercises. The New Hermeneutic and the New Criticism set in motion the shift in interpretation theory from the history to the language paradigm, but it was structuralism that gave the new model authority and popularity.

The structuralism we are describing begins with the 'revolutionary' French structural linguistics that reached a climax of sorts in Paris coincident with the student revolts there in 1968 but whose repercussions were felt in the English-speaking world throughout the next decade and beyond, until they were absorbed into the still more radical – and also largely French – poststructuralist strategies and became, ironically, part of the *history* of the eighties' 'critical theory' debate. In certain ways structuralism is an intensification of the New Criticism and the New Hermeneutic, for it takes their accent on language still more seriously. It proclaims the linguisticality of existence and urges the adoption of a/the linguistic paradigm to replace other models, above all the historical one.

One might have expected the formalist emphasis on the word and the biblical hermeneut's stress on the Word, therefore, to provide an easy transition from those older approaches to this new one, but this was not the case. It encountered bitter resistance in university literature and religion departments as well as in seminaries, and a major reason it did was the perceived threat of its central tenet, the theory of the arbitrary nature of the linguistic sign. The theory was formulated early in the century by the Swiss linguist Ferdinand de Saussure in his *Course in General Linguistics* (the name of an actual course offered at the University of Geneva as well as the title of a book compiled from Saussure's lectures by his students).[94]

According to Saussure, a linguistic sign is comprised of a signified, which is the unarticulated concept or field of expression, and a signifier, the 'sound-image' or vehicle of expression. But no natural relationship obtains between these two components of the sign. The sign is entirely arbitrary. That, for example, the blazing star that is the centre of our planetary system corresponds to the sound-image we pronounce and script as 'sun' is the result of accident and social convention. Further, because linguistic signs are arbitrary and one cannot depend on the old assumption of some natural equation between the word/symbol and what it represents, meaning must derive from the differences between signs and hence be understood as sheerly relational. This view is a long way from Tillich's theory of symbols as participating in the 'meaning and power' of the entities toward which they point, for in the differential system of structuralism the linguistic signs point only toward each other in an endless interplay of signification – a notion on which Derrida would elaborate as the rationale for his concept of dissemination.

Saussure was able to construct this system by 'freezing' language, in effect, and attempting to isolate its laws of interacting elements rather than continuing the wonted philological tradition that stressed etymologies, historical change and, inevitably, semantics. Saussure's choice of this synchronic over a diachronic approach is reinforced by his distinction between *langue* and *parole*. *Langue* is the whole abstract system of language, while *parole* is the actual expression of language in various utterances and discourses, and it is not incorrect to think of *langue* as the signified, the total potential of language to be expressed, and *parole* as the signifier, the concrete articulation, so that *langue* and *parole* together are the two interacting sides of language as a sign system.

Saussure's linguistic theory was seminal and immensely fruitful and was developed in a number of other fields. It stimulated the rise of literary narratology, of structuralist myth studies in the work of the anthropologist Claude Lévi-Strauss, and of structuralist psychoanalysis via the investigations of Jacques Lacan. It led to a deepening of poetics in the research of Roland Barthes and Roman Jakobson, and it helped to provoke both the deconstructive philosophy of Jacques Derrida and the theory of epistemic discourse advanced by Michel Foucault. This is not the place to treat all of these. They have, indeed, been exhaustively summarized and criticized in many books and essays over more than two decades, and the final chapter of this book will discuss in detail the debate over the theological possibilities generated by the writings of Derrida. Here we will sketch just three concepts out of the welter of structuralist influences that have particularly fascinated biblical and literary critics: the distinction between metaphor and metonymy, the theory of binary oppositions and the concept of deep structure.

The Russian-born linguist Roman Jakobson contributed a key distinction between metaphor and metonymy. In his landmark 'Linguistics and Poetics' essay,[95] he situates literary language within the framework of structural linguistics. He lists and describes six factors of verbal communication (e.g., addresser, context, addressee) and six corresponding functions (e.g., emotive, referential, conative) and states that the self-referential function of language, the focus of the message for itself, is the poetic function. In his *Fundamentals of Language*,[96] he elaborates Saussure's distinction between metaphor and metonymy as principles whereby one orders the linguistic components such as phonemes, morphemes and sentemes. Metaphor is connected to the principle of similarity, and to the 'vertical' plane of substitution, paradigm and opposition, while metonymy is related to contiguity and the 'horizontal' plane of linearity, syntagm and relation. Put oversimplified, in the realm of literary genres, metaphor characterizes (lyric) poetry, while metonymy marks narrative. Jakobson also describes the operations of metaphor and metonymy diagnostically in terms of two types of aphasia observed in children who could not substitute one element of language 'metaphorically' for another or who were unable to combine language elements contiguously or 'metonymically'. The distinction between the two principles has, of course, been adopted very profitably by readers of literary and biblical texts. The virtues of the metaphor/metonymy distinction in the interpretation of the New Testament parables, for example, are manifest.

Jakobson's observation that metaphor and metonymy correspond to condensation and displacement in the Freudian model of the unconscious is also fruitful for a structuralist literary-psychoanalytic hermeneutic. Metaphor merges images into new figures of signification, just as the dream conflates elements of waking reality into novel, concise patterns, and metonymy works associatively in a 'this reminds me of that' fashion, just as the dream replaces some element of waking experience with its contiguous image. Lacan, rereading Freud, identified metonymic displacement with desire (brought on by the lack left by the displacement) and metaphoric condensation with symptom (caused by the overabundance of the densely packed image). Such diagnostic attitudes towards literary and biblical texts have been attacked by Ricoeur, in what may prove to be one of the most telling critiques of the late twentieth century, as 'the hermeneutics of suspicion'.

The concept of binary oppositions, at one time so popular in structuralist interpretation, owes much to Jakobson's phonology, specifically to his theory of phonemic differentiation in which the pronunciation of the phonemic units is reduced to twelve fundamental levels in all languages and determined by pairs of contrasting sounds. This phonemic 'law' was quickly applied by others to meaning-units – to words, concepts and tropes – and even contributed to the speculation (expressed by Roland Barthes, among others) that humans *think* binarily, in terms of patterns of paired oppositions. Such binarism was exploited imaginatively by Lévi-Strauss and Edmund Leach in anthropological myth studies, and their examples provided the impetus for a plethora of biblical (particularly Old Testament) studies of oppositional patterns informing the structure of Hebrew myth narrative and poetry.

Literary and biblical interpreters were attracted no less to structuralism because of the allure of its 'deep structure' promise. Lévi-Strauss, foremost, argued that a text's/culture's surface structure covers another and different pattern of meaning underlying the obvious one and that in comparative, 'synchronic' readings of, for instance, the different versions of a myth narrative, the basic elements of that myth will emerge as the 'deep', real significance of what the story's sequentiality obscures.

Here one perceives a 'paraphrase' of the sort that the New Critics did not anticipate, but it is part of an attitude toward interpretation older than mid-twentieth-century structuralism. Marx's theory that a society's superstructure disguises its determinative substructural base, and Freud's conviction that the discourse of the person under analysis covers over the repressed but revelatory secrets of childhood causing neuroses and psychoses are earlier versions of the structuralist quest for the deep order to be found and laid bare. Literary and biblical scholars may have thought to recognize a theory of foundational meaning here congenial to traditional absolutist theories of symbols, yet the differences are crucial. The structuralist deep structure is not the ground of ultimate meaning or being but just the opposite. Determined by the notion of the sign's arbitrary nature, this deep structure is always finally a cultural accident/invention, the result of an infinite interplay of signs that denies (as Derrida would claim) the possibility of foundational meaning. Hence, the adoption of structural analysis by biblical and literary critics meant that they, if they applied the method rigorously, would be led to question the traditional basis of their hermeneutics. The structuralist 'paraphrase' of the text as its deep structure became the impasse (the 'aporia') that blocked the way back to the innocence of absolutist interpretation.

It is notable, and probably ironic, that in the literary application of structuralism the theory tends to obscure the interpretation. Or to put it another way, most applications, intentionally or not, turn into illustrations of how the theory works, and the accusation leveled against structuralism – that it proliferates theory at the expense of criticism – is in good part justified. Even (perhaps above all) the brilliant early textual readings of the French structuralists, such as Tzvetan Todorov's study, using a Greimas-oriented actantial model, of *Les Liaisons dangereuses*[97] and Gérard Genette's analysis of Proust in the three volumes of *Figures*,[98] demonstrate the preoccupation with theory.

In Roland Barthes's remarkable *S/Z*[99] a 200 page reading of 'Sarrasine', a 30 page short story by Balzac, the literary text is virtually overwhelmed by the theory, but it is a theory so ingeniously and engagingly spun out that the story is at last restored to something like its original lustre. This happens because Barthes does not provide *a* reading but a plenitude of them that is simultaneously a celebration of the reading process itself (a version of what he calls elsewhere 'the pleasure of the text'), a demonstration of how the linguistic interplay of signs can function at the level of literary analysis, and an example of how the notion of arbitrariness can be employed to turn a short work of fiction into a profound cultural critique.

Summarizing Barthes's method in *S/Z* is pointless in the space we have here. Suffice it to say that he invents and borrows five codes or voices (the hermeneutic, semic, symbolic, proairetic and cultural) and uses these as the organizing principle for commentary on 561 'lexia' (fragments) into which he divides the story.

Although structuralism in the form of, say, A. J. Greimas's structural semantics now seems quite cumbersome and forbidding, the Barthesian versions of it could be liberating, and they led in fact to the first significant interchanges of biblical and literary critics whereby literary scholars interpreted biblical texts and biblical scholars read literary texts with acumen. Louis Marin's *The Semiotics of the Passion Narrative*[100] and Barthes's own essay on 'The Struggle with the Angel: Textual Analysis of Genesis 32:23–33'[101] are examples of the former. In Barthes's treatment of the patriarch Jacob wrestling with his superhuman opponent he reveals particularly his indebtedness to structuralist narratology and to Lévi-Strauss's myth analysis.

An illustration of a biblical critic inspired by structuralism to engage literary texts is John Dominic Crossan's impressive *Raid on the Articulate*. As the subtitle, *Comic Eschatology in Jesus and Borges*, suggests, this study has a certain playfully subversive agenda, and Crossan himself, in the preface, says that it 'situates itself within this challenge posed by structuralist literary criticism to the monolithic ascendancy of historical criticism in biblical studies'.[102] Reading the parables and sayings of Jesus against the deceptive, self-reflexive fiction of the Argentine writer, Jorge Luis Borges, Crossan finds in both an iconoclastic use of language against institutions and tradition (including the institution of language itself) that, in yet another way, demythologizes religious and literary interpretations assuming the validity of foundational representation. To have Jesus emerge as an advocate of arbitrary signification is startling, but is also the kind of shock that readies one for the paradoxes of the parables that reveal gaps of transcendence.

Biblical scholars employing structuralism to interpret Scripture have been no less encumbered by the methodology than the literary critics but have managed more consistently to let the texts speak *through* (and not seldom in spite of) the jargon. Two examples are

Daniel Patte's *What is Structural Exegesis?*[103] and Robert Polzin's *Biblical Structuralism.*[104]

Patte, a pioneer in the introduction of structuralism to American biblical scholars, in this pivotal study presents structuralist analysis as a method designed to complement historical criticism and, after an overview of structuralist interpretive strategies based on the Saussurian theory of sign, etc., applies that method to exegeses of the Good Samaritan parable and Paul's Letter to the Galatians (1:1–10). Polzin, in a wide-ranging first half of his book, describes the nature of structuralism and its implication for biblical hermeneutics, then puts it to the formidable task of interpreting the Book of Job. Both Patte and Polzin typify the biblical structuralists' fondness for graphs, charts and algebraic formulas that complicate the method beyond its actual intricacies, but, fortunately, one can profit from the books without needing to absorb their technical aspects.

One must finally call attention to the role of *Semeia: An Experimental Journal for Biblical Criticism* in advancing the fortunes of structuralism in American biblical studies. Founded by Robert Funk in 1974 and guided by scholars such as Crossan, Patte and Via, *Semeia* was, throughout the seventies, the centre of an emerging biblical structuralism, until it moved with the currents of criticism and opened up to deconstruction, narratology, feminism, speech-act theory, reader-response criticism, etc., in relation to biblical studies. In the process it also served, and serves, as a journal where non-biblical critics such as Derrida, Frank Kermode and Susan Lanser join biblical scholars in dialogue.

It is reasonable to turn next to narratology, also called narrative poetics or simply narrative theory, since it had its genesis mainly in structuralism – even though it gradually outgrew that beginning. Narratology preceded or developed parallel to French structuralism in the work of Viktor Shklovsky, Roman Ingarden, Emil Staiger and Wayne Booth, as well as in that of the belatedly discovered Mikhail Bakhtin, but structuralist narrative theory was the force that truly invigorated a poetics of narrative. In Terry Eagleton's opinion, 'if structuralism transformed the study of poetry, it revolutionized the study of narrative. Indeed it created a whole new literary science – narratology.'[105]

Our sketch of narratology's role in the literary and biblical criticism interaction will take us far beyond structuralism into the complexities of poststructuralist hermeneutics (a concept that some would argue is oxymoronic), for a number of the leading narrative theorists nowadays have left structuralism or were never a part of it, and some, like Jean-François Lyotard, argue that narratology itself has no bright future in the postmodern world. We believe that the present study of narrative has tremendous potential and that it will increasingly influence hermeneutics at least well into the twenty-first century.

We will begin, however, with the Russian Formalist work on narrative that preceded and influenced the structuralists. Although Susan Sontag could write in the sixties that we had developed a theory of poetry but still lacked a poetics of narrative,[106] and be accurate for the Western context, the Russian Formalists had already, since the second decade of the century, been busy with a narrative theory that grew out of poetic theory and stressed the differences between poetry and prose fiction. Their greatest contribution was the distinction they drew in narrative analysis between *fable* (story) and *sujet* (plot) or, roughly between the story to be told and its manner of execution. That these are far from synonymous can be seen when we consider, for example, that the *fable* – the material or 'stuff' of a narrative – can be told in a vast variety of ways (e.g., via framing, flashbacks, multiple or unreliable narrators) that determine the nature of the story. Indeed, one could argue that without the *sujet* there is no *fable*.

This latter claim reminds one of the Saussurian definition of the linguistic sign, and one can create an analogy. The *fable* is something like the signified, the unarticulated potentiality of expression that needs the formative articulation of the signifier, the plot. It is not surprising that the French structuralists turned to aspects of Russian Formalism to shape their own narratology. Gérard Genette, in the Proust analysis mentioned above, modified Shklovsky's *fable – sujet* opposition into a difference among events that constitute a story (*histoire*), the actual story (*récit*) and the story's articulation (*narration*), with *récit* as the pivotal component from which the reader reconstructs *histoire* and anticipates *narration*. Genette then relates this triad to three aspects of verbs – tense, mood and voice – and shows how, for example, an examination of voice elucidates the relation of the narrator not only to *histoire* and *récit* but also to the story's characters and to its reader. Apart from the value of these distinctions in their own right for interpretation, they prepared the way for still more helpful concepts, such as that of focalization, for development by non-structuralist narratologists.

Genette and other structuralist theorists were at least as deeply indebted to another Russian, Vladimir Propp, for another direction of narrative investigation, that of actantial analysis. From Propp's *Morphology of the Folktale*, Greimas borrows seven character roles of folktale identified by Propp and adapts them (while reducing them to six) to a double syntactic-thematic pattern that purports to provide the foundation for interpreting all semantic actions – from those expressed in a simple sentence to those comprising a whole narrative. In Propp's schema the model was:

dispatcher   sought-after person   hero

↑

helper/giver   hero   villain/false hero

Greimas alters it to:

sender   object   receiver

↑

helper   subject   opponent

Although the model has obvious flaws (e.g., Greimas's derivation of the 'receiver' role from Propp's schema is tenuous), other structuralists such as Barthes (in his Genesis 32 essay on Jacob and the angel) and Todorov (in his interpretation of *Les Liaisons dangereuses*) have employed it in ways that expand our comprehension of characters' interaction and of the patterns of plotting, and it has enjoyed popularity among biblical scholars.

Lévi-Strauss's myth analysis and Barthes's code systems, both of which we touched on earlier, have relevance for the evolution of narratology, but we cannot pause to expand on them. Instead, we will move on to the work of Mikhail Bakhtin and Mieke Bal as examples of non-structuralist narratologists who are important for the literary/biblical interpretation nexus.

Although Bakhtin, who was in some ways a transitional figure between the formalists and the structuralists,[107] was writing criticism in the Soviet Union as early as the 1920s and well past mid-century, he began to exert influence in the West only since the seventies, following translation of works such as *Rabelais and His World* into English. One could say that whereas Barthes employs the study of prose fiction to identify a profusion of codes or voices of interpretation, Bakhtin finds these voices more deeply embedded in the very structure of the narrative text itself, which text then offers a complex, even subversive challenge to organic views of reality. Not surprisingly, given the apparently Marxist framework of Bakhtin's scholarship, his literary criticism is much concerned with the sociocultural dimensions of the text and with a desire to disclose the ideological implications of literature and its interpretation. Yet in fact we now know that his approach, so far from being a standard Marxist one, is deeply informed by his own Russian Orthodox background. It is not the class struggle in literature but rather the way language is made to disrupt all authority and liberate alternative voices that is his central concern.[108]

We will call attention first to Bakhtin's attack on Saussure's 'objectivist' *langue*-oriented linguistics and his alternative of an approach that stresses *parole*, the actual expressions of real persons in concrete social situations. The *parole*-oriented linguistic sign is far more complicated than Saussure's version. In his narratology, this unruly and multi-implicational sign expands into the polyphonic form typified by Dostoevsky's novels – in contrast to the monologic form of Tolstoy's works.[109]

It is the voices of Dostoevsky's characters that are polyphonic. They differ from each other by virtue of the ways they are distinguished from the author's voice, as for example by the use of techniques such as free indirect discourse. Although these voices are less controlled by the author than those of Tolstoy, their utterances do not produce chaos (although they often verge on anarchy) because they are always fundamentally in dialogue, and Bakhtin in fact refers as much to the dialogic as to the polyphonic form of the Dostoevsky type of novel.

This sort of heteronymy attacks the traditional definition of the novel itself, for some of the voices that are heard come from other genres, other kinds of discourse. This is as it should be, Bakhtin thinks: the novel should be rebellious and unsettling. It is a form of social upheaval. It is in this spirit that Bakhtin celebrates the 'carnivalization' of literary genres. In his study of the history of public festivity he emphasizes the anti-authoritarian, mocking, parodic language of carnival and finds this exemplified in ancient forms such as the Socratic dialogue and the so-called Menippean satire written by Lucian and revived by Dostoevsky.

It is apparent why Bakhtin, once his writing became available in English, gained popularity so quickly. His depiction of the subversive nature of the polyphonic novel is attractive to deconstructionist critics; his accent on dialogue appeals to those (for example, among the reader-response critics) seeking an interpretive community; his stress on the ideological complicitness of signifying systems and on the function of extraliterary voices within the novel speaks to the socio-historically oriented scholar. Also, as Eagleton points out, 'since all signs were material ... and since there could be no human consciousness without them, Bakhtin's theory laid the foundation for a materialist theory of consciousness itself.'[110] Versions of this theory are finding their way into materialist readings of the Bible undertaken in the context of a socio-historical approach that owes a good deal of its impetus to Marxist and socialist thought. In the essay collection *God of the Lowly*, for example, Kuno Füssel shows an awareness of Bakhtin's work.[111] One can also anticipate that Bakhtin's theory of polyphony, the many voices of a text asserting themselves with and against each other, will provoke interest among biblical scholars alert to the uses of the theory in treating not only the heterogeneous nature of the biblical canon but also the conflict of voices within the individual books themselves.

Julia Kristeva, in works such as *Desire in Language*, [112] continues some of Bakhtin's emphases, such as those on the ideological nature of literature and its value as social practice, and merges these with other insights drawn from Marxism, structural linguistics and psychoanalysis to forge a formidable and influential feminist hermeneutic. Although some of her writing is narratologically oriented (Todorov was her mentor), narratology is not her central concern, nor has she had significant impact on biblical studies. One must turn to Mieke Bal as a versatile scholar who combines innovative poststructuralist ('post' mainly in the sense of 'after') narrative poetics, biblical interpretation and feminist theory in compelling ways.

Trained in the Netherlands as a comparative literature scholar, Bal published her first major work in English on narratology in 1985, and burst into the awareness of English-language Bible scholars in the late eighties with three books in quick succession on women in the Hebrew Bible: her combative *Lethal Love*, the more sophisticated *Murder and Difference*, and the comprehensive and subtle *Death and Dissymmetry*.[113] In all of these the attack on male, 'patriarchal' scholarship is vigorous and solidly grounded in biblical research; her theses are both daring and persuasive and her range of competence daunting. Bal's *Narratology*[114] is a concise but thorough summary of state-of-the-art narrative theory of the structuralist (she is at home in Greimas's theory) and poststructuralist eras, a taxonymy along the lines of Seymour Chatman's *Story and Discourse*[115] and Shlomith Rimmon-Kenan's *Narrative Fiction*,[116] but superseding them. Since then she has refined her theory into a compact hermeneutical tool that appears as an appendix, a two-page 'Model for Narratological Analysis' at the end of *Death and Dissymmetry*. The model is too terse to be summarized; we will remark only that it attends to matters of language, voice and action in relation to role, position and action and stresses mainly focalization and the identities/roles of persons within the narrative. Although Bal is not beholden to Bakhtin, her research in *Murder and Difference* as well as in *Death and Dissymmetry* exposes the ideology – in this case sexist – in the texts' language as well as in their interpreters' modes, and encourages a reading that plays with the subversive heterogeneity and transfers such subversion to one's own exegesis.

In *Murder and Difference*, employing an orchestration of codes approach not unlike that of Barthes's *S/Z*, Bal undertakes a meticulous reading of Judges 4 and 5, the story of the Canaanite general Sisera's murder at the hands of the Hebrew woman, Jael. Arguing on the basis of philological, historical and generic evidence that the poetic 'Son of Deborah' version in chapter 5 is a female-composed older telling than the 'male', largely prose narrative of chapter 4, Bal proceeds to show how generations of male scholars have overlooked the obvious centrality of the female actors, marginalized them, and thus radically misread the passage as yet another instance of female duplicity. Bal, in contrast, wishes to amplify the prophetic, celebratory, simultaneously nurturing and destroying female voice of the narrative that, if heard along with other silenced women's voices in the canon, will change the nature of biblical scholarship. Her recent decision to leave this field for other research, almost as abruptly as she entered it, can only be regretted, for her contributions in the brief time of her involvement have been, in the best sense, carnivalesque as well as profound.

Leaving narratology, we turn to two prominent critics who have been subversive forces in another sense both in literary criticism and in biblical studies, Northrop Frye and René Girard. Frye's subversion began with an embracing archetypal theory of literature and culture expounded at a time (the fifties and sixties) when the New Criticism barely tolerated such 'extrinsic' interests. Girard threatened the literary establishment with a radical anthropological-psychological theory that appeared too harsh an assessment of human nature to be acceptable. Both men are prominent mavericks, powerful critics who have made few disciples and who are regarded with a mixture of scepticism and respect. Since an operative aspect of their works is a focus on myth in relation to Scripture as well as literature, we will examine representative aspects of their scholarship from that perspective and then continue the myth emphasis as a way of introducing, at last, Paul Ricoeur via his *Symbolism of Evil*.

Although Frye is occasionally identified as a structuralist, the designation in his case has virtually nothing to do with the French version but rather with the concern for structures and the general laws by which they work.[117] One of Frye's two central contributions to literary interpretation, in spite of a prolific production of books of criticism, remains his 1957 *Anatomy of Criticism*,[118] in which he, in effect, totalizes the New Critical creed of 'intrinsic' analysis and the eschewing of non-literary concerns by discovering in the history and structure of literature itself a 'scientific' system that categorizes (anatomizes) all periods, genres and components of literature. The laws that govern this system consist of quartets, triads and pairs of archetypal, mythic and symbolic patterns. For example, the rhythm of the four seasons and the associated *mythoi* of spring, summer, fall and winter generated, Frye argues, the corresponding basic narrative types of comedy, romance, tragedy and irony. Western culture has passed through all four of these genres as stages, having arrived at irony in the modern era, and is now poised to begin the cycle again by a descent into a new mythic phase.

Further, within each stage one can find a different status for the hero, and this information can be organized into a theory of literary modes. The mythic hero is superior to others in kind; the romantic hero in degree; the high-mimetic hero of tragedy and the epic super-ior to others in degree but not to his surroundings; the low-mimetic hero of comedy and realism on a par with his fellows; and the ironic hero inferior to his fellows. Running through all of this are three symbol patterns of the apocalyptic, the demonic and the anagogical – which have important bearing on Frye's Bible interpretation.

Frye's system is, patently, a combination of the ingenious and the facile; it is easy to criticize his system and there is a sense in which it comes very close to the old Arnoldian view of 'literature as a displaced version of religion'.[119] Indeed Frye fully intends to engage literature as an essential part of our belief system – for him it could not be otherwise. This programme is developed beyond *Anatomy of Criticism* in *The Great Code*, Frye's book on the Bible that com-prises his other major contribution to literary interpretation and, at the same time, to biblical studies. Scripture already figured promin-ently in the myth and archetype analysis of the *Anatomy*, in which Frye says that although the Bible involves elements of romance, irony and tragedy, its plot stresses the comic ('The sense of tragedy as a prelude to comedy seems almost inseparable from anything explicitly Christian'),[120] and contrasts Adam, 'the archetype of the inevitably ironic ... human nature under sentence of death', with Christ, 'The archetype of the incongruously ironic ... the perfectly innocent victim excluded from human society'.[121]

In *The Great Code* Frye attempts to show both how a myth and archetype approach reveals the overarching mythic unity of the Bible ('a gigantic myth, a narrative extending over the whole of time from creation to apocalypse')[122] and, conversely (and a bit reminiscent of Erich Auerbach's argument in *Mimesis* that the Bible is the foundation of Western literature and culture), how a mythic comprehension of the Bible provides a means of grasping the unity of culture, indeed of human behaviour. The Bible's mythic unity is determined by what one might call its progressive narrative structure and by an 'upward metamorphosis' whereby Scripture expands itself 'teleologically' (our term, not Frye's). The narrative progression passes through the five stages between creation and apocalypse (revolution/exodus, law, wisdom, prophecy and gospel), in which movement each phase absorbs and enlarges its predecessor, whereas the upward metamorphosis myth conveys the continuous supplementation of biblical materials, culminating in the encompassing of the Old Testament in the New and all previous metaphors gathered in the image of the body of the Messiah, the coming Christ who is and brings the end (the apocalypse) and the new beginning.

Not all modern critics have either presupposed or sought such unity, and some biblical scholars have seen in Frye's evolutionary framework the remnants of a Christian triumphalism,[123] and, though it is surely against Frye's intention, it is not difficult to translate the rewriting of Scripture in the dynamic of upward metamorphosis into an illustration of Derrida's concepts of supplementarity and dissemination: the constant rewriting goes on because the sign never finds its adequate referent, and dissemination comes to characterize this 'state of perpetually unfulfilled meaning that exists in the absence of all signifieds'.[124] In Richard Harland's terminology, what Frye sees, in faith, expressed mythologically in the Bible as a centripetal drive toward ultimate unity could be understood just as well as a centrifugal force exploding writing and meaning in endless dispersion.

Frye opens himself up to such a deconstructive critique because he does not consider language itself to be an essential part of the hermeneutical problematic. Thus, while the great code approach is valuable for sketching a Christian-biblical self-understanding, it does little for the impasse in the current scene of interpretation caused by a sense of the unreliability of language. René Girard, on the other hand, is acutely aware of the structuralist and poststructuralist challenges to traditional mimetic theories of language and literature and responds to them without yielding his contrary position. Rather than accommodating these challenges by seeking alternatives to representation theory, Girard instead moves deeper into an exploration of mimesis and finds in a more subtle 'conflictual' definition of it a means of turning the criticism back on his critics. Already in his *Deceit, Desire, and the Novel* he argues that 'desire itself is essentially mimetic, directed toward an other desired by the mode,'[125] and sees in the fictional playing out of this pattern of mimetic desire (a complicated version of Freud's 'family romance') a definition of the novel as 'an obsession transcended'.[126] More specifically, the triangulation of the hero's rivalry with the other for the desired object generates an acute threat of violence, one that can spill over into the pathological as the rivals find no way out of their Oedipal dilemma.

This violence writ large in culture and the history of culture is the subject of Girard's *Violence and the Sacred*, his 1977 (in English translation) book that had a far greater impact on the literary and biblical studies interaction than the earlier work. Whereas Frye looked for the genesis of all myth in the rhythm of the seasons and their progressive narrative-archetypal expression, Girard places it at the scene of sacrifice, where victim and victimizer interact in a communal resolution of the Oedipal fix. An interview with Girard in a 1978 issue of *Diacritics* displays how he advances his controversial thesis worked out in *Violence and the Sacred* and does battle with his many critics. He says:

Victimage ... becomes the sacred epiphany of the founding ancestor, or divinity, who was the first to transgress the laws he also brought to the community. He came first to chastise, then to educate and reward by showing how to practice ritual, how to kill substitute victims, in other words. The classical structuralists repress conflictual mimesis as much as anyone ever did. That is why the poststructuralists, beginning with Derrida, could turn mimesis into a weapon against the structuralist theory of the sign.... The new problematic of mimesis exceeds the problematic of signification in all directions. Lacoue-Labarthe and poststructuralism see mimesis as a factor of undecidability and this is not radical enough. As a result they never reach the other side of mimesis already perceived by religion but in a purely religious and fantastic light. They do not understand that mimesis can also play the crucial role in the genesis and practical stabilization of cultural differences.[127]

Later, the interviewer remarks, 'Clearly, certain texts of Judeo-Christianity – texts of the Hebrew prophets and of the Synoptic Gospels – have a privileged status in your work in that they reveal in full the sacrificial foundations of the primitive universe. In the wake of this revelation, what precisely is the nature of our modern inheritance?' Girard's response projects that biblical studies itself will be victimized:

Scapegoat demythologization alone is real. The biblical text alone carries it to its extreme conclusion. This is a harsh doctrine, no doubt, and it will take more time, more cultural disintegration for *la modernité* to take it seriously at all. The signifier is visibly playing against all of us, this time, and the irony is unbearable. Our most cherished beliefs are threatened. As the evidence of what I say becomes compelling, attempts will be made to re-arrange it in a manner more compatible with the self-esteem of an intelligentsia whose sole common ground and binding theme – *religio* – has become the systematic expulsion of everything biblical, our last sacrificial operation in the grand manner.[128]

Girard hopes that the West can still overcome the institutionalization of sacrifice in Judeo-Christianity – a ritualization that was an attempt to control violence but that also feeds it – and come to its senses, and hence his apocalyptic tone is tempered by some hope: 'The sacrificial misreading of the Judeo-Christian scriptures, common to Christian and anti-Christian thinkers alike has only retarded, we may believe, both the arrival of the ultimate *emergency* and the correct non-sacrificial reading of the biblical text.'[129]

The most comprehensive application of Girard's work in biblical studies has been by Burton L. Mack in *A Myth of Innocence.* Especially informed by Girard's 1982 book, *The Scapegoat*,[130] Mack uses Michel Foucault's *Archaeology of Knowledge*[131] linked with Derrida's *Of Grammatology* to uncover the voices in the text that tell stories about social moments in early Christianity reaching back to the time of Jesus. Through intertextual analysis, Mack detects significantly different social environments in early Christianity in the language of various collections of materials scholars have uncovered in the Gospel of Mark. The parables in Mark 4 reveal a social location where Christians perpetuate an alternative *paideia* which establishes a boundary between those on the inside who understand and those on the outside to whom all things appear as puzzling images.[132] The pronouncement stories exhibit a sociopolitical battle between Christians and Pharisees over the synagogue and the scripture in Galilee, an attempt at 'reform' by early Christians which failed.[133] The miracle stories exhibit an environment where Christians experienced no competition or hostility with Jewish leaders, but present Jesus as the founder of the new congregation of Israel using the 'great' traditions of Moses and Elijah.[134]

Underlying the passion narratives is the Christ cult from yet another social environment, especially cultivated by the apostle Paul, which provides no detailed information about Jesus's death in Jerusalem.[135] The author of Mark, in Mack's reading, was closest to the environment of the failure of the synagogue reform movement in Galilee. Using materials from the different social environments available to him from Syro-Palestinian Christian groups, 'Mark' transferred the hostility and anger of Christians in the Galilean situation in the sixties back to Jesus's death in Jerusalem 35 to 40 years earlier. In this manner, 'Mark' created a 'myth of origins' that introduces a rationale for the destruction of the Jerusalem temple based on the death of an 'innocent', Jesus in Jerusalem. Whatever was the nature of the entanglement of the Galilean Jew, Jesus, with authorities in Jerusalem that resulted in the crucifixion is completely covered over by socio-ideological dynamics coming out of the later social environment of Galilee that existed 30 to 40 years later. Bible scholars and theologians have barely begun to absorb this kind of intertextual analysis that assaults traditional reconstructions of the social history of earliest Christianity, but the effect of this work is likely to be highly significant during the coming decades of inter-pretation of early Christian texts.

If Girard is the aggressive myth-oriented scholar who battles his critics and Mack is the biblical scholar who has joined this active mode of engagement, Paul Ricoeur is the reconciler who addresses myth judiciously in the course of a career that has embraced many other cultural constructs as well. Ricoeur has absorbed the major movements of twentieth-century hermeneutics – phenomenology, existentialism, structuralism, linguistics, poststructuralism in its vari-ous guises – and synthesized them into his own still-evolving and expanding system. In a dismissive review of Ricoeur's magisterial three-volume *Time and Narrative*, J. Hillis Miller labels Ricoeur a reactionary who ignores the crucial current discussion of represent-ation and assumes 'the existence of stable monological texts of determinable meanings, meanings controlled in each case by the intentions of the author and by the text's reference to a prelinguistic "real world out there".'[136] More accurate, probably, is that Ricoeur's work will survive and prevail as among the great works of this century's mediatory interpretation – and the attention we pay to him in these concluding pages reflects our high regard for him.

His 1967 *The Symbolism of Evil*,[137] probably still the most widely read of his works, is a brilliant example of phenomenological myth criticism that exemplifies his synthesizing and mediating talents. *The Symbolism of Evil* is the third of a multivolumed phenomenology of the will that has taken many detours since its inception but appears now finished, a good quarter-century later, with *Time and Narrative* (especially volume 3), which at least approximates the projected (and concluding) poetics of the will. Whereas the first two 'will' studies, *Freedom and Nature* and *Fallible Man*, offer respectively an 'eidetics' and an 'empirics' of the will, *The Symbolism of Evil* introduces a 'hermeneutics' of the will as a third kind of reading that continues the analysis of the relationship of the will to self and other. Above all, the hermeneutical approach addresses its proper field, language itself.

This focus leads Ricoeur to concentrate on how the will can be further understood in terms of the human encounter with the reality of evil, an encounter which has been expressed through the symbolic-mythic language of the believer who 'confesses' his experience with that reality. This confession is conveyed through the three primary symbols of defilement, sin and guilt, each of which has a cosmological, oneiric (psychic) and poetic dimension. For example, in the primary symbol of guilt (which is a subjectivization of the sin symbol), the cosmological dimension is the feeling of the weight of guilt, the oneiric aspect is the experience of forgiveness or despair, and the poetic aspect is the imagery of a tribunal and of a scrupulously functioning conscience.

The particular relevance of *The Symbolism of Evil* for biblical interpretation becomes apparent in Ricoeur's next strategy, which is to examine the servile (passion-enslaved) will in the context of four myths of evil. Through this operation the narrative structure of myth itself provides a commentary on the archaic symbol of evil and enables the interpreter to employ the myths for her reflection on the nature of evil and its embeddedness in language. Discussing first cosmogonies and theogonies, Ricoeur finds in the Babylonian Gilgamesh epic the principle of evil existing in the chaos that marks the primordial state of things and entering the world through the creation of the gods. In the Hebrew Genesis myth, in contrast, Yahweh creates a good world and evil is generated by an act of human volition, even though the serpent's presence hints at an awareness of primordial evil already there. In the Greek Titan myths, evil originates somewhere in the uncertain realm between the human and the divine, a situation Ricoeur sees as similar to the Hebrew understanding of evil's genesis as an act of human volition and as already present.

In his analysis of three other myth genres – tragic myths, anthropological myths and myths of the exiled soul – Ricoeur employs the Adamic 'self-reflective' myth as central and as a contrast to the three other 'speculative' myths, a process through which he shows how the evil that humankind incorporates and initiates is also, paradoxically, already there as an other which man resists but which nevertheless invades him. The four myths interpreted together thus exemplify Ricoeur's voluntary-involuntary dualism: humankind acts to create the evil that is already its condition. In phenomenological terms, intending consciousness *apprehends* the evil that structures consciousness as well as the world.

The Symbolism of Evil concludes with Ricoeur's widely circulated essay, 'The Symbol Gives Rise to Thought', in which he argues the possibility of overcoming the impasse of the hermeneutical circle (one must believe in order to understand but understand in order to believe) by his famous wager of faith. Rather than attempting objective analysis, one needs to recognize one's implication in the interpretive process, take a position and work it through in the expectation that it will produce 'goodness'. Thus the exercise of the will becomes a key part of the hermeneutical process, illustrated here by Ricoeur's own 'faithful' decision to adopt the Genesis myth as his own and to undertake his symbol-myth interpretation of evil in the hope that it will lead to an experience of goodness – not any sort of primordial goodness but one imagined by the 'second naiveté'.

This wager-of-faith strategy, which we have described in an exceedingly simplified form, has continued to characterize Ricoeur's scholarship. What Miller and others see as a recalcitrant conservatism is really a firm openness to the examination of many positions from the tentative adoption of one of them, in the expectation of receiving correction and offering correction as well. This is a stance more open-minded and open-ended than that of the poststructuralists who have already closed off the dialogue (among whom we would not class Derrida) by presupposing the singular validity of deconstructive tactics – in which 'the dismantling of meaning and presence can become a *deus ex machina* every bit as predictable as the most triumphalist ontology.'[138]

In *Time and Narrative*, volume 3, Ricoeur develops his concept of 'mimesis 3' as 'the refiguration process through which the reader contributes to a text's meaning through his or her active questioning and response'. In 'Narrated Time' he writes, 'By refiguration I mean ... the power of revelation and transformation achieved by narrative configurations when they are "applied" to actual acting and suffering.'[139] Here is the ethical moment of hermeneutics that takes the place, for the committed interpreter, of speculation and restores the power of history. It is illustrated by Ricoeur's confession of horror at reading Holocaust literature – texts that, like those of the Bible, call for empathy rather than speculation and ask one to act in history to guide its future.

But this ethics of narrative has always been at least implicit in Ricoeur's thought and appears in earlier form in texts that connect his discussion of myth to biblical interpretation. In an essay from the early seventies entitled 'The Critique of Religion',[140] Ricoeur addresses the problem of false-consciousness in the thought of Marx, Nietzsche and Freud as part of a new critique of culture involving a hermeneutics of suspicion that is based on a doubt more radical than Descartes's:

Descartes doubts things but leans on the fortress of consciousness. . . . The problem of false-consciousness could only appear by way of a critique of culture whereby consciousness appears in itself as a doubtful consciousness. . . . What distinguishes a false-consciousness from error or falsehood, and what motivates a particular type of critique, of denunciation, is the possibility of signifying another thing than what one believes was signified, that is, the possibility of the masked consciousness.[141]

Discovering what this false-consiousness masks is what Ricoeur refers to as demystification, and he finds it at work in 'a Marxist critique of ideology, a Nietzschean critique of resentment, and a Freudian critique of infantile distress'.[142]

These three are 'the views through which any kind of mediation of faith must pass',[143] and to this external critique of religion Ricoeur adds an internal one that reacts to Bultmann and the demythologizing controversy. The false-consciousness of modern Christianity is that it identifies the ancient mythological world view as the hindrance to faith, but what this masks is the reluctance of the modern mind to face the decision to believe or disbelieve at all. In other words, we erect the implausible mythic view of the ancient world as an excuse not to consider the 'scandal' of belief, but this is a manoeuvre that the hermeneutics of suspicion will no longer permit us to practice. 'We have thus entered into an age when it is in interpreting, consequently in trying to discern what is announced through what has been said in a certain cultural language, that the faith of modern man is possible. We are, therefore, today in a situation where it is in reinterpreting that we can believe.'[144]

At this point, Ricoeur turns to the concept of the hermeneutic circle:

There is a circle because in order to understand the text, it is necessary to believe what the text announces. But what the text announces is given nowhere else than in the deciphering of the text and in this kind of struggle between the false and true scandal in the heart of the text itself; . . . this circle can only be broken by the believer in the hermeneutics when he is faithful to the community, and by the 'hermeneut' in the believer when he does his scientific work of exegesis.[145]

Hermeneutics then tries to re-establish the condition of belief by engaging the language of imagination that changes suspicion to

272   *Robert Detweiler and Vernon K. Robbins*

affirmation. Ricoeur declares that 'man is always sustained by his mythicopoetic core: he is always created and recreated by a generative word; . . . the circle of the atheistic hermeneutics recloses on the necessary, but the circle of the kerygmatic hermeneutics opens on the generation of possibility in the heart of imagination of our language.'[146] Ricoeur turns to the New Testament parables to disclose this force of a hermeneutics of affirmation. He finds in them an untranslatability (of the sort appealing to the New Critics) that subverts theological systematizing, but he also sees the parables as resisting easy moralizing, in ways that anticipate his ethics of 'mimesis 3' in *Time and Narrative.* 'If we look at the parables as at a word addressed first to our imagination rather than to our will, we shall not be tempted to reduce them to mere didactic devices, to moralizing allegories. We will let their poetic power display itself within us.'[147]

Without wishing to minimize the sharp differences between Ricoeur and Derrida, we point out nevertheless that they are, at least, intensely concerned with the same 'problematic' but with differing (the pun is instructive) views on language. It seems to us, further, that Ricoeur, in spite of the poststructuralist charge of conservatism, is actually the more expansive. As Champion remarks, 'Like the deconstructionists, Ricoeur seeks to explore the ambiguities and the concealing powers of language, but in relation to the vicissitudes and revelations within life itself and not only at the level of sign systems and textuality.'[148] One could argue, of course, that *écriture* has always meant more than sign systems and textuality for Derrida – or at least that the term now means more than that for him – but in any case, one way of explaining the difference between them is in terms of a recent turn of Jewish poststructuralist critics to the Bible.

Geoffrey Hartman and Harold Bloom are two who have done so, and Kevin Hart's essay in this volume offers a critique of Bloom's *Ruin the Sacred Truths* that contrasts the Hegelian, Christian model of interpretation with Bloom's 'Gnostic Jewish' model. Derrida has entered the discussion in his 'Of an Apocalyptic Tone Recently Adopted in Philosophy' essay and in his book on Heidegger, *Of Spirit.*[149]

Most New Testament scholars are nervous of adopting a fully poststructuralist mode of interpretation. Stephen D. Moore, for example, in *Literary Criticism and the Gospels,* fears that biblical interpreters will disqualify his interpretations as irresponsible.[150] The alternative, he accepts, is to argue that '[t]oday, it is biblical criticism itself that cries out for demythologizing,'[151] and he musters his courage thus:

Convinced now of the necessity of an iconoclastic moment in biblical studies (for myself, at any rate) – a revision, though not a rejection, of foundational concepts such as Bible and exegesis (a conviction that animates several of my chapters – I feel a spring-like quickening of my intellectual *and* spiritual sap such as I have not felt since historical criticism's first rude accostation mated my quest for Reality (I was a Cistercian monk at the time, and much taken with *The Cloud of Unknowing*) with a questioning. 'For to begin thinking such thoughts is to approach the boundaries of faith' (Kierkegaard, *Fear*, 269).[152]

Moore's book has no reference to Mack's *Myth of Innocence*, a book produced within the guild of biblical studies that has most thoroughly demythologized New Testament criticism of the Gospel of Mark. Meanwhile, Crossan has returned to source and redaction criticism in a deconstructive mode.[153]

Structural and poststructural investigations of the Hebrew Bible have remained much closer allied than in New Testament studies, perhaps because of the much larger corpus of material to investigate and the early, insightful studies by Edmund Leach and others in the Hebrew Bible.[154] In both Testaments, however, experiences of liberation attend the use of new methods that come from various spheres of human knowledge and investigation. This is well expressed by Renita J. Weems, who at the end of an exploration of marriage as a metaphor for the relation of YHWH and Israel states:

Finally, to the extent that religious language and metaphors are not bankrupt as some tend to suppose, that at least in some settings they continue to inspire, mobilize, convict, instruct, challenge, and transform, then the question of the insights and limitations of biblical metaphors should be priority for all theological enterprises devoted to liberation, especially those who propose to speak for the alienated. Biblical metaphors are not simply examples of grandiloquence, not just instances of literary embellishment where the prophet rather naively or in a moment of inspiration expressed somewhat overdramatically what could have been stated more directly. Instead, they are explicitly what all human language is implicitly, analogical, and therefore limited. Although already doomed to failure, religious language represents human beings' desperate attempts to comprehend and articulate what is in fact beyond comprehension and articulation, the Divine and our experience of it. Biblical metaphors such as one which depends on sexual violence to make its point simply highlight our defeat.[155]

At the beginning of this century, Bible scholars were liberating the Bible from dogmatic theology while literary scholars were establishing literature as religion. Now, near the end of the century, both Bible and literary scholars may be joining together in the liberation of women and men from ways of thinking that divide a people's sacred literature (that which celebrates the activity of the divine) from its artistic-aesthetic literature (that which explores the furthermost reaches of the spirit, body and mind). In the waning years of the twentieth century, and at the height (or depths) of secularization, the Bible is being reaffirmed and re-examined as one of Western literature's greatest texts. If it is a record of a language 'doomed to failure', it is a failure that may yet move us toward the boundaries of faith.

NOTES

1 Edgar Krentz, *The Historical-Critical Method* (Philadelphia, 1975).
2 Ibid., pp. 55–88.
3 Edgar V. McKnight, *Post-Modern Use of the Bible: The Emergence of Reader-Oriented Criticism* (Nashville, 1988), p. 167.
4 Lynn M. Poland, *Literary Criticism and Biblical Hermeneutics: A Critique of Formalist Approaches* (Chico, CA, 1985), pp. 22–3.
5 Burton L. Mack, *A Myth of Innocence: Mark and Christian Origins* (Philadelphia, 1988), p. 20.
6 Krentz, *The Historical-Critical Method*, p. 2.
7 Northrop Frye, *The Great Code: The Bible and Literature* (New York, 1981).
8 Robert Alter, *The Art of Biblical Narrative* (New York, 1981).
9 Meir Sternberg, *The Poetics of Biblical Narrative: Ideological Literature and the Drama of Reading* (Bloomington, 1985).
10 Harold Bloom, *Ruin the Sacred Truths: Poetry and Belief from the Bible to the Present* (Cambridge, MA, 1989).
11 Midrash means 'interpretation' of Jewish scripture-based study, search, investigation and inquiry; see Gerald L. Bruns, 'Midrash and Allegory: The Beginnings of Scriptural Interpretation'. In *The Literary Guide to the Bible*, ed. Robert Alter and Frank Kermode (Cambridge, MA, 1987), p. 628.
12 Geoffrey H. Hartman and Sanford Budick (eds), *Midrash and Literature* (New Haven, 1986).
13 Hugh C. White, 'The Joseph Story: A Narrative which "Consumes" its Content', *Semeia* 31 (1985), pp. 49–69.
14 Walter J. Ong. *Orality and Literacy: The Technologizing of the Word* (New York, 1982).
15 William K. Powers, *Sacred Language: The Nature of Supernatural*

Discourse in Lakota (Norman and London, 1986). See similarly Mircea Eliade, *Myths, Dreams and Mysteries: The Encounter between Contemporary Faiths and Archaic Realities*, trs. Philip Mairet (New York, 1967).

16 See pp. 218–19 above.

17 T. S. Eliot, *Selected Essays*, new edition (New York, 1960; 1964).

18 David Jasper, *The Study of Literature and Religion: An Introduction* (Minneapolis, 1989), p. 7.

19 Ibid., p. 8. For a fine further discussion of Eliot and other critics struggling to relate Bible-reading to faith, see Gabriel Josipovici, *The Book of God: A Response to the Bible* (New Haven and London, 1988) pp. 23–6.

20 Hendrikus Boers, *What Is New Testament Theology?* (Philadelphia, 1979), p. 56.

21 Poland, *Literary Criticism and Biblical Hermeneutics*, p. 44.

22 Ibid., p. 19.

23 Paul Tillich, 'Autobiographical Reflections', in *The Theology of Paul Tillich*, ed. Charles W. Kegley and Robert W. Bretall (New York, 1961), pp. 5ff.

24 Ibid., p. 14.

25 Paul Tillich, *Theology of Culture*, (New York, 1959), p. 75.

26 Ibid., p. 54.

27 Ibid., p. 59.

28 David H. Kelsey, *The Fabric of Paul Tillich's Theology* (New Haven and London, 1967), p. 48.

29 Ibid.

30 Paul Tillich, *The Dynamics of Faith* (New York, 1958), p. 49.

31 Robert Detweiler, *Story, Sign, and Self: Phenomenology and Structuralism as Literary-Critical Methods* (Philadelphia and Missoula, 1984), p. 44.

32 James M. Robinson, 'Hermeneutic Since Barth', In *The New Hermeneutic*, New Frontiers in Theology, vol. 2, ed. James M. Robinson and John B. Cobb, Jr. (New York, 1964), pp. 43–4, n. 113.

33 Rudolf Bultmann, *Jesus Christ and Mythology* (New York, 1958), p. 15.

34 Ibid., p. 18.

35 Quoted by Robinson in 'Hermeneutic Since Barth', p. 63.

36 Hans-Georg Gadamer, *Truth and Method* (New York, 1975; German original, 1960).

37 See, for example, Stanley Fish, *Is There a Text in This Class? The Authority of Interpretive Communities* (Cambridge, MA, 1980). Fish has been among the most prominent reader-response critics – an approach that, because of lack of space, we will not address. For work on reader-response criticism focusing on biblical and literary interpretation, see Robert Detweiler (ed.), *Reader-Response Approaches to Biblical and Secular Texts*, Semeia, 31 (Atlanta, 1985).

38 David E. Linge, 'Editor's Introduction', in Hans-Georg Gadamer,

Philosophical Hermeneutics, trs. David E. Linge (Berkeley, California, 1976), p. xxviii.

39 Ibid., pp. xxviii–xxix. See also Detweiler, *Story, Sign, and Self*, pp. 44–6 for the origins of this summary of Gadamer.
40 Robinson, 'Hermeneutic Since Barth', p. 55, n. 155.
41 Ibid., p. 58.
42 See ibid., pp. 58–9.
43 Ernst Fuchs, 'The New Testament and the Hermeneutical Problem', in Robinson and Cobb, *The New Hermeneutic*, pp. 143–4.
44 Gerhard Ebeling, 'Word of God and Hermeneutic', in Robinson and Cobb, *The New Hermeneutic*, p. 98.
45 Ibid., p. 100.
46 Ibid., p. 101.
47 Ibid., p. 103.
48 Ibid., p. 109.
49 Ibid.
50 Emil Staiger, *Die Kunst der Interpretation: Studien zur deutschen Literaturgeschichte* (Zurich, 1955; 2nd edn, 1957).
51 Robinson, 'Hermeneutic Since Barth', p. 69.
52 Amos N. Wilder, *Jesus' Parables and the War of Myths: Essays on Imagination in the Scriptures* (Philadelphia, 1982), p. 15.
53 Vernon Ruland, *Horizons of Criticism: An Assessment of Religious-Literary Options* (Chicago, 1975), p. 11. Wilder's 'The Uses of a Theological Criticism' appears in *Literature and Religion*, ed. Giles Gunn (New York, 1971).
54 Amos N. Wilder, *The Language of the Gospel: Early Christian Rhetoric* (New York, 1964).
55 Ibid., p. 34.
56 Ibid., p. 37.
57 Robert W. Funk, *Language, Hermeneutic, and Word of God: The Problem of Language in the New Testament and Contemporary Theology* (New York, 1966), p. 142.
58 Ibid., p. 143.
59 Ibid., p. 237. Funk states, in n. 52 on this page, that he owes this observation to Amos Wilder.
60 Ibid., p. 238.
61 Ibid., p. 244.
62 Ibid., p. 246.
63 Ibid., pp. 246–7.
64 Robert W. Funk, *Parables and Presence: Forms of the New Testament Tradition* (Philadelphia, 1982).
65 Robert W. Funk, 'The Form of the New Testament Healing Miracle Story', *Semeia*, 12 (1978), pp. 57–96.
66 Robert W. Funk, *The Poetics of Biblical Narrative* (Sonoma, CA, 1988).
67 Dan O. Via, Jr, *The Parables: Their Literary and Existential Dimension* (Philadelphia, 1967).

68 William A. Beardslee, 'Recent Literary Criticism', in *The New Testament and Its Modern Interpreters*, ed. Eldon Jay Epp and George W. MacRae (Philadelphia and Atlanta, 1989), p. 179.

69 William A. Beardslee, *Literary Criticism of the New Testament* (Philadelphia, 1970), p. 26.

70 Ibid., p. 31.

71 Ibid., p. 36.

72 Ibid., p. 50.

73 Ibid., p. 53.

74 Ibid., p. 57.

75 John Crowe Ransom, *The New Criticism* (Norfolk, CT, 1941).

76 I. A. Richards, *Science and Poetry* (London, 1926), p. 82; see David Robey, 'Anglo-American New Criticism', in *Modern Literary Theory: A Comparative Introduction*, ed. Ann Jefferson and David Robey (London, 1982; 1986), p. 76.

77 Cleanth Brooks, *The Hidden God: Studies in Hemingway, Faulkner, Yeats, Eliot, and Warren* (New Haven, 1963), p. 128.

78 Cleanth Brooks, 'Christianity, Myth, and the Symbolism of Poetry', in *Christian Faith and the Contemporary Arts*, ed. Finley Eversole (New York, 1962).

79 R. W. B. Lewis, 'Hold on Hard to the Huckleberry Bushes', in *Religion and Modern Literature: Essays in Theory and Criticism*, eds G. B. Tennyson and Edward E. Ericson, Jr (Grand Rapids, 1975), p. 62.

80 R. W. B. Lewis, *The American Adam: Innocence, Tragedy, and Tradition in the Nineteenth Century* (Chicago, 1955) and *The Picaresque Saint: Representative Figures in Contemporary Fiction* (Philadelphia, 1959).

81 C. S. Lewis, 'Christianity and Literature', in Tennyson and Ericson, *Religion and Modern Literature*, p. 48.

82 Ibid., p. 53.

83 C. S. Lewis, *An Experiment in Criticism* (Cambridge, 1961); *The Allegory of Love: A Study in Medieval Tradition* (Oxford, 1936), and *A Preface to Paradise Lost* (New York, 1942).

84 Ruland, *Horizons of Criticism*, p. 13.

85 Nathan A. Scott, Jr, *The Poetry of Civic Virtue: Eliot, Malraux, Auden* (Philadelphia, 1976), p. 108.

86 Robert C. Tannehill, 'The Magnificat as Poem', *Journal of Biblical Literature*, 93 (1974), pp. 263–75.

87 Robert C. Tannehill, *The Sword of His Mouth* (Philadelphia and Missoula, MT, 1975), pp. 67–77.

88 Ibid., pp. 88–101.

89 Robert C. Tannehill, 'Varieties of Synoptic Pronouncement Stories', *Semeia*, 20 (1981), pp. 101–19; 'Types and Functions of Apophthegms in the Synoptic Gospels', in *Aufstieg und Niedergang der römischen Welt*, ed. H. Temporini and W. Haase, II Principat, vol. 25, 2 (Berlin, 1984), pp. 1792–1829.

90 Robert C. Tannehill, 'The Gospel of Mark as Narrative Christology', *Semeia*, 16 (1979), pp. 57–95.

91 Robert C. Tannehill, *The Narrative Unity of Luke-Acts: A Literary Interpretation*, 2 vols (Philadelphia, 1986; 1989).

92 David M. Gunn, *The Story of King David: Genre and Interpretation* (Sheffield, 1978); *The Fate of King Saul: An Interpretation of a Biblical Story* (Sheffield, 1980); 'Joshua and Judges', Alter and Kermode, *The Literary Guide to the Bible*, pp. 102–21; 'In Security: The David of Biblical Narrative', in *Signs and Wonders: Biblical Texts in Literary Focus*, ed. J. Cheryl Exum (Atlanta, 1989), pp. 135–51; Danna Nolan Fewell and David M. Gunn, ' "A Son is Born to Naomi": Literary Allusion and Interpretation in the Book of Ruth', *Journal for the Study of the Old Testament*, 40 (1988), pp. 99–108; and 'Boaz, Pillar of Society: Measures of Worth in the Book of Ruth', *JSOT*, 45 (1989), pp. 45–59.

93 Robert C. Culley, 'Exploring New Directions', in *The Hebrew Bible and Its Modern Interpreters*, ed. Douglas A. Knight and Gene M. Tucker (Chico, CA, 1985), pp. 167–200.

94 Ferdinand de Saussure, *Course in General Linguistics* (New York, 1966; French original, 1916).

95 Roman Jakobson, 'Linguistics and Poetics', in *The Structuralists from Marx to Lévi-Strauss*, ed. Richard and Fernande De George (Garden City, NY, 1972).

96 Roman Jakobson and Morris Halle, *The Fundamentals of Language* (The Hague, 1956).

97 Tzvetan Todorov, *Littérature et signification* (Paris, 1967).

98 Gérard Genette, *Figures* (Paris, 1966; 1969; 1972).

99 Roland Barthes, *S/Z*, trs. Richard Miller (New York, 1974; French original, 1970).

100 Louis Marin, *The Semiotics of the Passion Narrative: Topics and Figures* (Pittsburgh, 1980; French original, 1971).

101 Roland Barthes, *Structural Analysis and Biblical Exegesis: Interpretational Essays* (Pittsburgh, 1974).

102 John Dominic Crossan, *Raid on the Articulate* (New York, 1976), p. xiv.

103 Daniel Patte, *What is Structural Exegesis?* (Philadelphia;, 1976).

104 Robert Polzin, *Biblical Structuralism: Method in the Interpretation of Ancient Texts* (Philadelphia, 1977).

105 Terry Eagleton, *Literary Theory: An Introduction* (Minneapolis, 1983), p. 103.

106 Susan Sontag, *Against Interpretation and Other Essays* (New York, 1969).

107 See Robert Scholes, *Structuralism in Literature: An Introduction* (New Haven and London, 1974), p. 75.

108 See Raman Selden, *A Reader's Guide to Contemporary Literary Theory* (Brighton, 1985), p. 17.

109 Mikhail Bakhtin, *Problems of Dostoevsky's Poetics*, trs. R. W. Rotsel (Ann Arbor, 1973).

110 Eagleton, *Literary Theory*, p. 117.

111 Kuno Füssel, 'Materialist Readings of the Bible: Report on an Alternative Approach to Biblical Texts', in *God of the Lowly: Socio-Historical Interpretation of the Bible*, ed. Willy Schottroff and Wolfgang Stegemann, trs. Matthew J. O'Connell (Maryknoll, NY, 1984), p. 25.

112 Julia Kristeva, *Desire in Language: A Semiotic Approach to Literature and Art*, trs. Thomas Gora, Alice Jardine and Leon S. Roudiez (New York, 1980).

113 Mieke Bal, *Lethal Love: Feminist Literary Readings of Biblical Love Stories* (Bloomington, IN, 1987; French edition, 1985); *Murder and Difference: Gender, Genre, and Scholarship in Sisera's Death*, trs. Matthew Gumpert (Bloomington and Indianapolis, 1988); *Death and Dissymmetry: The Politics of Coherence in the Book of Judges* (Chicago, 1988).

114 Mieke Bal, *Narratology: Introduction to the Theory of Narrative*, trs. Christine van Boheemen (Toronto, 1985).

115 Seymour Chatman, *Story and Discourse: Narrative Structure in Fiction and Film* (Ithaca, NY, 1978).

116 Shlomith Rimmon-Kenan, *Narrative Fiction: Contemporary Poetics* (London and New York, 1983).

117 Eagleton, *Literary Theory*, p. 94.

118 Northrop Frye, *Anatomy of Criticism* (Princeton, 1957).

119 'It is marked by a deep fear of the actual social world, a distaste for history itself, . . . the work of a committed Christian humanist (Frye is a clergyman), for whom the dynamic which drives literature and civilization – desire – will finally be fulfilled only in the kingdom of God.' Eagleton, *Literary Theory*, p. 93.

120 Frye, *The Great Code*, p. 215.

121 Ibid., p. 42.

122 Ibid., p. 224.

123 McKnight, *Post-Modern Use of the Bible*, p. 183.

124 Richard Harland, *Superstructuralism: The Philosophy of Structuralism and Post-Structuralism* (London and New York, 1987), p. 135.

125 René Girard, *Violence and the Sacred*, trs. Patrick Gregory (Baltimore, 1977; French original, 1972), p. 146.

126 René Girard, *Deceit, Desire, and the Novel: Self and Other in Literary Structure* (Baltimore, 1965; French original, 1961), p. 300.

127 *Diacritics*, 8 (Spring), 1978, pp. 33–4.

128 Ibid., p. 52.

129 Ibid., p. 53.

130 René Girard, *The Scapegoat*, trs. Yvonne Freccero (Baltimore, 1986; French original, 1982).

131 Michel Foucault, *The Archaeology of Knowledge and the Discourse on Language* (New York, 1972; French original, 1969; 1971).

132 Mack, *Myth of Innocence*, pp. 135–71.

133 Ibid., pp. 172–207.

134 Ibid., pp. 208–45.

135 Ibid., pp. 249–312.
136 Paul Ricoeur, *Time and Narrative*, vols 1 and 2, trs. Kathleen McLaughlin and David Pellauer (Chicago, 1984; 1985); vol. 3, trs. Kathleen Blamey and David Pellauer (Chicago, 1988; French originals, 1983; 1984). J. Hillis Miller, 'But Are Things as We Think They Are?', *Times Literary Supplement* October 9–15, 1987, p. 1104.
137 Paul Ricoeur, *The Symbolism of Evil*, trs. Emerson Buchanan (Boston, 1967; French original, 1960).
138 James Champion, 'The Poetics of Human Time: Ricoeur's *Time and Narrative*, vol. 3', *Literature and Theology*, 3 (November), 1989, p. 347.
139 Ibid., p. 343, from 'Narrated Time', *Philosophy Today*, 29 (Winter), 1985, p. 260.
140 Paul Ricoeur, 'The Critique of Religion', *The Philosophy of Paul Ricoeur: An Anthology of His Work*, ed. Charles E. Reagan and David Stewart (Boston, 1978), pp. 213–22.
141 Ibid., p. 215.
142 Ibid., p. 219.
143 Ibid.
144 Ibid., p. 222.
145 Ibid.
146 Paul Ricoeur, 'The Language of Faith', *The Philosophy of Paul Ricoeur*, p. 237.
147 Paul Ricoeur, 'Listening to the Parables of Jesus', *The Philosophy of Paul Ricoeur*, p. 245.
148 Champion, 'The Poetics of Human Time', p. 344.
149 Jacques Derrida, 'Of an Apocalyptic Tone Recently Adopted in Philosophy', *Semeia*, 23 (1982) 63–97; *Of Spirit: Heidegger and the Question*, trs. Geoffrey Bennington and Rachel Bowlby (Chicago and London, 1989).
150 Stephen D. Moore, *Literary Criticism and the Gospels: The Theoretical Challenge* (New Haven and London, 1989), pp. 159–70.
151 Ibid., p. 172.
152 Ibid., pp. 176–7.
153 John Dominic Crossan, *The Cross that Spoke: The Origins of the Passion Narrative* (San Francisco, 1988).
154 Culley, 'Exploring New Directions'.
155 Renita J. Weems, 'Gomer: Victim of Violence or Victim of Metaphor?' *Semeia*, 47 (1989), p. 101.

6

The Poetics of the Negative

Kevin Hart

I

What is the relation between literature and literary criticism? Simple though it seems, the question raises a cluster of problems that both organizes and perplexes a good deal of contemporary work in literary studies. It has not always been so. The question would have appeared idle to critics as diverse as Dryden, Johnson and Coleridge, and Arnold set the tone for many readers by observing that criticism is a secondary activity, always in the shadow of true creativity. It is not until we reach the sceptical late Victorians that the question begins to grow a sting in its tail. In a dialogue of 1890, 'The Critic as Artist', Oscar Wilde has a character, Gilbert, declare that 'Criticism is really creative in the highest sense of the word.'[1] The sideways glance at Arnold is unmistakable; yet Wilde's bold formulation was left to languish as mere wit. For it is only in recent years that Arnold's assumption that criticism ultimately serves literature has received intense scrutiny. The assumption takes various forms, so in rejecting it diverse futures for criticism present themselves. For some people, the upshot is that literature can now fully envelop criticism: one's essays on Wordsworth can be every bit as imaginative and creative as the poems discussed. Others conclude that criticism should do far more than reflect, in a scholarly and discriminating manner, on the fiction that has been accorded high cultural value by a society. Criticism, it is argued, should draw freely from the disciplines that surround it – anthropology, history, linguistics, philosophy and psychoanalysis – and, thus enriched, address itself to such apparently extra-literary topics as the representation of gender, race and class in writing from both high and popular culture. In this way, criticism becomes aware that writing, of whatever kind, occurs in particular social and historical circumstances, and so begins to acknowledge its political responsibilities. The argument is sometimes supported by reminders that criticism has traditionally concerned itself with more than the purely literary, and that the restriction of 'literature' to imaginative writing in a few genres is as recent as Romanticism. Yet as criticism incorporates a range of issues formerly treated under other rubrics, a problem emerges which some critics have not been slow to point out. For while literary criticism vouches for political or critical texts, it does so at a price, suborning them to appear only of aesthetic interest. Certainly one may learn an enormous amount about Marxism by studying *Capital* with all the rigour that a close rhetorical reading demands, though whether that kind of reading intensifies or diminishes the book's political impact is a disputed point. In short, there is a good case that, suitably framed, any kind of writing can be 'literary' and so available to the literary critic; while there are other arguments, equally persuasive in their own terms, that the critic has a moral responsibility to lead the reader from the enchantments of fine language to matters of local and ultimate concern.

As my example of Marx's *Capital* suggests, much discussion in literary theory turns on those texts which directly engage political questions. Philosophical texts provide another noteworthy site for controversy, typically those which seem to straddle the borders between philosophy and literature – writings by people as disparate as Plato, Rousseau, Kierkegaard and Nietzsche. Less often found in the forefront of recent debate about theory, although frequently exerting a force from a distance, are religious writings, especially the central religious document of Western culture: the Bible. Thus there are critics who wish to claim the Bible for literary study, finding its stories and poems as powerful as any they could name, while there are others who, for one reason or another, urge the separation of sacred and secular writings. It is easy to understand why some believers might be distressed to see holy writ treated on a par with a play by Shakespeare or a novel by George Eliot. For them, talk of biblical personages as 'characters' or salvation history as a 'narrative' constitutes a severe reduction of God's inspired word. The decisive thing about scripture is its truth value, they say, and its literary merit comes a very poor second. If fundamentalists believe that all scripture is uniformly inspired and therefore inerrant, others opt for a canon within the canon (the New Testament, the Gospels, the synoptic Gospels, Paul's Epistles ...). There always comes a point where literary value fades into the background. It is one thing to assert that Mark's story of Jesus's death and resurrection is sublime art, quite another to stake one's life on it. For the faithful, the first is not simply an inadequate response, it is a category mistake: one may or may not believe Mark's story, but one must read it as matter for belief.

On the other side of the fence, there are critics who try to keep believers and their Scriptures well away from literature. Q. D. Leavis, for one, attests that

There is no reason to suppose that those trained in theology ... are likely to possess what is essential in the practice of literary criticism, that 'sensitiveness of the intelligence' described by Matthew Arnold as equivalent to conscience in moral matters. A theological training seems to have a disabling effect and has subsequently to be struggled against when literary criticism is the concern.[2]

It all depends on the theological training, one is inclined to say. Leavis is worried by moral theology, that its range of response is set too narrowly for an adequate reading of fiction. But theology is, amongst other things, the study of the Bible, and a knowledge of patristic exegesis and the higher criticism, not to mention scrupulous philological work on both Testaments, would surely enhance one's ability to read a poem or a novel closely. Or would it? There are dangers in carrying interpretative procedures from one discipline to another. A course of studies that produced Empsonian 'Neo-Christians', squeezing biblical symbolism from every poem, would be just as harmful to criticism as a doctrinaire moral education. Paul de Man, one of the most consequent of recent American textual critics, takes the point further: 'I intend to take the divine out of reading. The experience of the divine is one that is totally conceivable, but which I don't think is compatible with reading ... Generally, the act of faith is not an act of reading, or for me is not compatible with reading.'[3] Where believers are disturbed by criticism denying the Bible its reference, literary critics seem worried that the Bible sets too insistent and determinate a reference for their activity.

We need to distinguish three tensions here: between the Bible and religious faith, between reading the Bible and other texts, and the relations between theology and criticism. Consider Paul de Man. There is no doubt that he believes religious questions to be the most redoubtable ones, even though his answers tend to be extremely sceptical.[4] All the same, he thinks, religious faith has no role to play in criticism. For when reading, 'we look for the delicate area where the thematic, semantic field and the rhetorical structures begin to interfere with each other, begin to engage each other', while when believing we supposedly trust that rhetoric and theme ultimately act in concert.[5] So when a critic reads a poem and claims to have found a determinate meaning, that reading is theological; while it is theoretically possible to tease out the conflicting significations of Mark's resurrection story and so produce a reading that is not theological. 'Faith', as de Man uses it, refers not to a set of beliefs about God, but about meaning, though, to be sure, the latter is historically influenced by the former. Polemics about faith and theology often come down to an anxiety about independence. In effect, Leavis and de Man represent one pole of the post-Romantic split between theology and literature discussed earlier, in chapter 4. They wish to establish a new discipline, literary criticism, and to do that, they feel, they must exorcise the ghost of theology. Leavis objects to a prescribed sense of morality in theology, and opposes it with a more vital and agile moral sensibility. De Man sees all moral and aesthetic readings as inherently theological, and favours philological and rhetorical criticism as the best way for criticism to be truly critical and not a disguised apology for something else. Perhaps no one has gone further to discredit theological categories than de Man; yet those same categories reappear in his works – a little askew, as when he confesses that 'The humility of the critic in relation to the work is total.'[6] Biblical critics may well exhibit a similar humility before Genesis or Revelation, though whether or not their faith commits them in advance to a style of reading is a question to place on notice. In the meantime, I turn to another contemporary critic who looks at this area from a rather different perspective.

Edward Said opens his influential *The World, the Text, and the Critic* with a discussion of 'secular criticism' and ends by invoking the spectre of 'religious criticism'.[7] In an interview with Said, Imre Salusinszky puts this antithesis under pressure. 'Are we really talking about "secular" versus "religious"', he asks, 'or are we talking more about "historicist" versus something that continues to believe in a supra-historical aesthetic effect?' To which Said replies, 'You can turn it any way you wish, but I think that it's not an accident that the three critics you just mentioned [Northrop Frye, Frank Kermode and Harold Bloom] all write about the Bible.' 'But one can't take exception to that,' Salusinszky objects. 'No, I don't agree,' comes the reply,

I think that it is, precisely, exceptional that the Bible should emerge in certain types of, shall we say, 'theological' thought, or thought that can be traced back to a God of some sort, to the divine ... Gnosticism, preciosity of language, obscurity of language – everything that comes out of modernism, which is now crystallized in biblical work – the privacy of interpretation, privileged or hierophantic language: all of these things are part of a clerical attitude.[8]

Said identifies a very familiar economy, the perpetual circulation of three elements – the Bible, literature and literary criticism – and he identifies it as dangerous. Or more exactly, dangerous to society; for, he suggests, social and political experience become occluded in regarding criticism this way. Whereas Frye, Kermode and Bloom propose to purify literature, Said is 'interested in … exactly the opposite of purification: not, as in Frye, literature as some kind of separate, total system, but literature as involved with many other things'.[9] And so, for him, the Bible functions in literary criticism as a powerful agent of exclusion and reduction. It need not be so: much twentieth-century biblical criticism has taken pains to situate Scripture in its cultural and political contexts, and a literary critic could well do the same. Yet literary theorists interested in Scripture have not, as a rule, taken the historical-critical scholarship of the Bible as a model for their own endeavours. Interestingly enough, Said sees contemporary 'biblical work' as stemming from Modernist literature and criticism. This is one way of looking at the matter, of freezing the economy at a given moment in literary history; yet Modernism itself, not to mention its prolongation into postmodernism, also draws deeply and variously from the Bible.

Towards the end of James Joyce's *Finnegans Wake*, the narrator utters a series of preemptory orders, one of which is 'Renove that bible.'[10] Taken out of context, it can stand as an emblem of how many twentieth-century writers have responded to the Bible 'Renove that bible': that is, renew that Bible; or, as Ezra Pound declared, 'Make it new,' let us have a new law and a new spirit in our writing. As always in *Finnegans Wake*, Joyce is punning, trying to evoke a particular historical situation for a special purpose. The reference here is to Oliver Cromwell who, on 19 April 1653, took a guard of soldiers into the House of Commons and forcibly dissolved it, thus ending the 'Rump Parliament'. After denouncing the members for corruption, Cromwell commanded that the mace, symbol of the Speaker's authority, be taken away: 'Remove that bauble.'[11] It would take some time to tease out the full implications of Joyce's pun. This much, however, is perfectly clear: the Bible no longer regulates men's and women's lives, and it is the writer's task to fill the abyss that is now apparent. One could argue whether Joyce intends the Bible to be displaced or dismissed, and, by nagging at details in the historical narrative, expand the tiny scene into an allegory of Modernism, but that is not my task. The crucial point at issue today is authority, and it can be resolved into several questions: what is the nature of the struggle between literature and the Bible? Is it a matter of priority or authority? Do the Bible and literature gain their respective authorities from the same source or from diverse sources?

For a second emblem, one that suggests the darker side of the twentieth century's response to religion, I choose an aphorism from Franz Kafka: 'What is laid upon us is to accomplish the negative; the positive is already given.'[12] I do not think that Kafka has the Bible specifically in mind here, although elsewhere he does have some revealing things to say about his relationship with Scripture. If he once confessed to his diary, 'the pages of the Bible don't flutter in my presence,' he also admitted, 'Only the Old Testament knows,' before checking himself – 'say nothing yet on it.'[13] Certainly Kafka was aware of the Kabbalah, for in an early diary entry he writes of 'Zohar, Bible of the Kabbalists',[14] and the Kabbalah may suggest one mode of negativity evoked by the aphorism: what we can call, following the mystics, a 'negative theology'. The name pertains to a wide range of Jewish, Gnostic and Christian practices, and has various nuances in each (some of which we will hear later), but is perhaps best introduced in Christian terms. In positive theology the Father is revealed by the Son in and through the Spirit, thereby establishing a God that can be described, albeit imperfectly, in positive and negative predicates. The negative theologian, however, is agitated by that imperfection, and tries to ascend to God through successive denials of the images of God disclosed in positive theology. Here both positive and negative predicates are put in question. Whereas positive theology follows a Spirit that descends and enlightens, negative theology beckons one to ascend to God through the darkness of unknowing. In positive theology one is concerned to represent God to His people; in negative theology one broods on the status, scope and strength of representation while trusting that, in doing so, one will find the God who is beyond the spheres of presence and representation. And because 'presence' and 'representation' have a proud philosophical heritage, there is always a moment when negative theology contests the privilege of philosophy to regulate our images of God.

What has all this to do with literature or literary criticism? If Leavis and de Man reject theology as a model for literary studies, it may be that negative theology can serve as a replacement. Roland Barthes, for one, judges that the task of criticism now is 'destruction in the larger sense of the word, as one speaks, for example, of negative theology'.[15] Harold Bloom, for another, reflects on a shift in critical orthodoxy. 'Our profession', he writes, 'is not genuinely akin any longer to that of the historians or the philosophers. Without willing the change, our theoretical critics have become negative theologians, our practical critics are close to being Agaddic commentators'.[16] Bloom's model, here and everywhere, is a highly eclectic Gnostic Judaism, one that does not fit at all neatly with the overtly Christian model of negative theology I have invoked by way of introduction. Even so, it is easy enough to see the contention. We have met it before in Said's diagnosis of modern criticism: 'What one discerns today is religion as the result of exhaustion, consolation, disappointment: its forms in both the theory and practice of criticism are varieties of unthinkability, undecidability, and paradox.'[17] The critic's fascination with absence and otherness, the drive to demystify and demythologize, the imperative that criticism must be revisionary – all these amplify and confirm Said's observations. All the same, one can also view the matter more positively, as part of criticism's desire for independence and renewal. As the negative theologian longs for the God beyond Being, that is, who is beyond all philosophical determinations of Being, so the literary theorist searches for a literature and a critical vocabulary that escape or thwart philosophical categories. And so, whether one has a regard for philosophy even while placing it at risk (as with Paul de Man), or whether one utterly rejects the vocabulary of philosophy in the context of criticism (as with Harold Bloom), one can see how literary theorists can, at a pinch, be taken for negative theologians.

Apparent regard and apparent rejection are varied modes of dialectic, and the criticism featured so far has tended to be dialectical rather than empirical. This marks a broad but important opposition with regard to reading the Bible. Empirical criticism treats the literary as already given; so, turning to the Bible, the common-sense critic finds a host of genres (proverbs, parables, psalms, and so forth) to take as literary, then brings his or her expertise to bear on those texts. Dialectical criticism, by contrast, takes 'literature' as a frame which critics use to read certain texts and by which some texts frame themselves. The frame is not immutable, but historically produced under changing circumstances. If one takes literature in the current Romantic sense, meaning (more or less) 'imaginative writing in the genres of prose fiction, poetry and drama', then whole sections of the Bible frame themselves as literature – Job, the Psalms and Jesus's parables, for instance. But the dialectical critic does not believe that the frame actually exists: there is neither any literature in and of itself, nor an essence of criticism. No wonder, then, that this kind of critic will look at both the accepted literature of the day and the conditions which render it acceptable. 'Literary criticism' thus becomes a rattle bag (containing ways of reading, systems of classification, ideas of history, rhetorical stances, code books, social theory and much else), and its object is any textual phenomenon, from high or popular culture. From this perspective, the Bible is a collection of texts and frames, all interchangeable – framing itself and other literature while, in turn, being framed by them.

Modern criticism has a way of absorbing and modifying ideas and techniques from other disciplines. Thus literary studies has appropriated a number of philosophical (or quasi-philosophical) stars and renamed them as literary theorists. In many English Departments, Jacques Derrida, Michel Foucault, Martin Heidegger, Julia Kristeva, Jacques Lacan and Friedrich Nietzsche are studied with as much zest as Chaucer, Spenser, Shakespeare, Pope, Johnson, Austen and Wordsworth. Once more the scope of literary criticism becomes an issue, and once more we must ask why some thinkers are taken up and not others. Why is it, for instance, that Emmanuel Levinas has not had an effect on anglophone literary studies whereas Jacques Derrida, who repeats and complicates a number of Levinas's themes, has become required reading, even for undergraduates? It may also be worth remarking that these philosophical figures, when read under the rubric of literary theory, can become little more than figures – metaphors for characteristic textual manoeuvres.

Some of these textual manoeuvres will prove to be of great interest as we continue, for in recent days (as in bygone days) literary theory has looked as often to biblical criticism as to philosophy for models of interpretation. Students of literature have long been used to study allegory both as a genre and as an interpretative procedure; and, as we have seen in earlier chapters, have been aware of how typology can organize literary as well as biblical texts. Only lately, though, have words like 'Haggadah', 'Kabbalah', 'Midrash', and 'Talmud' – signalling specifically Jewish modes of commentary – entered the critic's vocabulary. What do these various interpretative modes enable the critic to do? What problems do they raise for criticism? In trying to answer these questions, we will also find ourselves faced with others, raised earlier, concerning the competing authorities of literature and the Bible. Is there anything to prevent literary criticism entirely absorbing the Bible as literature? Are there any substantial variations between forming sacred and secular anons? More generally, is contemporary literary criticism committed to renewal, as Joyce's 'Renove that bible' suggests? Or does it carry a burden of negativity, as Kafka's aphorism might indicate? These are our guiding questions, and we can only follow them a little way, perhaps just to glimpse the vistas and also the labyrinths to which they lead. Finally, rather than keep a variety of biblical tales before us, I have chosen to focus on two texts, both by the so-called J author, that have haunted biblical and literary critics: the narrative of Jacob wrestling the angel (Gen. 32:22–32), and the story of the Tower of Babel (Gen. 11:1–9).[18]

II

Whether interpretation should be literary criticism's main subject is an open question today. In recent years, however, one could be forgiven for thinking that many critics had nothing other than interpretation on their minds. With characteristic rhetorical flourish, Stanley Fish ends an influential 1979 essay by saying, 'like it or not, interpretation is the only game in town.'[19] Yet it turns out that there are two ways of playing the game. On the one hand, there is a hermeneutic tradition, beginning with Schleiermacher and Dilthey, redirected by Heidegger, and elaborated by Gadamer and Ricoeur; while on the other hand, there is a structuralist tradition that derives from the Russian Formalists, Saussure, the Prague linguistic circle and Lévi-Strauss, and remains a powerful force by virtue of influential works by Barthes, Genette, Greimas and Todorov. All such lists are tendentious, and a more exact taxonomy would be both nicer and broader, discriminating between, let us say, narratology and poetics while also stepping back to observe cross-fertilization between hermeneutics and structuralism. More tendentious are the governing metaphors people use to indicate the relations between criticism and these theories of interpretation. It is common enough to hear that hermeneutics is a branch of continental philosophy, and that in looking to Heidegger or Gadamer literary criticism is seeking to ground itself in philosophy. Similarly, it is often said that critics want to base their discipline on structural linguistics. All these assertions are led astray by the metaphor of foundation. 'Nothing in my teaching', writes Northrop Frye, 'is more difficult to get across than the simple: "throw that metaphor away; it's the wrong metaphor". It always means that we have to get something established in another subject "before" we can study literature, which of course means we never get to study literature at all.'[20] We are always building 'some tower of Babel on a Marxist, Freudian or Thomist model', Frye laments, 'with a determination for its foundation and a confusion of tongues for its ground floor'. The 'safer metaphor' for criticism's relations with other disciplines, he advises, is that of interpenetration.[21]

Interpenetration, circulation, dialectic, exchange: these are the tropes we need for any interdisciplinarity. Hermeneutics and structuralism shape biblical and literary criticism, and are in turn shaped by them, as we shall see by looking briefly at each mode of interpretation. Over the last half-century, literary and biblical critics alike have greatly benefited from the work of Martin Heidegger, and it is with him that I shall begin. In the dialogue with a Japanese friend already cited in chapter 5 Heidegger responds to a question asking why he started to use the word 'hermeneutic' in his seminars and writings. 'The term "hermeneutics" was familiar to me from my theological studies,' he says. 'At that time, I was particularly agitated over the question of the relation between the word of Holy Scripture and theological-speculative thinking. This relation, between language and Being, was the same one, if you will, only it was veiled and inaccessible to me, so that through many deviations and false starts I sought in vain for a guiding thread.'[22] Heidegger explains to his Japanese friend that hermeneutics 'developed first and formatively in conjunction with the interpretation of the Book of books, the Bible', especially in the work of Schleiermacher, but that he has used the word in a far broader sense. That sense is specified in *Being and Time*:

The phenomenology of Dasein is a *hermeneutic* in the primordial signification of this word, where it designates this business of interpreting. But to the extent that by uncovering the meaning of Being and the basic structures of Dasein in general we may exhibit the horizon for any further ontological study of those entities which do not have the character of Dasein, this hermeneutic also becomes a 'hermeneutic' in the sense of working out the conditions on which the possibility of any ontological investigation depends. And finally, to the extent that Dasein, as an entity with the possibility of existence has ontological priority over every other entity, 'hermeneutic', as an interpretation of Dasein's Being has the third and specific sense of an analytic of an existentiality of existence; and this is the sense which is philosophically *primary*.[23]

By the time we reach that third sense it comes as no surprise to hear that the roots of 'hermeneutic' are used only derivatively. Heidegger is preoccupied by Being, not methodology: a distinction which was to become increasingly important to literary criticism in the twentieth century. This stress on Being informs Heidegger's vocabulary to the extent that he talks of '*Dasein*' rather than 'man'. *Dasein* is that entity for whom Being is an issue; unlike animals or natural objects, *Dasein* seeks to understand itself in Being. Hermeneutics, the study of understanding, enables us to redeem the Being of beings, to let Being appear as a coming into presence.

If all this talk about Being seems to take us a long way from literature and the Bible, it is only because they wait just around the corner and cannot be seen yet. We have come this far by following Heidegger, and have shadowed many literary and biblical critics who longed to see their chosen texts from a more rewarding perspective, one that sees writing as representing the experience of Being. That perspective may or may not be entirely satisfactory, depending on what one expects to see, but there are things to do before we can turn the corner and see for ourselves. Our immediate theme is Being, and (put crudely) two ways of regarding it: as conceived within metaphysics, and as thought hermeneutically. Quite clearly, Heidegger believes the metaphysical understanding of Being to be a profound misunderstanding. Our task then is to reformulate the question of Being, which requires a rethinking of the entire history of philosophy. 'If the question of Being is to have its own history made transparent', we are told,

then this hardened tradition must be loosened up, and the concealments which it has brought about must be dissolved. We understand this task as one in which by taking *the question of Being as our clue*, we are to *destroy* the traditional content of ancient ontology until we arrive at those primordial experiences in which we achieved our first ways of determining the nature of Being – the ways which have guided us ever since.[24]

The verb translated as 'to destroy' is *destruieren* which means 'to loosen up', and Heidegger is quick to detail its positive and negative resonances:

In thus demonstrating the origin of our basic ontological concepts by an investigation in which their 'birth certificate' is displayed, we have nothing to do with a vicious relativizing of ontological standpoints. But this destruction is just as far from having the *negative* sense of shaking off the ontological tradition. We must, on the contrary, stake out the positive possibilities of that tradition, and this always means keeping it within its *limits* ... On its negative side, this destruction does not relate itself towards the past; its criticism is aimed at 'today' and at the prevalent way of treating the history of ontology ... But to bury the past in nullity [*Nichtigkeit*] is not the purpose of this destruction; its aim is *positive*; its negative function remains unexpressed and indirect.[25]

Or as he says elsewhere, rather more simply, 'Destruction means –
to open our ears, to make ourselves free for what speaks to us
in tradition as the Being of being.'[26] As the injunction to open our
ears suggests, the hermeneutic approach to the history of ontology
requires attention to language. 'Language defines the hermeneutic
relation,' we are informed: not, to be sure, a relation between two
things, reader and text, for Heidegger above all wishes us to picture
Dasein listening to the voice of Being, becoming human only insofar
as he or she listens attentively and responds to its claim upon us.[27]

   That voice can be heard in many places: in writings by mystics
and poets, in the Bible, in some philosophical texts and elsewhere.
So if we are biblical or literary critics, it is plainly important to heed
that voice. Not everyone is capable of hearing it, though, since many
people do not open their ears; they are wholly governed by metaphysical ways of thinking, regarding them as the only ways in which
to think properly. What is metaphysics, then? How is it constituted,
and how did it gain this sway over us? The fundamental question of
metaphysics can be posed very simply. In Leibniz's words, 'Why are
there beings at all, and why not rather nothing?' Framed as it is, this
question can be answered only in terms of a first cause, the highest
ground of beings – what Aristotle calls the *theion*. Being is conceived
in terms of the highest being, thereby binding ontology to theology.
In Heidegger's idiom, metaphysics thinks Being by way of 'onto-
theology'. It has always done so, from Plato right up to Husserl,
because onto-theology enters philosophical thought at its ground
and origin. Within the West, onto-theology appears the natural,
inevitable and universal medium of thought; it defines in advance
what we can mean by 'reason'. Appearances, however, can be deceptive, for reason blocks rather than fosters true thought. Equally
deceptive is the word 'onto-theology' itself. Heidegger warns that it
'should not point to a connection with a discipline called "theology", but should indicate to us the most central thrust of the
problem of being'.[28] In Heidegger's vocabulary, even Nietzsche is a
theologian, while his slogan 'God is dead' remains 'an expression
not of atheism but of ontotheology'.[29]

   We must be ready to separate two senses of the word 'God'. There
is the God that enters philosophy at its inception, the *causa sui*, and
there is the God of faith. In abandoning the god of philosophy, the
thinker perhaps draws closer to the divine God. And so there is a
rapport between Heidegger's project and theology. '*Theology*', he
tells us,

is seeking a more primordial interpretation of man's Being toward God,
prescribed by the meaning of faith itself and remaining within it. It is slowly

beginning to understand once more Luther's insight that the 'foundation' on which its system of dogma rests has not arisen from an inquiry in which faith is primary, and that conceptually this 'foundation' not only is inadequate for the problematic of theology, but conceals and distorts it.[30]

As the allusion to Luther might suggest, Heidegger is principally thinking of Protestant theology, and we should recall that the relation between Scripture and speculative thought was one of his motivating questions.

The biblical criticism that Heidegger first encountered as a young man was largely influenced by Albrecht Ritschl; it reflected that theologian's distaste for viewing religion as a speculative system and his commitment to historical consciousness as the privileged means of understanding religious movements. Continuing in the spirit of Ritschl were Ernst Troeltsch and Adolph von Harnack, the most powerful representatives of Protestant liberal theology at the time: Troeltsch transmuting biblical criticism into a scientifically rigorous cultural history of religion, and Harnack attempting, by the judicious use of source studies, to separate the essence of Christianity from its accreted dogmas. The import of this serried historical scholarship was to break the borders between the sacred and the secular; the Church could be studied in the same way as any social movement, and Scripture could be approached like any other cultural document. Heidegger set himself firmly against the twin threats of reductionism and relativism, avowing the integrity of religious belief. Thus in his 1927 lecture, 'Phenomenology and Theology', he argues that theology is a positive science, oriented by faith in God, and irreducible to philosophical speculation or historical research. 'In no case', he contends, 'may we delimit the scientific character of theology by using an *other* science as the standard of evidence for its mode of proof or as the measure of rigor of its terminology.'[31]

Heidegger's interest in the Bible had surfaced earlier, in his theological training with the Jesuits (as a Gymnasium student then as a novice), but also in his 1920–1 lectures at Freiburg, 'Introduction to the Phenomenology of Religion', by which time he was in greater sympathy with Protestantism than Catholicism. In the second half of that course, he addressed himself to Paul's First Epistle to the Thessalonians, arguing that Christian belief, as Paul represents it, is completely unique and therefore cannot be usefully compared with other religious movements.[32] Of peculiar moment to Heidegger are Paul's thoughts on the parousia: 'But of the times and the seasons, brethren, ye have no need that I write unto you. For yourselves know perfectly that the day of the Lord so cometh as a thief in the night. For when they shall say, Peace and safety; then sudden destruction cometh upon them, as travail upon a woman with child; and they shall not escape' (I Thess. 5:1–3). What engrosses Heidegger is Paul's indifference to the date of the second coming. Far more significant than mere chronological time is the *chairos*, the stroke of decision that cannot be objectified. Christian experience is factical and historical, a matter of living rather than calculating. The same thoughts inform Heidegger's 1921 lecture series, 'Augustine and Neo-Platonism'. Harnack, Troeltsch and Dilthey are criticized precisely because they historicize Augustine, adjusting his claims for faith to the limits of his cultural milieu. They bring alien canons of content to a Christian who was motivated by performance, 'factical existence', and therefore misunderstand him.[33]

Although Heidegger lectured on Paul, and studied the fourth Gospel with his Marburg colleague Rudolf Bultmann, he never ventured to publish anything in the area of biblical criticism. Doubtless he would not have regarded his meditations on the New Testament as 'biblical criticism' in the first place, just as he set his illuminations of poems by George, Hölderlin, Rilke and Trakl apart from academic literary criticism. Paul Ricoeur wonders why Heidegger brooded for so long on Hölderlin while ignoring the Psalms and Jeremiah,[34] yet the answer is disarmingly simple: for Heidegger, Hölderlin's poems *are* sacred scripture.[35] Doubtless one may not approach '*Brot und Wein*' in the same spirit of faith one brings to the New Testament, but 'the poet in the time of the world's night utters the holy.'[36] As we have seen, Heidegger enforces a distinction between the secular and the sacred with regard to biblical criticism; however, when writing about poetry, especially Hölderlin, he lets the contrast fade. Poetry outside the biblical canon is treated as if it were sacred scripture. Indeed, in the same way that Heidegger bids to free the Bible from the all too ready accommodations of history, so he proposes to liberate poetry from literary history, a study for which he has very little time.

Harnack and Troeltsch listen to the Bible in the wrong way, it seems, confining God's word between the horizons of historical periods. Similarly, literary critics fail to grasp the proper relation between the poet's word and Being. 'Poetry is the saying of the unconcealedness of what is,' we are told, but not everyone is in a position to hear.[37] Hearing properly is a theme that runs through all of Heidegger's work. Thus in '... Poetically Man Dwells ...', an essay on a fragment supposedly by Hölderlin, we are informed that 'Poetry is a measuring.' When we first hear the sentence we are likely to think 'Poetry is presumably a high and special kind of measuring.'

But there is another possibility: 'Perhaps we have to pronounce the sentence, "Poetry is a *measuring*", with a different stress, "*Poetry* is a measuring".' Listening in this new way, we hear (or better, overhear) a unique message: 'In poetry there takes place what all measuring is in the ground of its being ... To write poetry is measure-taking, understood in the strict sense of the word, by which man first receives the measure for the breadth of his being.'[38] Heard in one way, poetry is a special kind of measuring man's dwelling on earth and under Heaven. Heard in another way, though, poetry reveals man's innermost being, that only he is 'capable of death as death'. Listening even more closely, we hear that poetry measures in a still stranger way: 'the unknown god appears as the unknown ... This appearance is the measure against which man measures himself,' and it is only through poetry that we can see this appearance.[39]

Literary and biblical critics alike are prone to find this sort of reading exasperating. After all, it is very hard to see how Heidegger can glean all this from the lines in question. Reproofs about critical rigour fall on deaf ears. 'Anything at all can be proved, depending only on what presuppositions are made:' so the master defends himself, while insisting he is merely attending to 'the poet's own words'.[40] One finds similar disclaimers by Philo Judaeus amidst highly imaginative exegeses of the Torah, and as even a cursory reading of Origen, Meister Eckhart, Moses de Léon or Isaac Luria would amply show, Philo is far from being alone in this respect. Heidegger diverges from these, though, in the way he theorizes his interpretative licence. We must leap from one interpretation, governed by metaphysics ('Poetry is a *measuring*'), to another interpretation that eludes metaphysics and marks its limits ('*Poetry* is a measuring'). While we can, and should, prepare for the leap, it can never be calculated in advance; it is a matter of having a good ear, of being able to discern the voice of Being, and of acting accordingly.[41] Reading poetry becomes like Kierkegaard working out his salvation in fear and trembling. It is all a matter of truth, not method.

We can place matters of hermeneutic violence to one side for now, and look instead at what Heidegger actually says in his exegesis of Hölderlin. It is this. Poetry allows us to glimpse the unknown God as unknown; we see the *deus absconditus* yet, rather than make him visible and knowable, guard him in his concealment. Plainly, it is not just any poetry that can do this. We have to read a poet who has deeply experienced Being. Using Hölderlin's '*Heimkunft*' as a touchstone, Heidegger argues that an engagement with Being must precede any encounter with God: 'the holy, which alone is the essential sphere of divinity, which in turn alone affords a dimension for the gods and for God, comes to radiate only when Being itself beforehand and after extensive preparation has been illuminated and is experienced in its truth.'[42] Which means, in short, that Heidegger effectively replaces the Bible with Hölderlin.

In the Bible or in poetry, Heidegger keeps watch for the event of the word. For it is the word that lets Being shine out. Opportunities to hear that word simply and directly are long since gone: the early Christians, in their childlike faith, were attuned to Being, but the more Christianity permitted itself to be explained and structured by metaphysics, the more theology stiffened into onto-theology; and the early Greeks, Parmenides and Heraclitus, could hear Being's message before it was scrambled in Plato's dialogues. From time to time, individual thinkers have partly recuperated what the tradition has forgotten, and it is in reading them that one can hear the voice of Being. That means, of course, reading in a special way – with two ears, as it were: one mindful of the metaphysical message, the other discerning the quieter, stranger voice of Being itself. *Destruktion* is therefore a way of reading; its negative aspect is revealed in recalling the metaphysics in a text to its proper limits, while its positive side is seen in affirming the truth of Being. That truth may be a dark one, bearing on a negative theology, as it was for Hölderlin; but in these days of God's default that is the best we may hope for.

Those biblical critics influenced by Heidegger, such as Rudolf Bultmann, put this hermeneutic to work in the New Testament, though not without some fairly close supervision, as we shall see a little later. The extent of Heidegger's influence on Bultmann can be overemphasized; we view the situation clearly when seeing Bultmann as a New Testament scholar (not a speculative theologian) responding to questions posed by a philosopher, questions which clarify issues that were already shaping his research. Like Heidegger, though independently of him, Bultmann defined himself against the liberal theology of his youth. 'The subject of theology is *God*,' he roundly asserted in 1924, 'and the chief charge to be brought against liberal theology is that it has dealt not with God but with man.'[43] Historical research into the Bible, as practised by Harnack and Troeltsch, 'can never lead to any result which could serve as a basis for faith, for *all its results have only relative validity*', and the figure of Jesus must be recognized as absolute for the decision of faith.[44] Where Troeltsch asks the believer to compare Christianity with other forms of faith, Bultmann urges us to respond to the Word. Denying that Christianity has a privileged access to the truth, Troeltsch would doubtless counter that claims for absolute value rest on a 'religious *a priori*', but Bultmann's categories are existential, not transcendental, and his debate with liberal theology is more of a conversation than a showdown. For Bultmann never denied that the Bible is an historical document. 'We must study the language of the Bible, the historical situation of the biblical authors,' he admitted, but such studies should always be subvened to our real concern: 'to hear what the Bible has to say for our actual present, to hear what is the truth about our life and about our soul'.[45]

'To hear': the verb recalls Heidegger's project of *Destruktion*, and indeed Bultmann's biblical criticism seems marked by that hermeneutic. What do people hear when they read the New Testament? Two things, Bultmann thinks. There is the voice of first-century Jewish culture, forever picturing the world by way of mythology and naive eschatology; and there is the kerygma, a proclamation addressed to the individual, calling him or her to repent and trust in Jesus. Our task is to heed that second voice, to see ourselves as the implied readers, and not be distracted by the first. 'This method of interpretation of the New Testament which tries to recover the deeper meaning behind the mythological conceptions I call *demythologizing* ... Its aim is not to eliminate the mythological statements but to interpret them.'[46] In the same way that Heidegger proposed loosening up the history of ontology, to release its positive possibilities, so too Bultmann in his own way continues the Reformation tradition of the trial of God's word by interrogating the New Testament. *Destruktion* 'is aimed at "today"', we were warned in *Being and Time*; similarly, 'demythologizing takes the modern world-view as a criterion.'[47] Heidegger found that some writers – including Augustine, Eckhart, Luther and Hölderlin – were already engaged in recovering Being from the metaphysical tradition; while Bultmann sees demythologizing occurring in the New Testament. The two discourses, one philosophical and one scriptural, resonate with each other.

III

And yet there are differences between Heidegger and Bultmann, salient differences, one of them being the relative weight each gives to historical research. For Heidegger, the history of ontology has greater authority than material history; he is far more interested in Being speaking to us through a text, than in that text's historical authenticity. (The lines on which he bases a long and detailed study of Hölderlin, '... Poetically Man Dwells ...', are classed by the editor as *'Zweifelhaftes'*, of doubtful authenticity.[48]) Bultmann has far greater respect for research, having affinities with nineteenth-century historical criticism. In addition to pressing ontological categories into the service of biblical studies, Bultmann is a major representative of *Formgeschichte*. 'Form criticism', as it is known, began in the early years of the century with Hermann Gunkel's pioneering work on Genesis, but no one has pursued his insights more tenaciously in the synoptic Gospels than Bultmann. The main tenet of form criticism is that the biblical authors did not so much compose their texts as gather and edit them. The Gospels, for example, were compiled from a range of traditional materials – miracle stories, apothegms, proverbs, apocalyptic sayings and so forth – which all answer to certain genres or 'forms', and which were originally related in a certain setting in discrete units. Seeking to locate the historical and geographical origins of these materials, the form critic also tries to picture how they were pieced together. It is easy to see why Bultmann would be sympathetic to this approach; for unless we know Jesus as he was known to his disciples – that is, before the Gospels were written – we are not in an ideal position to be directly addressed by his radical message of faith.

More suspicious about claims to recover the historical Jesus than most form critics, Bultmann nonetheless yields no ground to those who dispute that Jesus actually lived. If form criticism is pursued to its legitimate ends, without deviating from its methods, it will not lead to scepticism. True, we must admit that Jesus's character and personality are lost to us, but his message remains clear. 'Though one may admit the fact that for no single word of Jesus is it possible to produce positive evidence of its authenticity, still one may point to a whole series of words found in the oldest stratum of tradition which do give us a consistent representation of the historical message of Jesus.'[49] These old words, in which Bultmann places his full trust as a historical scholar, are the prophetic calls to repentance, those which demand a personal decision on the hearer's part.

The form critic endeavours to divide the evangelist's redactions from the prophetic words of Jesus, and is therefore akin to the demythologist. Both seek the purity of origins, and in Bultmann the two converge. Although he concentrates on the present, the time of decision, his scholarly tools are historical and literary, not structural. The form critic studies distinct literary types. 'It is self-evident that the laws of style governing a literary type are more or less elastic,' Bultmann tells us; 'at the same time each type has its own definite characteristics which may be observed in every example of the type, even though these characteristics are not all present in any one example.'[50] Where Bultmann is principally occupied with stylistic structures, another critic might probe the notion of structure a little more, and set out on a quite different kind of analysis: one that looks at a pericope or discrete biblical passage as it participates in larger narrative structures, not merely as a linguistic unit and its original context. The wider category of narrative does seem to forestall an obvious problem with form criticism. Why should the useful notion of a text's life situation, its *Sitz im Leben*, be necessarily restricted to the individual unit? Perhaps there are long passages or entire books composed with a special audience in mind. Thinking along these lines makes one link *muthos* to its original Aristotelian sense of 'fable'. Attention shifts from discredited beliefs in need of interpretation to the general medium of narrative in which beliefs are embodied.

The structural study of biblical narrative properly begins with Edmund Leach's essays on Genesis, which are broadly oriented by the structural anthropology of Claude Lévi-Strauss.[51] While mythical patterns have continued to captivate biblical critics, other structural models – such as A. J. Greimas's 'actantial analysis' and Vladimir Propp's 'functional analysis' – have gained attention. Of the many luminous readings of biblical stories that have emerged from structuralism, I choose just one, perhaps the most influential: Roland Barthes's 'Wrestling with the Angel'.[52] I say 'emerged from structuralism' because this essay is both an anthology of structural procedures (Propp's and Greimas's practices are neatly demonstrated) and a swerve away from those methods to 'textual analysis'. Since I will return several times to this story, I quote it here in full:

22 And he rose up that night, and took his two wives, and his two womenservants, and his eleven sons, and passed over the ford Jabbok.

23 And he took them, and sent them over the brook, and sent over that he had.

24 And Jacob was left alone; and there wrestled a man with him until the breaking of the day.

25 And when he saw that he prevailed not against him, he touched the hollow of his thigh; and the hollow of Jacob's thigh was out of joint, as he wrestled with him.

26 And he said, Let me go, for the day breaketh. And he said, I will not let thee go, except thou bless me.

27 And he said unto him, What is thy name? And he said, Jacob.

28 And he said, Thy name shall be called no more Jacob, but Israel: for as a prince hast thou power with God and with men, and hast prevailed.

29 And Jacob asked him, and said, Tell me, I pray thee, thy name. And he said, Wherefore is it that thou dost ask after my name? And he blessed him there.

30 And Jacob called the name of the place Peniel: for I have seen God face to face, and my life is preserved.
31 And as he passed over Penuel the sun rose upon him, and he halted upon his thigh.
32 Therefore the children of Israel eat not of the sinew which shrank, which is upon the hollow of the thigh, unto this day: because he touched the hollow of Jacob's thigh in the sinew that shrank.

Barthes begins by delineating three approaches to the passage. Historical criticism examines where the text comes from; structural analysis asks how it is made; while textual analysis ponders how it is unmade. Given Barthes's preference for the third approach, it is odd that this essay is so often held up as an example (or even a refinement) of structuralism.[53] True, we note how, following Greimas, one could distribute the characters in the narrative into the six formal classes of actants; and how, learning from Propp, the passage fits nicely into a series of narrative actions. Not only is the structural reading of the pericope quite feasible, it is also necessary if a textual reading is to follow. Yet Barthes is more interested in the rough surfaces of the passage than in the deep structures. In short, he responds most keenly to the kind of reading already demonstrated in *S/Z*, which searches for a text's difference, not its deep structure. Reading does not consist in determining a difference between two texts (a bourgeois exercise in discriminating taste) but within a text; and this requires a rethinking of interpretation. 'To interpret a text is not to give it a (more or less justified, more or less free) meaning, but on the contrary to appreciate what *plural* constitutes it.'[54] So reading becomes the art of unravelling a text's apparent unities, looking carefully for those moments when the text exceeds any interpretation which would foreclose its possibilities of meaning. The text is forever at work, deconstituting the language of communication and representation while producing another language which forever evades reductions to transitive meaning. The good reader follows the fault line between those two languages, admiring the limitless energy of the second, though never committing the violence that an act of understanding would wreak upon the text. Needless to say, this appreciation of plurality presupposes a revaluation of literary value; we must prize 'writerly' texts, which make the reader actively produce their meanings, and accordingly devalue those 'readerly' works which sit on our library shelves and cannot guide today's writers.[55]

Elsewhere, Barthes glories in the irreverent impulse behind this new conception of the text. 'We know now', he writes, 'that a text is not a line of words releasing a single "theological" meaning (the "message" of the Author-God) but a multi-dimensional space in which a variety of writings, none of them original, blend and clash.' Moreover, 'literature (it would be better from now on to say *writing*), by refusing to assign a "secret", an ultimate meaning, to the text (and to the world as text), liberates what may be called an anti-theological activity.'[56] One could easily mistake what is inferred here, by thinking that Scripture is playing the straight man to literature (especially today's literature: the *nouveau roman* of Alain Robbe-Grillet and Philippe Sollers); but Barthes's response to the Bible is a degree more complex. Scripture, it seems,

is a privileged domain ... because, on the one hand, theologically, it is certain that a final signified is postulated: the metaphysical definition or the semantic definition of theology is to postulate the Last Signified; and because, on the other hand, the very notion of Scripture, the fact that the Bible is called Scripture, Writing, would orient us toward a more ambiguous comprehension of the problems, as if effectivety, and theologically too, the base, the *princeps*, were still a Writing, and always a Writing.[57]

In cultural terms, then, the Bible is the readerly text *par excellence*: it is a work, a classic, something presented for passive reading. Nonetheless, it is a text, akin to literature, able to produce meaning endlessly, eluding all attempts to gather meanings into a totality. It is this ambivalence between the readerly and the writerly in Scripture that entices Barthes to offer close readings of biblical passages. Terry Eagleton relishes how Barthes will 'maliciously proceed to carve up the text of Genesis', but this places the accent in quite the wrong place.[58] For Barthes is not simply opposed to the great cultural monuments, as he explains when comparing *A la Recherche du Temps Perdu* with the Bible:

Proust is a complete world-reading system. This means that if we accept this system even in the slightest degree, if only because it is so seductive, then there is no situation which doesn't have its reference in Proust. Proust can be my memory, my culture, my language; I may constantly *remember* and *refer* to Proust, as the narrator's grandmother does with Madame de Sévigné. The pleasure of reading Proust – or rather of rereading him – is like consulting the Bible, abstraction made of the sacred and the respect it demands: it's the encounter between a present and what must be called, in the complete sense of the word, a *wisdom*: a knowledge of 'life' and its language.[59]

The connection is not altogether arbitrary. With all its carefully inlaid foreshadowings and redemptions, Proust's great novel develops a typology at least as elaborate as one finds in the Bible. We are used to reading both texts quickly, passing over hints, details, gaps and ambiguities, but if we return to them, attend to their typology and slow down the rhythm of our reading, we will find both links and lustres never noticed before.

At any rate, this is Barthes' intention when reading Gen. 32:22–32. His procedure is straightforward, working by way of a 'sequential analysis'. (Even though he distances himself from structuralism, he remains a narratologist through and through.) There are three sequences: the Crossing (vv. 22–4); the Wrestling (vv. 24–9); and the Namings (vv. 27–32). First of all, he pinpoints a crucial ambiguity: it is not clear whether Jacob fights the 'man' before or after crossing the ford. If before, the episode invites a folkloristic reading (Jacob must overcome a river spirit, say, and so prove his worthiness to cross the Jabbok); if after, the story foregoes a structural unity to attain a sense of religious finality: Jacob indicates his special relationship with Elohim by setting himself apart from the tribe. Both readings answer to the text, though they cannot be reconciled in an organic whole. Nor are they resolved as the narrative continues. There is a grammatical ambiguity in verse 26, since it is not immediately obvious to whom the pronoun 'he' refers. For Barthes, this is not a matter of style; it reflects the paradox at the heart of the struggle. To exhibit the paradox's structural *finesse*, he dwells on the story's logic. By all the conventions of narrative, the angel should win by dealing a decisive blow to Jacob; nevertheless, it turns out that the angel must depart at dawn, and cries to be released. Whereas the logic of the narrative requires the angel to be the victor, it is Jacob who actually triumphs. The sequence serves to unbalance the two wrestlers; the weaker defeats the stronger, though not with impunity, as he is marked on the hip.

Hence the creation of new meanings: the marking of Jacob encourages the development of a new language with God as a logothete and Jacob as a morpheme.[60] And so we have a new language: marked on Jacob's thigh; inscribed in the relation between Jacob and Esau (Elohim's blessing corroborates Isaac's), and more generally in the relation between Jacob and the Jews (they become 'the people of Israel'); imprinted on the landscape ('Peniel'); and in the creation of a new food taboo. The entire passage thus becomes an allegory of how form disseminates contents.

One intriguing aspect of Barthes's reading is its rhetoric of omission. He will not stage 'a methodological confrontation between structural or textual analysis and Biblical exegesis'; nor will he engage with the structural analysis he has left for textual analysis.[61]

And yet, almost despite itself, the essay does represent a struggle – between Genesis and Barthes. Right at the beginning of the paper Barthes says he will deal with structures 'in an underhanded way', and the text is definitely wounded by the encounter, its 'economico-historical range' being weakened, while it nevertheless gains victory over the reader by virtue of its intensified 'symbolic explosion' of meaning.[62] The struggle also results in a change of name: once known to its students as 'Work', Gen. 32:22–32 has become 'Text'. Crossing from structuralism to poststructuralism, Genesis has fought its readers and emerged triumphant. No one will ever be able to master its warring meanings.

For all that, the wound Barthes inflicts is serious; the text limps and the work did not. Biblical scholars may point out that gram-matical ambiguities in the passage result from a recension by J or E of earlier material. And biblical historians would refer Barthes to a range of commentators, in both Jewish and Christian traditions, who have lived quite happily with the idea that biblical texts do not release 'a single "theological" meaning'. The issue does not set plurality against singularity of interpretations, but concerns the role intention plays in reading. Jewish and Christian exegetes have lauded the Bible as polysemous, because as God's inspired word it must be inexhaustibly richer than human discourse, however heightened.[63] If Barthes's textual analysis defines itself against form criticism, addressing the text as a finished narrative (not as an ensemble of cultural documents), it also holds very different assump-tions from hermeneutics. Structuralism and textual analysis take their notion of 'text' from 'sign', whereas hermeneutics accents the primacy of 'work' and 'word'. Thus Heidegger: 'The nature of language does not exhaust itself in signifying, nor is it merely some-thing that has the character of sign or cipher. It is because language is the house of Being, that we reach what is by constantly going through this house.'[64] So it seems we find opposed ways of en-countering literature and the Bible. Is there a way in which they can be reconciled or at least thought together? And if so, how does this affect the way we read the Bible and literature?

IV

These questions direct us toward Paul Ricoeur who has explored the relations between interpretation, religion and literature with exemplary thoroughness. The split between structuralism and her-meneutics, he suggests, is a recrudescent dispute that began with

Dilthey's distinction between explanation (*Erklären*) and understanding (*Verstehen*). In drawing this antithesis, Dilthey hoped to
keep explanation at arm's length from the humanities, for there are
crucial methodological differences between research in chemistry,
say, and reading Keats. However, with the advent of structuralism
(and its chief instrument, semiotics), explanation has become a
privileged mode of intepretation in the arts as well as the sciences.
There are reasons why this move should be withstood, not the least
being an inherent logical difficulty in all semiotic analyses of texts.
As Ricoeur indicates, structuralism takes an element smaller than the
sentence (phoneme, grapheme or lexeme) as a model for analysing
texts which are larger than the sentence. In doing so, semioticians
forget how language actually works; since, as Frege made clear, it is
only by uttering a sentence that one performs a linguistic act. Structuralism does not bring the subject under critique, as is often
claimed. Rather, it omits the subject in its very choice of a model.[65]

One could object that semiotics respects the sentence when developing the idea of linguistic competence, for example; and it
would be more accurate to say that structuralism sets up a dialectic
between small lexical units and very large shapes such as plot and
genre. But these remarks do not entice Ricoeur from his main path.
A semiotic analysis, he contends, may be able to describe a text's
sense but can never grasp its reference. Contemporary literary criticism is committed to 'the destruction of reference', and without
reference there can be no truth.[66] This commitment may well have
precipitated a crisis in literary studies but, as Hans Frei has suggested, it has been a problem in biblical interpretation since the
Reformation. What Frei locates as an historical rupture in biblical
studies, Ricoeur furnishes as a transcendental condition for literature. 'It seems to be the function of a great deal of our literature to
"destroy" reality,' he avers,[67] and there is indubitably no hope of
establishing referents for *Finnegans Wake* or *The Trial*. For Ricoeur,
however, this suspension of ostensive reference is the negative condition of possibility for literature's true referential function. Poetic
discourse does refer – not to the historical world, but to the 'world
of the text', that unique sphere of experience described by the
narrator or narrators.

Reference is suspended in poetic discourse in much the same way
as the world is bracketed during the phenomenological *epoché*. In
that operation, Husserl thought, we cease making judgements about
the existence of things; we encounter the world as pure phenomenon, not as the ground of being. We return to the life-world
(*Lebenswelt*), the realm of untroubled freedom where consciousness

originates and properly belongs. No longer worried by questions of verification, we experience being as it unfolds before us and in us. Now when we read a literary work, Ricoeur suggests, we similarly find ourselves involved in a world that challenges us with fresh possibilities of experience and meaning. 'My deepest conviction', he tells us, 'is that poetic language alone restores to us that participation-in or belonging-to an order of things which precedes our capacity to oppose ourselves to things taken as objects opposed to a subject. Hence the function of poetic discourse is to bring out this emergence of a depth-structure of belonging-to amid the ruins of descriptive discourse.'[68] In other words, poetic language redescribes reality and calls us to recognize it as real.

'Poetic language' is not to be understood in opposition to prose. Rather, Ricoeur wishes to identify that capacity of language to elude reference while metaphorically naming reality. Biblical discourse is as poetic, therefore, as anything by Joyce or Yeats: 'Just as the world of poetic texts opens its way across the ruins of the intraworldly objects of everyday existence and of science, so too the new being projected by the biblical text opens its way across the world of ordinary experience and in spite of the closed nature of that experience.'[69] There is a rapport between the revelation that litera- ture offers and the more narrow biblical revelation. So it hardly takes one unawares to hear Ricoeur saying that 'the Bible is one of the great poems of existence.'[70] In this respect at least, we remain on speaking terms with Friedrich Schlegel and Herder. In another respect, however, we stand in the world of *Robert Elsmere* as evoked in chapter 4 by Stephen Prickett.[71] For, like Mrs Humphrey Ward, Ricoeur makes much of testimony: not, to be sure, in a psychological sense of the word, but as a semantic category. And it is here that Ricoeur redraws the contrast between the sacred and the secular that beforehand appeared, to all intents and purposes, to have been erased.

Ricoeur's work is best understood as a bold attempt to graft hermeneutics onto a tradition of reflexive philosophy, that style of thinking which takes self-understanding to be the central philo- sophical problem. The tradition begins with Descartes's *cogito*, is amplifed by the Kantian transcendental unity of apperception, then refined by Husserl in his theory of the transcendental subject. Re- flexion occurs when, through introspection, a subject perceives itself as a subject. At this point a familiar philosophical temptation is not far away: 'the idea of reflexion carries with it the desire for absolute transparence, a perfect co-incidence of the self with itself, which would make consciousness of self indubitable knowledge.'[72]

Resisting this temptation to let the subject ground itself in a moment
of immediate self-consciousness, Ricoeur counters that the self is
always mediated by signs. The move is worth pondering. Structuralism is not abandoned in favour of hermeneutics but integrated into a
larger framework: the act of interpretation involves two poles, one
objective (which structuralism helps explain) and one subjective
(where hermeneutics holds sway). It is at this point that reflexive
philosophy can be rethought, and that a hermeneutics of testimony
can be developed.

'What we recognize in testimony', Ricoeur tells us, 'is that it is the
expression of the freedom that we desire to be.'[73] Testimony is given
that the absolute has manifested itself in history; but the act has
passed, leaving only its meaning to be fathomed. In meditating on
that meaning, we must confront ourselves, for the testimony engages
us in relation to the absolute. And so the hermeneutics of testimony
is double: there is the historical event to be interpreted, and also the
subject who must interpret himself or herself in the light of that
event. Accepting the testimony, the subject divests itself of all claim
to be self-grounding, and risks believing that the signs to be interpreted constitute a trace of God. 'As a reader, I find myself only
by losing myself.'[74] The kenosis, or emptying out of the self, refers
equally to secular and sacred writing, although one cannot help
recalling Coleridge's apothegm that, of all books, the Bible seeks us
out the most. By what authority does it claim us? Not by dint of its
historical truth, but by virtue of the kind of text it is. Its performa-
tive dimension, what it makes us do, is the one in which we live and
move and have our being. That the Bible is fixed in writing, utterly
beyond revision, guarantees its authority; yet in the last analysis that
authority itself derives from two events: the one to which it attests,
and the one in which the reader accepts that testimony. Ricoeur is
not alone in holding this view; in their own ways Barth, Bultmann
and Heidegger make the same point.[75]

Without a manifestation of the absolute, the hermeneutic of testimony cannot commence; it would be only 'an interpretation of
interpretation . . . an infinite regress in a perspectivism with neither
beginning nor end'.[76] It is precisely this manifestation of presence
that Jacques Derrida reviews, and this seriality of interpretation that
he embraces. Not that Derrida breaks completely with Ricoeur. He
remains intrigued by hermeneutics and structuralism, by literature
and Scripture, but the pressure he puts on the idea of the absolute
revealing itself in history leads him to rethink their claims from a
different (and somewhat precarious) vantage point. The Bible as the

exemplary Book, and the notion of God leaving a trace in history, are themes that Derrida interrogates and refashions, as we shall see. Before turning to these issues, however, let us see how Derrida deviates from Ricoeur over the issue of testimony.

According to Ricoeur, the hermeneutics of testimony works with two subjects, both of whom can recognize themselves as subjects, even though they are mediated by signs. In listening to a testimony – the story of Jacob and the angel, say – one discerns a 'movement of liberation' that, formerly, could only have been posited as ideal; and this recognition 'permits us to speak of absolute actions which are senseless for historians'.[77] Picturing the relationship between the subjects by way of a letter passing between them, Derrida offers a counter-intuitive model of testimony:

> I do not make the hypothesis of a letter that would be the external occasion, in some way, of a meeting between two identifiable subjects – and which would be already determined. No, but of a letter which after the fact seems to have been cast toward some unknown recipient at the moment of its writing, a recipient unknown to himself or to herself, if one can say that, and who determines himself or herself, as you know how to do so well, on receiving the letter; this is quite different from the transfer of a message. Its content and its end no longer precede it. Here's the point, you identify yourself and you organise your life on the programme of the letter, or rather of a post card, of a letter that's open, divisible, at once transparent and encrypted. The programme says nothing, it doesn't announce or state anything, not the slightest thing, it doesn't even present itself as a programme. One can't even say that it 'does' programme, as far as appearances go, yet without having the air of a programme, it works, it programmes. Then you say: it's I, uniquely I, who can receive this letter, not that it is reserved just for me, on the contrary, but I receive as a present the chance to which this card surrenders itself. It chooses me. And I choose that it should choose me by chance, I wish to cross its trajectory, I wish to find myself there, I can and I want to ... Others would conclude: a letter thus finds its recipient, man or woman. No, one cannot say that the recipient exists before the letter.[78]

The audacity of the claim needs acknowledgement. Where Heidegger and Bultmann, Barth and Ricoeur, see the text mediating events or subjects, Derrida casts the text in the lead role: in some sense, *it* precedes subjects and events. Even so, there is no suggestion that we should abandon the concept of 'subject', for example. Subjectivity is assigned a new status, being regarded as a textual effect.

What Derrida offers, in short, is a critique of a very familiar model of communication, one that is common to readers of both the

Bible and literature. Written communication is usually understood as a passage between subjects; an author writes a text, and its meaning (however that be defined) is to be recovered by a reader. 'If we take the notion of writing in its currently accepted sense – one which should not – and that is essential – be considered innocent, primitive, or natural, it can only be seen as a *means of communication ... extending* enormously, if not infinitely, the domain of oral or gestural communication.'[79] So writing is figured as an aid, a supplement, to speech and gesture; nevertheless, Derrida proposes to think communication otherwise, seeing writing as foundational, not speech. The argument is straightforward. One can willingly admit that writing functions in the absence of author or intended audience. But if writing can signify without a designated sender or receiver, it can surely *always* signify without them; the possibility of their complete absence from the scene of reading is a structural feature of writing, any writing whatsoever.

One could restate the argument more dramatically by saying that death underwrites any text, any sign, any name. The proper name says death even when its bearer is alive and well: for it necessarily presupposes the bearer's death in order to function. It is this argument, first developed in *Speech and Phenomena*, that gave rise to Barthes's most popular doctrine, the 'death of the author'.[80] Now it seems only a short step from this to claiming that God – as the author of the world, history and Scripture – is dead. Or perhaps it is a very large step, and one Derrida does not choose to take. For although he has a case to prosecute against a dominant image of God, what Heidegger called the god of onto-theology, he seems to have no animus against the sacred and its valencies. If anything, one finds a sense of fine discrimination in Derrida's encounters with Judaeo-Christianity and its Scriptures, showing an awareness of the 'original, heterogeneous elements' that have persisted in both religions. Indeed, over the years these elements have been 'threatening and unsettling the assured "identities" of Western philosophy', working with deconstruction, not against it.[81] All the same, Judaism and Christianity are religions of the book, and Derrida has a case against the Bible as the exemplary book.

'Each "text" is a machine with multiple reading heads for other texts,' Derrida tells us,[82] and without a doubt the Bible has been used at one time or another to read the Western literary tradition. More precisely, a certain reading of the Bible has been so used, one that traces a single if complex narrative from Creation to Apocalypse, seen as flashes of full presence. (Marjorie Reeves amply discusses this aspect of the Bible's authority in chapter 1 of this book.)

This metaphysical reading derives from many sources, from the Church Fathers, of course, but ultimately from the Greeks. Nor has this reading been displaced by modern theories of interpretation. Structuralism remains in fee to it, forever invoking a centre which in determining the structure is undetermined by it. And hermeneutics, for all its professed liberality, places the play of the text under the surveillance of a consciousness. Maurice Blanchot describes the Bible under this gaze with customary clarity:

The book begins with the Bible, in which the logos is inscribed as law. Here the book achieves its unsurpassable meaning, including what extends beyond it everywhere and cannot be surpassed. The Bible takes language back to its origin: whether this language is written or spoken, it is always the theological era that opens with this language and lasts as long as biblical space and time. The Bible not only offers us the highest model of a book, the specimen that will never be superceded; the Bible also encompasses all books, no matter how alien they are to biblical revelation, knowledge, poetry, prophecy, proverbs, because it contains the spirit of the book; the books that follow it are always contemporaneous with the Bible: the Bible certainly grows, expands with itself in an infinite growth that leaves it identical, permanently sanctioned by the relationship of Unity . . .[83]

On the other side of the channel, T. S. Eliot's 'Tradition and the Individual Talent' chimes nicely with this. Eliot does not mention the Bible; he does not need to: the view that literary works form an 'ideal order', complete in itself, is plainly indebted to an influential idea of the biblical canon.[84] Canonical criticism, as practised by Eliot and Leavis, looks to the Book of books (as a guide which recommends which literature to read, and as the exemplary book). And yet sacred and secular canons do not go hand in hand all the way. Sometimes they diverge sharply: the canon of the New Testament, for instance, was authoritively decided only after years of broad consensus amongst the faithful; while literary canons are sometimes formed or adjusted in defiance of general usage or consent. When Eliot depreciated Milton and elevated Donne, he was responding to his own sense of literary value, not one long held by the literary community.

At any rate, it is this 'reading head', determining the Bible as the Book of books, that interests Derrida. He broaches a critique of the book from several directions – via Blanchot, Leibniz, Mallarmé and Hegel – always associating the book with premature closure, finality and delusive mastery, while affirming the text as an open network of signification. Perhaps his most revealing (because most equivocal) discussion of the book, though, is by way of the French poet Edmund Jabès. It is not hard to see what draws Derrida to Jabès. Such observations as 'Reading is impossible' and 'every page of writing is in some way the journal of a dead man', both from *The Book of Questions*, indicate a fellow-feeling between the poet and the critic.[85] Throughout Jabès's work we meet imaginary rabbis ruminating on God, writing, Judaism and exile. Of central importance is the way in which the book is represented: as the Hebrew Bible and as its ghostly double, literature. On the one hand we have, 'If God is, it is because He is in the book. If sages, saints, and prophets exist, if scholars and poets, men and insects exist, it is because their names are found in the book.'[86] And on the other hand, 'The book is made against the book, just as a word in a dialogue opposes the word which engendered it.'[87] Equally significant is the identification of Jew and writer. An extract from Yukel's Notebook tells us, 'First I thought I was a writer. Then I realized I was a Jew. Then I no longer distinguished the writer in me from the Jew because one and the other are only torments of an ancient word.'[88]

And yet there is a decisive difference between the rabbi and the poet. They examplify theories of interpretation which, though not opposed, are out of step:

In the beginning is hermeneutics. But the *shared* necessity of exegesis, the interpretive imperative, is interpreted differently by the rabbi and the poet. The difference between the horizon of the original text and exegetic writing makes the difference between the rabbi and the poet irreducible. Forever unable to reunite with each other, yet so close to each other, how could they ever regain the *realm*? The original opening of interpretation essentially signifies that there will always be rabbis and poets. And two interpretations of interpretation.[89]

This no doubt recalls Heidegger's two ways of listening to texts, one metaphysical and one seeking the outside of metaphysics. On Derrida's understanding, however, the two approaches are forever engaged in a struggle for dominance that neither can win. Metaphysics cannot control the meaning of a text, nor can there be a successful leap beyond metaphysics.

What does Derridean deconstruction mean for interpreting the Bible? Precisely this, ventures Geoffrey Hartman, 'that we no longer live in a world defined by certain writings having testamentary force and bending us authoritatively to their yoke. Today Old and New

Testaments are simply two "texts" in a series that is profane and endless ... and to which, say, *Krapp's Last Tape* is just another addition.'[90] But must we see deconstruction like this, as the great leveller? Not at all. Deconstruction redistributes distinctions by thinking them in terms of difference, not opposition; the sacred is not abolished by the new-found power of the profane. At the very least Derrida would ask us to see 'testamentary force' as a textual effect that requires analysis. Besides, he offers a more delicately nuanced account of biblical interpretation when reflecting on the Jew's dilemma:

The Jew is split, and split first of all between the two dimensions of the letter: allegory and literality. His history would be but one empirical history among others if he established or nationalized himself within difference and literality. He would have no history at all if he let himself be attenuated within the algebra of an abstract universalism.[91]

The problem has been around since Philo Judaeus weighed the demands of the Torah against the imperatives of Greek philosophy. For Derrida, the question of choosing between allegory and literality does not arise: the two must be taken in tandem. 'What emerges', Hartman says (and here he is on the right track), 'is an anti-allegoresis, and perhaps for the first time since Philo of Alexandria ... Interpretation no longer aims at the reconciliation or unification of warring truths.'[92]

One theme that runs through *The Book of Questions* is the negativity in God. *Deus absconditus, deus deceptor, deus definiri nequit* – all these, the darker threads of the Hebrew and Christian Bibles, weave in and out of Jabès's meditations, as do images of the Kabbalah and midrash. The same threads are also picked up and reworked by Derrida, whose interest in negativity hardly needs to be signalled, though it may require a good deal of explanation and some defence before it is correctly understood. This is something to ponder in a little while. Before then, though, it will be useful to see how Derrida goes about reading a text, sacred or secular, and to ask if that distinction remains intact during his reading.

V

One of the biblical narratives that has entranced Derrida is the story of the Tower of Babel. The tale serves as a proof text in a discussion of Walter Benjamin's theory of translation, and also features in a study of Joyce's *Finnegans Wake*, thereby allowing us to compare his treatment of biblical and secular writing. Let us begin with his reading of Scripture. Here is the biblical narrative (Gen. 11:1–9):

1 And the whole earth was of one language, and of one speech.
2 And it came to pass, as they journeyed from the east, that they found a plain in the land of Shinar; and they dwelt there.
3 And they said one to another, Go to, let us make brick, and burn them thoroughly. And they had brick for stone, and slime had they for morter.
4 And they said, Go to, let us build us a city and a tower, whose top may reach unto heaven; and let us make us a name, lest we be scattered abroad upon the face of the whole earth.
5 And the LORD came down to see the city and the tower, which the children of men builded.
6 And the LORD said, Behold, the people is one, and they have all one language; and this they begin to do: and now nothing will be restrained from them, which they have imagined to do.
7 Go to, let us go down, and there confound their language, that they may not understand one another's speech.
8 So the LORD scattered them abroad from thence upon the face of all the earth: and they left off to build the city.
9 Therefore is the name of it called Babel; because the LORD did there confound the language of all the earth: and from thence did the LORD scatter them abroad upon the face of all the earth.

For Derrida, this is a story about translation, the power of rhetoric, the laws of sacralization and the proper name, and the irreducible multiplicity of idioms. In short, it is a story that condenses much of what interests him under the rubric of 'deconstruction'. To begin with, one can read the narrative as an allegory of deconstruction; the story 'gives a good idea of what deconstruction is: an unfinished edifice whose half-completed structures are visible, letting one guess at the scaffolding behind them'.[93] In building their tower the Shem propose to make a name for themselves and, more pointedly, to impose their language on the whole world. Observing this, Yahweh opposes their name for the tower (Babel) with his own name (Bavel) which means confusion, and so disperses the Shem, 'disscheminating' them across the earth.[94]

In relating this story, J makes use of a popular Hebrew etymology in which the proper name 'Babel' derives from the verb '*balal*' meaning 'to confuse'. And so a problem in translation occurs: the proper name 'Babel' casts a shadow, the common noun for confusion. The proper name is forever untranslatable – it must remain 'Babel' in any language – yet in Hebrew it can be understood, by virtue of a pun, to mean 'confusion'. Along with the Shem, we find ourselves in a tricky situation:

> To translate Babel by 'confusion' is already to give a confused and uncertain translation. It translates a proper name into a common noun. Thus one sees that God declares war by forcing men, if you will, to translate his proper name with a common noun. In effect, he says to them: Now you will not impose a single tongue; you will be condemned to the multiplicity of tongues; translate and, to begin with, translate my name. Translate my name, says he, but at the same time he says: You will not be able to translate my name because, first of all, it's a proper name and, secondly, my name, the one I myself have chosen for this tower, signifies ambiguity, confusion, et cetera. Thus God, in his rivalry with the tribe of the Shems, gives them, in a certain way, an absolutely double command.[95]

There are several things worth noting here. In the first place, while considering a specific difficulty in translation, Derrida isolates a general problem of interpretation. No text, however simple or familiar, can be formalized without remainder: there will always be a supplement of signification that is overlooked or reduced. This marks what we could call the negative labour of deconstruction, the demonstration that no interpretation can totalize a text. In the second place, we see how a name which should properly expend its meaning entirely in reference begins, quite improperly, to join in the text's play of signification. And this reveals the positive aspect of deconstruction: it is a practice (or, better, an ensemble of practices) for reading and writing, one that works in between, across or around philosophical theses, showing how signification overruns nomination, exceeding it without return.

Neither the dark nor the light face of deconstruction seems at all disposed to look favourably on sacred texts. The word 'sacred' enters Derrida's vocabulary by way of Walter Benjamin's 'The Task of the Translator', although, by the end of the analysis, it no longer remains Benjamin's word purely and simply. What interests Derrida is the translatability of the sacred text:

> What comes to pass in a sacred text is the occurence of a *pas de sens*. And this event is also the one starting from which it is possible to think the poetic and the literary text which tries to redeem the lost sacred and there translates itself as its model. *Pas de sens* – that does not signify poverty of meaning but no meaning that would be itself, meaning, beyond any 'literality'. And right there is the sacred. The sacred surrenders itself to translation, which devotes itself to the sacred. The sacred would be nothing without translation, and translation would not take place without the sacred; the

one and the other are inseparable. In the sacred text 'the meaning has ceased to be the divide for the flow of language and for the flow of revelation'. It is the absolute text because in its event it communicates nothing, it says nothing that would make sense beyond the event itself. That event melds completely with the act of language, for example with prophecy. It is literally the literality of its tongue, 'pure language'.[96]

The sacred, for Benjamin, is the untranslatable; it is impossible to dissociate meaning and letter in a holy text, because the two are given in the one event. At the same time, though, the sacred text demands to be translated, so much so that it marks an ideal of all translation.

Now one can approach the sacred text from at least two directions. Like Benjamin and Barth, we can believe that the divine enters history as an absolute event, and that certain texts bear testimony to this supervention. More sceptically, we can refuse the character of absolute to the sacred and attend, rather, to the processes of sacralization or canonization that have made the text what it is. Derrida aligns himself with this second approach, though that by no means commits him to rejecting the order of the sacred. After all, it is quite possible to grant that texts, such as Genesis, have been subject to the complex processes of canonization and still maintain that, in some respect, they are nonetheless holy. What separates Derrida's view from that of Benjamin and Ricoeur is the status he attributes to the trace of the absolute.

Paul Ricoeur, as we have seen, argues that although the sacred event may be lost to us, its meaning remains to be interpreted in those texts which testify to it. There is a trace that lingers, and if correctly interpreted it will point to the divine presence to which it refers. Derrida diverges sharply from this. On his understanding (in which he is indebted to Emmanuel Levinas), the trace refers to the otherness of a past which has never actually presented itself to consciousness. In formulating the concept of the trace, Levinas has a biblical image in mind. 'The God revealed in our Judeo-Christian spirituality preserves all the infinity of his absence which is in the personal order itself. He does not show Himself except in his trace, as in the thirty-third chapter of Exodus. To go toward Him is not to follow the trace which is not a sign. To go toward Him is to go toward the Others who are in the trace.'[97] Unhappy with the implications of that biblical image, Derrida would prefer to rephrase the matter in a philosophical vocabulary. We cannot speak of a 'trace of a presence' because presence is incapable of presenting itself to consciousness. Instead, we must talk of a 'trace of a trace', *la différance*, a movement of pure negative difference and deferral which never enters the domains of presence.

For Benjamin, the sacred and the literary belong together in that both resist translation. Derrida agrees, even though he approaches the problem from another point: 'This is surely the relation we have to literature,' he says. 'The process of sacralization is underway whenever one says to oneself in dealing with a text: Basically, I can't transpose this text such as it is into another language; there is an idiom here; it is a work; all the efforts at translation that I might make, that it itself calls forth and demands, will remain, in a certain way and at a given moment, vain or limited. This text, then, is a sacred text.'[98] If this is true, the borderline between the sacred and the secular is equivocal and divided. And yet a question remains: what sort of translation is at issue here? Are we to think of translating a literary text from one language to another? That would certainly secure *Finnegans Wake*, say, as a literary work. Or is there another sort of translation being implied?

Meditating on Mallarmé's prose poem, 'Mimique', Derrida reflects that it could be read 'as a sort of handbook of literature' in that it extends 'the concepts of writing and reading ... to the point where nothing of what *is* can lie beyond them'.[99] And this tells us something valuable, 'that there is no – or hardly any, ever so little – literature; that in any event there is no essence of literature, no truth of literature.'[100] What marks that small corpus of literary texts, it appears, is a refusal to endorse philosophy as *magister ludi*. Following Socrates, the characteristic philosophical gesture has been asking, 'What is ...?' But, *pace* Sartre, literature declines organizing itself behind the question 'What is Literature?' and so keeps a distance from philosophical inquiry. To view the situation from another angle, whereas philosophy revolves around a thesis of translatability, that meaning can be transferred from one language to another without significant loss, literature forswears all translation.[101]

It is a point that has captivated Derrida since his first work on Husserl in which we find a deliberate contrast between two styles of writing. Both authors wish to capture a pure historicity: Husserl believing that only if a text's plurivocality is strictly controlled can it belong to a historical tradition; and Joyce favouring equivocity, using a language that summons the historical resonances in each word or even in each syllable.[102] Husserl exemplifies the philosophical path, Joyce the literary: the one submitting to a notion of translation, the other not yielding an inch of ground. A babelian writer, Joyce invokes the Tower of Babel in *Finnegans Wake* in a passage that tantalises Derrida:

And let Nek Nekulon extol Mak Makal and let him say unto him: immi ammi Semmi. And shall not Babel be with Lebab? And he war. And he shall open his mouth and answer: I hear. O Ismael, how they laud is only as my loud is one. If Nekulon shall be havonfalled surely makal haven hevens. Go to, let us extell Makal, yea, let us exceedingly extell. Though you have lien amung your posspots my excellecy is over Ismael. Great is him whom is over Ismael and he shall mekanek of Mak Nakulon. And he deed.[103]

How are we to read the words 'he war'? In what language are they written? If English they mean 'he wages war'; if German, 'he was', one of the meanings of Yahweh's proper name, or even, going out on a limb, 'truth' (from *wahr*).

This returns us to the issue, raised earlier in conjunction with Heidegger and Bultmann, of listening properly to texts. But *Finnegans Wake* is very improperly written in several languages at once, so how are we to hear it? 'Everything everywhere speaks of the ear, to the ear: what speaking means but first of all what *listening* means, to know how to strain one's ear (*e, ar, he, ar, ear, hear*) and obey the father who raises his voices.'[104] How Derrida derives 'ear' and 'hear' from 'he war' presents an exegetical problem, one that is later compounded:

The God of fire assigns to the Shem the necessary, fatal and impossible translation of his name, of the word with which he signs his act of war, of himself. The palindrome ('And shall not Babel be with Lebab?') overthrows the tower but also plays with the sense and the letter, the sense of being and the letters of being, of 'being' (*be, eb, baBEl, lEBab*), as with the sense and the letter of the name of God, EL, LE. The names of the father (*Dad, Bab*) are moreover dispersed over the same page, with those of the Lord (*Lord*) and of an Anglo-Saxon god (*Go to*, twice, *Gov*) which can spread out elsewhere into *governor* and scape*goat*.[105]

One might be tempted to say that Derrida reads *Finnegans Wake* as a sacred text, as the inaugural document of postmodernism. The signal detail, however, is that 'as'. Does it imply identity or similarity? By way of an answer, let us compare Derrida on Joyce with several rabbis on J. The first verse of the Babel story runs, 'And the whole earth was of one language, and of one speech [*ahadim*].' In the *Midrash Rabbah*, one rabbi take this to mean that the Shem spoke 'against two who were unique [lit. 'one'], viz. against *Abraham* who *was one* (Ezek. XXIII, 24) and against *The Lord our God, the Lord is One* (Deut. VI, 4).' Another gloss has it that 'they spoke sharp words (*hadim*).' In verse 7 the Lord says, 'Go to, let us go down, and there confound their language.' Rabbi Abba interprets this to mean, 'Through their own lips will I destroy them' by reading *nebalah* (meanness, 'obscenity', transferred sense, 'destruction') for *nablah* ('confound').[106] Similarly in the *Zohar*, a rabbi interprets 'And it came to pass, as they journeyed from the east', by hearing in 'from the east' [*miqqedem*: lit. from before] the word *quadmon*, signifying the Ancient One.[107] The verse therefore means that the Shem travelled away from Yahweh, and that begins to explain their degenerate behaviour.

Both Derrida and the rabbis follow the contours of the signifier, not the signified. All take their lead from paronomasia, deformations, acrostics, coupage and intertextuality. Whether or not Derrida has rabbinic modes of interpretation in mind when reading *Finnegans Wake*, his style of reading clearly serves to sacralize the text.[108] Not simply by bringing a sacred hermeneutic to bear on a novel, because those interpretative moves are already licensed by the text. When Joyce writes 'And shall not Babel be with Lebab?' he knows that the question can only be unravelled by the sort of imaginative leaps the rabbis use; he knows, for instance, that '*lebab*' is Hebrew for heart and recalls the Irish Gaelic for book ('*leabhar*'). By the same token, the rabbis work from the biblical text itself. For J hardly disdains wordplay: the story of Babel tells how the Shem build 'there' (*sham*), on the plain of Shinar, a tower to the 'heavens' (*sham-ayim*), in order to make a 'name' (*shem*) for themselves.[109]

Yet where the rabbis look to the inexhaustible fullness of God's word to sponsor their exegeses, Derrida appeals to a mode of negativity, *la différance*, which ceaselessly generates meaning. As we have seen, writing functions in the absence of any guiding presence, author or reader. It also operates in ways which we are not conditioned to see, following a thematic development while also working anthematically. Whereas themes are used to gather the text, even the whole Bible, into a unity, anthemes tend to disrupt that unity. One can use any antheme as a grid to help one through a text, and what one reads will differ from the text that arranges itself around a theme or group of themes.[110] In biblical midrash, all apparent anthemes necessarily become themes. (To take a rather extreme example, Rabbi Aqiba contended that nothing in the Scriptures is superfluous; any graphic element, even decorations to the letters of Scripture, can become meaningful when read in the right way.) Not so with a text like *Finnegans Wake* which does not posit a divine author to underwrite endless meaning. We could say that Joyce writes 'scrypture', not Scripture. Because in this particular text all of history is encrypted, in syllables and anthemes as well as words and themes, to be called up by a style of reading as irruptive as its style of writing. And also because, in any case, the text encrypts itself, taking its apparent outside (title, date or signature) and showing it to be already working within the text, producing secret meanings only the initiated, the most devout of Joyce scholars, will try to uncover.

Reading Hölderlin, Heidegger thought that poetry teaches us, in this dark time, to see the unknown god as unknown. Poetry points us, by a negative way, toward the holy. Derrida, too, thinks that literature has an irreducible secrecy; it 'unveils a secret only to confirm it there as a secret, withdrawing, protected from hermeneutic exhaustion'.[111] This is not a consequence of hermeticism but of the irreducible idiom that makes a text literary. No interpretation, however agile, thorough and cogent, can formalize a text without remainder. If Genesis or *Finnegans Wake* is literary it is because of an idiom, a singularity, in the text, not by virtue of any special teaching contained there. And the same would be true if we decided to call either or both those texts 'sacred'. For Derrida, 'literary' and 'sacred' are two ways of ascribing originality. Literary and sacred writings alike function as proper names; on the one hand they resist translation, clinging to their singularity, while on the other hand, they allow themselves to be transformed and deformed, 'Babel' becoming 'balal' or – amazingly enough – Genesis becoming *Finnegans Wake*.

VI

That a clash between Jew and Greek coordinates the study of the Christian Bible hardly need be stressed. Increasingly, though, the distinction plays an important role in literary criticism: partly in response to the Bible, and partly in rejoinder to philosophy. Erich Auerbach's urbane comparison of one passage in each of the *Odyssey* and Genesis, in which the Greek poem is all visible, palpable foreground while the Hebrew narrative remains 'fraught with background', intent on moral positions, not physical locations, has become a *locus classicus* of stylistic criticism and a certain kind of historicism.[112] For him, Greek and Jewish habits of perception, not to mention the aesthetic value of their stories, are equal and symmetrical. The historicizing of aesthetic value and its rider of waiving cultural difference has been a recognizable theme from Vico to Auerbach. The idea is as bewitching in its democratic appeal as its erudition is humbling, but intellectual history, at least since Hegel, tends to tell another story, one strongly biased toward the Greeks. And as the mention of Hegel indicates, it is a story written by philosophers.

Emmanuel Levinas puts the issue very sharply when observing that 'Greek philosophy is the way that people speak in the modern university the world over. That is speaking Greek. They all speak Greek, even if they don't know the difference between alpha and beta.'[113] Greek has provided us with a vocabulary which, whether we like it or not, defines intelligibility in whatever Western language one happens to know. At the same time, there is another language that offers itself to us, that of the Hebrew Bible. But since Greek determines what counts as intelligible, it is supremely difficult to talk of this other tradition. Not because it is wholly other, which would present its own problems, but because it has already been incorporated into the Greek tradition and must be recovered. There is no 'biblical language', pure and simple, nowadays, though that cannot stop one from seeking the God of the patriarchs and the prophets: 'to hear a God not contaminated by Being is a human possibility no less important and no less precarious than to bring Being out of the oblivion in which it is said to have fallen in metaphysics and in onto-theology.'[114] Thus Levinas redistributes the priorities that Heidegger placed on the agenda for discussion. There is still time and there is still hope. 'All one can say is that the Septuagint is not yet complete, that the translation of biblical wisdom into the Greek language remains unfinished.'[115]

Also incomplete, one might add, is the translation of literature into philosophy. 'Many critics flee to philosophy or to linguistics,' sighs Harold Bloom, 'but the result is that they learn to interpret poems as philosophy or as linguistics.'[116] One way of curbing that rush to philosophy, to Greece, and of keeping the Septuagint incomplete, is to introduce uniquely Jewish modes of reading. We have seen how Derrida may, perhaps against his intentions, have contributed to that project. But, as Levinas suggests, the hellenistic model of intelligibility is extremely pervasive, no less so in criticism than in philosophy. One of the most powerful critics in the twentieth century is Northrop Frye who, as it happens, is also unreservedly committed to Holy Writ, or, as some of his detractors might say, somewhat reductively, hellenistic interpretations of Scripture. Certainly all of Frye's work revolves around the Bible, closely or at a distance, and by 'Bible' one must understand that he always means both Testaments. 'The Bible', he tells us, 'considered in its literary aspect, is a definitive encyclopaedic poem starting with the beginning of time at the creation, ending with the end of time at the Last Judgement, and surveying the entire history of man, under the symbolic names of Adam and Israel, in between.'[117] It is the book to which all his favoured writers, from Milton to Blake, refer time and time again, finding there, in one form or another, their imaginative universe. For Frye as for Blake, the Bible is 'the great code': a unified structure of narrative and imagery; and since the only way such a unity can be conferred is by the study of types, it is typology that becomes the proper way of reading Scripture. Nothing could be further from Auerbach's aesthetic historicism than Frye's grand, self-sufficient imaginative structure, where literature feeds off literature. More generally, there is little contact between the gimlet eye of stylistic criticism (whatever its sociological reach may be) and the olympian study of archetypes.

After the sober conclusions of the higher criticism, and the heady Modernist elevation of the fragment, the Bible remains for Frye a *book* in the full sense of the word, even though, as he happily admits, it may be a hotchpotch of inconsistent texts. For the Bible has 'traditionally been read as a unity, and has influenced Western imagination as a unity', though if one pauses to ask 'Whose tradition?' and 'Whose imagination?' one quickly discovers a Protestant tradition intersecting a high literary canon.[118] Frye's Christian Bible rearranges and subsumes the Hebrew Bible, making it a wonderful prologue to the New Testament; and here we can see, very clearly indeed, how various responses to the Bible structure much contemporary literary criticism. 'I deplore,' Harold Bloom says (with Frye in mind), 'a reading of the Bible in which the Hebrew Bible vanishes and there is only the Christian Bible.'[119] So it might be expected that when Bloom tackles his sometime master it is over his reading of a passage in the Hebrew Bible – Jacob's wrestling with the angel.

'The inference for the reader,' Frye tells us, 'seems to be that the angel of time that man clings to until daybreak (Genesis 32:36) is both an enemy and an ally, a power that both enlightens and cripples, and disappears only when all that can be experienced has been experienced.'[120] Bloom replies that Frye minimizes the terror of the tale, the ferocity of the fight and the angel's desperate cry, 'Let me go, for it is daybreak!' Frye idealizes the story, as he must when granting typology such amplitude. But it would be wrong to see this as a disagreement over one scriptural passage, or even about biblical criticism. It is a struggle between opposed views of literature: one that posits a 'myth of concern' which absorbs anxieties of obligation, and another that presents anxiety as central to an understanding of literature, that is, how texts become canonical, whether they be sacred or secular:

Frye's ultimate idealization, always, is his moving faith that 'imaginative literature' is *not* an 'anxiety structure'. He concludes *The Great Code* by saying that man builds anxiety-structures around his religious and social institutions. What Frye cannot or will not see is that artistic institutions (including canons, and academies, and traditions) are necessarily anxiety-structures also. The Bible, like any real literary canon, is *an achieved anxiety*, and not a program to release us from anxiety. For what can a canon, or an academy, or a tradition be unless it has some residual authority over us?[121]

Earlier in this essay Bloom recalls that he has written twice before on the story of Jacob and the angel. In fact, he continually alludes to it, renaming in the process his two main exemplars, Emerson and Freud, as 'Wrestling Waldo' and 'Wrestling Sigmund'.[122] What attracts Bloom to the story is how closely it figures the relation between poets. 'Wrestling Jacob could triumph,' we hear, 'because his Adversary was the Everliving, but even the strongest poets must grapple with phantoms.'[123] These phantoms are the mighty dead, made all the more appealing by their distance from us. So Wordsworth's great immortality ode is 'the angel with whom Shelley wrestles in his *Ode to the West Wind*', and if Shelley is to triumph, albeit precariously, it can only be at the cost of being wounded by Wordsworth's lyric.[124]

The Talmud relates that when the angel cried out to be released, Jacob accused him of being a thief, only to hear, 'I am an angel, and this is my first turn since my creation to sing praises.'[125] Bloom tells a more sublime story, that Jacob confronts the angel of death, and that all modern poets must do the same if they are to win the blessing of poetic strength.[126] That blessing, paradoxically enough, is not a new name but one's own proper name, so that the author of 'Ode to the West Wind' may rightly be called Shelley and not Wordsworth. The struggle is to become oneself, which demands following the *via negativa*: not the simple negation of the precursor, but the repression of his influence. Bloom is thinking of Freudian *Verneinung* here, the process whereby the repressed is thought while nonetheless remaining repressed. And this psychoanalytic conception of negation is elected over and above all philosophical determinations of the negative, especially that propounded by Hegel. 'We can call

Hegelian negation perhaps the most profound of all Gentile idealiz-
ations, after Plato, and then say of the Freudian (and Kafkan) mode
of negation that always it reenacts the ambiguities of the Second
Commandment.'[127]

Negativity, Hegel teaches, is 'the energy of thought, the pure ego',
and it has a formidable power, permitting 'what is bound' to obtain
'an existence all its own, gain freedom and independence on its own
account'.[128] The negative is the very means of creation:

Death, as we may call that unreality, is the most terrible thing, and to keep
and hold fast what is dead demands the greatest force of all. Beauty which
lacks strength hates the understanding [*Die kraftlose Schönheit den Ver-
stand*], because the latter exacts from it what it cannot perform. But the life
of the mind is not one that shuns death, and keeps clear of destruction; it
endures death and in death maintains its being.[129]

Self-consciousness is absolute negativity, though it does not come
without a struggle. 'For this consciousness was not in peril and fear
for this or that moment of time, it was afraid for its entire being; it
felt the fear of death, the sovereign master.'[130] One reason why
Bloom rejects the Hegelian negative is that, at some points, it anticipates his theory of poetic influence. Hegel shows us a strong self (a
severe poet, if you like) who confronts the mighty dead and emerges
victorious from the struggle. Why then does Bloom prefer J's vision
of the archetypal struggle to Hegel's? Because it stresses there can be
no victory without a wound?

Yet that is a truth that Hegel knew well enough. In the *Phenomenology* he spoke of 'the seriousness, the suffering, the patience, and
the labour of the negative', especially as it affects God's internal
life.[131] And here we come upon a crucial difference between Hegel
and Bloom: the one proposes a Christian model, in which the
suffering of Jesus modifies the impassivity of the Godhead; while the
other elects a Jewish model – a story, moreover, not a piece of
theology. I say 'Jewish model' though 'Gnostic Jewish' would be
better. The Hegelian dialectic inevitably idealizes truth, Bloom
thinks, regarding it as a universal, an abstraction. 'But Gnosticism
would not accept this shifting of the truth to a universal. The
warrant for the truth remains personal, indeed *is* the true personal,
the *pneuma* of the Gnostic, his self as opposed to his mere *psyche* or
soul. Shall we say, against the philosophers, that Gnosis is the rapid,
impatient labour of the Negative?'[132] Against the philosophers, yes,
but it is often difficult to know who the philosophers are; they might
have names like 'Coleridge' and 'Shelley' as often as 'Plato' and
'Hegel'. For the Romantics in particular, creativity is commonly

identified with the *nous* rather than the *gnosis*; yet Bloom is always keen to redeem poetry from philosophy, even against a poet's will, and pits his sense of 'gnosis' against Plato's. To put it another way, Bloom is not interested in epistemology (and therefore in deconstruction) precisely because he is so absorbed with gnosis. And by 'gnosis' he means, at root, poetic knowledge.

What has poetry to do with Gnosticism? Both are radical manifestations of negative theology.[133] Pseudo-Dionysius may appear the most rigorous, the most violent, in his negations; yet his is not the most radical theology the West has known:

Gnostic negative theology is more drastic because Gnostic transcendence really needs a word beyond transcendence to designate so hyperbolic a sense of being above the world, 'that world', our mere universe of death. Gnostic metaphor depends therefore upon the most outrageous dualism that our traditions ever have known. In a Gnostic metaphor, the 'inside' term or *pneuma* and the 'outside' cosmic term are so separated that every such figuration becomes a catachresis, an extension or abuse of metaphor.[134]

For Pseudo-Dionysius, God is beyond the reach of all predicates, positive or negative, though one can approach him by remorselessly following the negative path. This is the way of faith, yet gnosticism is concerned with knowledge, not faith. It is not a knowledge of God, or anything outside the self, solely a quest for the divinity within. We must discriminate between the *psyche* and the *pneuma*. The former is a rhetorical fiction, inviting then yielding to deconstruction, while the latter is a spark that cannot be extinguished. The theoreticians of the negative, from Hegel to Derrida, have failed to recognize this *pneuma*; and so we must look to another tradition of negativity: one which includes gnostics like Basilides and Valentinus; the bizarre braiding together of Neo-Platonic and Gnostic motifs which is the Kabbalah; and, in modern days, Emerson and Freud.

Let us take our lead from the Kabbalistic tradition, especially the writings of Isaac Luria; for it is here, in this strange commentary on Scripture and the *Zohar*, that Bloom finds his model for reading secular and sacred literature. Of particular interest is Luria's theory of creation as catastrophe. It has three main phases. First, *Zimzum*: God's withdrawal into himself, his act of pure concentration that opens a space wherein creation (that which is not God) can occur. Second, *Shevirath ha-kelim*, or the breaking of the vessels, when creation is smashed because Yahweh's proper name is stronger than his works. Third, and most important, *Tikkun*: man's restoration of creation. What this arcane theory offers us, Bloom says, is a very practical way of reading poetry, because since the Enlightenment all major poems work in a rhythm of limitation, substitution and representation which is exactly how Luria describes creation. That same rhythm can be matched by the vocabularies of rhetoric and of Freudian psychoanalysis. Consider the initial move. *Zimzum* marks the young poet's (or as Bloom says, ephebe's) swerve away from the precursor's work: the too powerful presence must be imagined as an absence, a space for creation. All strong poems begin with an ironic displacement of their great originals, and that irony bespeaks what Freud called 'reaction formation' in which a repressed desire is countered by the irruption of a fiercely opposing attitude. The irony, therefore, is not simply a matter of structure; it involves the ephebe's willful concentration on what the precursor has failed to see in his or her own work. The instant of creation is doubled: a movement of withdrawal and intensification, of desire and defence.

There is no original goodness, then, only an original fall. Salvation must be by a negative path, and for the poet that means using rhetoric as the negative way to poetic knowledge. It is a knowledge that leads directly to the self, the *pneuma*, the poet-in-a-poet. Only by moving inwards, approaching a deep solipsism, can the poet attain the strength that allows him or her to write. The weak poet believes in something outside the self (God, literary history, culture, whatever); the strong poet, a visionary, knows that God is within. Literary history thus becomes a story of visionaries and their revisions: a narrative of deviations, perversity and striking reductions. If one major index of poetic strength is the ephebe's degree of swerve from the precursor, another is transumption, the eerie trope that undoes literary history, making the precursor seem indebted to the ephebe. Thus there are times when Wallace Stevens almost appears to have been reading too deeply in John Ashbery; or, more disturbingly, when Milton's supreme poetic power transforms Genesis 'into a midrash on Milton'.[135] The highest power is the strong self; for Bloom, even the Bible is a commentary on the self, and when he intones, 'There are no texts. There are only ourselves,' one hears Coleridge stressing the primacy of subjective experience.[136]

Since the acerbic exchanges between the theologians of Alexandria and Antioch in the third century, arguments about Scripture have often turned on whether one prizes allegory or typology. In recent times, the deconstructionists have rethought allegory, and so become the Alexandrians of the twentieth century. Paul de Man's *Allegories of Reading* acknowledges a debt to Benjamin and Hegel, though due restitution has still to be paid to Origen, St Dionysius of Alexandria and St Gregory Nazianzen. Against the deconstructionists, and as a belated Antiochian, Bloom offers a remarkable displacement of typology. Literary history, he argues, is not a series of types that are eventually fulfilled by later poets. Rather, we must reconceive history in terms of revision, which may deform or deflect earlier texts but which may never fulfill them. Hence Bloom's vivid reaction to claims that the New Testament fulfills the Old:

The Old Testament is far too strong, as poetry, to be fulfilled by its revisionary descendant, the self-proclaimed New Testament. 'New' means 'Early' here and 'Old' means 'Late', and precisely what the New Testament lacks in regard to the Old is a transumptive stance, which is why the New Testament is a weak poem. *Figura* is supposed to work by making Joshua late and Jesus perpetually early. This works well enough for Joshua and Jesus, since the prior figure is less central, but would have had more difficulty if Moses had been taken as the *figura*. The entire point of the theory of *figura* must be that the second term of fulfilment is the truth, and the first term of *figura* only a shadowy type of the truth.[137]

Not quite a reverse typology, this, where later texts would always fall away from earlier texts, for that possibility is precluded by transumption. There is an interplay between the old and the new, the early and the late; although the game is played to the bitter end, with every available stratagem enlisted to gain victory. One of the greatest dangers for literary historians, Bloom suggests, is to think that biblical typology might prove a useful model for reading all secular literary history. Of course, as Stephen Prickett argues in chapter 4, typology did provide a common means of organizing the English novel well into the nineteenth century; but Bloom's point concerns literary history as a whole. Simply to lay a typological grid over all literary history would be to overspiritualize texts, as serious a distortion as the radical despiritualization that motivates Derrida and de Man.

For all that, the Hebrew Bible (especially those sections written by J) remains for Bloom the strongest, most sublime text of Western literature. Does this square with his insistence on the absolute priority of the self? One could point out that J is more likely to name a tradition than an individual, and that even the strongest texts by J are possibly revised by E, but such objections would not fault Bloom's trust in the strong individual. That trust is directed to writing today, at the very end of Western literary history, a state so belated that individual strength is the only way to survive. In any case, Bloom perhaps has a greater fear, that Derrida may be right in a way of which even he is not aware: that the New Testament is a dangerous supplement to the Hebrew Bible, adding to it with bad intent, only to form an 'Old Testament'. Yet Bloom is more of a polemicist than a reader when faced with the New Testament, so when he exclaims 'I am an enemy of the New Testament' one hears a tone, not an argument.[138] What does that tone respond to? It is not easy to say. Here is one approach to an answer, by way of Bloom's observations on pitting the secular against the sacred.

I myself do not believe that secularization is itself a literary process. The scandal is the stubborn resistance of imaginative literature to the categories of sacred and secular. If you wish you can insist that all high literature is secular, or, should you desire it so, then all strong poetry is sacred. What I find incoherent is the judgement that some authentic literary art is more sacred or more secular than some other. Poetry and belief wander about, together and apart, in a cosmological emptiness marked by the limits of truth and of meaning.[139]

This is not a programme sanctioning 'the Bible as literature', or an attempt such as Benjamin's and Derrida's to identify high secular literature with the sacred. More radically, Bloom is suggesting that the category of poetry precedes all rifts between the sacred and the secular, and that these distinctions serve to occlude what we read. As he departs, Bloom leaves ajar the door into Herder's study; but Herder would be just as likely to slam the door shut from his side.

Perhaps hastily: because Bloom does not simply erase all the boundaries between the sacred and the secular. 'Literary authority, however we define it, has no necessary relation to spiritual authority,' he says, before suggesting that Kafka commands spiritual authority.[140] That authority seems to come from Kafka's sense of the negative which, in turn, ultimately derives from the most negative of negative theologies, that propounded by the Gnostics. Bloom approaches the question of authority via Kafka's uncanny parable, 'Before the Law', the story of a man from the country who asks to be admitted to the Law, only to be refused entrance year after year until he dies. At the moment of death, the doorkeeper roars in his ear, 'No one else could ever be admitted here, since this gate was made only for you. I am now going to shut it.'[141] The parable is shattering, both in its vision and its authority, and we recall what Kafka told us, right at the beginning of this chapter, 'What is laid upon us is to accomplish the negative; the positive is already given.' The positive is the Law or, as Bloom says, normative Judaism; and what Kafka offers in 'Before the Law' is a vision of the negative: the radiance of the Law forever blocked by petty officials who are – who knows? – perhaps in the secret service of the Law. Kafka's spiritual authority stems precisely from the integrity of that vision.

Or, better, revision: since Kafka teaches that one interprets rather than sees, that the doorkeeper's message concerns interpretation – deferral, not simple denial. Spirituality, if there can be any in the twentieth century, must go by a negative path of misreading, more tortuous than even that followed by the Kabbalists. It is at this point that Bloom's reading of Kafka crosses Derrida's. 'What is deferred forever till death,' Derrida tell us, 'is entry into the law itself, which is nothing other than that which dictates the delay. The law prohibits by interfering and deferring the "ferance", the reference, rapport, and relation. What *must not* and cannot be approached is the origin of *différance*: it must not be represented and above all not penetrated.'[142] If the law, for Bloom, is normative Judaism and its burden of interpretation, for Derrida it is *différance*, that which permits and limits interpretation. Bloom and Derrida both read Kafka as Scripture. Bloom finds a negative theology there; it is as though he hears (for once with Heidegger), '*Poetry* is a measuring,' meaning that the unknown god appears as unknown. Reading the same passage of Kafka, Derrida makes out something still more negative than a negative theology, that which legislates from the dark realm of the transcendental, not from the heights of transcendence.

Which is not to say that negative theology has no deconstructive power. How much power it has depends entirely on the theologian. Meister Eckhart and St John of the Cross show some regard for the *theion*, the highest ground of all that is, even while denying it the predicate of existence; but Pseudo-Dionysius goes still further, putting at risk both the proper names of philosophy and the divine names. Derrida would argue that no negative theologian, not even Pseudo-Dionysius, follows deconstruction with complete rigour, and that the Kabbalah need not be understood spiritually.[143] Bloom, on the other hand, sees modern poetry pursuing a negative theology that is more cunning, more supple, than anything so far proposed by the theoreticians of the negative. Where the negative theologian whispers, 'How can I be sure that when I speak of God, I am speaking of *God* and not a graven image?', Bloom asks, 'How can I know I talk of poetry, not an idealization of poetry?'

VII

Negativity: the concept has appeared in various guises throughout this discussion, though always with positive goals in mind. The Heideggerian programme of *Destruktion*, for all its air of violence, is directed towards a more satisfactory understanding of the history of

Being; and Derrida's translation of Heidegger's project, deconstruction, is also affirmative, engaging with plurality and never glancing back at unity with nostalgia. To affirm plurality is one thing, many biblical critics might say, while all the time wondering, 'At what cost?' Too much for more biblical than literary critics, it would seem. At any rate, biblical criticism (in the Protestant Churches) has followed the train set in motion by Bultmann. Demythologizing sets out from what now appears as the conservative side of Heidegger, the desire to find an authentic meaning in a text; and once this is realized, it becomes increasingly hard to discern kerygma amidst the *mythos*. After demythologizing comes dekerygmatizing, and after that what forgiveness? None from the Greeks, for another force that is channelled through hermeneutics is a steady stream of dehellenizing, an attempt (began by Harnack) to isolate and renew the specifically Jewish religious experience, and one that continues in the word of writers as unmatchable as Levinas and Bloom.

'Depatriarchalization', as Phyllis Trible calls it, belongs to the same general pattern. If one has read Heidegger, Bultmann or Derrida its rhetoric is easily recognizable:

Depatriarchalizing is not an operation which the exegete performs on the text. It is a hermeneutic operating within Scripture itself. We expose it; we do not impose it. Tradition history teaches that the meaning and function of biblical materials is fluid. As Scripture moves through history, it is appropriated for new settings. Varied and diverse traditions appear, disappear, and reappear from occasion to occasion. We shall be unfaithful readers if we neglect biblical passages which break with patriarchy or if we permit our interpretations to freeze in a patriarchal box of our own construction. For our day we need to perceive the depatriarchalizing principle, to recover it in those texts and themes where it is present, and to accent it in our translations.[144]

The project easily moves in several directions at the one time: identifying the subjection and abuse of women in ancient Israel; tracing a critique of patriarchy already broached in Scripture; and telling the stories of biblical women *in memoriam*, from a sympathetic viewpoint. This, then, is a rhetorical criticism used in tandem with a cultural critique. The Bible is understood to be a literary composition, susceptible to the rigours of close reading, and the feminist reader part of a broad prophetic movement, judging misogynist behaviour while calling for repentance.

In broad terms, Trible remains an empirical critic: at no time does the concept 'literature' come under any examination. Her readings gain authority from the closeness with which she listens to the biblical word. Yet, as we have seen, a good listener attends not only to what is said but also to what is not said. Thinking along these lines, Mieke Bal occasionally finds Trible's readings falling well within the orbit of male interests,[145] and proposes a way of reading the Bible which is thoroughly feminist and thoroughly dialectical. Thus in her searching study of the Book of Judges, *Death and Dissymmetry*, we find a style of criticism which gives weight to silence as much as voice. Bal finds most commentary on Judges obsessed by attempts to restore a coherence in the form of a military and political chronology in the book, but her project is not limited to subverting that enterprise. 'I will primarily focus on what is left out, repressed, by such readings,' she says, 'I want to explain why the political coherence is a tool – or should I say weapon? – in the politics of the critics: a politics of coherence.'[146] That explanation develops a 'countercoherence': we are requested to shift our attention from the political struggle the book depicts to the social revolution that affects the relations between men and women. In this way, Bal displaces the dominant ideology of the text. Questions of female society are recalled from their ancient silence, and brought to the front of the stage where they may engage contemporary readers. Negativity and renewal are to be thought together.

There is a sense in which the story of wrestling Jacob speaks of this dialectic between the negative and the positive. Jacob is lamed then named; his victory is real, but limited – and that, we are to remember, is the very best we may hope for. Perhaps literary critics have recognized their activity in the story of Jacob more than in any other single biblical tale. Roland Barthes sees a story of textual criticism, how an underhanded blow makes a work into a text. Harold Bloom recognizes agonistic criticism, a struggle between strong poem and strong reader in which one gains one's proper name by an ironic swerve from one's opponent then confirms that name by transumption. Maurice Blanchot finds in the story the very dialectic between solitude and otherness that motivates his criticism. When, after leaving Peniel, Jacob sees Esau, it is his brother's human presence that moves him: 'this other Presence is Other, no less inaccessible, separated and distant than the Invisible himself ... Who sees God is in danger of dying. Who encounters the Other can only relate to him by mortal violence or by the gift of the word in his welcome.'[147] Similarly, Geoffrey Hartman reads the tale as a struggle between Scripture and literature; it is a 'struggle for the text – for a supreme fiction or authoritative account stripped of inessentials, of all diversions'. The view should not surprise us, coming, as it does, from a critic whose recent career has been a struggle between two demands: the just claim of texts to be read as texts, and the equally legitimate call to value tradition and to see that names do name and that words can wound.[148]

What is surprising is that such a tale of male power is taken as a guide for feminist criticism. 'As a paradigm for encountering terror, this story offers sustenance for the present journey,' writes Trible at the outset of *Texts of Terror*.

> To tell and hear tales of terror is to wrestle demons in the night, without a compassionate God to save us. In combat we wonder about the names of the demons. Our own names, however, we all too frightfully recognize. The fight itself is solitary and intense. We struggle mightily, only to be wounded. But yet we hold on, seeking a blessing: the healing of wounds and the restoration of health. If the blessing comes – and we dare not claim assurance – it does not come on our terms.[149]

It all makes perfect sense. The story of wrestling Jacob plainly offers itself as an allegory of the critical act, almost regardless of what particular act it is.

That so many critics turn to a biblical narrative for a paradigm of their reading practice tells us something about that story and about literary criticism. What attracts people to Gen. 32:22–32 is not so much its capacity for manifold readings as its resistance to the charm of literature. That resistance is tacitly acknowledged in the awkward phrase 'the Bible as literature' where the 'as' hints at all manner of evasions. The Bible has literary charm, of course, because it *is* literature; yet it also admonishes us not to be so enchanted by fine writing that we do not address matters of local and ultimate concern. We can denude a text of its reference, its testimony, even its author; however, as Derrida reminds us, all these return like ghosts and must be taken seriously as textual effects. Doubtless Scripture can be read for its aesthetic charge, but to restrict the aesthetic to questions of style and taste is a drastic reduction of its scope. Since Kant, the realm of aesthetic judgement has linked epistemology and ethics, so that discussions which turn on beauty and the sublime inevitably involve questions of knowledge, morality and politics. In answering those questions, we begin to frame Scripture in one way or another, appealing to contexts like Church, State and education which are in turn modified by the reading of Scripture. Of these contexts, which are as much inside Scripture as outside it, the most powerful is the Church. If parts of the Bible resist being read like other literature it is because they are invested by the Church with an authority (or an effect of authority) which cannot be overlooked when reading, yet which can make us overlook the textuality of what we read. It is that tension between authority and textuality which cannot fail to attract the critic, who sees there, more vividly than in secular writing, what happens when we read literature. In becoming aware of the differences between sacred and secular writing we also begin to realize that those differences structure secular literature.

And so, while there may not be an *a priori* distinction to divide sacred from secular texts, there remain *a posteriori* reasons why that distinction cannot be altogether abandoned. Indeed, it is as much use to literature as Scripture; for there is no reason to suppose that, in their effects, some literary texts do not have as much spiritual authority as certain biblical passages. Which of the following is the most spiritually powerful text: Job, the 23rd Psalm, the Lord's Prayer, Johnson's 41st *Idler*, Kafka's 'Before the Law', or Wallace Stevens's 'Final Soliloquy of the Interior Paramour'? If that question is at all difficult to answer, it may be because we are more used to secular than sacred canons, although we draw strength from both and often cannot tell the difference between them.

NOTES

I wish to thank my research assistant, John Jacobs, for his tireless work in locating material, checking sources and proofreading the entire essay.

1 Oscar Wilde, 'The Critic as Artist', in *Oscar Wilde's Plays, Prose Writings, and Poems*, introd. Hesketh Pearson (1930; rpt, London, 1967), p. 24.
2 Q. D. Leavis, 'Charlotte Yonge and "Christian Discrimination"', *Scrutiny*, 12 (1944), p. 158.
3 Robert Moynihan, 'Interview with Paul de Man', *The Yale Review*, 73 (1984), pp. 586–7. Cf. Nietzsche's aphorism, 'The humor of European culture: one holds *this* to be true but does *that*. E.g., what is the point of the arts of reading and criticism as long as the ecclesiastical interpretation of the Bible, Protestant as well as Catholic, is cultivated as ever?' *The Will to Power*, trs. Walter Kaufmann and R. J. Hollingdale, ed. Walter Kaufmann (New York, 1968), p. 139.
4 J. Hillis Miller makes this point in several places. See, for example, his interview with Imre Salusinszky in the latter's *Criticism in Society: Interviews with Jacques Derrida, Northrop Frye, Harold Bloom, Geoffrey Hartman, Frank Kermode, Edward Said, Barbara Johnson, Frank Lentricchia, and J. Hillis Miller* (New York, 1987), p. 232.

5 Paul de Man, 'Time and History in Wordsworth', *Diacritics*, Winter, 1987), p. 5, n. 4.
6 Moynihan, 'Interview with Paul de Man', p. 592.
7 Edward W. Said, *The World, the Text, and the Critic* (London, 1984), pp. 1–30; 290–2.
8 Salusinszky, *Criticism in Society*, pp. 140–1.
9 Salusinszky, *Criticism in Society*, p. 141.
10 James Joyce, *Finnegans Wake*, 3rd edn (London, 1964), p. 579:10.
11 Although Joyce clearly thought that these were Cromwell's exact words, there is considerable disagreement about what Cromwell actually said. According to Algernon Sidney he ordered, 'Take away these baubles'; according to Bulstrode Whitelock, 'Take away that fool's bauble the mace'; whereas Edmund Ludlow has him ask, 'What shall we do with this bauble? There, take it away.'
12 Franz Kafka, *The Great Wall of China: Stories and Reflections*, trs. Willa and Edwin Muir (New York, 1946), p. 167.
13 Max Brod (ed.), *The Diaries of Franz Kafka, 1914–1923* (New York, 1949), pp. 130; 158.
14 Max Brod (ed.) *The Diaries of Franz Kafka, 1910–1913*, trs. Martin Greenberg with Hannah Arendt (New York, 1949), p. 226. Kafka's probable knowledge of the Kabbalah is examined by Ritchie Robertson in his *Kafka: Judaism, Politics, and Literature* (Oxford, 1985), pp. 195f. Also see in this regard Jean Jofen. *The Jewish Mystic in Kafka*, American University Studies, Series I, Germanic Languages and Literature, vol. 41 (New York, 1987).
15 Roland Barthes, '*L'Express* talks with Roland Barthes' (31 May 1970), in *The Grain of the Voice: Interviews 1962–1980*, trs. Linda Coverdale (New York, 1985), p. 92.
16 Harold Bloom, *A Map of Misreading* (New York, 1975), p. 29.
17 Said, *The World, the Text, and the Critic*, p. 291.
18 All quotations from the Bible will be from the King James Version. J is variously taken to be an author, editor, school and tradition. Although certain commentators, most notably Harold Bloom, stress J's individuality, recent biblical scholarship has preferred to speak in terms of a community. It is also worth mentioning that not everyone thinks all of the Jacob pericope, for instance, is wholly written or revised by J. Thus Gunkel, for one, contends that the short exchange between Jacob and the angel in vv. 27–9 is a later addition by E.
19 Stanley Fish, 'What Makes an Interpretation Acceptable?', in *Is There a Text in This Class? The Authority of Interpretive Communities* (Cambridge, MA, 1980), p. 354.
20 Northrop Frye, *Spiritus Mundi: Essays on Literature, Myth, and Society* (Bloomington, 1976), p. 106.
21 Ibid., p. 107.
22 Martin Heidegger, 'A Dialogue on Language', in *On the Way to Language*, trs. Peter D. Hertz (New York, 1971), pp. 9–10.

23 Martin Heidegger, *Being and Time*, trs. John Macquarrie and Edward Robinson (Oxford, 1973), p. 62.

24 Ibid., p. 44.

25 Ibid., p. 44.

26 Martin Heidegger, *What is Philosophy?*, trs. and introd. William Kluback and Jean T. Wilde (New York, 1962), p. 73.

27 Heidegger, 'A Dialogue on Language', pp. 30; 40.

28 Martin Heidegger, *Hegel's Phenomenology of Spirit*, trs. Parvis Emad and Kenneth Maly (Bloomington, 1988), p. 100. See Heidegger's 'The Onto-Theological Constitution of Metaphysics', in *Identity and Difference*, trs. Joan Stambaugh (New York, 1969). I examine the concept 'onto-theology' in some detail in Kevin Hart, *The Trespass of the Sign: Deconstruction, Theology and Philosophy* (Cambridge, 1989), ch. 3.

29 Martin Heidegger, *Nietzsche*, vol. iv, trs. Frank A. Capuzzi, ed. David Farrell Krell (San Francisco, 1982), p. 210.

30 Heidegger, *Being and Time*, p. 30.

31 Martin Heidegger, 'Phenomenology and Theology' in *The Piety of Thinking*, trs. James G. Hart and John C. Maraldo (Bloomington, 1976), p. 16.

32 Otto Pöggeler presents a lucid exposition of Heidegger's lecture courses at Freiburg in his *Martin Heidegger's Path of Thinking*, trs. Daniel Magurshak and Sigmund Barber (Atlantic Highlands, NJ, 1987), pp. 24–7. I am indebted to his discussion. Also valuable in this regard is Jeffrey Andrew Barash's *Martin Heidegger and the Problem of Historical Meaning* (Dordrecht, 1988), ch. 4. Barash refers to previously unpublished material by Heidegger and Bultmann.

33 For more detail, see Barash, *Martin Heidegger and the Problem of Historical Meaning*, pp. 178f.

34 Paul Ricoeur, 'Note introductive' in *Heidegger et la question de Dieu* ed. Richard Kearney and Joseph Stephen O'Leary (Paris, 1980), p. 17.

35 In 'Heidegger's Exegeses of Hölderlin', Paul de Man observes that 'Hölderlin is the only one whom Heidegger cites as a believer cites Holy Writ,' *Blindness and Insight: Essays in the Rhetoric of Contemporary Criticism*, 2nd edn, revised (London, 1983), p. 250. De Man's response to Rousseau's texts sometimes comes close to the same kind of veneration.

36 Martin Heidegger, 'What are Poets For?' in *Poetry, Language, Thought*, trs. and introd. Albert Hofstadter (New York, 1971), p. 94.

37 Martin Heidegger, 'The Origin of the Work of Art', in *Poetry, Language, Thought*, p. 74.

38 Martin Heidegger, '... Poetically Man Dwells ...', in ibid., pp. 221–2.

39 Ibid., pp. 222–3.

40 Ibid., p. 222.
41 Heidegger discusses the leap in detail in his discussion of the principle of ground, *Der Satz vom Grund* (Pfullingen, 1965), ch. 7. A similar kind of analysis to that performed on 'Poetry is a measuring' is undertaken with 'God is the Absolute' in Heidegger's *What is Called Thinking?*, introd. J. Glenn Gray (New York, 1968), p. 156. I discuss the two tones in which one hears the principle of ground, and how one leaps from one to the other, in Hart, *The Trespass of the Sign*, ch. 8.
42 Martin Heidegger, 'Letter on Humanism', in *Basic Writings: from 'Being and Time' (1927) to 'The Task of Thinking' (1964)*, ed. and introd. David Farrell Krell (New York, 1977), p. 218.
43 Rudolf Bultmann, 'Liberal Theology and the Latest Theological Movement', in his *Faith and Understanding*, ed. and introd. Robert W. Funk, trs. Louise Pettibone Smith (London, 1966), p. 29.
44 Ibid., p. 30.
45 Rudolf Bultmann, 'Modern Biblical Interpretation', in *Jesus Christ and Mythology* (New York, 1958), p. 52.
46 Rudolf Bultmann, 'The Message of Jesus and the Problem of Mythology', in *Jesus Christ and Mythology*, p. 18.
47 Rudolf Bultmann, 'The Christian Message and the Modern World-View', in *Jesus Christ and Mythology*, p. 35.
48 Friedrich Beissner, *Hölderlin: Sämtliche Werke* (Stuttgart, 1951), vol. 2, part 1, pp. 372–4.
49 Rudolf Bultmann, 'The Study of the Synoptic Gospels', in *Form Criticism: Two Essays on New Testament Research*, trs. Frederick C. Grant, 1934 rpt (New York, 1962), p. 61.
50 Ibid., p. 36.
51 See Edmund Leach, *Genesis as Myth and Other Essays* (London, 1969). In a later essay, Leach indicates the ways in which he differs from Lévi-Strauss in certain methodological respects. See his introduction to Edmund Leach and D. Alan Aycock, *Structuralist Interpretations of Biblical Myth* (Cambridge, 1983).
52 Roland Barthes, 'Wrestling with the Angel: Textual Analysis of Genesis 32:23–33', in *The Semiotic Challenge*, trs. Richard Howard (Oxford, 1988), pp. 246–60. A list of other prominent structural studies of biblical narratives would include the following: Claude Chabrol, 'Analyse du "texte" de la Passion', *Langages*, 22 (1971), pp. 75–96; and Louis Marin, 'Essai d'analyse structurale d'Acts 10, 1–11, 18', *Recherches de science religieuse*, 58 (1970), pp. 39–61.
53 See, for example, Richard Jacobson, 'The Structuralists and the Bible', in *A Guide to Contemporary Hermeneutics: Major Trends in Biblical Interpretation*, ed. Donald K. McKim (Grand Rapids, Michigan, 1986), pp. 290–3; Wolfgang Roth, 'Structural Interpretations of "Jacob at the Jabbok" (Genesis 32:22–32)', *Biblical Research*, 22 (1977), pp. 51–62; and Hugh C. White, 'French Structuralism and

OT Narrative Analysis: Roland Barthes', *Semeia*, 3 (1975), pp. 99–127.

54 Roland Barthes, *S/Z*, trs. Richard Miller and pref. by Richard Howard (New York, 1974), p. 5.

55 Ibid., p. 4. Also see Barthes's discussion of work and text in his 'Theory of the Text', in *Untying the Text: A Post-Structuralist Reader*, ed. and introd. Robert Young (Boston, 1981), pp. 39–42.

56 Roland Barthes, 'The Death of the Author', in *Image Music, Text*, trs. Stephen Heath (New York, 1977), pp. 146–7.

57 Roland Barthes, 'The Structural Analysis of Narrative: Apropos of Acts 10–11', in *The Semiotic Challenge*, p. 242.

58 Terry Eagleton, 'Meaning and Material', *Times Literary Supplement*, 2 May 1986, p. 477.

59 Roland Barthes, 'Roland Barthes versus Received Ideas' (*Le Figaro*, 27 July 1974), in *The Grain of the Voice* (London, 1985), p. 194.

60 Barthes, 'Wrestling with the Angel', p. 255. In an interview Barthes provides a useful gloss on *logothete*: 'What I can say here is that a logothete is not only and not even necessarily a writer who invents words, sentences that bear his stamp, in short, a style; a logothete is someone who knows how to see in the world, in his own world (social, erotic, or religious), elements, traits, "units" in the linguistic term, which he combines and arranges in an original fashion, as if he were producing the first text of a new language,' 'Roland Barthes versus Received Ideas', p. 193.

61 Barthes, 'Wrestling with the Angel', pp. 247–8; 256; 259.

62 Barthes, 'Wrestling with the Angel', pp. 247; 260.

63 Consider Gershom Scholem's observation: 'Here revelation, which has yet no specific meaning, is that in the word which gives an infinite wealth of meaning. Itself without meaning, it is the very essence of interpretability', *The Messianic Idea in Judaism and Other Essays in Jewish Spirituality* (New York, 1971), p. 295.

64 Heidegger, 'What are Poets for?', p. 133. Hans-Georg Gadamer extends Heidegger's critique of language as a sign system in *Truth and Method*, ed. Garrett Barden and John Cumming (London, 1975), pp. 366–78.

65 For a more comprehensive account of Ricoeur's critique of structuralism and his reinterpretation of hermeneutics, see my 'Ricoeur's Distinctions', *Scripsi*, 5 (1989), pp. 103–25.

66 Paul Ricoeur, *The Rule of Metaphor: Multi-Disciplinary Studies of the Creation of Meaning in Language*, trs. Robert Czerny with Kathleen McLaughlin and John Costello, SJ (London, 1978), p. 224. Ricoeur is plainly thinking of formalist criticism such as structuralism. Cf. Barthes: 'Our object is not the philosophical or historical document, custodian of a truth to be found, but the text's *signifying* volume,' 'Wrestling the Angel', p. 256.

67 Paul Ricoeur, 'Philosophical and Theological Hermeneutics', *Sciences religieuses/Studies in Religion*, 5 (1975), p. 25.
68 Paul Ricoeur, 'Toward a Hermeneutic of the Idea of Revelation', in *Essays on Biblical Interpretation*, ed. and introd. Lewis S. Mudge (Philadelphia, 1980), p. 101.
69 Ibid., p. 104.
70 Ibid., p. 104.
71 For further discussion of Mrs Ward, see Stephen Prickett, *Words and The Word: Language, Poetics and Biblical Interpretation* (Cambridge, 1986), pp. 237–40.
72 Paul Ricoeur, 'On Interpretation', in *Philosophy in France Today*, ed. Alan Montefiore (Cambridge, 1983), p. 188.
73 Paul Ricoeur, 'The Hermeneutics of Testimony', in Mudge, *Essays on Biblical Interpretation*, p. 151.
74 Paul Ricoeur, 'The Hermeneutical Function of Distanciation', in *Hermeneutics and the Human Sciences: Essays on Language, Action and Interpretation*, ed. trans. and introd. John B. Thompson (Cambridge, 1981), p. 144. Cf. 'Toward a Hermeneutic of the Idea of Revelation', p. 115.
75 The only one of this group not discussed beforehand is Karl Barth. For his views on Scripture, see his *Church Dogmatics*, vol. 1, *The Doctrine of the Word of God*, trans. G. T. Thomson (Edinburgh, 1936), pp. 124–35.
76 Ricoeur, 'The Hermeneutics of Testimony', p. 144.
77 Ibid., p. 152.
78 Jacques Derrida, 'Télépathie', in *Psyché: Inventions de l'autre* (Paris, 1987), p. 240. My translation.
79 Jacques Derrida, 'Signature Event Context', in *Limited Inc* (Evanston, IL, 1988), p. 3.
80 See Jacques Derrida's *Speech and Phenomena: And Other Essays on Husserl's Theory of Signs*, trans. and introd. David B. Allison (Evanston, IL, 1973), ch. 7.
81 Jacques Derrida, 'Deconstruction and the Other', in Richard Kearney, *Dialogues with Contemporary Continental Thinkers: The Phenomenological Heritage* (Manchester, 1984), p. 117.
82 Jacques Derrida, 'Living On: Border Lines', in *Deconstruction and Criticism*, ed. Geoffrey Hartman (London, 1979), p. 107.
83 Maurice Blanchot, 'The Absence of the Book', in *The Gaze of Orpheus and Other Literary Essays*, pref. Geoffrey Hartman, trs. Lydia Davis, ed. P. Adams Sitney (Barrytown, NY, 1981), p. 151.
84 T. S. Eliot, 'Tradition and the Individual Talent', in *Selected Essays*, 3rd edn, (London, 1951), p. 15. Interestingly enough, as James Barr argues, canonical criticism of the Bible, as practised by B. S. Childs, sometimes seems to answer to the new criticism. See his *Holy Scripture: Canon, Authority, Criticism* (Oxford, 1983), p. 77. I am indebted to Barr's discussion of canon-formation throughout this essay.

85 Edmond Jabès, *The Book of Questions*, vol. 7, trs. Rosemarie Waldrop (Middletown, CT, 1984), pp. 18; 93. Derrida's meditations on Jabès centre on the first three books of *The Book of Questions*; all seven books, however, are much of a piece in so far as they relentlessly interrogate the status of 'Book', 'writing' and 'God'.

86 Edmond Jabès, *The Book of Questions*, vol. 1, trs. Rosemarie Waldrop (Middletown, CT, 1976), p. 31.

87 Edmond Jabès, *The Book of Questions*, vol. 6, trs. Rosemarie Waldrop (Middletown, CT, 1983), p. 235. For a clear account of what Jabès owes to Jewish interpretation, see Susan Handelman's essay, '"Torments of an Ancient Word": Jabès and the Rabbinic Tradition', in *The Sin of the Book: Edmond Jabès*, ed. Eric Gould (Lincoln, 1985).

88 Edmond Jabès, *The Book of Questions*, vol. 3, trs. Rosemarie Waldrop (Middletown, CT, 1976), p. 195.

89 Jacques Derrida, 'Edmond Jabès and the Question of the Book', in *Writing and Difference* (London, 1979), p. 67. Derrida expands on these 'two interpretations of interpretation' in 'Structure Sign and Play', pp. 292–3.

90 Geoffrey Hartman, *Saving the Text: Literature/Derrida/Philosophy* (Baltimore, 1981), p. 63.

91 Derrida, 'Edmond Jabès and the Question of the Book', p. 75.

92 Hartman, *Saving the Text*, p. 51.

93 Jacques Derrida et al., *The Ear of the Other: Otobiography, Transference, Translation*, ed. Christie V. McDonald and trs. Peggy Kamuf (New York, 1985), p. 102.

94 Ibid., p. 103. Translator's note: 'Derrida condenses at least four senses in this invented word: dissemination, deschematization, de-"Shemitizing", and derouting or diverting from a path (the word *chemin* meaning path or road).'

95 Ibid., p. 102.

96 Ibid., p. 204.

97 Emmanuel Levinas, 'On the Trail of the Other', *Philosophy Today*, 10 (1966), p. 46.

98 Derrida, *The Ear of the Other*, p. 148.

99 Jacques Derrida, 'The Double Session', in *Dissemination*, trs. and introd. Barbara Johnson (London, 1981), p. 223.

100 Ibid., p. 223.

101 In 'Plato's Pharmacy' Derrida writes of 'a violent difficulty in the transference of a nonphilosopheme into a philosopheme', *Dissemination*, p. 72; and he expands on this in *The Ear of the Other*, pp. 119–20; 140.

102 See Jacques Derrida, *Edmund Husserl's 'Origin of Geometry': An Introduction*, trans. and pref. John P. Leavey, Jr, ed. David B. Allison (Stony Brook, 1978), pp. 102–3.

103 Joyce, *Finnegans Wake*, p. 258. Derrida also finds a babelian motif in Philippe Sollers's *Nombres*. See *Dissemination*, p. 341.

104 Jacques Derrida, *Ulysse gramophone: deux mots pour Joyce* (Paris, 1987), p. 35. My translation.
105 Ibid., p. 39. My translation.
106 H. Freedman (trs.) *Midrash Rabbah. Genesis*, vol. 2 (London, 1939), pp. 304–9.
107 *The Zohar*, trs. Harry Sperling and Maurice Simon, vol. 1 (New York, n.d.), p. 259.
108 Derrida denies that he has any direct knowledge of rabbinical interpretation. When asked about his familiarity with the Talmud he responded as follows: 'one can amuse oneself wondering how someone can be influenced by what he doesn't know. I don't preclude that. If I regret so much not knowing the *Talmud*, for example, perhaps it's because it knows me itself, because it knows all about me.' Quoted in John P. Leavey, Jr, *Glassary*, with essays by Gregory L. Ulmer and Jacques Derrida (Lincoln, 1986), p. 30c. However, also see Derrida's remarks on the Torah in Jacques Derrida *et al.*, *Affranchissement du transfert et de la lettre* (Paris, 1982), pp. 47–8. Finally, Derrida's wordplay can seem rather tame when compared with that of the Hebrew literature: gematria, notrikon, atbash and others take the primacy of the signifier to further extremes than one finds in Derrida's texts. For details of wordplay in the Hebrew Bible, see *The Interpreter's Dictionary of the Bible*, Supplementary Volume, p. 968.
109 Michael Fishbane, *Text and Texture: Close Readings of Selected Biblical Texts* (New York, 1979), p. 38.
110 For Derrida's discussion of anthemes, see Jacques Derrida, *Glas*, trs. John P. Leavey Jr, and Richard Rand (Lincoln, 1986), p. 208bi.
111 Jacques Derrida, *Schibboleth: Pour Paul Celan* (Paris, 1986), p. 50.
112 Erich Auerbach, *Mimesis: The Representation of Reality in Western Literature*, trs. Willard R. Trask (Princeton, 1953), ch. 1.
113 Tamra Wright, *et al.*, 'The Paradox of Morality: an Interview with Emmanuel Levinas', trs. Andrew Benjamin and Tamra Wright, in *The Provocation of Levinas: Rethinking the Other*, ed. Robert Bernasconi and David Wood (London, 1988), p. 178.
114 Emmanuel Levinas, *Otherwise than Being or Beyond Essence*, trs. Alphonso Lingis (The Hague, 1981), p. xliii.
115 Richard Kearney, 'Dialogue with Emmanuel Levinas', in *Face to Face with Levinas*, ed. Richard A. Cohen (Albany, 1986), p. 19. For some useful caveats on contrasts between Jewish and Greek modes of thinking, see James Barr's *The Semantics of Biblical Language* (Oxford, 1961), esp. pp. 8–20.
116 Harold Bloom, 'The Breaking of Form', in Hartman, *Deconstruction and Criticism*, p. 9.
117 Northrop Frye, *Five Essays on Milton's Epics* (London, 1966), p. 8.
118 Northrop Frye, *The Great Code: The Bible and Literature* (London, 1982), p. xiii.
119 Salusinszky, *Criticism in Society*, p. 64.

120 Frye, *The Great Code*, p. 198. Frye also refers to this passage in *Spiritus Mundi*, p. 280, and *The Secular Scripture: A Study of the Structure of Romance* (Cambridge, MA, 1976), p. 61.

121 Harold Bloom, 'Criticism, Canon-Formation, and Prophecy', in *Poetics of Influence: New and Selected Criticism*, ed. and introd. John Hollander (New Haven, 1988), p. 419.

122 See Harold Bloom, *The Breaking of the Vessels*, the Welleck Library Lectures at the University of California, Irvine (Chicago, 1982), pp. 35, 42–70.

123 Bloom, *A Map of Misreading*, p. 17.

124 Ibid., p. 149. As Bloom makes plain, however, the central struggle of the Western poetic tradition is with Milton: 'The older Romantics at least thought that the struggle with Milton had bestowed a blessing without a crippling; to the younger ones a consciousness of gain and loss came together,' 'Keats and the Embarrassments of Poetic Tradition', in *The Ringers in the Tower: Studies in Romantic Tradition* (Chicago, 1971), pp. 131–2.

125 Paul Isaac Hershon, *Genesis: With a Talmudical Commentary*, The Pentateuch According to the Talmud (London, 1883), p. 396.

126 Harold Bloom, *Ruin the Sacred Truths: Poetry and Belief from the Bible to the Present* (Cambridge, MA, 1989), p. 6.

127 Ibid., p. 151.

128 G. W. F. Hegel, *The Phenomenology of Mind*, trans. and introd. J. B. Baillie, new introd. George Lichtheim (New York, 1967), p. 93.

129 Ibid., p. 93. Translation modified.

130 Ibid., p. 237.

131 Ibid., p. 81.

132 Harold Bloom, 'Lying Against Time: Gnosis, Poetry, Criticism', in *Agon: Towards a Theory of Revisionism* (New York, 1982), p. 60.

133 Harold Bloom, 'A Prelude to Gnosis', in *Agon*, p. 15.

134 Bloom, 'Lying Against Time', p. 61.

135 Bloom, *Ruin the Sacred Truths*, p. 97.

136 Salusinszky, *Criticism in Society*, p. 73.

137 Harold Bloom, 'Shelley and His Precursors', in *Poetry and Repression: Revisionism from Blake to Stevens* (New Haven, 1976), p. 88.

138 Harold Bloom, 'Before Moses Was, I Am', Hollander, *Poetics of Influence*, p. 388.

139 Bloom, *Ruin the Sacred Truths*, p. 4.

140 Ibid., p. 179.

141 Franz Kafka, 'Before the Law', in *The Penguin Complete Short Stories of Franz Kafka*, ed. Nahum N. Glatzer (Harmondsworth, 1983), p. 4.

142 Jacques Derrida, 'Devant La Loi', trs. Avital Ronell, in *Kafka and the Contemporary Critical Performance: Centenary Readings*, ed. Alan Udoff (Bloomington, 1987), p. 141.

143 For Derrida's strictures on negative theology see 'Comment ne pas

340   *Kevin Hart*

parler' in *Psyché*, and for his observations on the Kabbalah, 'Dissemination', in *Dissemination*, p. 344. The description of the Kabbalah as a 'document' is questionable (see Preface, p. 9).

144 Phyllis Trible, 'Depatriarchalizing in Biblical Interpretation', *Journal of the American Academy of Religion*, 41 (1973), p. 48.

145 See Mieke Bal, *Lethal Love: Feminist Literary Readings of Biblical Love Stories* (Bloomington, 1987), pp. 2–3.

146 Mieke Bal, *Death and Dissymmetry: The Politics of Coherence in the Book of Judges* (Chicago, 1988), p. 5. Bal's methodology is partly indebted to Pierre Machery's influential *A Theory of Literary Production*, trs. Geoffrey Wall (London, 1978), esp. pp. 82–8.

147 Maurice Blanchot, 'Etre Juif', in *L'Entretien infini* (Paris, 1969), p. 189. My translation.

148 Geoffrey H. Hartman, 'The Struggle for the Text', in *Midrash and Literature*, ed. Geoffrey H. Hartman and Sanford Budick (New Haven, 1986), p. 16. Also see Hartman's *Saving the Text*, ch. 5.

149 Phyllis Trible, *Texts of Terror: Literary-Feminist Readings of Biblical Narratives* (Philadephia, 1984), pp. 4–5.

Index